DATE			
DEC 0 4 1995			
MAY 1 0 2001			

Professional Forestry
In the United States

Professional Forestry in the United States

c. 1

Henry Clepper

Published for Resources for the Future, Inc.
By The Johns Hopkins Press, Baltimore and London

Resources for the Future is a nonprofit corporation for research and education in the development, conservation, and use of natural resources and the
improvement of the quality of the environment. It was established in 1952
with the cooperation of the Ford Foundation. Part of the work of Resources
for the Future is carried out by its resident staff; part is supported by grants
to universities and other nonprofit organizations. Unless otherwise stated,
interpretations and conclusions in RFF publications are those of the authors;
the organization takes responsibility for the selection of significant subjects
for study, the competence of the researchers, and their freedom of inquiry.

Henry Clepper, now a consultant, retired in 1966 as executive secretary of
the Society of American Foresters and managing editor of the *Journal of
Forestry*. His work on this book was supported by a grant to the Forest
History Society, Inc. The index was prepared by Margaret Stanley.

RFF editors: Henry Jarrett, Vera W. Dodds, Nora E. Roots, Tadd Fisher.

The Johns Hopkins Press, Baltimore, Maryland 21218
The Johns Hopkins Press Ltd., London

Library of Congress Catalog Card Number 70-171107

International Standard Book Number 0-8018-1331X

Contents

Preface

Having been professionally educated in forestry and having devoted my career to the management of natural resources, I find the annals of the conservation movement endlessly fascinating. I attempted this book because I hoped to transmit this sense of attraction to others and to stimulate the perception of history as indispensable to an understanding of the role of natural resources in the making of the United States.

A need for a history of forestry has been expressed at various times by teachers, students, librarians, and practicing foresters themselves. The subject is a rich domain. Since forest preservation gave impetus to the whole conservation movement, workers in other fields of natural resources management may find in the record of forestry useful lessons to guide policies and techniques in their own disciplines.

This work, then, aims to be more than an account of woodland management over the years; it aspires to relate forestry to the general natural resources environment. But because it is fundamentally about forestry, other aspects of conservation are brought in only when they impinge on forestry. Similarly, little is said about developments in resource utilization that are significant to economic growth but not to forestry.

As a forester, I have fought woods fires; raised seedlings in a nursery; planted trees; logged timber and harvested pulpwood; operated a small sawmill; administered a state forest that contained parks and recreational areas; combated forest tree diseases and insect infestations; constructed roads, trails, and fire towers. In short, I have performed many of the duties incidental to the management of a forest property.

My experience has spanned an arc in time that began in 1921 with employment under Gifford Pinchot in the Pennsylvania Department of Forests and Waters. It has been my good fortune to have known, or at least to have met, most American foresters of prominence in administration, education, research, and policy formation during the present century. Admittedly, acquaintanceship with leaders of forestry confers no special competence on me as the author of this book. It has not earned me the right to speak for American forestry. But it has given me a richly informed sense of the kinds of men who made forestry history.

Certain traits were common to these men—strong convictions, sincere dedication, and high integrity. They had a love for the land, they cherished the outdoors, and they strove to preserve and protect all natural resources. Their involvement with resources was less for the production of wealth than for the production of those things that safeguarded and improved the natural environment. All the foresters mentioned in this book, living and dead, are treated as historical figures—without offense, I hope.

Many foresters of the first half of the present century came from small rural towns and backwoods villages whose values and virtues they understood. After college, they were happy to start their careers in these small communities. The remote logging camp or hamlet that a city-oriented man might find intellectually stifling and unendurable in its provincialism was not a cultural wasteland to them. Their social consciousness found outlet in service on school boards, Boy Scout councils and civic committees, and in work with religious and sportsmen's groups.

Some of these foresters attained executive and policy-making positions in education, government, and industry. The decisions they fashioned in later life were sometimes too idealistic and sometimes wrong, but always they were based on the realities both of the foresters' experience and of the lives of the people whose existence and income would be affected. In the term of reference of this book, the decisions of these men had historical consequences.

This book, then, is an attempt to get inside the living past of American forestry. The exploration of this past is essential to our understanding of the contribution of the forest and of related resources to our national culture and economic growth. I have endeavored to present the significant events in American forestry, not its minutiae, making numerous and necessary compromises along the way. Occasionally, I have permitted personal sentiment to flavor my comments because I believed it would aid the reader's understanding of certain events. Since this work is not intended to be a basic textbook history, it can be best understood as a supplement to, and a commentary on, other books on the history of American forestry.

I hope I have resisted the temptation to inflate or romanticize the role of forestry in terms of history. If I have unconsciously performed this disservice to my profession it is because of my enduring enthusiasm for the power of forestry to contribute to our national social and economic progress.

I am most grateful for the counsel of many colleagues—foresters, historians, and general conservationists—who kindly read portions of this work in progress. As the number of these reviewers totals more than a hundred, I cannot list them all. I would be remiss, however, if I did not acknowledge my heavy reliance on the comments of the following individuals, although none is responsible for any mistakes I may have made: Keith A. Argow, George B. Amidon, Henry Bahr, Henry I. Baldwin, Sam R. Broadbent, Marlin H. Bruner, C. Raymond Clar, William K. Condrell, James B. Craig, Paul M. Dunn, Walt L. Dutton, Hugh Fowler, Tom Gill, James C. Gritman, W. D. Hagenstein, Lawrence S. Hamilton, V. L. Harper, Clarence S. Herr, Frank Heyward,

George M. Jemison, George S. Kephart, Fred H. Lang, Austin N. Lentz, David T. Mason, Richard E. McArdle, James C. McClellan, Arthur B. Meyer, Howard A. Miller, Robert B. Moore, Earl Porter, Carrow T. Prout, Jr., Perry E. Skarra, C. B. Stott, Wilson B. Sayers, Lloyd W. Swift, M. N. Taylor, Philip L. Thornton, Z. W. White, Ralph Wible, Robert K. Winters, and Ross A. Youngblood.

I made extensive use of the papers of Herman H. Chapman and of Henry S. Graves in Sterling Memorial Library at Yale University, and some of the papers I have quoted were unpublished heretofore. Transcripts of oral histories in the Bancroft Library of the University of California and in the Forest History Society (formerly at Yale University, now in Santa Cruz, California) provided valuable sources of information.

Additionally, I am indebted for the use of documents in the archives of The American Forestry Association; Brown Company; Conservation Center of the Denver Public Library; International Paper Company; National Forest Products Association; regional headquarters of the U.S. Forest Service in Denver, Portland, Oregon, and San Francisco, and Forest Service offices in Washington, D.C., and Rosslyn, Virginia; Oregon Historical Association; University of Oregon Library; National Archives; St. Regis Paper Company; and Society of American Foresters.

I am grateful to Resources for the Future for the funds that supported this project and to the Forest History Society for its administration of the project. During the three years I worked on the book, RFF generously provided me with desk space in its Washington, D.C., headquarters, where I was accorded the status of visiting scholar assigned to the Program in Land Use and Management. I thank Marion Clawson, the genial director of the program, for many kindnesses; Tadd Fisher for editorial guidance; and Miriam Seagle and Diantha Stevenson for efficient typing service. Finally, I owe much to my two associates in the Forest History Society—Elwood R. Maunder, executive director, and Joseph A. Miller, editor of *Forest History*—for their ever-helpful criticism and suggestions.

In slightly different form, several chapters of this book were published as magazine articles in *American Forests, Journal of Forestry, Forest Farmer, Northern Logger,* and *Unasylva.*

June 1971   Henry Clepper

Professional Forestry
In the United States

Introduction

Several events during the closing decades of the nineteenth century launched the forest conservation movement.

With the organization in 1875 of The American Forestry Association, a citizens' crusade began for the preservation of the nation's forest resources. One year later, under the leadership of the American Association for the Advancement of Science, the first forest investigations were started by the federal government when F. B. Hough was appointed special forestry agent in the Department of Agriculture.

About this time, intimations of a timber famine were heard throughout the land. Spokesmen prominent in national affairs, such as Secretary of the Interior Carl Schurz, voiced warnings that timber resources long believed to be inexhaustible might be depleted within a century by cutting, fire, and other destructive forces. This apprehension was repeated later with rousing effect by Gifford Pinchot, Theodore Roosevelt, and other concerned conservationists.

Another historical event of significance was the first move by Congress in 1891 to halt spoliation of the public lands of the West; it resulted in the creation of forest reserves (now the national forests). The second advance was made in 1897, when Congress was induced to provide for the protection and administration of the reserves.

Meanwhile, numerous woods fires that caused loss of life and incalculable property damage constituted an evil that public-spirited citizens demanded should be suppressed. As laws for fire prevention and control were passed by the states, state forestry agencies were created to enforce them and to provide protection of the woodland from fire.

Briefly, these were some of the regnant influences that contributed to the forest conservation movement of the past century. All are dealt with in detail in later chapters. But forest conservation is not forestry. And since this book is about the origins and growth of forestry in America, the beginnings of forestry must be established also.

It seems an accurate assessment to assert that the creation of national forests from the public lands of the West laid the foundation for the practice of forestry in the United States. The national forests created a need for foresters that led to the founding of schools of forestry, which in turn led to the formation of a profession of forestry.

Except in a few minor instances, lumber companies and other private owners of timberland had shown little interest in employing trained forest managers. Thus, if the Forest Service had not created the need for technical men, the establishment of schools of forestry would not have occurred when it did. For the first time in America, men who obtained technical training in forest management could look forward to careers in forestry.

With the beginning of education in forestry, a second need arose—a need for more information about tree growth, forest soils, forest diseases and insects, wood utilization, and means of forest renewal and harvest. In addition to teaching, faculty members began investigations that pointed up the need for systematic research. It logically followed, then, that from education and research a profession of forestry was born.

Then, around the turn of the century, the beginning acquisition of state forests and the organization of state forestry departments increased employment opportunities. Interest mounted with the publicized activities of The American Forestry Association and the organization of state forestry associations. Another manifestation of forestry's promise was the creation in 1900 of the Society of American Foresters. It is to be noted that, although there were less than a dozen Americans at that time who had received professional education in forestry, they nevertheless brought into being a professional society.

The actual practice of forestry[1] may be said to have started when Gifford Pinchot and Carl A. Schenck made the first applications of silviculture at Biltmore, North Carolina, during the late 1890s. Thus, the art and science of forestry have been applied for only seven decades. As of 1969 approximately 20,000 professionally educated foresters were practicing their profession or were working in closely allied fields. About half were in private practice and employed by industrial organizations and associations. An equal number were employed by federal, state, county, and municipal governments. This division of employment illustrates the pattern of forestry development, and from it may be drawn the inference that forestry is definitely not a government enterprise decreed by law.

On the contrary, forestry has been a cooperative development. From its inception, it has been characterized by cooperation between government agencies on the one hand and private landowners and the forest industries on the other. This cooperative design has been further extended to encompass close working relations between these groups and the forestry schools and experiment stations.

1. As defined by the Society of American Foresters in *Forestry Terminology*, forestry is "the scientific management of forests for the continuous production of goods and services." *Forestry* is more comprehensive than *forest management*, which is "the application of business methods and technical forestry principles to the operation of a forest property."

Forestry in America is the achievement of politically independent citizens living under a democratic form of government with the economic advantages of a free enterprise system. This is not to say that forestry and the forest products business have flourished without legal restrictions. But, in general, forestry as a business has been free to organize and to operate competitively for profit with a minimum of regulation by federal and state governments. Forestry has flourished, not through the coercion of law, but through the absence of it. To be sure, forestry is an important function of government because it is in the public interest. But the reason forestry is practiced by tens of thousands of landowners—small farmers and big corporations alike—is because it yields profits. To understand the nature of American forestry, then, one must realize that it is a matter of concern and interest to a host of public agencies, businesses, conservation organizations, institutions of learning and research, individual landowners, and ordinary citizens.

Forestry in the United States is a multifaceted enterprise. In the federal government alone, five departments and seven independent agencies, boards, and commissions employ foresters. Many units have woodland under forestry management. In the Department of Defense, for example, the army, the navy, and the air force each has extensive holdings of woodland under the supervision of foresters. The Department of the Interior has seven bureaus which together employ more than 1,000 foresters.

In most of the fifty states there are state forests, state forest preserves, state parks, state game lands, and other categories of state-owned woodland. Almost without exception these holdings are under professional supervision. Additionally, many counties own woodland, as do municipalities and townships. Generally, such properties are operated as public parks and forested watersheds, but there are several hundred community forests that are managed for products as well as for recreation and water supply.

The point is that most of these holdings, regardless of ownership, receive multiple-use management.[2] Whereas the quality and intensity of silviculture vary, all the tracts get a high degree of protection from fire. Los Angeles County, California, affords an example of an integrated system of fire control. Within the county boundaries are national forest, county forest, and city-owned forest land. Here, a large fire on a forested watershed might be fought by suppression crews of the U.S. Forest Service, the state Department of Conservation, and the county protection forces.

A stranger examining American forestry for the first time might see it as a disorganized and fragmented undertaking without a dominant guiding policy—a pattern of conflicting and overlapping administrations. This view might be held in particular by a visitor from a nation where only a strong central authority is deemed capable of organizing programs for economic and social welfare.

---

2. Multiple-use (sometimes referred to as multiple-purpose) forestry is defined by the Society of American Foresters in *Forestry Terminology* as "the practice of forestry which combines two or more objectives, such as production of wood or wood-derivative products, forage and browse for domestic livestock, proper environmental conditions for wildlife, landscape effects, protection against floods and erosion, recreation, production and protection of water supplies, and national defense."

In point of fact, forestry is distinguished by a cohesiveness which may not be apparent to an outsider but which nevertheless exists. Contributing to this unity have been the influence and activities of the 65,000-member American Forestry Association and the 16,000-member Society of American Foresters. Through meetings, publications, and educational activities, these organizations have served as forums for the discussion of techniques and the formulation of policies. Meanwhile, numerous regional, state, and local conservation groups have added their weight to the decision-making process that is so fundamental to democratic procedure.

The driving force that enables this complex forestry operation to function is the forestry profession. If the pages that follow have one special message to impart, it is this: The history of the forestry profession is a chronicle of experimentation, of practical ideals of public service, of imaginative conceptions of a society enriched by scientific resource management, of constant technical innovation, of policy making by the democratic trial and error process, and of faith in the financial profit to be derived from the practice of silviculture. Lest this statement imply that a summit has been reached, it should be added that forestry is still a young profession and is still in the evolutionary process.

Of the many and varied tangible achievements of American forestry, several stand out:

- The greatest system of managed national and state forests and parks of any nation on earth.
- The largest number of professionally educated foresters practicing their profession.
- The largest number of universities offering professional curriculums in forestry and its allied fields.
- The largest number of federal and state forest experiment stations with the most personnel engaged in research.
- The most extensive area of privately owned forest land under management.

In the brief span of seventy years, forestry has made notable contributions to the economic growth of the nation and to its social welfare. But professional foresters are not complacent about the status of forest practice. They realize that they have made only a modest beginning.

With the expanding population and the inexorable rate of encroachment of urban spread on woodlands, the profession must practice more intensive silviculture so that the goods and services that forests provide may continue to contribute to the American way of life. Wood and fiber are needed in greater volume each year. So is water from our forested watersheds for industry and households. So are forest browse and forage for domestic livestock, and food and habitat for wildlife. Besides these needs, the heavy impress of recreational use must increasingly have a place in management plans.

Multiple-use forestry—a form of practice that combines two or more objectives—is both a technical term and an omnipresent reality. The forester, whether in industry or government, could not escape its demands even if he wanted. But he does not wish to escape. Aided by an enlarging body of research, he must try to apply multiple-purpose management, as effectively as he knows how, regardless of what the dominant use of the forest may be.

CHAPTER 1

Plunder of the Pineries

Acquisition of the public domain began in 1781 when the thirteen original states ceded to the federal government extensive portions of their largely unexplored lands lying west of the Allegheny Mountains. The acquisition process continued with various purchases and annexations; with the purchase of Alaska in 1867, the total area of public lands rose to 1,838 million acres.

Concurrently with the first acquisition of public lands, the government began disposing of them. Veterans of war, for example, were rewarded by gifts of forest to be cleared for agriculture. Tracts were often offered to volunteers as an inducement to enlist for military service. Vast acreages were sold outright to obtain funds to help run the government and to pay off the public debt.

The acquisition, disposal, and supervision of the public domain constitute a colorful and confused chapter in the annals of U.S. forestry. For instance, the number of laws dealing with the public lands may have exceeded 5,000, although the precise total is unknown. One thing is certain: the disposal of these lands was a chaotic business, subject to constant abuse and badly in need of orderly and honest administration.

But we are concerned here with the acts of Congress affecting the public lands only as they influenced the development of forest conservation. With characteristic bluntness, Gifford Pinchot claimed that "some of these laws were good, but all of them were badly, and more often than not, corruptly administered. Yet upon these laws and their administration depended the future of forestry."[1]

In 1849, Congress created the Department of the Interior. The General Land Office, formerly in the Treasury Department, was transferred to Interior and given responsibility for the administration of the public lands. This act was followed in 1850 by a decision of the Supreme Court that declared constitutional an earlier law of 1831[2] that prohibited the removal of timber

1. *Breaking New Ground*, p. 79.
2. *Antitrespass Law of March 2, 1831* (4 Stat. 472).

from public land. This decision, which was to have significant repercussions, originated from a theft committed by one Ephriam Briggs of Michigan.

Briggs was accused by the government of stealing timber from the public domain contrary to the law of 1831 that provided for the punishment by fine and imprisonment of anyone unlawfully cutting, destroying, or removing live oak and other timber or trees reserved for the navy. Although the full title of the law referred only to timber on naval reservations, the broad provisions of the act included penalties for cutting or removing timber anywhere on the public domain.

This law had an interesting genesis. In 1827, Congress had authorized the president to reserve lands containing live oak and other timber species in suitable quantity for the use of the navy. After certain areas were reserved in Florida and elsewhere in the South, Congress next passed the law of 1831 to protect them. The law imposed a fine of not less than three times the value of the timber cut or removed and a sentence of imprisonment for up to one year. According to forester-lawyer J. P Kinney, this act "has remained until today the fundamental law as to the offense of cutting, wantonly destroying, or removing timber from public lands of the United States."[3]

In accordance with the Supreme Court's decision, special agents were appointed in the new Department of the Interior to stop timber trespass; to stop, in short, the stealing of forest trees from the federal estate. Few government officers before or since have had more difficult or hazardous or frustrating assignments than the agents appointed to suppress the plundering of the nation's forest resources. The wonder is not that they accomplished so little but that they were able to accomplish anything at all.

This was the era in which the legend of timber inexhaustibility was generally believed. During the decade prior to the Civil War, settlers were trekking into the Middle West and the Lake States. The western trend of settlement depended on cheap land and cheap wood. Both lay waiting for pioneers hardy enough to take them, but often the pioneers took them without legal right. Many were farmers who needed rails and posts to fence their fields and boards to build their homes and barns. New towns, new railroads, new industries were springing up. All needed wood.

Forest trees were available in abundance. Loggers followed the settlers; indeed, they often moved in first. Penetrating the dense coniferous woods of Michigan, Minnesota, and Wisconsin, they set up sawmills on the rivers and began a brisk trade in logs, lumber, poles, shingles, and other products.

After all, the government owned the land. The government wanted the land developed. Was it not logical, then, that the government should condone, if not encourage, the exploitation of the resources that belonged to the nation? This, in a nutshell, was the opinion of most people who gave any thought to the matter at all. Not many did.

Politicians were less worried about the legality of forest plundering than that the West should be won. Typical of the political sentiment was the viewpoint of Congressman Ben C. Eastman of Wisconsin in 1852: "Upon the

3. *The Development of Forest Law in America*, p. 240.

rivers which are tributary to the Mississippi, and also upon those which empty themselves in Lake Michigan, there are interminable forests of pine, sufficient to supply all the wants of the citizens in the country, from which this supply can be drawn for all time to come."[4]

Since Mr. Eastman believed that the pineries of his and adjoining states could supply wood for all time to come, he was opposed to policing them. He charged that his constituency was harassed by timber agents appointed by the President without authority. He complained that an honest pioneer could be waylaid by a government agent for "cutting a sapling for a rooftree for his humble cabin." He warned that his constituents were ready for open revolt because of the timber agents "let loose upon this devoted class of our citizens" (meaning the lumbermen).[5]

And Congressman Eastman was not alone. Delegate Henry Sibley from the Territory of Minnesota denounced the attempts by timber agents to enforce the law in Wisconsin and Minnesota as an outrage and a disgrace to the country. Senator Augustus Dodge of Iowa regretted having voted to create the Department of the Interior; he too denounced the government's harassment of settlers and lumbermen who cut timber on the public domain.

This was a rough era when only tough-fibered men could survive. To many of the frontiersmen, violence was a way of life. They were not outlaws in the usual sense, but they were often lawbreakers by force of circumstance, the circumstance being that law was both remote and little regarded. The federal government was far away and federal authority, for all practical purposes, nonexistent.

Isaac Willard, Timber Agent

One of the timber agents appointed was Isaac W. Willard of Paw Paw, Van Buren County, Michigan, where timber theft was widespread. He was selected by Secretary of the Interior Robert McClelland, a Michigan lawyer who served three terms as a representative in Congress, who was elected governor of the state in 1851, and who resigned to accept appointment on March 7, 1853, as secretary of the interior. This background gave the secretary special knowledge of the public land laws as they applied to his state, and he held decided opinions about their enforcement. Hence, his instructions of March 14, 1853, to Isaac Willard, describing in detail Willard's duties as timber agent, are of more than casual interest.

The Department does not design by these agencies to interfere, in any manner, with any of the legitimate rights of bona-fide settlers, intending to acquire title by preemption, in cutting timber for the purpose of building, fencing or the construction of bridges, etc., but to compel the purchase of the lands of the United States by speculators whose sole object and pursuit are the manufacture and exportation of lumber, for their own profit, without compensation to the government or benefit to the country whence it is taken. To effect this object, the proceeding will be by indictment, or by seizure, under proper process, of the lumber or timber cut, either upon the ground, at

4. *Congressional Globe*, 32 Cong., 1 sess. (1852), p. 851.
5. Ibid.

the mills to which it may be carried, or wherever else it can be found and identified as having been taken from the public lands, and you will, therefore, give immediate information to the United States District Attorney or Marshal as the case may require, of the result of your observations and discoveries with a particular description of the lot on which the lumber or timber is to be seized, or on which the depredation may have been committed, the name of the trespasser and his ability to respond in damages, the amount of the trespasses, the names of witnesses to prove them, place of residence, etc., and you will also make regular monthly reports to the Department of all your proceedings.[6]

Born in Massachusetts and later a resident of Vermont, Willard had emigrated to Michigan in 1827 at the age of twenty-four. From 1836 to 1841, he was postmaster at Kalamazoo. In 1840 he erected a sawmill at Paw Paw and engaged in lumbering. He also operated a flour mill and a store. He was the first clerk of the U.S. Court in the western Michigan Territory.

Following his appointment as timber agent in March 1853, Willard went promptly to work. On April 1, he left Paw Paw to visit lumbering operations on Lake Huron, at Saginaw, on the east shore of Lake Michigan, and at Green Bay. He "ascertained that about fifty millions feet of lumber had been robbed from the public domain, between the mouth of Grand River and the Menomonee River in Green Bay, besides two to three millions of railroad ties, telegraph poles, and fence posts. During the trip he seized, in logs, shingle bolts, and lumber, from thirty to thirty-five millions feet, and placed the lumber so seized in charge of persons in his employ."[7]

Depredations on such a scale were proof of the fatuity of Congressman Eastman's complaint that government agents were waylaying honest pioneers for cutting sapling rooftrees for their humble cabins. This was thievery on a monumental order, organized and financed by business interests that did not hesitate to use bribery, intimidation, and violence to make a dishonest dollar. In a court deposition Willard later asserted that the greater portion of the lumber he had seized was retaken from his men.

Attempting to enforce the law, Willard found his authority severely challenged. Unlike some agents and their deputies, he could not be bribed, nor would he accept payment for stumpage, which would have meant pocketing the money for himself. Consequently his life was threatened, and on one occasion his enemies nearly succeeded in murdering him. The open revolt predicted by Congressman Eastman eventually erupted. During this insurrection one deputy was murdered. Three others died mysteriously.

"All the more credit is due Willard for his behavior in the face, first, of attempted bribery, then of intimidation," historian Jenks Cameron wrote. Cameron described the agent, who for years had been "a lumberer himself," as bluff and incorruptible. "Possessing unquestionably a strong slant for the pioneer viewpoint, his forthright character could not be budged from what he conceived to be his duty. He left behind him a reputation for kindly humor, stubborn honesty, and utter fearlessness. . . ."[8]

6. "Interior Department, Public Land," Land Office Records, National Archives.
7. *Detroit Free Press*, June 14, 1854.
8. *The Development of Governmental Forest Control in the United States*, p. 147.

Timber Stealing Rampant

Two of the localities where timber thefts were flagrant were Grand Haven and Manistee on the eastern shore of Lake Michigan. Agent Willard arranged for a showdown.

In May 1853, he seized two million board feet of lumber at a mill at Manistee owned by R. Canfield & Co. of Chicago, together with some 20,000 logs. The lumber and logs had been taken illegally from the public lands by company employees. Willard estimated the value of the lumber at $15,000 and the logs at $10,000. He deposed that the remote location of the logs, which were in booms and in creeks, made it impossible for him to realize their full value for the government. He could not get fair value for the lumber for lack of competitive bidding.

In its day, this company came under the category of big business, and its owners were ruthless in their efforts to defy the law that threatened their interests. As the *Detroit Free Press* reported:

The affidavits show that R. Canfield & Co. are large lumber dealers in Chicago, and own two or three steam mills on the Manistee river in Michigan, capable of sawing, in the aggregate, 40,000 feet of lumber per day; that a large extent of the country about these mills, and up the Manistee river and its branches, for a distance of thirty miles, has been despoiled of its choicest timber by men in their employment and others. And that by far the largest portion of all the lumber they cut at their mills belonged to the government, that they disregarded the Timber Agent, and put him at defiance; that after the lumber was seized by him they took it away by force, and in defiance of the men put in charge of it. The affidavits also show a most conclusive case of bribery and corruption, and that a fund has been raised, and agents employed, to corrupt witnesses and officers of the Court; and that the Canfields themselves are, and have been, the prime movers, the backers of the mob, and the instigators of the principal villainies committed.[9]

In the summer of 1853, after warning trespassers that timber theft would have to stop, Willard next demanded that stolen lumber on hand be surrendered. His demand went unheeded. Moreover, he himself was warned that the lumberers would continue to cut public timber and the government be damned.

When Willard seized lumber and placed it under guard, it was either carried away or burned. When he tried to sell it, purchasers were afraid to buy or even bid on it. At this stage, with public opinion and even local law officers against him, a less courageous or less obstinate man might have backed down. But Willard seems not to have been the stuff of which a quitter is made.

Agitation by local people, abetted by newspapers, made Willard's position as a government official almost hopeless. The *Chicago Tribune*, for example, even advocated resistance by force.

Willard's next attempt to enforce the law by "seize and sell" was a disaster. In the name of the government, a sizable quantity of lumber and shingles had been confiscated and offered for sale at prices calculated to

9. From affidavits filed in the U.S. District Court for the District of Michigan, as reported in the *Detroit Free Press*, June 8, 1854.

attract buyers. A purchaser having come forward, Willard was able to deliver a small amount of lumber to him, but most of it was burned or stolen.

Checked but not beaten, he obtained warrants for the ringleaders among the lawbreakers; he had already arranged indictments in the federal court at Detroit. Then, accompanied by a U.S. marshal, George W. Rice, he went to Manistee to put them under arrest.

Like his previous attempts, this too ended in failure, but not for want of courage and resolution on his part. Some of the thieves and the masters of lumber boats whom he apprehended were set free by local mobs armed with clubs and guns. In the brawls the officers were roughed up. Some prisoners who had been seized and held aboard boats chartered to the government were aided by the crews to escape.

Mob Insurrection

Rice was the U.S. marshal for the District of Michigan, at Kalamazoo. In a deposition made in the U.S. District Court at Detroit on June 1, 1854, he described his experience with Willard when they went to the Manistee region to make arrests. He had twenty writs to serve. He arrested John Canfield; two lumber boat captains, William Higgie and Harrison Clark; and four others. He reported that "the greater number took to the woods and avoided the service of process."[10]

The men arrested agreed to go quietly provided they could make temporary arrangements before leaving, "but instead effected an organization to resist."[11] Captain Higgie went aboard his vessel and actually started loading it with lumber that had been seized. The crew resisted the marshal and refused to give Higgie up. Captain Clark also went aboard his vessel and with the backing of his crew refused to surrender.

Later, the marshal rearrested Higgie together with Captain Charles Hammond of the schooner *Barnum*, which also was engaged in transporting stolen lumber. Taken to Chicago, these two worthies escaped the next day.

In his sworn statement, Marshal Rice testified that he had been approached with a bribe by one Henry A. Mitchell, who may have been a deputy marshal, then or earlier (the record is not clear). If Rice and Willard would delay or discontinue proceedings against the Canfields, the latter would pay $1,500.

Walter Durkee of Paw Paw had been deputized by Willard as an assistant. In an affidavit before the U.S. commissioner, Durkee related how he and Willard, who had papers and other documents relating to the timber thefts, stopped overnight at the home of Stillman Stubbs at the mouth of the Manistee River. At 2:00 A.M., the house was set on fire in several places by persons throwing cotton balls soaked in turpentine and oil in the windows. Had it been successful, this murderous attempt would have killed not only Durkee and Willard but the Stubbs family as well.

Durkee also told how one George Foster, deputized by Willard, arrested and took away John Canfield, who managed to escape despite handcuffs.

10. Ibid.
11. Ibid.

Foster returned to Manistee seeking Canfield and met with sudden and mysterious death.

Finally, Durkee swore that one Levi Conroe offered him twice the wages paid by Willard and a year's pay in advance to abandon his services to Willard and leave the country.

By this time, Willard's authority had disintegrated. In the face of mob incitement and the risk of physical harm, he found it impossible to arrest local timber thieves without assistance from people other than those inhabiting the pineries or those doing business with residents who were in the lumber trade. For the culprits, escape or successful resistance was quite certain when so many people were united in their determination to continue trespassing on public lands.

Momentous was the decision now before him: whether to call retreat—in itself an admission of defeat—or to hit the lawbreakers again, and hit them hard. Using a novel expedient, he again took the offensive. He obtained the help of the U.S. Navy.

Enforcing the Law

The *Michigan*, the first iron warship built for the navy (in 1843), operated on the Great Lakes. She was a side-wheel steamer with a three-inch gun, a well-armed crew, and a brig. A request having been made to the Navy Department for her aid, it was granted. Thus began what was certainly one of the most remarkable peacetime missions of the pre–Civil War navy.

Willard obtained additional indictments, at least fifty, from the federal court in Detroit. With the help of the U.S. marshal, he was able to begin making arrests in earnest.

In an order dated August 23, 1853, the secretary of the navy directed Commander Abraham Bigelow, master of the *Michigan*, to cooperate with the U.S. marshal in arresting certain "depredators upon the public land." Acting promptly on his orders, Bigelow notified the secretary on August 25 that "Mr. Rice the U.S. Marshal for Michigan is now on board and informs me that the depredations on the public lands are being committed at Manistee. . . . I have invited the Marshal to take passage on the Michigan and shall proceed with him to the scene of the depredations and render him all the aid he may require in executing the laws."[12]

On August 31, Bigelow wrote that at Herring River, twenty miles north of Manistee, the master of a lumber vessel was arrested, but several other persons escaped to the woods. Two vessels then came up to take away forcibly a quantity of shingle bolts, but "got under way at our approach and left the coast." He continued, "I think the appearance of this vessel [the *Michigan*] to aid the authorities, being an evidence that it is the intention of the Government to sustain its officers in executing the laws, will put a stop to the nefarious practice of plundering the public domain, which has prevailed so long in this community."

Commander Bigelow wrote the secretary of the navy on September 14: "The Marshal and Timber Agent find a favorable change in their position

12. Commanders' Letters, Naval Records Collection, National Archives. Subsequent references in this section to the naval action are to this source.

since this vessel has been ordered to cooperate. The tone of the marauders is changed, and they have ceased to abuse those employed by the Government to protect the Timber. Public opinion in this matter seems also to have undergone a change, and they no longer find advocates in the editors of public prints. I am told that in consequence of this movement . . . large quantities of Timber Lands in this region are being entered." By *entered* he meant the lands were being acquired legally.

On October 1, 1853, Isaac Willard, signing himself "U.S. T Agent for Michigan," notified Commander Bigelow that he would have no further use that season for the *Michigan*, adding, "I beg of you to accept my very grateful acknowledgement for the very prompt and efficient aid you have at all times so cheerfully rendered me in the execution of my duties."

Writing from the *Michigan*, then berthed at Chicago, on October 8, 1853, the commander briefly and routinely reported to the secretary of the navy that he had been several times to the coast of Michigan and Milwaukee. He had received aboard a number of prisoners arrested by the agents of the marshal, the prisoners having been sent to Detroit by railroad.

On October 26, Bigelow dispatched a longer report to the secretary from Erie, Pennsylvania, commenting that his vessel had been usefully employed, in his opinion, in cooperating with the federal marshals "in suppressing the plunder of the public lands" in Michigan. "The effect will no doubt be to induce the Lumber Dealers to enter the lands they require, and hasten the period when the system of wholesale plunder which has prevailed so long in that region will have ceased." The commander, who like Isaac Willard had been defamed and libeled for having faithfully performed his duties, continued: "The employment of this vessel to aid the Marshal and his Deputies in executing the laws has excited towards me the ill will and resentment of a class of men who have grown rich from profits of this nefarious business and I have been subjected to abuse in a low paper, the Chicago Tribune, which is their *organ*. . . . The better portion of the Community both in Illinois and Wisconsin, however, condemn this system of plunder, and are glad to find the Government taking decisive steps to put a stop to it."

Verdict of the Court

The final issue was anticlimactic. During the summer of 1854, the defendants were tried in the Detroit federal court. Convictions were obtained, but the sentences handed down were light in comparison to the offenses committed. The fines were small. The jail terms ranged from one day to one year. True, the government's case did not fall to pieces in the court. But the penalties meted out hardly hurt at all. What Isaac Willard thought when he realized that his arduous exertions, even at the risk of his life, amounted to so little is not recorded.

During his short and turbulent career as a timber agent, Willard endured calumny, attempted bribery, assault, and attempted murder. He was maligned in the press, and accused of blackmail before his superiors in Washington. But he was defended by newspapers, too. The following appeared in the *Detroit Free Press*, May 20, 1854:

Mr. Isaac W. Willard, the United States Timber Agent for this State, is a scrupulously honest man, as hundreds of his neighbors can attest. . . . He has, within a single year since he entered upon the discharge of his duties, entirely broken up and driven off the bands of plunderers who were despoiling the public lands, and has saved the treasury department thousands of dollars, obtained for the timber that was in the process of removal; and he has, besides, brought to the bar of justice some scores of persons who persisted in timber depredations.

Although Isaac Willard is scarcely remembered today, except perhaps by an occasional historian, at least he is remembered with respect.[13]

Judgment of Time

In the long march of time, a minor episode like this one and a minor character like Isaac Willard have little individual significance. But they are worth noting because they gave impetus to the emerging conservation movement. The Willard episode clearly showed that the public land could be defended from plunder if the government wanted to enforce the law. Conversely, it also showed that political expediency often interfered with law enforcement, for when the politicians put pressures on the secretary of the interior, the secretary dismissed all the timber agents. Also dismissed was the commissioner of the Land Office, to whom the secretary had delegated the duty of protecting the federal forests. In addition, the secretary stopped the arrests and suits for timber theft, leaving law enforcement to local officers, which meant practically no enforcement at all. Some of these officers were bribed by lumbermen to do nothing.

The Willard incident—and there would be many more like it—was a triumph of politics over the common welfare. Resource protection had taken a tentative step forward, then was brought to a halt, not to advance again until the 1890s.[14] The government's machinery for conducting its own public-land business was defective and would not start to function with even partial efficiency for another half-century. Eventually, the dawn of conservation's day would break. Meanwhile, thinking citizens in increasing numbers began to criticize the government for shabby handling of its forest estate.

In summary, the Isaac Willard case is worth noting for two reasons. First, the case marks a turning point in the government's responsibility toward its own lands. Second, it reveals something of the difference in values that once separated politicians from conservationists, and indeed still does on occasion.

13. Willard died April 8, 1879.
14. On December 24, 1855, the General Land Office issued a policy circular that was to govern the administration of the public timberlands for more than twenty years. In short, what resulted was a haphazard job of law enforcement. For an interesting account of this period, see Lucile Kane, "Federal Protection of Public Timber in the Upper Great Lakes States," *Agricultural History*, vol. 23 (1949), pp. 135–39. This article was republished in Vernon Carstensen (ed.), *The Public Lands: Studies in the History of the Public Domain* (University of Wisconsin Press, 1963), pp. 439–47.

CHAPTER **2**

Forestry's Uncertain Beginning

In 1864, George Perkins Marsh established the basic principles of resource conservation—principles that have endured for more than a century—in his remarkable book *Man and Nature.*[1] A scholar with wide-ranging interests, a thoughtful observer with ability to analyze and describe what he saw, he laboriously explained the relationships of water, soil, and vegetative cover. He demonstrated by hundreds of references to European scientific knowledge how changes in grass and tree cover cause changes in soil and water; in short, how man was changing the physical condition of the earth.

Marsh's book does not include the word *forestry*, which was scarcely known in America. His chapter "The Woods" has 200 pages; it contains a section on "Sylviculture." He used the word *sylviculture* as meaning much the same thing as forestry; to describe what is now known as forest management, he employed the term *system of forest economy*. He was one of the first Americans to discuss forest conservation principles, although he did not use that term.

Marsh assembled an impressive miscellany of facts and opinions about the relationship of woodland to civilization and presented a wealth of data bearing on the decline of agriculture, of water supplies, of cities, and indeed of whole civilizations. In his opinion, and in that of the scientists and other observers he quoted, the cause was deforestation. His massive evidence indicated that the cutting of forests, fire, and overgrazing had ruined extensive areas of once-productive land in China, Europe, and North Africa.

Citing instances from ancient and contemporary history, he drew the conclusion that denuding the mountain slopes of forests led to floods in the valleys, that flooding followed by arid conditions ruined fields for agriculture, and that, consequently, communities and even cities fell into decay. Among his examples were provinces in China where erosion caused by overcutting had turned formerly dense forests into wastelands. He also described the

1. Charles Scribner, 1864. For the modern edition of this classic, see David Lowenthal (ed.), *The Earth as Modified by Man's Action* (Harvard University Press, 1965).

shortage of wood for agriculture and local industries and of fuel for home use that resulted from destructive felling in France, Italy, Portugal, Spain, North Africa (especially along the borders of the Mediterranean), Great Britain, Bavaria, Prussia, Switzerland, Japan, and even well-wooded Finland.

Marsh was joined by other scientists and "natural philosophers" in presenting the case for forest preservation as the support of American civilization. Pointing out the connection between soil erosion and stream siltation, for example, they called attention to the disappearance of trout streams and salmon runs in New England rivers. They explained the chain of cause and effect connecting the clearcutting of forests to repeated fires, to the drying up of springs, to the rapid runoff of water from bare slopes, to the sedimentation of rivers. Coastal waters once navigable by sizable vessels were no longer usable for commerce. Ports on tidal creeks, where schooners formerly called to load lumber, tobacco, and other agricultural crops, became ghost towns. One did not need a scientific education to perceive the relationship between forest devastation on the one hand and soil erosion, the gullying of land, and stream siltation on the other.

To Marsh, it was "a matter of the utmost importance that the public, and especially land owners, be roused to a sense of the dangers to which the indiscriminate clearing of the woods may expose not only future generations but the very soil itself." Like other thinking men of his era, he had no hope that the government would halt the plundering of its own forests and the destruction of woodland generally. "For prevention of the evils upon which I have so long dwelt," he warned, "the American people must look to the diffusion of general intelligence on this subject and to the enlightened self interest, for which they are remarkable, not to the action of their local or general legislators."[2]

Although certain officials in government and members of Congress were aware of the resource destruction going on around them, the government itself was not the motivating force in conservation. In truth, the federal government did little until scientists, such as Marsh, and other public-spirited citizens began to call for action to protect the forests from spoliation. Thus, the indifference of public officials in high places created an enormous inertia difficult to overcome. How could it have been otherwise in an era when the logger's double-bit ax and the crosscut saw were symbols of progress?

Destiny Shaped by Scientists

Loomis Havemeyer of the Yale University Sheffield Scientific School forthrightly assigned the credit to those entitled to it.

The modern conservation movement is the direct result of the work of scientific men. The great question of conservation has been forwarded more by the rapid reduction of our forests than by any other cause. The forests are the natural resource whose rapid destruction made scientists realize as early as in the seventies that, if existing practice were continued, the end was in the not far distant future.[3]

2. *Man and Nature*, pp. 234, 303.
3. *Conservation of Our Natural Resources*, p. 5.

Among the small group of scientists who helped bring the forestry movement to the attention of the government and their scientific peers was a Yale professor of agriculture. For the United States census of 1870, William Henry Brewer of the Yale Sheffield Scientific School prepared a special report, "The Woodlands and Forest Systems of the United States," published in the *Statistical Atlas* in 1874. It contained most of the knowledge on the subject available at that period. A botanist, chemist, and geologist, Brewer began as early as 1873 to give lectures on forests and forestry at Yale, perhaps the first such instruction to be offered in an American university.

In a paper written a half-century after his own entry into forestry, Henry S. Graves reminisced about some of the men who had been active in promoting the forest conservation movement of the 1870s and 1880s.

Gifford Pinchot and I were the first Americans to take up forestry as a profession, and we often have been given too much credit for initiating the national forestry movement. In point of fact the swift advance in forestry in the nineties and subsequently would not have been possible if there had not been the background of activities by scientists, educators and other public spirited citizens over a period of 20 to 25 years before we came on the ground.[4]

Graves then mentioned "Edward A. Bowers, a Yale man, who left in his will a fund for the Forestry School, used for the construction of Bowers Hall, a wing of the main forestry building. In the early days Bowers was a special agent of the Government in prosecution of violations of the public land laws." Additional men mentioned by Graves, "whose influence in forwarding the movement cannot fully be appraised," were Brewer; Clarence King, author of *Mountaineering in the Sierra Nevada* (1874); John Muir; F. B. Hough; C. S. Sargent; and Nathaniel S. Shaler, state geologist of Kentucky, who wrote a book on the forests and trees of Kentucky, and who later was influential in the establishment of the Harvard forestry school in 1904.

One of the earliest and most successful efforts by the scientific community to arouse Congress to the urgency of governmental action for forest preservation stemmed from an address by Franklin Benjamin Hough of Lowville, New York. This many-sided man was a physician who had served during the Civil War. Historian, naturalist, and statistician, he was an indefatigable writer of articles, letters, and speeches. Presumably, he became interested in forest preservation while serving as superintendent of the New York State Census and as a member of a commission appointed in 1872 to look into the possibility of a state park in the Adirondacks.

In 1873, the American Association for the Advancement of Science (AAAS), which had been organized in 1849, held its annual meeting in Portland, Maine. In his address, "On the Duty of Governments in the Preservation of Forests," Hough described the severe damage suffered by other nations following deforestation, particularly of mountain slopes, and then proposed that the United States retain in government ownership its extensive forest lands in the West. He concluded with the suggestion "that this Association

4. "Background of a New Profession," March 14, 1947 (Graves Collection, Sterling Memorial Library, Yale University).

might properly take measures for bringing to the notice of our several State Governments, and Congress with respect to the Territories, the subject of protection to the forests and their cultivation, regulation, and encouragement"; and that it appoint a committee for this purpose.[5] In the history of American conservation, it is doubtful if any document presented by an ordinary citizen had more immediate and lasting effect than Hough's paper. It set in motion a series of events whose direct consequences are perceptible nearly a century later.

The AAAS voted to appoint a committee "to memorialize Congress and the several State Legislatures upon the importance of promoting the cultivation of timber and the preservation of forests, and to recommend proper legislation for securing these objects."[6] Hough was named chairman of the committee. The other members were Professor Brewer; George Barrell Emerson, a retired educator who had written a comprehensive report of the trees and forests of Massachusetts, first published in 1846; Asa Gray, recently retired Harvard professor of natural history, America's foremost botanist, and author of the impressive *Manual of Botany* (1848); and Eugene W. Hilgard, professor of agriculture at the University of Michigan and an eminent soil scientist.

Promptly going to work, the committee prepared a memorial that emphasized that "the preservation and growth of timber is a subject of great practical importance to people of the United States, and is becoming every year of more and more consequence, from the increasing demand for its use; and while this rapid exhaustion is taking place, there is no effectual provision against waste and for the renewal of supply."[7] Then followed a request for the creation of a federal commission of forestry—a proposal that doubtless was influenced by the establishment by Congress in 1871 of the Commission of Fish and Fisheries. During the following winter, the committee visited Washington, saw President Grant, and submitted the memorial and the draft of a joint resolution for the appointment of a federal commission to investigate forest conditions.

President Grant referred the memorial and the proposed joint resolution to the secretary of the interior. The secretary, in turn, passed them down to the commissioner of the General Land Office, who reported back that he concurred in the plan suggested. The secretary of the interior then informed the president that he concurred with the views of the commissioner and suggested the propriety of laying the matter before Congress.

The president transmitted the memorial and the departmental reports to Congress in February 1874 with a special message. In the House of Representatives the documents were referred to the Committee on Public Lands. Within a month, the committee reported out a bill providing for the appointment of a commission of inquiry into forest destruction and the measures necessary

---

5. AAAS, *Proceedings*, 22nd annual meeting, Portland, Maine, August 1873 (Salem, Mass.: 1874), p. 10.
6. Ibid., p. 429.
7. Ibid.

for timber preservation. But the bill died aborning, less the victim of Congressional opposition than of indifference.

Resubmitted in the next Congress, the bill fared no better. Hough in his "Report upon Forestry," published in the *Proceedings* of the 1878 meeting of the AAAS, wrote: "Although several of the members expressed opinions favorable to the subject, the Committee made no report, and in view of the issues then pending, on the eve of a presidential election, it soon became apparent that the occasion would not be favorable for the inauguration of new measures."[8]

Herbert A. Smith, historian for the Forest Service, commented in 1929: "For some reason the bill which would have placed the new work in the Interior Department failed, at two if not three sessions of Congress, [but] finally went through in somewhat modified form when attached as a rider to the free seed clause in the Agriculture Appropriation Act."[9]

First Forestry Agent

Congressman Mark Hill Dunnell of Minnesota, chairman of the Public Lands Committee, accomplished by a political stratagem what he knew he was unlikely to obtain by the conventional procedure of guiding the bill through his committee and onto the floor for a vote. Since the latter possibility appeared remote, he added an amendment to a pending appropriation bill. Among other things, the bill provided for free seed distribution for agricultural experimentation, and it was to this clause that Congressman Dunnell attached the rider.

And so it happened that forestry by the federal government got its start under the Appropriations Act of August 15, 1876, which authorized $2,000 to be expended by the commissioner of agriculture. What Commissioner Frederick Watts was expected to obtain with this modest sum was the service of a superior kind of American, whose qualifications and duties were outlined as follows:

> ... some man of approved attainments, who is practically well acquainted with methods of statistical inquiry, and who has evinced an intimate acquaintance with questions relating to the national wants in regard to timber to prosecute investigations and inquiries, with the view of ascertaining the annual amount of consumption, importation, and exportation of timber and other forest products, the probable supply for future wants, the best means adapted to their preservation and renewal, the influence of forests upon climate, and the measures that have been successfully applied in foreign countries, or that may be deemed applicable to this country, for the preservation and restoration or planting of forests, and to report upon the same to the Commissioner of Agriculture, to be transmitted by him in a special report to Congress.[10]

Samuel T. Dana commented: "Thus did the promotion of forestry become a function of the Department of Agriculture through a rider attached to

---

8. AAAS, *Proceedings*, 26th annual meeting, St. Louis, Mo., August 1878 (Salem, Mass.: 1879), pp. 29–40.

9. "Federal Organization for Forestry Work," March 22, 1929 (Manuscript Division, Sterling Memorial Library, Yale University).

10. *Appropriations Act of August 15, 1876* (19 Stat. 143, 167).

a minor item in an appropriation bill without debate and probably without even the knowledge of most members of Congress.[11]

The initial amount of $2,000 appropriated by Congress for 1876 was not renewed for the following year. Indeed, for four years the forestry program was kept going by allocations from general appropriations to the Department of Agriculture. In 1877, the allotment was $2,000; it was $2,500 for each year thereafter. At last, this uncertain period was ended in 1881 when Congress made $5,000 available and then increased the sum to $10,000 for another two years.

On August 30, 1876, only fifteen days after the bill became law, Hough accepted the assignment to prepare the forestry report for Congress. He immediately began gathering data on the subjects specified by Congress and invited the collaboration of persons having knowledge about them. In a letter published in the magazine *Forest and Stream* (May 10, 1877), he asked the cooperation of botanists, entomologists, and other observers of natural history. Explaining his appointment, he requested information on the principal native tree species, on second growth following cutting, on the effect of forests on climate, on experiments in forest planting, and on forest destruction by insects and disease.

Hough submitted his first official *Report upon Forestry* to Congress the next year. Although the voluminous document filled 650 pages, Congress authorized the printing of 25,000 copies, an unusual press run for that era for a report on a new and little-understood subject. He wrote another report that was published in 1880. These reports comprise a miscellany of data, mainly on the forest resources of the United States, but also of Canada and Europe. He advocated stations for research, investigations of forest fire, and observations of weather to learn about the influence of wooded areas on climate. Hough went to Europe in 1881 to study forestry practices and to learn how they might be applied in America. An account of his European observations was printed in his third and last report of 1882.

In 1881, Hough's minuscule agency was advanced to the status of a separate Division of Forestry in the Department of Agriculture. Even so, he had practically no staff or facilities for field research and precious little money for travel. Yet, he did get around the country to call on governors and state officials to gather data on forest conditions and to try to induce them to pass laws for forest preservation. Through these meetings and by correspondence he garnered much valuable information, not previously available in any one place, for study and interpretation. In the main, his contributions were of two kinds: fact-finding and reporting on the one hand, and urging action by the federal and state governments on the other.

A prolific writer as well as a prodigious worker, his production was amazing. For example, in 1882 his book *The Elements of Forestry* was published at a time when he was fully occupied with his governmental duties. Also in 1882, he started the *American Journal of Forestry*, which was published for one year only and failed for lack of financial support. But he prophesied that the time would come when a similar enterprise would be

11. *Forest and Range Policy*, p. 81.

sustained. Twenty years later, a technical journal of forestry was launched successfully.

Hough's prescience with respect to the development of a professional forestry journal was faulty with regard to the future of professional education. In 1883, he advocated lectures on forestry in secondary schools but saw no need for instruction at the technical level. He doubted that persons especially trained in forestry, as in the forestry schools of Europe, would find employment in the United States. Yet, within two decades, three curriculums in forestry were being offered in New York, North Carolina, and Pennsylvania.

In 1883, Hough was replaced as head of the Division of Forestry by Nathaniel H. Egleston of Jamaica Plain, Massachusetts, a Congregational minister and former teacher with an interest in forests and rural life. Egleston had helped organize The American Forestry Association and was one of its vice presidents, but he had little experience in, or knowledge of, forestry—if any.

Hough's replacement by Egleston prompted Samuel T. Dana to comment, "Whatever the reasons for the change, they were not based on the relative competence of the two men."[12] Gifford Pinchot, never one to hesitate calling a spade a spade, referred to Egleston as "one of those failures in life whom the spoils system is constantly catapulting into responsible positions" and spoke of his tenure as "three years of innocuous desuetude."[13] Dr. Egleston was replaced on March 15, 1886, by Bernhard E. Fernow, a native of Germany who had graduated from the Prussian Forest Academy at Münden.

Forest Reserves Created

During the mid-1870s, while the AAAS was spearheading action in forestry on behalf of the scientific community, a citizens' organization was getting started that would spearhead action in behalf of the general public. This organization was The American Forestry Association, which came into existence largely through the imagination and energy of a doctor of medicine, John Aston Warder of Ohio. In addition to being a physician, Dr. Warder was a practicing farmer with a special interest in horticulture and forestry. Following a trip to Europe in 1873 to attend an international exhibition in Vienna, he wrote an official report for the government on his observations of European forests and forestry. The American Forestry Association was founded in Chicago in September 1875, and Dr. Warder became its first president, serving for seven years.

In his announcement of the organizing meeting, Dr. Warder proposed that one object of the association should be "the fostering of all interests of forest planting and conservation on this continent."[14] It is noteworthy that the word *conservation* as specifically applied to forests was used, probably for the first time.

In *Breaking New Ground* Gifford Pinchot devoted a chapter to "The Birth of Conservation." According to him, the concept of conservation

12. Ibid., p. 83.
13. *Breaking New Ground*, p. 135.
14. W. N. Sparhawk, "The History of Forestry in America," in U.S. Department of Agriculture, *Trees: The Yearbook of Agriculture*, p. 705.

flashed through his head while he was riding horseback in Rock Creek Park in Washington, D.C., on a winter day in 1907. Describing it as a "newborn idea," he later discussed it with Overton Price and other advisers and then took it to President Roosevelt, who "understood, accepted, and adopted it without the smallest hesitation." Pinchot claimed that "launching the Conservation movement was the most significant achievement of the T. R. Administration, as he himself believed."[15]

But according to William N. Sparhawk, "the term 'forest conservation' [as used by Dr. Warder] . . . was in use more than 30 years before it was taken up and popularized by Gifford Pinchot and Theodore Roosevelt."[16] It can be no detraction from the Pinchot–Roosevelt program, so revolutionary in concept, so grandiose in scale, to insert this footnote to history and assign credit for the birth of conservation where it is due: to John A. Warder and The American Forestry Association.

The American Association for the Advancement of Science, which in the 1870s had led the drive to establish a forestry agency in the Department of Agriculture, undertook another drive in the 1880s. Its goal was to obtain Congressional authority to reserve as public forests those government-owned timberlands in the West that had not already passed into private ownership. In this movement, the AAAS was supported by The American Forestry Association. Because of the value of these lands as watersheds, the proposal was also endorsed by water irrigation interests in the West.

As early as 1878, Secretary of the Interior Carl Schurz had unsuccessfully proposed a forest reservation bill. Numerous additional bills advocating the reservation of public timberlands were introduced. Although they all failed,[17] they patently had educational value; some Congressmen became aware that forest reserves were a live issue and that influential elements of the public believed the time had come for a revision of the land laws.

At the meeting of the AAAS in Toronto in 1889, B. E. Fernow, chief of the Division of Forestry, delivered an address entitled "Need of a Forest Administration for the United States." Following this speech, and doubtless influenced by it, the AAAS adopted a memorial advocating forest reservations and delivered it to President Harrison, who transmitted the memorial to Congress early in 1890. Congressman Dunnell, whose rider attached to the Agriculture Appropriations Act of 1876 started the forestry work in the federal government, introduced a bill based on the AAAS memorial, but without result.

About this time, another group of professional people became interested in the forest conservation movement. The American Economic Association, organized in 1885, held its fourth annual meeting in Washington, D.C., December 26–30, 1890.[18] One session with the theme "Government and

15. *Ibid.*, p. 325.
16. Sparhawk, "The History of Forestry," p. 705.
17. These abortive legislative attempts are discussed by John Ise in *The United States Forest Policy.*
18. The origins of the American Economic Association and its early interest in conservation and land policy are discussed by Henry C. Taylor and Anne Dewees Taylor in *The Story of Agricultural Economics in the United States, 1840–1932* (Iowa State College Press, 1952), pp. 856–70.

Forestry" was arranged jointly with The American Forestry Association. Three papers of consequence were presented: "Government Forestry Abroad," by Gifford Pinchot; "The Present Condition of the Forests on the Public Lands," by Edward A. Bowers; and "Practicability of an American Forest Administration," by B. E. Fernow.

In addition to these three papers, the Association published a proposed bill for protecting and administering the forests of the public domain. The bill provided for a federal commissioner of forests and four assistant commissioners, who would constitute a forestry board. Also proposed were the establishment of forest reserves, the restoration of forest lands, and the prevention of unlawful cutting of public timber.[19]

Edward A. Bowers, a lawyer employed by the General Land Office in 1886, worked closely with Fernow, becoming so interested in forest conservation that he was elected secretary of The American Forestry Association. With Fernow he prepared a comprehensive plan for the administration of the public domain timber, and was probably the author of the bill mentioned above. In his paper, he described the condition of the public forests as bad and criticized laws that provided neither for adequate protection of the public timber nor for its proper utilization.

In reviewing the public land policies prevailing during the period up to 1890, a student of government is likely to be both appalled and incredulous. Railroads having government land grants or rights of way were permitted to cut adjacent timber for construction purposes. Timber cutting on mineral lands by bona fide residents was also permitted. But in the vast territory from the Missouri River to the Pacific states, settlers were without legal right to cut public timber. Consequently, to obtain the wood necessary for their existence they simply had to steal it.

As a former inspector of the Public Land Service in the General Land Office, Bowers' conclusions were those of a responsible citizen and honest public servant fed up with politicians.

This condition of affairs is not the fault of the officers of the Interior Department or the General Land Office having charge of these lands, but of Congress, which persistently ignores the calls of these officers for such a change in the laws as will enable them to protect the public timber. While this is so, it is the duty of this Association to agitate this question until reform is accomplished.[20]

According to Bowers, during the period 1881–87, the value of timber reported stolen from government land was in excess of $36 million and the amount recovered was $478,000. Although the annual appropriation for protection against trespass and theft was barely sufficient to employ an average of twenty-five timber agents, they were expected to protect 70 million acres of public timberlands. Worse yet, they were appointed for political reasons

19. *Publications of the American Economic Association,* vol. 6 (May 1891), pp. 184–285.
20. Edward A. Bowers, "The Present Condition of the Forests on the Public Lands," *Publications of the American Economic Association,* vol. 6 (January and March 1891), p. 157.

and were without knowledge or fitness for the work, as instances cited by Bowers proved.

Finally, on March 3, 1891, Congress passed the bill that Gifford Pinchot was to call "the most important legislation in the history of Forestry in America," although when first introduced, the act that inspired this encomium contained nothing whatever about forest reserves. It was simply a bill to repeal obsolete timber culture laws already in the statute books.

What happened was this: Congress was about to adjourn. A conference committee of the Senate and the House of Representatives was designated to resolve certain discrepancies in the proposed legislation. This committee hastily inserted a new section that authorized reservations. Section 24 read as follows:

That the President of the United States may, from time to time, set apart and reserve, in any State or Territory having public land bearing forests, in any part of the public lands wholly or in part covered with timber or undergrowth, whether of commercial value or not, as public reservations, and the President shall, by public proclamation, declare the establishment of such reservations and the limits thereof.[21]

In a pertinent comment about Section 24, S. T. Dana observed: "That it was prepared in considerable haste is indicated by the fact that it is not even a complete sentence, the transitive verbs 'set apart and reserve' not being followed by any object. This grammatical slip, however, has not led to any question as to the intent or the validity of the act."[22]

The insertion of Section 24 clearly violated a Congressional rule prohibiting the addition by committee conferees of matter not in the original bills. "It was almost a miracle," Herbert A. Smith said of Section 24. "To this day no one knows exactly who wrought it, but in one way or other it slipped through Congress, doubtless through the inattention of the legislators interested on the other side, as an obscure rider attached in the crowded closing hours of a short session of Congress to an important and elaborate general act."[23]

Pinchot was more certain than Herbert Smith as to how the law came about.

In 1891 the most important legislation in the history of Forestry in America slipped through Congress without question and without debate. It was an amendment to the Act of March 3, 1891, . . . and it authorized the creation of Forest Reserves. This was the beginning and basis of our whole National Forest system.

Secretary Noble of the Interior Department, and Edward A. Bowers, at that time a Special Agent in the General Land Office, who suggested it, deserve the credit for this fundamental legislation.[24]

21. 26 Stat. 1095.
22. *Forest and Range Policy*, p. 101.
23. "Federal Organization for Forestry Work" (memorandum to the chief of the Forest Service, March 22, 1929).
24. *Breaking New Ground*, p. 85. John Willock Noble, who had been a brevet brigadier general in the Union Army during the Civil War, was practicing law in St. Louis when President Harrison appointed him secretary of the interior. He held the post during the period 1889–93.

Pinchot could on occasion be less than generous in giving credit to those who differed with him, and he neglected to mention Bernhard E. Fernow. Yet, on the basis of the historical record, Fernow is entitled to at least equal credit with Noble and Bowers, and some students would give him the most.

In the weekly AAAS journal, Fernow reviewed the events leading to the passage of the historic legislation. For a quarter-century, he said, every secretary of the interior and every commissioner of the General Land Office had asked that the public lands be safeguarded. "Bill after bill," he wrote, "had been introduced for the protection of the public timber, but most of these never found consideration even in the committees, much less on the floor of the two Houses of Congress."[25]

Fernow told how in 1887 the secretary of The American Forestry Association had drafted a detailed bill providing for the withdrawal of all public domain timberlands from entry or other disposal, setting them aside as reservations. The bill provided for a special agency in the Department of the Interior to administer the proposed forest reserves; protect them from fire and theft; regulate their use by prospectors, miners, and herders; and permit the cutting and sale of timber under "rational forestry methods."

"Of this radical yet reasonable legislation," Fernow went on, "all that could be obtained was the enactment of a brief clause, inserted at the last hour of the 51st Congress into 'An Act to repeal Timber-culture laws and for other purposes.' The credit for securing this recognition belongs to the then Secretary of the Interior, Hon. John W. Noble." According to Fernow, Secretary Noble managed to insert Section 24 into the act as follows:

My memory is, that at the time the story was current, Mr. Noble declared at midnight of March 3, in the Conference Committee, that he would not let the President sign the bill (for abolishing the timber claim legislation) unless the Reservation clause was inserted. Since these things happen behind closed doors, only someone present can tell what happened, Secretary Noble or one of the conferees. All we, that is, Bowers and myself, can claim is that we had educated Noble up to that point.[26]

J. P Kinney called Section 24 "a half-concealed but radical step in the national policy" and gave credit for it to B. E. Fernow and "his associates in the American Forestry Association."[27]

Administration of the Reserves

At a meeting of The American Forestry Association in Springfield, Massachusetts, September 4–5, 1895, Gifford Pinchot read a paper on the condition of forest reserves and the need for action to protect them. He held that, since past efforts of the association had been largely ineffectual, the proper method of procedure would be through a three-man Forest Commission to be created by Congress, as had been proposed by Robert Underwood Johnson of

25. "The Forest Reservation Policy," *Science*, March 26, 1897, p. 490. At this time Fernow was chairman of the Executive Committee of the American Forestry Association.
26. Ibid.
27. *The Development of Forest Law in America*, p. 244.

Century magazine. Fernow, chief of the Division of Forestry, strongly opposed Pinchot's views on the ground that immediate action was needed, rather than a Congressional investigation. The association, however, passed a resolution for the establishment of the commission.[28]

In a letter to Johnson, Fernow later recalled this episode with some bitterness:

It was in that year [1895] at the Springfield meeting, Mr. Pinchot appeared, with you to support him, to tell us we didn't know our business, that we had done nothing. You may remember my protestations to the charges of a man who had never up to that time done a thing to forward the work of the Association. At the time when we were almost successful in establishing a real forest administration, we were asked to stultify ourselves by asking for a commission to suggest such an administration. . . .

Our Executive Committee at Washington was dismayed at the action of the Springfield meeting, finding fault with me for having given way to this unwarranted change of method. I was anxious at that time to secure the good will of everybody interested in the subject, especially Messrs. Sargent and Pinchot, who had taken an offish position for reasons which I now understand better than I did at that time.

P.S. I want to accentuate that most credit for the conservation policy is due friend Bowers, which I have recognized in the dedication of my book to him![29]

Although Pinchot praised the act of 1891, the legislation only partially solved one problem and soon raised others. The future of the millions of acres of public domain timberlands was only apparently secured. What Congress could do it could also undo. Certain affected interests badgered and bedeviled the president and Congress to rescind or nullify the reserves that had been established. In short, the so-called Forest Reserve Act raised several fundamental issues that had to be resolved before a national forestry policy could be firmed up.

Perhaps no man, inside or outside government, was better informed about these momentous developments than Fernow. Writing not as the chief of the Division of Forestry but as chairman of the executive committee of The American Forestry Association, he recorded the salient events.

In the fall of 1895, finding that the arguments for legislation did not procure its enactment, the Secretary of the Interior was induced by the Executive Committee of the Forestry Association to call upon the National Academy of Science [sic] for an expression of advice as to the need and methods of a proper administration of the public timberlands, in order to secure the weight of authority of that body to the proposition. The Academy, as customary, appointed a committee, asked an appropriation of $25,000 for the purpose of field examination, and members of this committee visited the regions where the public lands are situated.[30]

28. From the report of B. E. Fernow, chairman of the Executive Committee, American Forestry Association, December 28, 1895.

29. August 15, 1908 (Johnson Collection, Bancroft Library, University of California at Berkeley). For forty years, Johnson had been associated with *Century* magazine and was editor during the period 1909–13. He aided campaigns to promote Yosemite and Sequoia National Parks.

30. "The Forest Reservation Policy," p. 490.

The committee submitted its report[31] to the secretary of the interior on May 1, 1897. Doubtless because of the eminence of the committee members[32] in the scientific community, the editors of *Science* published an analysis of the report in the issue of June 11, 1897.

In his letter of February 15, 1896, Secretary of the Interior Hoke Smith had asked the National Academy three questions:

1. Whether it was desirable and practical to preserve from fire and to maintain permanently as forest land those portions of the public domain[33] then bearing wood growth for the supply of timber. The committee reported that it was not only desirable but essential.

2. What influence forests had on climate, soil, and water. The committee replied that forests are necessary to prevent destructive spring floods and low water in summer and autumn.

3. What specific legislation should be enacted. The committee presented a series of recommendations for action by Congress.

Regarding the need for better protection of the public forests, the committee pulled no punches. Its comments on the inadequacy of Interior's custody of the forests and the incompetence of the politically appointed employees were scathing:

Our examination of the Western forests shows that existing methods and forces at the disposal of the Interior Department are entirely inadequate to protect the forests of the public domain. Civil employees, often selected for political reasons and retained in office by political favor, insufficiently paid and without security in their tenure of office, have proved unable to cope with the difficulties of forest protection, and the reserves are practically unguarded. Excluded from the provisions of the general land laws and without protection, they invite trespass of every kind and demoralize without benefitting the community.[34]

"To reduce the number and restrict the ravages of forest fires in the Western States and Territories," the committee recommended that details from the army should be used permanently, or until a body of trained forest guards or rangers could be organized. The committee declared flatly that it was not "practicable or possible to protect the forests of the public domain with the present methods and machinery of Government."[35]

---

31. "Report of the Commission Appointed by the National Academy of Sciences upon a Forest Policy for the Forested Lands of the United States," *Report of the National Academy of Sciences for the Year 1897*, S. Doc. 57, 55 Cong., 2 sess. (1898). Although "commission" is used in the title of the report, the NAS group was originally appointed as a committee.
32. Charles S. Sargent of Arnold Arboretum, Harvard University, was the chairman. The other members were Henry L. Abbot, Alexander Agassiz, William H. Brewer, Arnold Hague, Gifford Pinchot, and Wolcott Gibbs.
33. At that time, the public domain contained 600 million acres of open and unappropriated public lands, nearly all in the West. Less than 20 million acres were in forest reserves.
34. "Forest Policy for the Public Lands of the United States," *Science*, vol. 5 (June 11, 1897), pp. 895–96.
35. Ibid.

Going further, the committee recommended that a Bureau of Public Forests should be established in the Department of the Interior and staffed with specially selected and qualified officers. It recommended also that a Board of Forest Lands be appointed by the president to determine what portions of the public domain should be reserved permanently as forest lands. Public lands more valuable for the production of timber than for agriculture and mining should be withdrawn from sale, settlement, and other disposition and held for the growth and sale of timber. Finally, the committee proposed that portions of the Rainier Forest Reserve and the Grand Canyon Forest Reserve should be set aside as national parks.

To back up for a moment: The committee of the National Academy of Sciences held a meeting on October 24, 1896. Although the committee's report was not yet ready, the members unanimously agreed to recommend the establishment of new forest reserves. This action could be taken by presidential proclamation, as authorized by Section 24 of the 1891 act, and would not require passage of legislation by Congress. Chairman Charles S. Sargent conveyed the recommendation to President Wolcott Gibbs of the National Academy on January 29, 1897. Gibbs in turn passed it on the Secretary of the Interior David R. Francis, who had succeeded Hoke Smith. On February 6, Secretary Francis proposed that President Cleveland, who would soon be going out of office, issue proclamations on Washington's birthday "establishing these grand forest reservations."[36] Cleveland did so on February 22, 1897, creating thirteen new reservations containing more than 20 million acres.

Congress did not accept the committee's recommendations for administration of the forest reserves. But it passed the law of June 4, 1897, the basic legislation on which the administrative structure of the Forest Service was later built. This law, known as the Forest Reserve Act of 1897 was also a rider, in this case appended to the sundry civil appropriations bill. It was passed largely in retaliation for Cleveland's proclamations, which were unpopular among some congressmen and had set off a storm of criticism. The 1897 law suspended Cleveland's proclamations until March 1, 1898, and authorized President McKinley to revoke or modify them. But it did more than that. It instructed the secretary of the interior to protect the reserves against fire and depredations, and authorized him to make regulations for their administration.

Although McKinley was granted authority to annul the reserves established by Cleveland, and was indeed of a mind to do it, he did not. Instead, he accepted the counsel of the eminent botanist Charles Sprague Sargent, chairman of the committee of the National Academy of Sciences. Years later, in a letter to Henry S. Graves, Sargent described how this committee interceded with President McKinley to safeguard the forest reservations set aside by President Cleveland.

36. Letter, David R. Francis to Grover Cleveland (Department of the Interior Records, Lands and Railroads Division, National Archives).

There was a strong pressure on McKinley to annul Cleveland's action and our Commission called on him two days after his inauguration. He was bent on returning Cleveland's reservation to the public domain and told us that he was going to do it. After our interview was over I went back alone and had a private interview with McKinley which lasted I think an hour. When it was over he had decided to let the reservation stand and take no action in the matter. I have always felt that this was the best day's work I ever put in for this country. I do not think I have ever spoken of this to any one and it is hardly a matter for publication. It is good history nevertheless.[37]

Strong opposition arose in the states where these extensive acreages had been put into reserves. Since many of these lands were occupied by mining and lumber companies, their appropriation threatened to close local businesses and to curtail employment. Complaints mounted; Congress heard them.

Meanwhile, petitions for a number of additional reservations had been prepared but were not proposed until legislation could be obtained for their proper use and administration. Bills to establish the necessary policies and administrative procedures were introduced but fared badly. Again, Congress neglected the simple custodial chores that would protect the government's most valuable real estate.

It is one of the ironies of conservation history that the three fundamental acts of Congress establishing a United States forestry policy came about through a combination of circumstances in which chance and opportunism were the controlling influences. It is incredible that these important statutory goals had to be reached by such devious routes.

Fortunately, scientists, professional men, and other citizens of good will prevailed on a largely indifferent Congress to establish forestry policies in the public interest. They firmly planted the conception of forest conservation in the minds of thinking Americans, a conception so well rooted that today conservation has become part of the American way of life.

Golden Era of Conservation

John Ise called the decade following the passage of the Forest Reserve Act the "golden era" of the conservation movement, "for more was accomplished during this decade than during any similar period in the history of that movement."[38]

In 1897, there were a few technical foresters in the United States— Fernow, Pinchot, Schenck, and Graves—who had received technical training. But there were none who could be described as professional foresters, because they lacked the kind of education in forestry that is available today. The Division of Forestry, under Fernow, had thirteen employees, six of whom were clerical staff. It was largely an office for gathering information and conducting investigations.

When Pinchot became chief of the old Division of Forestry on July 1, 1898, he promptly started to stimulate improved forestry practices on private lands by assigning the technical men in the Division to the assistance of

37. September 7, 1921 (Graves Collection).
38. *The United States Forest Policy*, p. 143.

landowners who might request such aid. Because of limited personnel, the aid consisted mainly of plans of management, called working plans, and demonstrations of silviculture on the ground. Three years later, when the Division was renamed the Bureau of Forestry, it obtained broader authority and increased funds for making working plans for private owners. This cooperative work by the Forest Service was a key activity for the simple reason that in order to practice forestry the foresters had to do it on private lands. The foresters were in Agriculture; the forest reserves were in Interior.

Pinchot had been in office as chief of the Division of Forestry only one year when the Appropriation Act of 1899 directed the secretary of agriculture to submit a detailed report on the work of the Division and on the practical results of the forestry investigations that had been initiated under Fernow. Certain Congressmen seriously contemplated abolishing the investigations, and the call for the report was virtually a summons to show cause why Congress should not put an end to them.

During Fernow's twelve years as chief, the Division had undertaken research in dendrology; experiments in tree planting, especially in the Plains States; and investigations in timber physics. Realizing that forestry required a scientific underpinning, Fernow had obtained the advice of scientists, and the investigations that Congress was now questioning were the start of the program in research that the Forest Service was later to expand to nationwide proportions.

In transmitting the requested report to Congress, Secretary James Wilson pointed out that, since Pinchot's appointment, the work of the Division had been directed into different channels. In his annual report of 1898, Pinchot outlined new plans. The secretary told Congress that he fully approved of the plans.

Under Pinchot's kinetic leadership, the Bureau of Forestry began to expand. From 11 employees in 1898, the number grew to 821 in 1905. Appropriations, which were $28,520 in 1898, increased to $439,873.

Up to this time, the government's supervision of its forest activities was divided between two departments and was spread over three bureaus. In addition to the Bureau of Forestry in the Department of Agriculture, there was a Forestry Division in the General Land Office of the Department of the Interior, but surveying and mapping were the responsibility of Interior's Geological Survey.

These conflicts and overlapping of functions were resolved when administration of the forest reserves was transferred from Interior to Agriculture in 1905. The Bureau of Forestry became the Forest Service, and two years later the reserves were named national forests.

Henry S. Graves, later chief of the Service, described the formidable job confronting the foresters and other technicians:

This was wildland, much of it in frontier country that had never been surveyed or, from the standpoint of character and condition of the forests, accurately described. It was an immense task to organize the management of these areas. It involved problems of determination of boundaries; land surveys; construction of roads, trails, and telephone lines; construction of ranger stations and other buildings; exploration and description of the forests; development of specific policies and procedures for disposal of timber; control of use of forage for livestock, and a multitude of other features of forest utilization; problems of building an adequate and competent administrative personnel; initiation of organized fire control; and development of techniques in applied forestry, range management, and protection of wildlife.[39]

By 1911, when Pinchot left the government, the national forest system had a net area of 170 million acres spread over twenty-one states and territories.

39. *Problems and Progress of Forestry in the United States*, p. 4.

CHAPTER **3**

Biltmore: Cradle of Forestry in the United States

Most of the important forestry beginnings in the United States have been small ones—almost inconsequential, it would appear at times. Looking back, we see that successful and well-established forces were presaged by minor or casual incidents. And thus it was with Biltmore in North Carolina, the first forest in the United States to be put under technical management. The events leading to the historic occasion when the first native forester undertook to apply the first silvicultural practices to private woodland make one of the fascinating chapters in the annals of American forestry.

The chronicle begins in 1889. That year, Gifford Pinchot graduated from Yale at the age of twenty-four. Because he wanted to go on to get a forestry education, he sought the advice of B. E. Fernow, who had been appointed chief of the Division of Forestry in the Department of Agriculture three years earlier. Fernow advised him to study in Europe, since no American college or university offered a curriculum of technical caliber. Pinchot left for Europe in October 1889. He soon met the renowned forester Sir Dietrich Brandis, who until 1883 had been inspector general of the Imperial Forest Service of India. At Brandis's suggestion, Pinchot enrolled in the National School of Waters and Forests at Nancy, France.

This institution was a logical choice, for Pinchot was of French ancestry. After six months at Nancy, he made a tour with Brandis and a party of students through the forests of Germany and Switzerland. Pinchot's European forestry instruction, in classroom and field, appears to have totaled not more than thirteen months.

On his return to the United States, he declined an offer from Fernow to become the latter's assistant in the Division of Forestry at an annual salary of $1,600. Instead, Pinchot accepted an appointment to take charge of George W. Vanderbilt's Biltmore Forest, which in Fernow's opinion was "a kind of impracticable fad."[1]

1. Letter, B. E. Fernow to Gifford Pinchot, February 2, 1892 (Pinchot Papers, Library of Congress).

Later, Fernow would be generous in acknowledging the pioneer work done at Biltmore. In a letter of July 20, 1893, he told Pinchot that "forest management has not been put into operation on any other area in this country except Biltmore." But he also told Pinchot: "If you can 'make forestry *profitable*' under the conditions of Biltmore within the next ten years, I shall consider you the wisest forester and financier of the age."[2]

This goal was beyond Pinchot's attainment during the few years he had direction of forestry at Biltmore.

First Managed Forest

In *Biltmore Forest*, a fifty-page report bound in hard covers and privately printed in Chicago in 1893, Pinchot described the results of the first year's work. He called it the first practical application of forest management in the United States.

In this item of forestry "incunabula," Pinchot provided the outline of his working plan for the estate of 7,282 acres, of which 3,891 acres were in timber. Prior to its acquisition by Vanderbilt, the property consisted mostly of farm woods, wastefully cutover for sawlogs, fuel wood, and fencing. Moreover, it had been destructively grazed by cattle and frequently burned for pasturage. Pinchot noted wryly that the condition of a large part of the forest was deplorable. In retrospect, we see it as an unlikely site to attempt the premier demonstration of private forestry for profit.

During his first year of supervision, Pinchot trained a nontechnical assistant and a crew of woodsmen, started improvement cuttings, constructed roads, and undertook the many chores essential to building up the productive capacity of a run-down stand. Because of the low quality of the timber, marketable products from the defective trees were hard to obtain and seldom profitable.

Discouraging difficulties similar to those faced by Pinchot would later confront hundreds of foresters in the eastern states. The almost insoluble problem was not so much how to make a profit from the management of low-grade hardwood second growth but how to undertake the necessary improvement and break even financially. Many well-qualified foresters would be defeated by this problem during the following seventy-five years, for the situation did not change until pulpwood markets became available.

Pinchot noted that the economic output of Biltmore Forest was unfavorable. Biltmore's products were of low grade and were in competition with the low-class products from the large area of surrounding timberland. Firewood was of little value, yet much of the product of Biltmore Forest would be firewood for many years to come. In addition to cordwood for a local brickworks, the forest produced railroad ties, fence posts, and lumber and shingles for use on the estate, all in competition with similar products sold on the open wood markets for the region.

Expenses for operating the forest during the period from May 1, 1892, to April 30, 1893, were $9,911. Pinchot's consulting fees were not included in his expense report. Woods labor was paid $1 a day; the rate for mules was 75

2. Quoted in Gifford Pinchot, *Breaking New Ground*, p. 50.

cents a day. Income for the year, including products on hand, was $9,519. The book loss was $392.

Approximately 1,000 acres of wasteland and clearings were included in the working plan for planting to forest trees. A nursery had been started; it contained 1.8 million seedlings of twenty species. But the expense of operating this nursery is not included in Pinchot's forest management costs. These costs were probably assigned to the work of Frederick Law Olmsted, the landscape architect of the estate, who had established an arboretum and had begun to plant the trees and shrubs that were to make Biltmore one of the show places of the Appalachians.

In his report and in his subsequent work for Vanderbilt, Pinchot was clearly intent on establishing the business basis of forest management. He believed that it was possible and necessary to prove that forestry was practical and could be commercially profitable. Biltmore Forest offered an opportunity, the first one, to demonstrate his beliefs.

Unfortunately, Biltmore Forest was precisely what its name implied—a rich man's estate. It had little possibility under a system of strict cost accounting of becoming a profitably managed forest. This is not to say that the work started by Pinchot was not technically sound; it doubtless was. But profitable it was not.

Management of Biltmore Forest was not Pinchot's sole assignment. He made reconnaissance surveys throughout the mountains to obtain information about forest conditions. Vanderbilt had plans to purchase additional woodland, and, like his plans for the estate, they were not little ones. On the basis of Pinchot's reports and recommendations, Vanderbilt acquired the Pisgah Forest of 80,000 acres, named for Mount Pisgah, a well-known landmark of western North Carolina. Eventually, Vanderbilt's forest holdings totaled 120,000 acres.

Having obtained permission from Vanderbilt to engage in an outside consulting practice, Pinchot opened an office in New York City in 1893. Then, after two years as Vanderbilt's forester, Pinchot "with other irons in the fire and characteristically beginning to tire of the routine at Biltmore, persuaded Vanderbilt of the need for a resident forester at Biltmore."[3] As Pinchot himself was the sole native American with technical training in forestry, it was necessary to look elsewhere for a suitable replacement, and he sought the advice of his former mentor Sir Dietrich Brandis. Sir Dietrich recommended Carl Alwin Schenck, to whom Vanderbilt offered the job early in 1895.

Enter Dr. Schenck

Born in 1868 in Darmstadt, Germany, Schenck studied forestry at German universities during the period 1886–90 and entered the state forest service of Hesse–Darmstadt. He was granted the degree of Doctor of Philosophy by the University of Giessen in 1894.

British Empire students who were preparing for the Indian Forest Service customarily studied forestry practices in France, Germany, and Switzerland, as Pinchot was to do. On their tours, they were instructed by Sir Dietrich.

3. Nelson M. McGeary, *Gifford Pinchot*, p. 30.

While a student at Giessen in 1889, Schenck met Brandis, who invited the young man to accompany him as his assistant on the tours of western Europe. Schenck spoke some English. With his scientific education and forestry knowledge, he was a valuable lieutenant and completely won the leader's high regard.

Schenck's salary at Biltmore was to be $2,500; additionally, he would be provided with a house for living quarters and two saddle horses and their feed. Pinchot would continue as a consultant at $1,000 per year, although, according to Schenck's memoirs, Vanderbilt told Schenck soon after the latter's arrival at Biltmore "that Pinchot's connection with the Biltmore Estate had ended" and that Schenck "was in no way subject to his orders or to his supervision."[4]

In *The Biltmore Story*, Schenck tells of his successes and failures in his attempts to practice profitable forestry in the Pisgah Forest. As a *doktor* of a great Germany university, an army officer on reserve duty, and a European of energy and ambition, Schenck was perhaps fated to make mistakes in dealing with Appalachian mountaineers, local businessmen, and others who stood between him and the prompt attainment of his goals. Thus, it is understandable that his relations with Pinchot and later with Fernow would become abrasive in time. But he seems to have had, up to a point, the good will and support of Vanderbilt, even when some of his forestry experiments— for example in seeding and planting—ended in failure.

It is unimportant at this remove of time to dwell on the personality conflicts that developed between Schenck and Pinchot. They are mentioned for one reason only: because they had a curious bearing on the direction that certain aspects of forestry would take.

In his memoirs, Pinchot wrote:

Schenck came in the spring of 1895. I did my best to break him in, but never quite succeeded. Being a German with official training, he had far less understanding of the mountaineers than he had of the mountains and the woods. He thought of them as peasants. They thought of themselves as independent American citizens—and, of course, they were right.

The Prussian point of view dies hard. After two years it prevailed with me, and after four years with Vanderbilt, who let Schenck go in 1899 [sic].[5]

If Pinchot considered Schenck an arrogant Prussian, he himself is revealed in his writings as one not above playing the role of *grand seigneur* on occasion. And, strangely enough, this clash of character traits probably influenced the development of America's first experiment in nonprofessional, or applied, forestry education.

The Biltmore Forest School

Seemingly by chance, an event occurred in 1895 that was to have interesting consequences. Twenty miles from Biltmore, a young college graduate named Overton Westfeldt Price was in residence on another estate. He too

---

4. *The Biltmore Story*, p. 34.
5. *Breaking New Ground*, p. 65. Schenck left Biltmore in 1909, not in 1899 as reported by Pinchot.

wanted to be a forester, but since there were no American schools of forestry, he applied to Schenck for permission to work for him as an apprentice without pay.

Schenck took him on and in 1896 accepted a second apprentice named Edward Merriam Griffith. Later, Overton Price became Pinchot's trusted deputy and second in command in the Forest Service. E. M. Griffith became state forester of Wisconsin.

Schenck established a formal school in 1898 and issued a catalog. Heretofore, he had given instruction on an informal basis to the young men who assisted him in the management of the forest. But with an increase in the number of applicants for training, he arranged the combined work and instruction in an organized curriculum, and thus the Biltmore Forest School came into existence.

The school offered a one-year curriculum. Classroom courses in theory were supported with practical field instruction, and the degree of Bachelor of Forestry was awarded. Every second year Schenck led a group of students on a tour of European forests.

George Herman Wirt of Pennsylvania enrolled as a student at Biltmore on January 9, 1900. He had been induced to study forestry by Joseph Trimble Rothrock, commissioner of forestry, later known as the Father of Forestry in Pennsylvania. Wirt paid $200 tuition. In later years, he recalled the circumstances.

Dr. Schenck had a regular course and it didn't make any difference if you entered that course at the end or the beginning. You covered the field and when you got through you could leave, or you could stay as long as you wanted to—repeat if you wanted to.[6]

The school had an office on the second floor in a real estate building of the Biltmore Estate. Lectures were given there, and it was considered to be the school headquarters. About ten or twelve students were taking the course during Wirt's period.

Wirt went to Germany with the class in the summer of 1900 and completed the course in March 1901. He then was appointed state forester of Pennsylvania—the commonwealth's first—in April 1901 at a monthly salary of $60.

It must be remembered that Schenck's position was that of manager of the Pisgah forest. His students were, in effect, apprentice foresters and performed many of the needful technical chores, such as surveying, making growth studies, and laying out roads and trails. In general, they prepared themselves through practical experience for employment by the forest products industries.

Schenck left Biltmore in 1909 but continued the school four years longer without a fixed headquarters. The students moved from Germany, to the Adirondacks, to North Carolina, to the Lake States, and even to the West. The school ceased operation in 1913, for financial reasons principally.

6. Transcript, interview with George Wirt by Charles D. Bonsted, March 1959 (Forest History Society, Santa Cruz, Calif.).

Schenck went on active duty with the German army when World War I broke out.

During its existence, the Biltmore Forest School gave forestry instruction to about 350 students. Among its instructors were Homer D. House, a botanist; Clifton D. Howe, later dean of the Faculty of Forestry at the University of Toronto; and numerous short-term visiting scientists who lectured on forest entomology, geology, forest pathology, wood utilization, and the many subjects adjunctive to forestry. But the institution was primarily a "master school" in the European tradition with Schenck as the headmaster. Although he emphasized its purpose as that of providing specially trained men for industry, many of its graduates went into public forestry service. To be sure, dozens of its graduates actually did enter industry and found careers there. Founded to prepare men for private forestry work, the school was ahead of its time, because industrial demand for foresters did not open up for another two decades.

The Biltmore Plantations

Experiments in forest planting began at Biltmore in 1889 under the supervision of Frederick Olmsted. During the next year, 300 acres were reforested. The stock used was mostly white pine. These pineta and others subsequently established were among the first successful commercial forest plantations, although there were other plantations undertaken for horticultural or ornamental purposes. The Stephen Girard Estate had started extensive forest plantations in Columbia and Schuylkill Counties, Pennsylvania, as early as 1877. But they had practically disappeared fifty years later. The author, then a forester with the Pennsylvania Department of Forests and Waters, could find only vestiges remaining.

In 1922, writing from Lindenfels, Germany, where he then made his home, Schenck complained bitterly to H. H. Chapman at Yale about the loss and destruction of the early forestry records: "When I left Biltmore in fall 1909, all the records of the Forest Department were also left. As I understand it, all detailed records of cutting, year by year and compartment by compartment, were then destroyed; all records of planting, going back to 1894, were destroyed; all working plans were destroyed. . . ."[7]

Fortunately, he was wrong; all was not lost. Ferdinand W. Haasis of the Appalachian Forest Experiment Station at Asheville, North Carolina, was able to reconstruct the records of the Biltmore plantations, and his findings were published in 1930.[8] He described the plantations as one of the nation's earliest large-scale reforestation projects under private initiative. The planting continued until about 1911.

Haasis reported that the first 300-acre planting in 1890 had been made by an Illinois nursery company and that Pinchot had added a few plantations in 1895. But the greater part of the planting was done under the direction of Schenck, who took over the work in 1895. From then until he left the estate

7. Chapman Papers, Sterling Memorial Library, Yale University.
8. Ferdinand W. Haasis, *Forest Plantations at Biltmore, North Carolina*, U.S. Department of Agriculture, Misc. Pub. 61 (1930).

in 1909, Schenck made plantings or sowings every year; forty different species were tried, half hardwoods, half conifers.

The total area planted was about 3,000 acres. Of the successful plantations remaining in 1930, most were of white pine and shortleaf pine. The hardwoods were generally unsuccessful. The remnants of the plantations still in existence are among the showplaces of Biltmore.

Protecting the property from fire was always a major problem in the management of Biltmore. On April 8–9, 1909, for example, fires were reported as having been "disastrous." The fires "were set by incendiaries who, it is supposed, had been offended by some of the forest employees, or had been prevented from hunting and fishing on the Vanderbilt preserve."[9] Schenck wrote that the reports of the fire losses had been exaggerated. He said only two acres of plantations were destroyed, although "12,000 acres of primeval forest were run over by fire." But he admitted, "All our fires were of incendiary origin."[10]

Assessment of Time

Pioneer silviculture and the beginning of technical forestry education at Biltmore were unsuccessful, but both attempts laid the groundwork for other ventures that would succeed. Schenck's system of forest management, although adapted from European practices, demonstrated the principles of treating native second growth to obtain financial returns and at the same time to regenerate and improve the stand. His methods of harvesting, thinning, and planting, if not always successful, had both a scientific and a practical basis. Not a great deal was known about the properties of soils, the influence of light, and the silvical characteristics of the tree species, but Schenck utilized any available knowledge that appeared to have empirical value.

However much other early foresters, such as Fernow and Pinchot, might have differed from Schenck on forestry policy, the existing records of those who visited Biltmore and who were competent to judge the quality of silviculture practiced there indicate that they considered Schenck an able woods manager. Practical forestry, the kind that emphasized revenue and profit, was his goal.

During his fourteen years at Biltmore, he started the first sustained-yield program in forestry ever attempted in the United States. Although the program was not continued by Vanderbilt, the property was adapted to management for continuous production. Schenck claimed in his memoirs that "Biltmore Forest was made fit for a sustained annual yield as reliably as any forest in central Europe."[11]

Fernow began the first college-level professional curriculum in forestry at Cornell University in September 1898. Theoretical where Schenck was pragmatic, Fernow considered forestry to be a science; Schenck thought of it as an art. Fernow was ambitious for forestry to attain the status of a profession. And he knew that forestry would never attain recognition as a profession if

9. "Biltmore Forest Fire," *Conservation*, vol. 15 (May 1909), p. 296.
10. "The Biltmore Fires," *Conservation*, vol. 15 (June 1909), p. 369.
11. *The Biltmore Story*, p. 175.

educational preparation for a career was based on a one-year or even a two-year curriculum with no minimum entrance standards.

Nevertheless, Schenck's experiment in the empirics of forestry instruction, his leading the students daily into the woods, and his emphasis on the apprentice kind of training by which the student learned by doing had a popular appeal during this formative period. Essentially, then, Schenck was training forest technicians, who were quite as much needed in the early years of forestry as were the university-educated foresters. The so-called ranger schools and the forest technician schools that later sprang up in the United States and Canada, particularly during the post–World War II years, were direct descendants of the Biltmore Forest School of 1898.

In 1911, Congress passed the Weeks Law, which appropriated funds for the federal government to acquire forest lands on the headwaters of navigable streams. A year later, the Forest Service began buying woodland in the southern Appalachians. In 1914, nearly 80,000 acres of Vanderbilt's Pisgah Forest became the nucleus of the present 479,000-acre Pisgah National Forest. A half-century later, on September 26, 1961, the purchase of the first tract of national forest in the East was commemorated by ceremonies held at Asheville and at the Pink Beds, an area of spectacular natural beauty covered with beds of mountain laurel. At the Pisgah National Forest Secretary of Agriculture Orville L. Freeman and Richard E. McArdle, chief of the Forest Service, broke ground for a visitor center and museum to mark the beginning of forestry in the United States. The visitor center was erected at the site of the little community where the summer headquarters of the Biltmore Forest School formerly stood. Outdoor displays and nature trails aid the visitor to visualize the tract as it once was. Recreational facilities are available.

On July 11, 1968, President Lyndon Johnson approved an act of Congress (Public Law 90–398) that established the Cradle of Forestry in America. It commemorates both the birthplace of forestry (by Pinchot) and of forestry education (by Schenck). The area of 6,800 acres includes the site of the old Biltmore Forest School.

CHAPTER **4**

The White House Conference on Natural Resources

On May 13–15, 1908, the first national conference on the conservation of natural resources met in the White House in Washington, D.C. Called by President Theodore Roosevelt, it was officially known as the Conference of Governors.

The president predicted that it would be "among the most important gatherings in our history in its effect upon the welfare of our people."[1] And so it was, for the conference awakened Americans to what was happening to the nation's natural resources and to the pressing necessity for conservation.

Gifford Pinchot said: "The Governors' Conference on Conservation was the first of its kind—the first not only in America, but in the world. It may well be regarded by future historians as a turning point in human history. Because it introduced to mankind the newly formulated policy of the Conservation of Natural Resources, it exerted and continues to exert a vital influence in the United States, on the other nations of the Americas, and on the peoples of the whole earth."[2]

What was the genesis of this notable assemblage? Whose idea was it? How did it come about? And what did it accomplish?

In October 1907, President Roosevelt accompanied members of the Inland Waterways Commission on an inspection trip down the Mississippi River. The president's purpose in making this journey was to focus public attention on the need for development of the nation's river systems. During the previous March, when he created the commission, he had directed it to study "the relations of the streams to the use of all the great permanent natural resources and their conservation for the making and maintenance of prosperous homes."[3]

1. *Proceedings of a Conference of Governors in the White House, Washington, D.C., May 13-15, 1908* (1909), p. x. Throughout this chapter, information about the conference and quotations from conference papers are from the *Proceedings*.
2. *Breaking New Ground*, p. 352.
3. Ibid., p. 328. Quoted from Roosevelt's letter of March 14, 1907, to the members of the commission.

39

Gifford Pinchot, head of the Forest Service for the past decade, was a member of the commission. Another member was Frederick H. Newell, chief engineer of the Reclamation Service. Newell had earlier proposed to the commission that it call a national conference on natural resources in Washington, D.C., during the coming winter. The commission agreed to this suggestion. Congressman (later Senator) Theodore E. Burton of Ohio was commission chairman. He and Pinchot were named as a committee to convey the matter to the president as "an expression of the view of the Commission, leaving him to decide how the call shall issue."[4]

On October 5, 1907, the presidential party made a stop in Memphis where the president addressed an audience that included a score of state governors. Taking advantage of this opportunity, Roosevelt announced his intention to call the conference:

As I have said elsewhere, the conservation of natural resources is the fundamental problem. Unless we solve that problem it will avail us little to solve all others. To solve it, the whole nation must undertake the task through their organizations and associations, through the men whom they have made specially responsible for the welfare of the several states, and finally through Congress and the Executive. As a preliminary step, the Inland Waterways Commission has asked me to call a conference on the conservation of natural resources, including, of course, the streams, to meet in Washington during the coming winter. I shall accordingly call such a conference. It ought to be among the most important gatherings in our history, for none have had a more vital question to consider.[5]

The commission promptly appointed a conference committee. Pinchot was named chairman. The other members were Newell and W J McGee. Dr. McGee, secretary of the commission, was in charge of soil erosion investigations for the Bureau of Soils in the Department of Agriculture; he later served as the capable recording secretary of the conference and edited the 451-page *Proceedings*.

In November, Roosevelt invited the governor of each state and territory to attend a three-day conference in Washington, D.C., May 13–15, 1908, and to select three citizens as advisers. The president then issued invitations to "a limited number of leading associations of national scope concerned with our natural resources" to send one representative each to take part in the discussions.

The conference committee prepared a syllabus to guide the speakers and experts in the preparation of their statements. This syllabus, which served as the agenda for the conference, covered all the natural resources. In condensed outline, it was as follows:

> Mineral Resources
> Mineral Fuels
> Ores and Related Minerals

4. Ibid., p. 344.
5. Ibid., quoted, p. 345.

Land Resources
  Soil
  Forests
  Sanitation
  Reclamation
  Land Laws
  Grazing and Stock Raising
Water Resources
  Relation between Rail and Water Transportation
  Navigation
  Power
Conservation as a National Policy

When finally convened on May 13, 1908, in the East Room of the White House, the conferees included the Cabinet; the Supreme Court; many members of the Congress; fifty-two governors of states, territories, and dependencies; the representatives of seventy associations, societies, and labor organizations; twenty-one representatives of the periodical press; fifty-two special and general guests; and the members of the Inland Waterways Commission.

Keynoting the Issues

In his opening address, President Roosevelt declared that the conservation of the nation's natural resources is "the chief material question that confronts us, second only—and second always—to the great fundamental questions of morality." He went on:

This Conference on the conservation of natural resources is in effect a meeting of the representatives of all the people of the United States called to consider the weightiest problem now before the Nation; and the occasion for the meeting lies in the fact that the natural resources of our country are in danger of exhaustion if we permit the old wasteful methods of exploiting them to continue.

Andrew Carnegie opened the second session with an address on the conservation of ores and related minerals. John Mitchell, the eminent labor leader, spoke on coal. John Hayes Hammond, famous mining engineer of that period, discussed the depletion of the nation's mineral resources. Secretary of State Elihu Root and several governors were then heard.

James J. Hill, financier and railroad builder, opened the third session, whose theme was the natural wealth of the land. His address was followed by a keynote statement, "Forest Conservation," by R. A. Long, a prominent lumberman, head of the Long–Bell Lumber Company of Kansas City, Missouri, and president of the National Lumber Manufacturers Association.

Long was an unfortunate choice to present a general paper on this broad subject. Much of his speech, which was written in a florid and pretentious style, was devoted to forest aesthetics and forest influences. He denounced the critics of the "lumber trust," which he denied existed, while proposing governmental price supports for lumber and a high tariff on lumber imports from Canada.

But the nub of his talk was his prophecy about the future of the nation's timber production. He said his investigations led him to predict that Lake States timber would cease to contribute to the lumber supply within a decade, and that southern yellow pine would cut "no great figure in our lumber supply" in another two decades. As for Pacific Coast timber, he said its life would be about four decades. Long did make one necessary and practical proposal. Calling for a detailed, national forest inventory, he asked, "Should a nation as rich as ours hesitate to furnish the means required for information of such great value?"

Keynote speakers for the fourth session included H. A. Jastro, president of the American National Livestock Association, whose speech was about grazing on the public lands. Although representing livestock interests that were often critical of federal management of national forest ranges, Jastro praised the Forest Service for its administration of the forage and water resources of the West.

The Governors' Declaration

The practical results of the conference showed up in the fifth session. Under the chairmanship of Governor Newton C. Blanchard of Louisiana, a resolutions committee had prepared a declaration of views and recommendations. The salient features of the declaration are worth noting.

With the "firm conviction that this conservation of our natural resources is a subject of transcendent importance," the governors agreed on the principles that should guide the use and protection of resources. Moreover, they asserted "that the sources of national wealth exist for the benefit of the People, and that monopoly thereof should not be tolerated." Concerned not alone with physical resources, they went on record in favor of natural beauty too, saying that it must be protected and preserved.

Subsequently, the following paragraphs of the declaration had great influence on national and state conservation policy:

We agree that further action is advisable to ascertain the present condition of our natural resources and to promote the conservation of the same; and to that end we recommend the appointment by each State of a Commission on the Conservation of Natural Resources, to cooperate with each other and with any similar commission of the Federal Government.

We urge the continuation and extension of forest policies adapted to secure the husbanding and renewal of our diminishing timber supply, the prevention of soil erosion, the protection of headwaters, and the maintenance of the purity and navigability of our streams. We recognize that the private ownership of forest lands entails responsibilities in the interests of all the People, and we favor the enactment of laws looking to the protection and replacement of privately owned forest.

Subjects Shunted Aside

The sixth session—on water resources—began with "Conservation of Life and Health by Improved Water Supply," a paper by George M. Kober, M.D., professor of hygiene at the Georgetown University School of Medicine. Dr. Kober presented a fearful but factual account of stream pollution and its effect on public health. And it is a sad but true commentary that his description of the defilement of the Potomac River by domestic and industrial pollutants is as applicable to conditions today as it was in 1908.

In reading the papers of this session, however, one gets the impression that the conferees were more concerned about navigation, power development, and water transportation than with water quality. In the statements by the several governors who discussed water resources, precious little was said about pollution or its control. Pollution appears to have been a nasty subject that they preferred not to dwell on. Certainly, they could not have been unaware of it.

For example, in a long paper on conservation progress in New York State, Governor Charles E. Hughes (later unsuccessful candidate for the presidency) gave a learned and legalistic account of the Adirondack Forest Preserve and the development of water resources for power and for flood control. Despite the awful condition of the Hudson and of other rivers in his state, he did not once mention pollution.

Governor Charles S. Deneen of Illinois, then as now a state notorious for its polluted waters, told of plans for the improvement of navigation and waterpower and of the millions of dollars to be spent on water-related public works. But he barely mentioned public health, and water pollution was not mentioned at all.

These comments are not made as criticism of the speakers and their lack of knowledge about the resources they were discussing. A careful reading of the many papers shows clearly that the governors were mostly concerned with the economic development of resources, particularly water, and hardly at all with resources for social improvements, such as public health, recreation, and scenic beauty. One senses that, as politicians, they were not opposed to these indirect values; they, or at least some, were simply unaware of their existence.

Supplementary statements by speakers who were not on the regular agenda were presented at this final session. Governors not previously heard and other representatives took advantage of this opportunity to submit what were called "additional expressions."

Samuel Gompers, president of the American Federation of Labor, gave convincing arguments for the conservation of human resources. John Allison, an adviser to the governor of Tennessee, proposed immediate governmental acquisition of the Appalachian Forest Reserve. (The land recommended by Judge Allison subsequently was purchased under the provision of the Weeks Law passed in 1911.)

Among the "additional expressions" one paper stands out; it is as timely now as it was then. Entitled "The Preservation of Scenic Beauty," it was presented by George F. Kunz, president of the American Scenic and Historic Preservation Society. Dr. Kunz criticized logically and justly the despoliation of the nation's scenic resources, a form of criticism that was heard at the White House Conference on Natural Beauty nearly six decades later.

States' Rights Oratory

Since many of the speakers were politicians, the speeches contain a great deal of oratory, flowery and orotund. Most governors exploited the opportunity to vaunt the wonders of their own states and the exemplary virtues of the citizenry. Some gave lip service to conservation, while denouncing federal administration of those regulatory measures essential to conservation management.

A conspicuous example was Governor Edwin L. Norris of Montana, who was all for preserving the forests but declared, "We do protest and we do object to the employment of a forest reserve as a means for the regulation of the ranges of the West." In other words, this governor was objecting to the Forest Service charging fees for permits to graze stock on the forest reserves. According to his specious argument, since the forest reserves belonged to all the people, all the people should pay for their protection and management, and the stockmen should have the right to graze their herds on public land without charge.

In rebuttal, James R. Garfield, secretary of the interior, asked:

Why should a great resource owned, as the Gentleman admits, by the People at large, be used by private interests, by somebody who is looking only to his own benefit, and not to the People of the country? The principle applies not only in the forest reserves, so far as grazing is concerned; it applies equally well to the use of the water powers of this country, in the conservation first, and afterward in the use of those water powers.

Governor Bryant B. Brooks of Wyoming took a strong states' rights stand on water resources. He asserted that "the people of Wyoming believe the Federal Government can exercise no control over the waters of Wyoming, and that certainly the Forestry Department [sic] has no right to charge for power privileges or for water which runs from various forest reserves."

Secretary Garfield apparently expressed the consensus of the conference when he declared:

. . . in the progress of our country we have found that the powers given the Federal Government must be used to develop those natural resources for the greatest good to the greatest number which do not lie simply within one State but extend into several States, and which, as in the case of water, must be considered as for the use of all the States with the given watershed rather than for the special States through which the water runs or in which the water rises.

Governor Frank F. Gooding of Idaho questioned the federal government's rights in the public lands. He claimed that "the interests of the whole country would be best served if Congress would turn over to the States all of the public domain, under proper laws looking to the protection of the forest and the range, to be administered and developed by the citizens of those States."

Fortunately, not all the governors were so self-seeking as these honorable delegates. Governor John Burke of North Dakota pointed out that "there are some delegates who want to give the States the control of the National Forests." Affirming the constitutional right of the federal government to establish national forest reserves, this enlightened governor urged the government "to retain absolute control over such territory . . . and to conserve the whole in the interests of those who are to come after us as well as those who are now enjoying its benefits." Appropriately enough, Governor Burke was elected honorary secretary of the conference.

The National Conservation Commission

The information provided in the speeches and discussions opened the conference delegates' eyes to conditions and opportunities to which many had previously been blind. Most conferees, aware that they were participating in a historic event, rose to the occasion by putting politics aside in order to present a united front. Impressed by the importance of resource conservation, they felt impelled to help advance it. Also, since the principle of conservation was universally accepted and therefore politically accredited, it became a firm policy of the Roosevelt administration and of most subsequent administrations. As a matter of fact, conservation as a popular crusade may be said to date from 1908.

Most important, the conference recommended that each state appoint a commission on the conservation of natural resources. According to Pinchot, forty states did set up commissions or similar bodies to deal with their resources.

Acting for the federal government, President Roosevelt immediately (June 8, 1908) appointed a National Conservation Commission. It was organized in four sections: water resources, forest resources, resources of the land, and mineral resources. Pinchot was elected chairman of the commission, which had forty-eight members. Each of the four sections was chaired by a member of Congress.

Doubtless for political reasons, politicians were well represented in the sections. The forests section, chaired by Senator Reed Smoot of Utah, had twelve members, including Senator Albert J. Beveredge of Indiana, Congressman Champ Clark of Missouri, Congressman Charles F. Scott of Kansas, and former Governor Newton C. Blanchard of Louisiana.

Also appointed to the forest group were Irving Fisher, a professor of political economy at Yale; William Irvine, a lumberman from Wisconsin; Gustav H. Schwab, a merchant of New York City; and J. B. White, a lumberman from Missouri. Charles Lathrop Pack of New Jersey, later to become president of The American Forestry Association, was the only member, not a forester, who was identified with forest conservation and was active in the movement.

If the two members who actually were professional foresters were in the minority, they nevertheless were the ones who probably had most to do with the section's report on forests. They were Henry S. Graves, dean of the Yale School of Forestry, and Overton W. Price of the Forest Service.

When he created the National Conservation Commission, the president asked its members to investigate the condition of the country's natural resources, to advise him of their findings, and to cooperate with other bodies created for similar purposes. Although the commission was wholly without funds, Pinchot's executive committee immediately made plans for obtaining an inventory of the resources.

This work was started on July 1 with the cooperation of the federal resources bureaus, similar agencies in the states, and industry. With characteristic energy Pinchot pushed the work along so that, under the direction of the four section secretaries, it was completed by autumn.

On December 1, 1908, a meeting of the full commission was held. Summaries of the four section inventories were accepted and combined into a report[6] that became the basis for a joint conservation conference in Washington, D.C., on December 8–10.

The personnel of this conference totaled nearly 500. Included were 22 state governors; 11 personal representatives of governors; 98 representatives of 31 state conservation commissions; 105' representatives of 59 scientific, professional, and labor organizatons; 38 chiefs and experts of 16 federal bureaus; and 68 delegates at large.

On balance, the personnel of the Joint Conservation Conference were better informed and generally more knowledgeable about resources than were the participants in the White House Conference held in May. In forestry, for example, several representatives were professional foresters who attained positions of some eminence in later years.

Among these were Henry E. Hardtner of Louisiana, pioneer practitioner of industrial forestry in the South; Herman Von Schrenk of Missouri, America's first forest pathologist and an expert on timber preservation; Philip W. Ayers of New Hampshire, later head of the Society for the Protection of New Hampshire Forests; Alfred Gaskill, state forester of New Jersey; and Joseph T. Rothrock, the esteemed commissioner of forestry in Pennsylvania. Among the foresters representing the Forest Service were William T. Cox, William L. Hall, Royal S. Kellogg, and Edwin A. Ziegler, all subsequently prominent in the profession.

At the first session on December 8 in the Belasco Theater, President-elect William Howard Taft, who would be inaugurated on March 4, 1909, served as chairman. President Roosevelt gave the opening address, in which he specified work that should "be done without any further delay:"

First, to provide for a comprehensive waterway development; second, to begin at once on work already planned that will surely fit into the larger plan; third, to provide amply for forest protection against fire, against reckless cutting, against wanton or reckless destruction of all kinds, and as a prime incident of this third provision to secure without delay the Appalachian and White Mountain National Forests.[7]

The commission's first two section reports—on minerals and lands—were presented at the second session on December 9, Pinchot presiding. At the final session on the following day, Pinchot called for the reports on forests and waters. The conference then approved all four reports.

The combined reports of the National Conservation Commission were endorsed "as a wise, just, and patriotic statement of the resources of the nation, of the thoughtless and profligate manner in which some of these resources have been and are being wasted, and of the urgent need for their conservation in the interests of this and future generations, to the end that the prosperity and perpetuity of the nation may be assured."[8] In addition,

6. *Report of the National Conservation Commission*, 3 vols., S. Doc. 676, 60 Cong., 2 sess. (1909).

7. Ibid., vol. 1, p. 128.

8. Ibid., pp. 241–42.

the conferees went on record as favoring the maintenance of conservation commissions in all the states, and urged on the Congress the desirability of maintaining a national commission on the conservation of resources.

In a special message to Congress on January 22, 1909, the president transmitted the report. He invited the attention of the Congress to the resolutions and urged the appropriation of $50,000 to cover the commission's expenses. Congress, however, declined to appropriate funds for the commission. Worse than that, Congress prohibited all bureaus from doing work for any presidential commission, board, or similar body appointed without congressional legal approval. This action put the commission out of business.

The opprobrium felt by conservationists then and later for this hatchet job attaches to James A. Tawney, a Republican Congressman from Minnesota. One of Tawney's most caustic critics was Charles Richard Van Hise, president of the University of Wisconsin, an eminent educator and geologist, a member of the National Conservation Commission, and chairman of the Wisconsin State Conservation Commission, who wrote:

Under the system in vogue in Congress, by which it is difficult to fix responsibility, with the exception of one man we cannot certainly designate the individuals who are most guilty of halting the conservation movement. This exception is Mr. Tawney, of Minnesota, who introduced the objectionable section, and advocated its adoption. We should hold him responsible to the people for doing all possible to render ineffective the conservation movement. All good citizens who know the facts should spread the truth abroad as widely as possible in order that he may receive the profound public condemnation which is his just due.[9]

Tawney's congressional record showed opposition to conservation during the nine terms in which he served, from 1893 until 1911 when he was defeated for renomination.

In addition to Tawney, Dr. Van Hise condemned the House Committee on Printing, of which James B. Landis, a newspaper editor and Democrat from Indiana, was chairman. The Senate had passed a resolution authorizing the printing of 25,000 copies of the report of the Conservation Commission. But the Committee on Printing refused to report the resolution favorably to the House. According to Van Hise: "These men should be held responsible to the public for doing all that lay in their power to block the conservation movement, of such vital importance to the nation."[10] Congressman Landis had served in Congress from 1897; when his term expired in March 1909, he was an unsuccessful candidate for reelection. Fortunately, his committee could not block the printing of the record, which was issued in three volumes in 1909 as Senate Document 676.

The Doctrine of Scarcity

The Governors' Conference and its sequel, the Joint Conference on Conservation, had an interior theme that persisted throughout the programs and the keynote speeches. This theme was the doctrine of resource scarcity.

9. "The Future of Man in America," *The World's Work*, vol. 18 (June 1909), p. 11719.
10. Ibid.

Pinchot and many others firmly believed in the imminence of a timber famine. Members of the committee that prepared the agenda and selected the speakers for the Governors' Conference were unmistakably influenced by their belief that resources were being wastefully used and depleted. This notion was a recurring one; it is prominent in the president's announcement that he would call the conference, in his letters of invitation, and in his opening speech. In his speech, he said: "The prosperity of our people depends directly on the energy and intelligence with which our natural resources are used. It is equally clear that these resources are the final basis of national power and perpetuity. Finally, it is ominously evident that these resources are in the course of rapid exhaustion."

James J. Hill, the railroad magnate, claimed that the nation was "consuming yearly three or four times as much timber as forest growth restores." He predicted the supply of some species would be practically exhausted in from ten to twelve years, and that the present century would see the end of the others unless reforesting were done.[11]

Strangely enough, the Governors' Conference failed to include wildlife among the major resources discussed. This omission was curious in view of the fact that President Roosevelt, an ardent hunter and an influential force in conservation, had been a founder of the Boone and Crockett Club and had used his presidential authority to establish wildlife refuges.

The oversight was corrected in the report of the National Conservation Commission, which contained a comprehensive statement, "Relations of Birds and Mammals to the National Resources," by C. Hart Merriam, chief of the Biological Survey. Dr. Merriam emphasized the economic importance of birds and fur-bearing animals. He also discussed economic losses caused by such animals as wolves, coyotes, and cougars, which prey on livestock, and by rodents, which ruin farm crops. Despite the omission of wildlife from the program, the Governors' Conference together with the Joint Conservation Conference stimulated the creation of state game agencies.

Results: Direct and Indirect

If the Conference of Governors failed to produce immediate and direct results in the improvement of resource conservation, it was notable for its numerous indirect influences. Thus, historically, the conference was the single greatest stimulus to resource preservation and management. And this stimulus, be it noted, not only affected the federal and state governments; private interests also took action.

Of the utmost significance was the increased attention given to fire detection and control, particularly by the states. Up to 1908, state action in fire control was inadequate almost everywhere. The best results had been accomplished in Minnesota, New Jersey, New York, Pennsylvania, and Wisconsin. Hardly 1 percent of the 450 million acres of woodland in private ownership

---

11. A shrewd and interesting analysis of the fear of resource exhaustion that marked the Governors' Conference was made by Thomas B. Nolan, director of the U.S. Geological Survey, in "The Inexhaustible Resource of Technology," in Henry Jarrett (ed.), *Perspectives on Conservation.*

had organized fire protection systems. And the federal lands, outside the national forests, were no better. On the great public domain, for example, the Department of the Interior had no fire prevention and control facilities.[12]

During the decade following the conference, new or improved state forestry agencies were created in all regions. This state action was largely the result of the Weeks Law of 1911, which provided funds for the secretary of agriculture to cooperate with the states in forest fire protection. States that had previously lacked satisfactory fire control laws were induced to adopt such legislation and to create forces for fire prevention, detection, and control. Within two decades after the passage of the Weeks Law, thirty-six states had forestry agencies or departments that dealt not only with protection matters but operated state forest tree nurseries, administered state forests, and provided assistance to private owners in the management of their properties.

Without exaggerating the effect of the Governors' Conference and the National Conservation Commission on citizens' actions, one can identify a number of occurrences that either had their origins in these meetings or were probably influenced by them. In 1908, the word *conservation* suddenly appeared in newspapers, magazines, legislative gatherings, and the conversation of thinking citizens. Thus, it followed that certain desirable matters, previously discussed but never acted on, were brought to fruition in the favorable climate then prevailing. The time for action on these affairs had come.

Early in 1909, the Western Forestry and Conservation Association was organized. State forestry associations were formed in North Carolina in 1911, in Texas in 1914, and in additional states during the coming years.

In 1916, the long-advocated National Park Service was created by Congress and placed in the Department of the Interior. Three years later, the National Parks Association—a citizens' body for the promotion of public support for the park system—came into being.

It is difficult to assign specific causes to the stimulus in forestry education that occurred up to, and immediately following, the White House Conference. Up to 1908, sixteen forestry curriculums had been started. Within the next five years seven more universities began offering undergraduate instruction.

This early proliferation of forestry schools resulted from two main influences. The first was the rapid expansion in employment in the Forest Service following the transfer of the forest reserves from Interior to Agriculture. Then, as recruitment by the states expanded, especially with the passage of the Weeks Law in 1911, technical foresters were not only in demand but had wider career choices.

In December 1909, Pinchot called the first national conference on forestry education in Washington, D.C. A committee of five, with Henry S. Graves as chairman, was designated to study the standardization of instruction. A supplementary conference was held two years later, with delegates

12. Clyde Leavitt, "Forest Fires," *Report of the National Conservation Commission*, vol. 2, pp. 390-468. This was the most comprehensive account of the subject up to that time.

from sixteen U.S. and Canadian institutions. The committee's report, submitted in 1912, noted that twenty-four institutions offered courses leading to a degree in forestry, and about forty others included forestry in the curriculum. How much of the interest in forestry education during the period 1909–12 stemmed from the White House Conference is problematical, but the sudden concern of the Forest Service and of educators about the need for charting the course of education was more than simple coincidence.

As noted earlier, the declaration of the governors encouraged private forestry. A more comprehensive statement, "The Duty of the Private Owner," was included in the section on forests of the report of the National Conservation Commission. There can be no doubt that these developments stimulated private owners, particularly in industry, to think about forestry. How much they influenced the application of management practices is less certain. Examples, however, can be cited.

Henry E. Hardtner, president of the Urania Lumber Company in Louisiana, was a delegate to the Joint Conservation Conference. Afterwards, he started a program of organized fire detection and suppression on the company's extensive holdings. He was one of the first lumbermen in the South to take action of this kind. His company was one of the first to buy cutover land in order to grow trees; this was in 1912 at a time when most lumber companies were trying to sell their logged lands for whatever price they could get.

In the North, on December 29, 1908, the directors of the International Paper Company voted "to manage [the company's] timberlands and those of its subsidiary companies under methods of practical forestry, so as to insure a permanent growth of timber thereon."[13] The company's Department of Woodlands was directed to carry out the policy and to conduct its operations so as to minimize the danger of fire.

Other industrial owners, as well as owners of farm woodland and similar small acreages, were taking tentative steps in forest management during the second decade of the present century. Many of these are known to have been inspired by the Governors' Conference and the work of the National Conservation Commission.

Because of the standing of the conferees in the business and political world, the Governors' Conference received wide press coverage. Some of the nation's most eminent magazines were represented in the persons of their editors, and newspaper editorials were numerous and almost wholly favorable to the conservation movement.

In addition, agricultural, professional, technical, and trade journals reported the conference, giving its work their editorial blessings. For the benefit of people who knew little about conservation—indeed, many had never even heard of it—the country's newspapers and magazines were remarkably successful in interpreting and explaining it. All in all, the American press was for conservation, at least in principle.

In the fields of information and public education, the Governors' Conference and the National Conservation Commission gained immediate and wide-

13. "Minute Book of the Board of Directors," December 29, 1908 (International Paper Company, New York City).

spread results. To promote conservation as a public policy, the federal and state governments stepped up their dissemination of literature. The three-volume report of the Conservation Commission was in itself the most timely and comprehensive body of information about the four resources (water, land, forests, and minerals) ever compiled.

In 1910, Charles Van Hise published a useful book, *Conservation of Natural Resources in the United States*. It was the first popular work on the subject. Other books and popular writings followed: Pinchot's *The Fight for Conservation* (1910) and Overton W. Price's *The Land We Live In* (1911). B. E. Fernow's history of forestry appeared in 1913; primarily intended as a textbook, it was the first American treatise on the subject of forestry history. Pinchot's *The Training of a Forester* (1914) was the first American book to offer career guidance in natural resources.

Not all the publications were general in scope. A stream of books, bulletins, and monographs flowed forth, giving directions for the application of specific forest practices. They included guides on tree planting, logging techniques, fire control methods, and many other practices. An example was *Forestry in New England—A Handbook of Eastern Forest Management* (1912) by R. C. Hawley and A. F. Hawes. The first textbook on farm woodland management—*Farm Forestry*, by John A. Ferguson—was published in 1916. A year later, *The Development of Forest Law in America* by J. P Kinney was issued.

There are grounds for the presumption that numerous publications on forestry and related topics were spin-offs from the Governors' Conference and the report of the National Conservation Commission. If not directly inspired by these two events, the publications attracted receptive readers and stimulated extraordinary interest in resources.

In his keynote speech at the Governors' Conference, R. A. Long had proposed that the government take an inventory of the country's timber supply. Soon after the National Conservation Commission was created, the Section on Forests, of which Overton Price was secretary, immediately began an inventory of the country's forest resources. In point of fact, it was less an inventory than an office estimate. There was no time for field work, because the results were needed for a commission meeting on December 1. Nevertheless, in less than six months, considerable data were accumulated and later published in the *Report of the National Conservation Commission*. Volume II of the report contained several factual chapters on various aspects of the forest resource by Forest Service personnel.

In 1909, the Forest Service published a twenty-four-page circular, *The Timber Supply of the United States*, by R. S. Kellogg. This was followed in 1911 by a summary of the first of a three-part *Report of the Commissioner of Corporations on the Lumber Industry*. Part I, "Standing Timber," when issued in its entirety by the Department of Commerce and Labor, had 300 pages. Parts II and III on timber ownerships were published in 1914. Since 1920, additional periodic reviews of the timber situation have been published by the Forest Service.[14]

14. A list of these documents will be found in U.S. Forest Service, *Timber Resources for America's Future* (1958), p. 5. The most recent was *Timber Trends in the United States* (1965).

As forestry developed in the United States, reliable figures on forest growing stock, growth, and drain were essential for setting policy and for many other aspects of the decision-making process. Hence, forest inventories would have been necessary whether or not a Governors' Conference had ever been held. However, it is to be noted that the conference provided the seminal influence for the first appraisals, another example of the weight it had in the formation of forestry as an art and a science.

Another outgrowth of the two conferences held in 1908 and of the report of the National Conservation Commission was the North American Conservation Conference, held in Washington, D.C., on February 18, 1909. It was a closed meeting with attendance restricted to official delegates from Canada, Mexico, Newfoundland, and the United States. Representing the United States were Robert Bacon, secretary of state; James R. Garfield, secretary of the interior; and Gifford Pinchot, forester, Department of Agriculture. President Roosevelt opened the proceedings with a speech in which he emphasized the need for international action to preserve each nation's wealth in natural resources.

At the close of the conference, a declaration of principles for the North American nations was adopted. In general, the principles were similar to those recommended by the National Conservation Commission. In behalf of their four governments, the commissioners adopted proposals for public health, forests, waters, lands, minerals, and game.

The commissioners went on record for forest reservations under government supervision, for the early completion of timber inventories, for the extension of technical education, and for decisive action in forest fire control. Apart from fire, they declared wasteful cutting to be the principal cause of forest destruction. They considered it most important that lumbering operations be conducted under a system of rigid regulation. One sees here the influence of Pinchot, who firmly believed in the need for timber cutting under government control.

A permanent conservation commission for each country was also recommended. And the final recommendation was for still another conference—a world conference. Declaring that resource conservation should become nationwide in scope, the commissioners suggested "that all nations should be invited to join together in conference on the subject of world resources and their inventory, conservation, and wise utilization."[15]

Taking the initiative, the U.S. Government canvassed the other nations, asking whether they would send delegates to such a conference. Favorable responses having been received, President Roosevelt, with the approval of the Netherlands government, proposed that the interested nations meet at The Hague in September 1909 to consider resource conservation on a global front. The Taft administration took office shortly thereafter; the conference was never held. Pinchot said flatly that Taft killed the plan.[16]

As a footnote to this abortive episode, it should be added that Pinchot never forgot the good that might flow from such a world conference, and on

15. Loomis Havemeyer (ed.), *Conservation of Our Natural Resources*, p. 541.
16. *Breaking New Ground*, p. 367.

several occasions suggested to President Franklin D. Roosevelt that one be held. Following the creation of the United Nations, a world conference was finally convened. Known as the United Nations Scientific Conference on the Conservation and Utilization of Resources, it was held at Lake Success, New York, August 17–September 6, 1949. Gifford Pinchot had died in 1946, but Mrs. Pinchot was in attendance. Professional resource workers, including foresters, from all over the world discussed techniques for the scientific utilization of resources for human welfare.

Despite the the many obstacles that the conservation movement would encounter over the years, it would never lose the momentum and vitality generated by the Governors' Conference. When begun in the 1870s, the movement was almost wholly concerned with saving the forests. The White House Conference enlarged and extended the scope of conservation to other natural resources—grazing lands, minerals, water, wildlife, and scenery.

Looking back on the composition of the Governors' Conference, of the National Commission on Conservation, and of the Joint Conference on Conservation, one can detect a core of activists who were guiding—not to say manipulating—the conservation movement. Led by Pinchot and functioning with Theodore Roosevelt's hearty approval, they were young, remarkably energetic, and wholly dedicated. Most were scientists and professional men. In the early forestry records, particularly of the fateful year 1908, these names crop up:

1. Henry Gannett, a geographer in the U.S. Geological Survey, who supervised the compilation of the natural resources inventory and edited the three-volume report of the National Conservation Commission;

2. Joseph A. Holmes, a geologist in the Geological Survey, formerly state geologist of North Carolina, and a loyal Pinchot supporter, who first proposed federal acquisition of the Appalachian Forest Preserve;

3. W J McGee, geologist and hydrologist, who was referred to by Pinchot as "the scientific brains of the conservation movement all through its early critical stages";[17]

4. Frederick H. Newell, chief engineer of the Reclamation Service, who conceived the idea of the Governors' Conference;

5. Overton W. Price, associate chief of the Forest Service, who was later an officer of the National Conservation Association;

6. Thomas R. Shipp, a former newspaperman and one-time Forest Service editor, who was executive secretary of the Inland Waterways Commission, general secretary of the Governors' Conference, and secretary of the Joint Conference on Conservation;

7. Harry Slattery, who was a long-time Pinchot lieutenant, later undersecretary of the interior and director of the Rural Electrification Service.

Recognizing that the conference would give conservation a new and greater dimension, President Roosevelt, in his opening speech, singled out one individual for commendation for having brought it about:

17. Ibid., p. 359.

Especial credit is due to the initiative, the energy, the devotion to duty, and the farsightedness of Gifford Pinchot, to whom we owe so much of the progress we have already made in handling this matter of the coordination and conservation of natural resources. If it had not been for him this convention neither would nor could have been called.[18]

Pinchot and Roosevelt gave the movement unity and coherence. Henceforth, conservation would be understood to comprehend not only the preservation and restoration of resources but their development and wise use under scientific management. In all his long fight for conservation, Pinchot never advocated locking up resources. But he did demand that they be properly used for the benefit of all the people and not exploited for the profit of a few.

18. *Proceedings*, p. 10.

CHAPTER 5

The Forest Service:
Its Struggle for Survival

Richard A. Ballinger of Seattle, former commissioner of the General Land Office in the Department of the Interior, was appointed secretary of the interior by President Taft in March 1909. During the summer of 1909, Louis R. Glavis, a field officer in the Land Office, charged Ballinger with fraud in the administration of public lands in Alaska. At issue were coal claims in the Chugach National Forest; thus, the Forest Service was involved.

Forester Gifford Pinchot and Associate Forester Overton W. Price publicly supported the charges against Ballinger. The ensuing dispute became known as the Ballinger–Pinchot controversy. On January 7, 1910, Taft directed the secretary of agriculture to dismiss Pinchot and Price for insubordination.[1]

Pinchot had hardly been let out before the secretary of agriculture made certain changes that put limitations on the powers of the Forest Service. For example, he ordered that all legal activity be put under the supervision of the department's solicitor. Philip P. Wells, law officer of the Forest Service, resigned. Accounting and disbursing functions were ordered to be put under the chief of the department's Division of Accounts and Disbursements. Significantly, too, the secretary promptly took charge of all Forest Service publicity activity.

Although not an egotistical man, Henry S. Graves had a nice appreciation of his own worth. He realized that the Forest Service, without the forceful Pinchot at its head and without the friendly interest of the White House, would be vulnerable to its enemies. As dean of the School of Forestry at Yale, he had stood apart from Pinchot's row with Ballinger; hence he was not publicly identified with the critics of the Taft administration. Moreover, he was recognized as being, after Pinchot, the most influential forester in the United States. He, if anyone, could run the Forest Service as a transition

---

1. Among the many articles, monographs, and books about this celebrated dispute, an interesting case history is Alpheus Thomas Mason's *Bureaucracy Convicts Itself.*

chief, meanwhile keeping the office out of politics. If a politician without a forestry education were named as chief, a precedent would be set that could cause the Forest Service to become another bureau subject to political patronage. Graves decided to seek the job and was appointed forester on February 1, 1910.

In a personal memoir, he frankly stated that he had solicited the appointment. His account of this episode was prepared for a meeting of The Dissenters, a New Haven literary group of which he had long been a member.

When Gifford Pinchot was dismissed from the Forest Service by President Taft in January 1910, I was asked to take his place. I think it was Anson Stokes who suggested my name to Mr. Taft. I have an idea that I suggested my name to Anson. The Yale Corporation gave me a year's leave of absence. My idea was to help in straightening out the confused situation, protect the position from political appointment, and, when a successor were found, I would return to Yale. I remained ten years. . . .

I found the Forest Service badly demoralized. The Chief, the Assistant Chief, and another high officer of the Bureau had been dismissed; and Phil Wells, head of the legal division of the Service, had resigned in sympathy. The Secretary, James Wilson, and his immediate staff felt a lack of confidence in the Forest Service, and were imposing new restrictions in various procedures. The political and personal enemies of the Service were jubilant and looked forward to smashing the whole system of National Forests. In this category were strong elements among the organized mining interests of the West, the stockmen, the water power group, and especially land speculators of all kinds. And their interests were well represented in Congress.

The Secretary did not want to appoint me, but was overridden by Mr. Taft. . . . I soon found that the Secretary had been conducting a sort of personal investigation of the Service. He had been corresponding direct with many of my field officers regarding various matters, and had arranged for a later tour with my Regional Foresters, all without consulting me. This fitted in with various incidents that indicated a definite trend on the part of the Secretary to go over my head in my own field of administration. I was so stirred up about the situation that I went to the President himself, thus going the Secretary one better in violating the principles of administration. Mr. Taft wrote a letter to Mr. Wilson to straighten out the matter with me. Of course there was a painful interview, but I took the initiative and told the Secretary that if he would give me his confidence, he would never find anyone more loyal. He saw that I meant it and we soon were working in fine harmony. The incident was never mentioned in our later close association together.[2]

When Graves and the secretary agreed to bury the hatchet, it stayed buried during the remainder of Wilson's administration and through that of his successor, David F. Houston. According to Graves, Houston "was a new type of Secretary of Agriculture. He was an economist and an able executive. He was not popular with politicians or with farmers. . . . Houston always gave me fine backing in my various administrative problems."[3]

Proposed Cession to the States

After Henry Graves made peace with the secretary of agriculture, harassment from that quarter stopped. But attacks from outside the federal estab-

2. Personal recollections, written in late 1942 or early 1943 (Graves Collection, Sterling Memorial Library, Yale University). Anson Phelps Stokes, Jr. (1874–1958), was a prominent clergyman and educationist and onetime secretary of Yale University.
   3. Ibid.

lishment continued. The Forest Service was on the defensive almost continuously during Graves's administration. "One of the favorite charges against
the Forest Service," Graves wrote, "was that there was a great aggregate area
of agricultural land in the National Forests and that the withdrawal of this
land shut out the homesteader and blocked development. The most grotesque
misrepresentation of conditions were repeated in the Western press and in
Congress. . . ."[4]

On April 10, 1911, Congressman Abraham Walter Lafferty of Oregon,
who had taken office the previous month, introduced H.R. 2980, a bill to
convey the forest reserves to the states in which they were situated. Although
the bill failed to pass, it was typical of a succession of similar proposals that
had to be fought off over the years. On December 19, 1912, Graves wrote to
Charles Lathrop Pack of Lakewood, New Jersey, commenting with some
bitterness on current proposals to transfer the national forests to the states:

This movement is for the most part inspired by interests which have
consistently opposed public control of the natural resources and have argued
for private control. . . . A leading part in the attempt to bring this policy
forward has been played by certain water-power interests which desire to
secure public land privileges of great value. Recently a series of attacks on the
Forest Service has been made by certain mining interests which seek to prevent officers of the government from examining mining claims to determine
whether the law has been complied with. The entire movement is in the
interest of those who seek special privilege and the opportunity to secure
public property or rights in public property for private purposes.[5]

The movement, Graves pointed out, was most conspicuous in Colorado
where it was better organized than elsewhere in the West. Governor John A.
Shafroth was a militant advocate of state control. Delegates from Colorado
were in the majority at the second Public Lands Convention in Denver in
1911 and made an issue of the transfer of public resources to the states. A
number of western Congressmen had pledged themselves to bring about the
proposed grant of national forests to the states. They had been pressured to
take this stand by two recent mining conventions where resolutions were
adopted in support of granting federal resources to the states. Graves termed
it "a definite movement which must be met squarely and fought to a conclusion." The values were tremendous:

So far as the National Forests alone are concerned, the proposed transfer
means the grant outright by the people of the country to the individual states
of at least two billion dollars worth of property. It means the surrender by
the nation of all control over the resources now contained in the National
Forests. It means also that the Nation will lose control over the protection of
the headwaters of navigable streams and other very important national and
interstate interests.[6]

But this was not all. Another threat was embedded in the proposal; a
threat to the growing profession of forestry and to the corps of dedicated
foresters in the Forest Service. Transfer of the national forests to the states

4. Ibid.
5. Graves Collection.
6. Ibid.

would set back the notable progress being made in building a profession based on civil service and the merit system.

In 1912, only a few states, such as Connecticut, Maine, New York, Pennsylvania, and Wisconsin, had forestry departments that were reasonably well financed and reasonably free from political influence. Their forestry departments were mainly concerned with fire prevention and control. Forest management as applied to the state lands was largely custodial; the practice of silviculture was sporadic indeed. Moreover, most of the states with experience in forest management under technical foresters were in the eastern half of the country. The states containing national forests and lacking either personnel or policies competent to administer them were in the West. To be sure, the professional foresters then employed by the states were as dedicated as federal foresters, but there were fewer of them and their tenure was uncertain. The future of forestry in America, both as a public policy and as a profession, was at stake. Graves summed it up with a discouraging prediction: "The transfer would break up a strong, compact organization of trained and experienced men and create twenty new organizations, probably many of them in political hands, with many untrained men and new and varied policies."[7]

In fighting off this threat to the integrity of the national forests, the Forest Service had to face formidable challenges. Other members of Congress who persistently advocated turning the forests over to the states were four powerful senators—Joseph W. Bailey of Texas, William E. Borah and Weldon B. Heyburn of Idaho, and Albert B. Fall of New Mexico. Railroader James J. Hill was another who added his influential voice to the pressure for cession to the states.

As an example of what the Forest Service had to combat, W. B. Heyburn was a senator whose sense of legislative poise would have been amusing if, because of his high office, he had not had so many possibilities for committing serious injury. His accusations against the Forest Service varied from the libelous to the ridiculous. He accused rangers of shooting at citizens and of committing other "atrocities." He claimed that forest officers conspired to defeat him for reelection. He denounced the Service for causing squirrels to starve to death by robbing their nests of tree seed for growing new forests. It was characteristic of this politician when he was not sure what he was saying was true to say it louder and with greater conviction.

Forests versus Farms

Another serious Congressional attack on the national forests was made in 1912 by Senator Knute Nelson of Minnesota, who proposed an amendment to the Agricultural Appropriations Bill that year. Under the terms of the amendment, the secretary of agriculture would have been required to select, classify, and segregate all national forest lands that were suited for agriculture. Then, under the homestead laws, all such lands that could be used for agriculture would be opened for settlement. Irrespective of their value for

7. Ibid.

other uses or their need for public use, all national forest lands fit for agriculture would be vulnerable to exploitation. Densely wooded areas of little potential worth for agriculture, even if the value of the timber were many times the value of the land when cleared, would have been opened for settlement. However well-intentioned Senator Nelson's amendment may have been, it would have resulted in irremediable dismemberment of the national forests, if not their virtual eradication.

Opposing this proposal at the National Conservation Congress held in October 1912 at Indianapolis, Graves charged that it would block, not facilitate, agricultural development. But worse than that, he warned that its result would be the transfer of timberlands and waterpower sites to powerful private interests, thus giving resources then under public control to private monopoly. Fortunately, Nelson's amendment was reworded by the House of Representatives in keeping with the principles of the Forest Homestead Act of 1906, which had authorized the withdrawal of national forest lands for agriculture upon the request of an applicant and after examination and approval by the Forest Service. The service continued to be plagued, however, by the cant of politicians and to be harassed by the self-seeking criticism of stockmen, miners, and water users.

Interior Covets the Forest Service

Early in 1911, President Taft appointed Walter L. Fisher of Chicago as secretary of the interior to succeed Ballinger, who had resigned. Fisher was no stranger to forestry. Having been active in Pinchot's National Conservation Association, he was a Pinchot supporter in conservation as well as in politics. But this did not prevent him from proposing to Graves in October 1911 that the Forest Service be transferred to the Department of the Interior—a proposal Pinchot never would have approved. Graves, naturally, also resisted such a move.

From the records it is not clear whether this proposal was made by Fisher with President Taft's approval, or even knowledge. Elmo R. Richardson, in *The Politics of Conservation*, pointed out that the president gave Fisher a free hand in policy decisions because Fisher generally had the goodwill of conservationists. In any case, Graves had reason to look upon the proposal as another instance of higher authority in the government threatening the integrity of the Forest Service.

In a letter to Secretary of Agriculture James Wilson on October 21, 1911, Graves commented on a conference of national park superintendents held in Yellowstone Park in September 1911, during which the secretary of the interior "expressed himself as in favor of the transfer of the Forest Service to the Department of the Interior." In reprisal for the results of the Ballinger–Pinchot controversy, the Secretary of the Interior "boldly moved to bring the Forest Service and the national forests under its control."[8]

That the backlash against the Forest Service was not imaginary is evident from the writings and recollections of many people both inside and outside

8. Ibid.

the service. The following excerpts from a memorandum to Secretary of Agriculture David Houston, on June 19, 1916, recount the frustrations and difficulties Graves had to contend with:

During the past year the forces of reaction, which have never ceased their efforts to undermine the National Forest System, have made such headway that unless vigorous steps are taken to counteract this adverse movement the most serious consequences are imminent.

I do not recall any session of Congress when so many measures damaging to the National Forests have been given serious consideration, or when there was such a spirit of yielding to the demands of private interests for special grants and privileges on the public property; or when there was such a tendency to turn from the present day point of view back to the old nineteenth century indiscriminate policy of land distribution.

The situation is that a number of such bills have already passed either the House or the Senate with very strong support and little opposition; most of them have passed by unanimous consent. These adverse measures do not take the form of directly abolishing the National Forest system. Such an attack would doubtless arouse opposition. The drive on the Forests is more subtle and insidious. It is a process of attrition which will cripple or make inefficient the administration of the Forests, or break up their integrity and finally cause the system to crumble to pieces. . . .

I attribute the present situation in part to a general reaction against conservation. I attribute it in part also to the failure of the Executive departments to make it clear that they are definitely opposed to legislation which constantly nibbles at the National Forests. Most of the measures which constitute, as I see it, the greatest danger to the National Forests have been approved by the Secretary of Interior [Franklin K. Lane]. The Department of Agriculture has in its official reports expressed strong disapproval of these measures. The support given them by the other Department has entirely neutralized the action of the Department of Agriculture.[9]

Bills were introduced in Congress in 1916, 1918, 1919, and 1921 to transfer the national forests back to Interior. Although none of these bills was passed, the considerable time spent by the higher officials of the Forest Service in fighting them was diverted from other policy and technical matters.[10]

Conflicts over Parks

Equating conservation with preservation, some conservationists, even some historians, have assumed that in everything touching on forests and related resources Gifford Pinchot was a preservationist. He was not. He favored the utilization but not the exploitation of resources. As a forester, he knew that timber cutting could be carried on in the national forests or in commercial forests with benefit to the economy and with improvement to the stand. He advocated opening the national forests to orderly and scientific development, not only as sources of wood products, but as areas for grazing and for waterpower as well—always under adequate safeguards, however.

9. Ibid.
10. These bills and other overt attacks on the Forest Service and its administration of the national forests constituted an anticonservation movement that is well-documented and discussed at length by John Ise in *The United States Forest Policy*.

So uncompromising was his position on "conservation through wise use" that he made statements that alienated influential wildlife and park enthusiasts. For example, he told an audience in New York State that "forestry has nothing whatever to do with the planting of roadside trees, that parks and gardens are foreign to its nature, that scenery is altogether outside its province."[11] Robert Shankland described Gifford Pinchot as "a 'practical' (as differentiated from an 'aesthetic') conservationist and no particular friend of the national parks."[12]

In the early 1900s, the main concerns of the few professional foresters in America were the management of timber and the administration of forest land. As outdoorsmen, they appreciated natural scenery and are on record in letters, reports, and other writings as to the place of aesthetics in their way of life. Thus, in asserting that forestry had little to do with parks and scenery, Pinchot was speaking for himself, not for foresters generally. But since he was the doyen of the forestry profession, his voice was the one that the public heard and listened to. Park enthusiasts, in particular, were not impressed.

Acting both in his own behalf and as head of the Bureau of Forestry, Pinchot proposed putting the existing national parks, as well as the forest reserves, under the jurisdiction of the Department of Agriculture. President Theodore Roosevelt himself had recommended to Congress that the forest reserves be transferred from Interior to Agriculture. Roosevelt set up a Committee on the Organization of Government Scientific Work, appointing to it Charles D. Walcott, director of the Geological Survey; James R. Garfield, secretary of the interior; and Pinchot, as secretary. In a report of July 20, 1903, the committee proposed not only that the national forest reserves be transferred but that the national parks also be entrusted to the Department of Agriculture. When one reads of Pinchot's alleged opposition to the national parks and of his known conviction that they would be better managed under forestry principles in Agriculture, one must remember that his was not a lone voice. Two of the highest officials in Interior itself were willing to recommend such action to the president.

It is also a matter of record that Pinchot opposed the creation of a separate bureau for national parks, especially if it would be put in Interior. Although he opposed the bill to create a national parks bureau in Interior, he was willing to support legislation that would put it in Agriculture. This was also the recommendation of Secretary of Agriculture David Houston, and doubtless reflected the viewpoint and hope of the Forest Service.

During the two decades following Pinchot's departure from federal service (1911–30), the Forest Service suffered backlash from the preservationists and national park enthusiasts who resented Pinchot's opposition to the proposed bureau of national parks. Moreover, well-known wilderness advocates, such as the highly respected John Muir and J. Horace McFarland, had been rebuffed by Pinchot when they proposed that the forest reserves be in fact reserved from lumbering and other commercial development.

11. *Breaking New Ground*, p. 71.
12. *Steve Mather of the National Parks*, p. 48.

Wildlife preservationists, led and supported by President Theodore Roose-velt, advocated that the forest reserves be made inviolate wildlife refuges under military protection, in the manner of Yellowstone National Park. Pinchot was able to convince Roosevelt of the impracticability of such a policy, countering that under proper forest (including wildlife) management, with hunting permitted, game habitat and populations would improve. The soundness of this decision has been vindicated over the years; the national forests are among America's sources of breeding stocks of big game and indeed of all native wildlife species. Nevertheless, at the time, a certain ele-ment in the wildlife conservation movement was alienated, and the Forest Service was long subjected to criticism.

The attitude of the Forest Service toward national parks was outlined by Graves during a conference of district foresters held in Salt Lake City, Febru-ary 10-16, 1916.

I wish to reiterate my feeling that we should not take any position which is antagonistic to a *proper* National Park extension program. We must, how-ever, recognize that there is a very definite movement on foot to induce the Government to embark upon a very extensive National Park policy. This movement is led by a small, but fairly well organized, group, bringing to-gether various field organizations and interests, supporting the creation of certain individual parks, but with no great understanding of, or concern in, the broader aspects of the general National Park problem itself. . . .

Any movement looking to the setting aside of a great natural wonder as a National Park will be supported, but the boundaries of any park which has my support must be so drawn that the Park administration will not be com-pelled to practice Forest administration. Some of the Park bills now before Congress will be opposed on this ground.[13]

By act of Congress on August 25, 1916, the National Park Service was established in the Department of the Interior, and the next year Stephen T. Mather was designated the first director.

Mining Interests: Legitimate and Otherwise

Another area of conflict with the Department of Interior involved patents to claims on national forest land for mining or other special purposes. The General Land Office in Interior functioned as a land court in approving these claims. The Forest Service, which managed the national forests, had the un-pleasant task of investigating the claims to verify that the requirements of the law were upheld. This exercise of administrative responsibility led to frequent outcries during Graves's administration that the Forest Service was shutting out the homesteader and miner, hence blocking the development of the West.

There are hundreds of examples of the fight waged by forest officers to impose standards of efficient and honest management on the lands put in their charge. One of the problem areas was the Black Hills National Forest of South Dakota. On July 1, 1909, a young forest assistant named George A. Duthie began his assignment at the Black Hills Forest headquarters in Dead-wood at $1,000 a year. Like most forest officers, Duthie kept a diary, and,

13. Graves Collection.

when he retired, he drew on it to write a sketch of his Forest Service career. He explained:

There had been strong opposition to the establishment of a national forest in the Black Hills both from the homesteaders and the mining interests. The opposition of the latter was influential enough to suspend the reservation for one year and during that period a very large part of the Black Hills was covered by mining locations. There was a theory, widely circulated, that these locations automatically nullified the national forest reservation and therefore the Forest Service had no jurisdiction over land covered by the mineral entries. Upon this premise any kind of trespass, the cutting of timber, grazing of livestock or occupancy for any purpose was justified. This, of course, resulted in many trespass cases. This conflict with the mining interests was the natural outgrowth of the free and easy attitude toward the appropriation of government land and resources which had grown up through the years of settlement. It simply fell to the lot of the Forest Service to be the first agency to enforce the principle that the public has vested rights in the public domain which individuals must respect.[14]

Duthie's first assignment was to a timber survey crew of fifteen rangers and assistants who estimated the timber cut in trespass from mineral locations by the Safe Investment Gold Mining Company. This company, whose operations were mainly promotional stock selling, rather than mining, had located some 6,000 acres under mineral entry and cut the standing timber from a large part of the area before the Forest Service stopped it. The court rendered a judgment in favor of the Forest Service and stopped the company's stock sales, after which the enterprise passed into oblivion. In many of these conflicts, local newspapers championed the cause of the mining promoters and attacked the Forest Service.

The consequences of unrestricted entry were made clear by a continuing investigation of claims patented before the national forests were transferred to the Department of Agriculture. The chief forester's annual reports for 1912, 1913, and 1914 are filled with examples of fraudulent claims uncovered by Forest Service investigators.

"The mining laws," Graves wrote in his annual report for 1913, "afford the greatest cloak for land frauds in the National Forests, and have been more commonly misused than the other laws."[15] Patents to mining claims were repeatedly applied for by persons wanting to get control of timber, water supplies, power sites, sites for dwellings and resorts, even town sites, or simply a hole in the ground in order to sell mining stock. Naturally, these gentry were harshly critical of the Forest Service. Graves countered their charges with pages of facts in his annual reports and once led a field trip to inspect a supposed manganese claim in the Olympic National Forest. The manganese claim proved nonexistent. Legitimate prospectors and the responsible elements in the mining industry had few reasons to defame the service, but their views did not seem to reach the newspapers or the halls of Congress.

Graves personally inspected forest homesteads on the St. Joe and Coeur d'Alene National Forests of Idaho in the summer of 1914. On the St. Joe,

14. Manuscript Division, Conservation Library Center, Denver Public Library.
15. U.S. Forest Service, *Report of the Forester* (1913), p. 5.

208 of 264 homesteads had passed into the hands of lumber companies within three years after being patented. These disclosures did not spare the Forest Service from the criticism of special interests or from the cant of politicians, but opposition faded gradually as the benefits of Graves's avowed policy of putting "every foot of land in the forests" to productive use became evident.

Education or Propaganda?

During both the Pinchot and Graves administrations, but particularly during the latter, the Forest Service was persistently attacked for its alleged extravagance in spending funds for propaganda. Representative Frank W. Mondell of Wyoming and Senator Heyburn charged repeatedly that forestry officials were traveling about the country on unnecessary junkets giving speeches before societies, conventions, and associations, telling them how to run their affairs. Parallel with this criticism was the complaint that the Service devoted too much time and money to writing bulletins and newspaper and magazine articles.

From its beginning, federal forestry work was based on investigating and reporting. This was the assignment Congress gave F. B. Hough when he was appointed special agent in 1876. His first *Report Upon Forestry* in 1877 was followed by a stream of additional reports, articles, bulletins, and speeches by him and his successors. On becoming chief of the division in 1886, B. E. Fernow immediately started on a busy career as lecturer and publicist. In his campaign of public information to enlighten people about forest conservation, he was ably assisted by The American Forestry Association. Much credit is due him for helping to create the favorable public interest that subsequently aided the phenomenally rapid growth of forestry and the Forest Service. But more than that, Fernow started the investigations in wood utilization, timber physics, and related subjects that resulted in an impressive series of technical bulletins and monographs. This work, in fact, marked the beginning of the Forest Service's comprehensive research program.

Pinchot, Fernow's successor, was an indefatigable publicist. Supported by President Roosevelt, he broadcast the conservation message across the land. These two astute leaders realized that well-informed people were those most likely to support the government's conservation policies. The Forest Service was pioneering in the formulation of policy, not only in forest management, but in range management, water management, and wildlife management as well. The why and how of these new ventures had to be explained to all who were interested in them or affected by them. Consequently, the Service had staff men whose jobs it was to write and edit speeches and material for publication—for government bulletins and circulars on the one hand, and for newspapers and magazines on the other. Herbert A. Smith, a Yale graduate and close friend of Pinchot's, joined the old Division of Forestry in 1901 as an editor and writer. During his nearly four decades with the service, he did as much as any other single employee to inform the country about government forestry policy and the operations of the Forest Service. His writings were informative, factual, and honest.

Royal S. Kellogg also entered the old Division of Forestry in 1901 and had a successful career both as a government forest officer and later as an industry association executive. But he claimed that much of the energy of the staff in the Washington office was directed toward building up sentiment for forestry. "When I was in the Forest Service," he said, "I think I talked to more organizations than any other man in the Service. And I wrote more bulletins that had wider distribution than any other man in the Service during that particular period." [16]

In 1910, the Washington office of the Forest Service compiled a document listing criticisms directed at the Service and answers in rebuttal. There were thirteen criticisms about livestock and grazing administration; eighteen about reforestation, timber sales, assistance to states and private owners; ten about forest fires, personnel, organization, and improvements; and nineteen about land administration.

Ranging from the trivial to the consequential, the criticisms were all answered at length with citations from the law, statistics, and other sources of authority. The criticism, for example, that squirrel stores were robbed when tree seed was collected was answered with the admission that robbing the squirrels was the cheapest way to obtain seed needed for reforestation, and that it was not inhumane because only a small portion of the seed stored by squirrels is found. Other criticisms made and answered were that forest fires were neglected by forest officers (untrue); that extravagant expenditures were made for ranger stations (untrue; the law prohibited spending more than $650 for any building erected by the Forest Service); that reforestation is impracticable and a useless waste of money (some methods were acknowledged to have failed, but success had been general and 7.5 million acres of unproductive land needed planting).

Only an organization sensitive to its good name and its responsibility to the public would have gone to the trouble to document the minor as well as the major criticisms levelled against it and to provide explanations in defense of its practices. Who made use of this volume outside the forester's office is not known. [17]

Most of the speeches given by forest officers at meetings and conventions were in response to invitations by citizens simply wanting information and by users of the national forests, such as lumbermen, stockmen, and water consumers, seeking clarification of regulations. This employment of funds and personnel was not only a legitimate activity; it was essential in the education of the public.

Nevertheless, the criticism continued, though in time it became less hostile in tone, except for a few politicians who never ceased their carping. Under Graves's administration, the Forest Service was under frequent attack for alleged extravagance in "advertising."

16. Interview with Elwood R. Maunder of the Forest History Society in Palmetto, Florida, April 16, 1955.
17. The copy in the Graves Collection apparently was inherited by Graves when he succeeded Pinchot as chief forester in 1911.

Morale Declines

During this decade (1911-20), as never before or since, the development of forestry and the growth of the forestry profession were bound to the success of the Forest Service and the application of forest practices on the national forests. Had the bitter anticonservation hostility to the Forest Service prevailed, forestry, both as a developing public policy and as an emerging profession, could have been set back for decades. While it is idle at this late date to speculate about what might have happened, from the record of this turbulent era it is clear that the foes of the national forests were the foes of forestry.

Such politicians as Senator Heyburn were openly committed to the dismemberment of the system of forest reserves. Although men of education, the anticonservation Congressmen were unable or unwilling to comprehend what the Forest Service was trying to do: to develop the resources of the national forests for the permanent good of all the people. Their hostility to the Forest Service derived from the service's unwillingness to permit the resources to be exploited for the immediate and temporary benefit of a few.

Senator Henry Moore Teller of Colorado, a former secretary of the interior (1882-85), might have been expected to have shown some consideration for the interests of future generations in the natural resources of the West. But in 1909 he declared, "I do not believe there is either a moral or any other claim upon me to postpone the use of what nature has given me, so that the next generation or generations may have an opportunity to get what I myself ought to get."[18]

As the architect of the national forest system, Pinchot fought effectively to preserve and extend it, loyally supported by ex-President Theodore Roosevelt and many additional leaders in public opinion. Politically oriented as he was, Pinchot championed the Forest Service as a bureau ably administered and essential to the efficient administration of the national forests. In short, he fought for a continuation of sound public policy.

Graves was fighting for these things too. Like Pinchot, he staked his official position on the defense of the Forest Service as an agency of sound policy in the public interest. But Graves, it must be remembered, was on leave as dean of the Yale School of Forestry. He viewed the strengthening of the Forest Service as the strengthening of the young forestry profession. If the Forest Service went under, so might the profession, which up to this time had scarcely gained recognition as a profession and which numbered almost all its members as employees of the service.

Inman F. Eldredge, who began his career in the Forest Service in 1905 and became one of the profession's most respected and beloved members, was a shrewd and candid observer of early forestry trends. Because he had endured the backlash as a field forest officer in the West, his outspoken comment is noteworthy: "The lowest ebb in the Forest Service," he said, "when morale and money and everything else went into a deep dip was during Taft's administration after the Pinchot controversy with Ballinger. Then we were

18. *Congressional Record*, daily ed., February 26, 1909, p. 3226.

punished, and I mean in every possible way; the Department of Agriculture just went after our scalps. There were years when nobody got a promotion in the Forest Service. It went on from 1910, I should say, until close to 1920 before we commenced to get our heads up."[19]

In his report for the fiscal year ending June 30, 1918, Forester Graves was pessimistic about the future of Forest Service personnel.

... With conspicuous and devoted loyalty the bulk of our force, outside of those who have gone into the Army or Navy, have chosen to stand by the Service, although they might almost to a man have obtained much better-paying positions elsewhere.... The National Forest force is now underpaid, and its members are hard pressed by high living costs. Without relief, the standards of administration and protection are bound to deteriorate greatly and rapidly.... The forest ranger receiving $1,100 or $1,200, required as he is to own from one to three horses, finds himself, even with the greatest economy, unable to pay his essential bills.[20]

In 1919, Aldo Leopold, who had left the Forest Service, noted that during the previous five years the low salaries paid by the service had caused a shortage of competent men in the national forests. Because of the almost negligible promotions allowed by Congress, there was an increasing annual exodus of leadership, experience, and ability into other fields. He feared that the poor salary situation threatened the ultimate success "of our great experiment in national forestry." Moreover, Leopold contended that the Forest Service salary scale was a menace to the whole forestry movement. He predicted that "the collapse of the great experiment in national forestry would have widespread effect. State forestry, private forestry, forest schools, the profession in general, and even other fields of conservation would be profoundly affected."[21]

Leopold's warnings were substantiated by *Field Program*, a Forest Service quarterly that listed all work assignments, including appointments and promotions. Resignations during 1919 included 2 assistant district foresters, 46 supervisors and deputy supervisors, 152 forest rangers, 5 logging engineers, 23 forest and grazing examiners, 3 forest assistants, and 25 wood technologists and engineers.

Although the Forest Service contained as loyal a group of workers as the federal government had anywhere, the shabby treatment they received affected morale. The concern of the field forces was evident in Chief William B. Greeley's annual report for 1920:

... The inadequacy of the salaries paid to employees of the Forest Service led to such discouragement and so many resignations that complete demoralization of the Service was threatened.... The Forest Service has exhausted every means at its disposal to adjust salaries to present living costs and the responsible duties demanded of its employees. The employment situation has been improved, but it cannot be met effectively without radical increases in

19. Elwood R. Maunder, "Ride the White Horse—Memoirs of a Southern Forester," an interview with Inman F. Eldredge, *Forest History*, vol. 3, nos. 3 and 4 (Winter 1960).
20. U.S. Forest Service, *Report of the Forester* (1918), pp. 3-4.
21. "Forest Service Salaries and the Future of the National Forests," *Journal of Forestry*, vol. 17 (April 1919), pp. 398-401.

the rates of compensation fixed by statute. . . . The Government demands of a forest supervisor, paid on an average $2,368 per year, including the temporary war-time bonus, the honest and efficient handling of public property worth 15 to 20 million dollars. . . . No organization can perform miracles; and the public Forests of the United States can not be effectively protected from fire, developed, and administered to meet the tremendous demands being made upon them without a field force whose compensation is on a par with the work demanded.[22]

At the time Greeley was writing, the forest ranger's average salary was $1,516 per year.

Notwithstanding the backlash endured by the Forest Service during the period 1910–20, notable advancements in forest conservation were made. The first of consequence in Graves's administration was the establishment in 1910 of the Forest Products Laboratory at Madison, Wisconsin. Then, in 1911, Congress enacted the far-reaching Weeks Law which provided for federal and state cooperation in protecting forests from fire and for the acquisition of national forests on the headwaters of navigable streams.

In 1915, the Branch of Research was created in the Forest Service. It not only correlated all the experimental field work being done throughout the country but gave research a status equal to the service's administrative branches. With the entry of the United States into World War I, the Forest Service undertook increased responsibility for the production of wood and for research in its war uses. Henry Graves was assigned by the War Department to help organize a regiment to engage in logging and milling in France. During part of 1917, he held the temporary rank of lieutenant colonel.

Following the war, Graves put the influence of the Forest Service behind a campaign for public regulation of timber cutting on private land. This was a controversy that he would periodically be engaged in for the next quarter-century, but not as chief of the Forest Service. He resigned in March 1920.

In accepting appointment as forester, Graves considered himself a transition chief, a temporary custodian of the office during a critical period. His supreme achievement was that he kept the national forests from becoming the spoils of politicians and the Forest Service from going under.

22. U.S. Forest Service, *Report of the Forester* (1920), pp. 3–4.

CHAPTER 6

Battles with the Stockmen

The Forest Service faced some of its most difficult problems in its relations with the livestock industry. Regulated grazing on the national forests began in 1906 under a system of fees and permits promulgated by the secretary of agriculture. Grazing control was essential if there was to be consistency and stability in national forest administration and progress in the livestock industry. Basically, the form of regulation was simple and equitable. The Forest Service instituted a permit system which required stockmen desiring to graze livestock on national forest ranges to obtain permits for specified numbers of animals and to pay a fee for the grass grazed. It was also the job of the Forest Service to enforce the rules governing the issuance of permits and the payment of fees.

Under the old "free use" custom, stockmen had turned their cattle and horses loose to roam at will. Sheep were handled differently; they were herded in bands, but the bands were moved about with little regard for the condition of the range. They went wherever there was sufficient grass and water. "Dead lines," established in the early range wars between cattlemen and sheepmen, separated cattle ranges from sheep ranges. Almost everywhere, grazing on the public lands was a chaotic business.[1] Those defending the system and wanting to perpetuate it were almost wholly the large and strong outfits capable of enforcing their "rights."[2]

These and other livestock groups were critical of government regulation as an invasion of their American freedom. They maintained that it was their

1. U.S. Forest Service, *The Western Range*, S. Doc. 109, 74 Cong., 2 sess. (1936).
2. In delineating some of the influences that brought about improved range administration on the national forests and other federal lands, the author is aware that, in the light of present knowledge, early reports of range conditions were on occasion distorted and technically in error. The angry concern of those charged with the protection of the public lands may have led to exaggeration, but it demonstrated the need for improved management to prevent destructive grazing. During the period with which this chapter deals, sensationalism helped overcome the apathy and indifference of the responsible policy makers.

right by custom to graze livestock on public land without restriction. Predictably, they were supported in this opinion by certain politicians, by certain newspapers, and by a certain segment of the general public.

Some stockmen refused to apply for grazing permits or to pay grazing fees. Without permits, they were in trespass on the national forests, and the Forest Service sought to enforce the regulations by taking the offenders to court.

Other stockmen accepted the regulations and tried to make them work. They realized that the traditional "free range" of the frontier was destructive of the resource, wastefully competitive, and uneconomic. They could see the massive range depletion and erosion that followed unrestricted grazing. For profitable livestock production, they knew that a system of range management had to replace the ruinous chaos that had so long prevailed.

One group that resisted the permit system and the payment of grazing fees was the Grand Valley Stock Growers Association of Colorado. Fred Light, a homesteader and president of the association, refused to take out a permit or to pay a fee for grazing his cattle on the Holy Cross Forest Reserve (now the Holy Cross Ranger District, White River National Forest). Moreover, he contended that the federal government was required by the law of Colorado to fence its land if it wanted to prevent trespass by livestock. This contention was supported by the Colorado Stock Growers Association and the American National Live Stock Association.[3]

Light became the defendant in a test case brought by the Forest Service in federal court, a case that developed into a *cause célèbre*. Newspapers throughout the West kept interest at the boiling point. The circuit court decided in the government's favor and enjoined the defendant from letting his stock go into the national forest. Under pressure from the stockmen, the Colorado legislature appropriated funds to carry the case to the Supreme Court. On May 1, 1911, the Supreme Court affirmed the lower court's decision.

In delivering the opinion of the court, Justice Joseph Rucker Lamar noted that Light engaged in wanton and willful trespass.

He could have obtained a permit for reasonable pasturage. He not only declined to apply for such a license, but there is evidence that he threatened to resist efforts to have his cattle removed from the Reserve, and in his answer he declares that he will continue to turn out his cattle, and contends that if they go upon the Reserve the Government has no remedy at law or in equity. . . . Under the facts the court properly granted an injunction. The judgement was right on the merits, wholly regardless of the question as to whether the Government had enclosed its property.[4]

---

3. Public opinion, as reflected by the local newspapers, was not all on the side of Fred Light. In an editorial on March 21, 1908, the *Aspen* (Colo.) *Times* accused Light of demanding the discharge of two Forest Service riders, I. W. Foster and W. S. Cyphers, from the Snow Mass district of the Holy Cross Forest Reserve. The editorialist claimed that Light wanted the riders to be replaced by men who could be handled more easily. Foster was fired and Cyphers resigned. According to the *Times*: "Fred Light has waged war against the forest service since it was started. He has been its bitterest enemy."

4. *Report of U.S. Supreme Court*, 220 U.S. 523 (1911).

In brief, this Supreme Court decision upheld the right of the secretary of agriculture to require stockmen wishing to graze animals on national forest ranges to take out grazing permits and to pay fees for them. It also upheld the authority of the Forest Service to undertake management practices for rehabilitation of the range. One might assume, then, that this historic decision forced the stockmen to comply with the regulations and to cooperate with local forest officers for their mutual benefit. On the contrary, resistance to the Forest Service and harassment of its officers in the enforcement of the regulations continued.

An editorial, "The Forest Reserve Decision," in the *Great Falls* (Mont.) *Tribune* on May 4, 1911, criticized the Supreme Court for invading the sovereignty of the states. Montana, like Colorado, had a law that required owners to fence their range land if they desired to prevent trespass by wandering cattle. The law obligated the landowner to go to the expense of excluding unwanted cattle; it put no responsibility on stockmen to keep their cattle off other private or public land. This law the *Tribune* considered to be right and proper:

The supreme court decides that the federal government by order of its officials has the right to defy the statute concerning fencing and abrogate the range law. It is another step in invasion of state sovereignty. The public lands of the federal government are held to be exempt from the sovereignty of the state, so far as this particular case involves the question of state sovereignty. It is one more step in a long line of judicial decisions by which the powers of the federal government are augmented, and the sovereignty of the states invaded.

At conventions of livestock, mining, and waterpower associations, resolutions continued to pour forth denouncing both government policies and government officials who were trying to prevent further damage to the range and to build it up. The National Livestock Association and the National Woolgrowers Association continued to whip up opposition to the Forest Service even after numerous stockmen throughout the West began to perceive the value of grazing regulations and the need for them.

Local permittees ceased their opposition and cooperated with the forest officers as the improvements from better range practices became evident. Among the improvements brought about by the Forest Service were facilities for water supplies, access roads and trails, drift fences to control the movement of stock, and the eradication of poisonous weeds. Permittees had assurance that their use of the range would be protected even if reduction in their herds became necessary. A certain stability, not enjoyed by the industry under its former competitive, unregulated customs, began to emerge. In time, even the big national livestock associations dropped their dissent against improved range management on the national forests and gave grudging approval of it.

Theodore Shoemaker, a career forest officer who entered the Forest Service in 1907, described an episode following his appointment (probably in 1913) as supervisor of the Pike National Forest. When he arrived at headquarters in Denver, he immediately encountered the antagonism of stockmen who still resented the grazing regulations.

"The Platte Canyon district of the Pike was one of the hotbeds of this opposition," Shoemaker noted, "and all attempts at overcoming it had failed." It would take all the tact and firmness he could muster to enforce the unpopular rules and overcome local hostility, for he was in the stronghold of E. M. Ammons who later became governor of Colorado "mainly on the strength of the bitterness with which he attacked the Forest Service and the principle of federal control of the public lands." Ammon's relatives and neighbors looked to him "to back them in thwarting regulations at every point."[5]

Shoemaker found it impossible to get an accurate count of the cattle each man owned, and he knew—as everyone did—that the stockmen were paying fees for only a fraction of their grazing cattle. Some areas were being damaged by overgrazing; others were scarcely used at all.

The new supervisor was hard put to decide "how to set about dealing with people who either would not speak to a forest officer or spoke only to insult and belittle." Studying the problem for a year, he decided to call a meeting of the stockmen in a local schoolhouse.

They turned out to a man, and they didn't wait to be called to order. They cursed the Forest Service up one side and down the other. They strode about the schoolroom, most of them wearing side arms. One of the biggest owners, an aged old-timer, after delivering an especially blasphemous tirade, stalked out the door and we heard his spurs clanging down the walk. He didn't come back.

After an hour or more of blustering and blowing off steam things quieted down somewhat, and one of the stockmen who had taken no part in the tirade arose and asked to speak. . . . The gist of his remarks was that since the call for the meeting by the representatives of the Forest Service indicated there were problems in the matter of range allotments, use of the range, issuance of permits, etc., which they wished to discuss, that they had arranged for the use of the schoolhouse for the meeting, and had listened to everybody's remarks respectfully, it was only fair to listen to what "they" had to say. . . .[6]

Thanking the men for attending the meeting and for frankly stating their views, Shoemaker explained that he "had to deal on some basis" with them because they were grazing their cattle on government land. He expressed his hope for friendly cooperation on both sides and reminded the men that others depended on the range "since every acre of it was on the watershed from which 200,000 people in Denver got their water." He warned that he and the stockmen alike "were sure to hear from the folks in Denver" if the stockmen "left dead critters in the streams," let the forests burn, or permitted cattle to overgraze the range and cause erosion.[7]

"I suggested that since this was our common problem we should get together and face it squarely," Shoemaker recalled. In order to better utilize the range, he recommended that they reduce overgrazing and distribute their stock more efficiently. Then he let them know that they could no longer run

5. Theodore Shoemaker, "Some of My Experiences in the Forest Service, 1907–1938" (Manuscript Division, Library of Congress).
6. Ibid.
7. Ibid.

more stock than their permits called for and that they must pay fees for all grazing animals. Shoemaker concluded this episode by remarking that in time the stockmen's distrust was replaced by "friendliness and even comradeship."

Paul H. Roberts, range management specialist in the Forest Service for many years, once wrote: "Grazing use, since the creation of the Forest Service, has been the most difficult activity to administer. There has never been a time in the experience of this writer when some segment of the livestock industry was not in a battle with the Forest Service over local or national issues."[8]

Hoofed Locusts

Henry Graves was particularly bitter toward some of the sheepmen who used the national forests. They were among the most destructive users of the forest ranges, the least responsive to supervision, and the most unreasonable in their criticism of the service's efforts to rehabilitate the resource by reducing and regulating the number of sheep permitted to graze. In later years, Graves wrote:

I recall very vividly seeing the effect of unregulated grazing of sheep in the eastern Oregon forests in 1896. On dry summer days one would see here and there clouds of dust rising above the tree tops like the smoke of a forest fire. Bands of two to three thousand sheep, moving in compact masses, tramped the dry soil and destroyed the protective cover of humus and upper layer of undecomposed needles of the conifers. No wonder that the sheepmen opposed the system of regulation of grazing on the National Forests inaugurated by Gifford Pinchot when he was Chief Forester; and they redoubled their attacks when I succeeded Pinchot in 1910.[9]

Next to wildfire, the worst enemy of the western forest reserves was the sheep. Overgrazing by sheep destroys grass and results in erosion. The sharp hoofs of sheep cause compaction of the soil, which slows natural revegetation. Sheep also break and trample tree seedlings, thus preventing natural regeneration. On some forest reserves they were a scourge.

Clearly, the sheep problem had to be solved before the forest reserves could be put under conservative management. As custodian of the reserves, the Department of the Interior had scant success in applying effective grazing policies. Part of the difficulty arose from the unsatisfactory—and almost unenforceable—laws and regulations under which the reserve officers were compelled to function. Part of the difficulty stemmed from the ineffectiveness of those put in charge of the reserves.

The sheepman was responsible not only for the enormous damage done by his animals but for widespread fire losses as well. L. A. Barrett, assistant regional forester in the California Region of the Forest Service, compiled a comprehensive record of early fires in California forests and brush lands. No agency recorded fires and their causes before the establishment of national forests, he said, but "it is well established, through newspaper items, which commented only on unusually large fires, by statements of mountaineers

8. *Hoof Prints on Forest Ranges*, p. 151.
9. Graves Collection, Sterling Memorial Library, Yale University.

familiar with conditions and occurrences at that time and by writers who realized the damage being done, that the largest percentage of the most destructive fires in the mountains of California were caused by sheepmen during the thirty years preceding the establishment of the National Forests."[10]

In the absence of a clear-cut workable law and of specific police power applicable to such a shifting problem as protection of the forest from sheep, officials were put to unusual expedients in order to perform their duties. Gus Knight was one of the early special agents of the California State Board of Forestry in San Bernardino County. In a report of 1888, he stated:

I have done all in my power to keep down fires, and I have succeeded in keeping sheep off of the most of the State and Government land in and about Bear Valley, one of the finest timbered and watered districts in the mountains, by placing friends of mine on timber claims in various places through the mountains, so that sheep could not get in without infringing on their claims, and by so doing have kept the mountains almost free of fires, as the sheep men are the cause of nine-tenths of the fires in the mountains.[11]

The extensive injury to the public domain caused by nomadic sheep husbandry had been clearly brought to the attention of the Department of the Interior in the impressive report on forest policy submitted May 1, 1897, by the special commission of the National Academy of Sciences. (See chapter 3.) A section of the report was devoted to a discussion of the serious damage caused by the great bands of sheep that were driven each spring from the valleys into the high ranges.

Every blade of grass, the tender, growing shoots of shrubs, and seedling trees are eaten to the ground. The feet of these "hoofed locusts," crossing and recrossing the faces of steep slopes, tread out the plants sheep do not relish and, loosening the forest floor, produce conditions favorable to floods. . . .

In California and Oregon the injury to the public domain by illegal pasturage is usually increased by the methods of the shepherds, who now penetrate to the highest and most inaccessible slopes and alpine meadows wherever a blade of grass can grow, and before returning to the valleys in the autumn start fires to uncover the surface of the ground and stimulate the growth of herbage. . . .

In every Western State and Territory the nomadic sheep men are dreaded and despised. Year after year, however, they continue their depredations. . . .

The pasturage of sheep on the national domain has been so long allowed, however, that the men who benefit by it have come to believe they have acquired vested rights in the public forests, and their trespass can only be checked by the employment of vigorous measures.[12]

In 1898, Paderson Y. Lewis was appointed a ranger on the Stanislaus Reserve in California at a monthly salary of $60. His primary responsibility

---

10. Typescript, 1935 (History File, U.S. Forest Service, Region Office, San Francisco). Barrett noted that stockmen, particularly sheepmen, raised the greatest objections to the creation of forest reserves.

11. Typescript (History File, U.S. Forest Service, Region Office, San Francisco).

12. "Report of the Commission Appointed by the National Academy of Sciences upon a Forest Policy for the Forested Lands of the United States," *Report of the National Academy of Sciences for the Year 1897*, S. Doc. 57, 55 Cong., 2 sess. (1898), pp. 45–46.

was to evict trespassing sheep owners from mountain areas that had suffered the devastating effects of fire and overgrazing for twenty years. Many of the sheepmen were Basques; that is, aliens who owned no land and paid no taxes. They literally got their living from the public lands by stealing feed from national parks and forest reserves, ruining the mountain pastures in the process. Too few rangers were available to watch over the immense expanses of mountain country. Hence, bands of sheep were easily hidden in the remote and rugged valleys. But even when found illegally on government land, the herders were defiant of law and official authority.

In the annals of public land administration, few officials had a more frustrating experience than the early forest reserve ranger. If he located a sheepman running stock in violation of the regulations, he could not make an arrest but had to appear before a U.S. commissioner with an affidavit. If the commissioner was willing to issue an injunction forbidding the herder to trespass, the forest officer then had to ride back to the mountains, hunt up the trespasser, and present the injunction. Should the trespasser refuse to leave the green pastures, the ranger had to return to the commissioner with another sworn statement in writing to show contempt of the injunction. Then a U.S. marshal might be sent to arrest the herder, provided the trespasser could be found.

These trips might involve a hundred or more miles of horseback riding or stagecoach and train travel back and forth between the range, the forest supervisor's office, and the commissioner's office. Meanwhile, the trespasser might have a month or more in which to graze his sheep, and might be far distant from the original scene of the trespass when the warrant arrived.

Some commissioners refused to permit criminal prosecution of trespassers on the ground that the Interior Department regulations were delegations of authority and therefore unconstitutional. The commissioners would allow civil suit for contempt only. Sheepmen were willing to pay a moderate fine of $100 when such civil cases came to trial. And to make law enforcement even more difficult, owners exchanged fraudulent bills of sale for sheep, making ownership and responsibility hard to determine. Moreover, they altered wool brands, and some pretended inability to understand English. Crooked officers were paid off by sheepmen to ignore trespass. Thus, the job of honest rangers was made almost hopeless. The disheartening nature of the work, coupled with the low pay, caused many rangers to quit.

But with the transfer of the reserves from the Department of the Interior to the Department of Agriculture, the campaign for law enforcement began to succeed. Five days after the transfer, on February 6, 1905, Congress gave the forest reserve and national park officers power to arrest without warrant for violation of the laws and regulations.[13]

This power, combined with the determination of the Bureau of Forestry to use it, led to a solution of the migratory sheep dilemma in the forest reserves of California and other western states. In his report of 1905, Forester Pinchot predicted the act would result in better protection of the forest reserves. And it did.

---

13. R. F. Feagans, *Laws, Decisions, and Opinions Applicable to the National Forests*, U.S. Department of Agriculture, Office of the Solicitor (1916).

R. L. P. Bigelow was another old-time forest ranger who left behind a record of the rangers' war with the sheepmen. Entering the Forest Service in the fall of 1902, he was assigned to the Sierra Forest Reserve in California. His immediate job was to protect the reserve from trespass by transient sheep outfits. It was a tough assignment.

A year after Bigelow began his duties, a ranger found it necessary to shoot a sheepman in order to protect a fellow ranger. The sheepman recovered from his wound, but the Forest Service gave orders that rangers were not to use force to prevent sheepmen from entering government reserves; they were to withdraw and report if the trespassers refused to leave.

Bigelow wrote: "We rangers had to pack guns to protect ourselves. We did not like the orders to withdraw and there were no withdrawals that I ever heard of."[14]

One evening in May 1904, Bigelow found nine bands of sheep inside the forest boundary. At daybreak the next morning, Bigelow and a group of rangers and local cattlemen drove the sheep out of the forest. The men caught three bands of ewes and lambs, mixed them together just inside the boundary, and turned them over to the herders. It was a fifteen-mile drive to the nearest corrals at Fort Independence, and it took the herders a week to separate the bands. This was the beginning of the end of the transient sheep business in California.

Law Enforcement on the Yellowstone

Although enforcement of Department of the Interior regulations was discouragingly difficult, a bold and ingenious forest officer could make them stick. One such was A. A. Anderson, first superintendent of the Yellowstone Forest Reserve. Emigrating to Wyoming as a young man, he bought a cattle ranch, then became active in the preservation of the forest resources of the state. Having been appointed special forest superintendent of the reserve by President Theodore Roosevelt, July 1, 1902, Anderson was unrelenting in his efforts to eliminate the unrestricted trespass of sheep and to suppress forest fires.

When the reserve was established in 1902, it surrounded Yellowstone Park. Its area in three states—Idaho, Montana, and Wyoming—was approximately 9,500 square miles, a domain twice as large as Connecticut. Appalled at the many raging fires that swept through the timber prior to the creation of the reserve, Anderson sought ways to stop them. He discovered that most of the fires "had been deliberately started by wandering sheepmen, who were setting fire to the dense pine forests for two reasons: first, because it would be easier thereafter to trail their sheep; and second, because when the forest was burned the resultant weeds which sprang up would afford better pasturage."[15]

The situation became critical. As Anderson described it:

A few wandering sheepmen were jeopardizing not only the forests and wild game but the prosperity of the farmers, the very life of the State. They were

14. Typescript (History File, U.S. Forest Service, Region Office, San Francisco).
15. "The Yellowstone Forest Reserve," *Annals of Wyoming*, vol. 4 (April 1927), p. 378.

doing this at the expense of the local sheepmen. . . . For the wanderers, bringing their sheep across country after shearing time, could poach upon the ranges of the home sheepmen only until snow fell—a period of about two and a half months. And in that short time, their sheep rendered the home ranges useless for a period of nine months after.[16]

During the summer of 1904, Anderson was informed by telegram from Washington that 60,000 sheep had been put into the Teton division without permit. The sheep belonged to four large outfits in Utah and were herded by forty armed men.

In a ten-page letter to the commissioner of the General Land Office, Anderson responded to a request for a report on action taken against the Utah trespassers and gave a colorful account of how government regulations were applied on the frontier. He said that one A. A. Covey had come to the reserve office at Jackson the year before to say that some of his sheep were near the line of the reserve. Covey told Anderson that he had not known that Utah sheep must be kept off the reserve. The sheep were without feed, he said, and he could not possibly find another range for them that season. Anderson gave Covey and his brother a permit to graze 35,000 sheep, emphasizing that after the close of the 1903 season the sheep could not be put on the Yellowstone Forest Reserve. In 1904, however, the Coveys were back with even more sheep.

"I have every reason to believe that their intention was to place so large a number of sheep upon Reserve that it would be impossible for the rangers to remove them," Anderson told the commissioner. "When sued for trespass, they would plead guilty expecting to get off with a small fine." The Coveys, he said, "drove their sheep, at once, to extreme easterly boundary of Reserve, expecting to have several weeks grazing on return trip." Anderson decided to waste no time in taking action, "as unless the rules of the Department could be inforced in this instance, next year the Reserve would be overrun by hundreds of thousands of sheep from adjoining States."[17]

By July 20, Anderson had assembled two supervisors and twenty rangers at Cottonwood Creek in the Green River Valley, which was about 125 miles from Jackson. The sheepmen had expected only one or two rangers to ride into their camp and order them to leave the reserve, and they instructed the herders to refuse. If the rangers insisted, the herders were to turn the sheep over to the forest officers. Without dogs, for one or two men to attempt to drive a band of 3,000 sheep in that mountainous and timbered region was of course impossible.

Anderson rode into their camp with twenty-two men, the rangers all well-mounted and in uniform. Having previously located the various bands of sheep, he gathered up a band belonging to each sheepman, in all 15,000 head, and proceeded to put the sheep off the reserve at the nearest point, which was on the Green River side.

Now, the sheepmen feared the cattlemen living on Green River, having suffered considerable loss at their hands. When Anderson started the sheep

16. Ibid., p. 379.
17. September 27, 1904 (History File, U.S. Forest Service, Region 2 Office, Denver).

for the river, the herders struck their camps, leaving with all possible speed. "It was a regular stampede," he wrote, "some of their bunches getting mixed up, but in three or four days they were off the Reserve, having, in that time, covered a distance, which when I first talked with them, they said would be impossible to travel in twelve or fourteen days."[18]

He drove the remaining bands to the easterly line of the reserve, where he expected to receive an injunction from the United States Court, which he had applied for on August 1. It had not arrived. Two weeks later a district attorney, accompanied by a U.S. marshall, reached the camp and served an injunction on the owners and herders, restraining them from returning to the reserve. Fear of the cattlemen prevented the sheepmen from driving their bands down Green River Valley, and to return to Utah across the reserve would place them in contempt of court.

Anderson concluded: "As soon as the injunction had been served I sent the rangers back to their respective districts, leaving the sheepmen to decide upon which horn of the dilemma they would throw themselves. Of one thing I am quite confident; the Utah sheep owners will not attempt to trespass upon the Yellowstone Forest Reserve the coming season."[19]

Although Pinchot was in the Department of Agriculture and had no jurisdiction over Interior's forest reserves, he and his colleagues in the Division of Forestry were interested in the protection and administration of the reserves. It was common knowledge that a movement was afoot to transfer the reserves to Agriculture, and, as noted earlier, certain officials in Interior strongly favored the proposal. Superintendent Anderson was one of them. On the same day he sent his report to the commissioner of the General Land Office, he sent a copy to Pinchot with the following covering letter:

I received your letter regarding sheep trespass and was very glad to learn that you are still interested in the Yellowstone Forest Reserve and had not lost sight of my work in this portion of the mountains.

At time I received your letter I was in the southern portion of the Reserve teaching Utah sheepmen a lesson and think I have done this so effectually that we are not likely to be troubled by any farther trespass from that quarter.

I inclose a copy of my report to the Department on the subject, as I thought perhaps it would interest you to know what I have been doing.[20]

The Supreme Court Decides

Final and absolute control of grazing on the national forests was not obtained by the Forest Service until 1911 when the Supreme Court handed down two historic decisions. One decision was in the Light case in Colorado, involving cattle, and the other was in the Grimaud and Inda case in California, which involved sheep. The latter case[21] arose when Pierre Grimaud and Antonio Inda, Basque sheepherders, grazed their sheep on the Sierra National Forest without a permit and in defiance of regulations issued by the secretary of agriculture.

18. Ibid.
19. Ibid.
20. Ibid.
21. *United States v. Grimaud; U.S. v. Inda*, 220 U.S. 506 (1911).

The manner in which this case developed throws light on the early career of one of the nation's eminent foresters. In 1906, William B. Greeley, who fifteen years later would succeed Henry Graves as chief of the Forest Service, was appointed supervisor of the Sierra South Reserve (now the Sequoia National Forest) in California.

Fire was his knottiest administrative problem, but not far behind was the almost insoluble one of how to handle trespassing sheep. Large bands were overrunning ranges already allotted under permit to local ranchers. The sheep not only overgrazed the range but disrupted the system of grazing controls that the Forest Service had worked out to bring order to the industry and to conserve the resource.

Early each spring, according to long-established custom, herders drove the sheep from winter pasture in the San Joaquin Valley eastward to the Sierra foothills and then into the high ranges for summer pasture. It was a big country, rough and difficult to patrol, and even large bands of sheep could be concealed in the broken terrain. They might be driven into national forest ranges for days or even weeks, then taken off again. According to Greeley, "They played hide-and-seek with the forest rangers all summer."[22]

During the winter, Greeley's officers plainly marked 100 miles of eastern forest boundary and posted "no trespass" signs in English and Spanish at half-mile intervals. Then, in the spring, while the rangers watched from lookout points, 9,000 sheep under a dozen herders moved across the boundary into the forest. After the sheep were well inside and bedded down, forest officers and deputized federal marshals arrested the herders and took them before the U.S. Commissioner at Bakersfield.

San Francisco lawyers who represented large California land companies, the actual owners of the sheep, promptly came to the defense of the herders. The lawyers challenged the authority of the secretary of agriculture to require a permit to graze on the forest reserve.[23]

Criminal indictments were brought against Pierre Grimaud, J. P. Carajous, and Antonio Inda for grazing sheep on the Sierra Forest Reserve without having obtained permission. The defendants entered a demurrer on the ground that the Forest Reserve Act of 1891 was unconstitutional insofar as it delegated to the secretary of agriculture power to make rules and regulations and made a violation of these rules a penal offense. Although sustained by the U.S. District Court for Southern California, the demurrer was eventually knocked down by the Supreme Court of the United States. A unanimous decision delivered by Justice Joseph Rucker Lamar, on May 3, 1911, sustained the right of the government to enforce grazing regulations by criminal prosecution.

In delivering the opinion of the court, Justice Lamar put into the record certain statements which would seem obvious and commonplace today but at that time were crucial to the development of long-range forestry policy. When the court gave legal authorization to the forest and range regulations, it showed that it understood what the national forest officers were trying to do to conserve and improve the range resources. This decision, then, was basic to

---

22. *Forests and Men*, p. 79.
23. In 1907, the forest reserves were renamed national forests.

all of the scientific research and range improvements that the Forest Service would undertake during the decades ahead. The following statements of Justice Lamar are significant in the foregoing context:

The defendants were indicted for grazing sheep on the Sierra Forest Reserve without having obtained the permission required by the regulations adopted by the Secretary of Agriculture. . . .
To pasture sheep and cattle on the reservation, at will and without restraint, might interfere seriously with the accomplishment of the purposes for which they were established. But a limited and regulated use for pasturage might not be inconsistent with the object sought to be attained by the statute. The determination of such questions, however, was a matter of administrative detail. What might be harmless in one forest might be harmful in another. What might be injurious at one stage of timber growth, or at one season of the year, might not be so at another. . . .
These [grazing] fees were fixed to prevent excessive grazing and thereby protect the young growth, and native grasses, from destruction, and to make a slight income with which to meet the expenses of management. . . .
The subjects as to which the Secretary can regulate are defined. The lands are set apart as a forest reserve. He is required to make provision to protect them from depredations and from harmful uses. He is authorized "to regulate the occupancy and use and to preserve the forests from destruction." A violation of reasonable rules regulating the use and occupancy of the property is made a crime, not by the Secretary, but by Congress.[24]

In an editorial, "The Forest Service Upheld," the *Ogden* (Utah) *Examiner* on May 3, 1911, presented the following comments on the outcome of the Grimaud case:

The opinion handed down by the United States supreme court on Monday, on the power of the government to establish and regulate forest reserves, makes permanent one of the best branches of our government. Had the decision been adverse and had congress failed to supply that which the court would have taken away, then the forest service, as we know it, rapidly would have fallen into dry rot and finally would have disappeared. As it is, the conservation policy has been made impregnable, unless congress should decide to undo what has been done to conserve the resources which are the richest heritage of this people.
From a purely selfish standpoint, we have cause to be thankful; from the broader view of the worth of the service to the American people, particularly to the western livestock owner, we have a right to rejoice.

On May 3, 1911, editorial approval of the decision also appeared—surprisingly enough— in *The Breeder's Gazette*, a weekly stock journal.

This sweeping decision puts an end to one of the most bitter controversies that ever raged. . . . Rangemen have so long made free use of public lands that many persuaded themselves that they had vested rights in the matter. The conflict has raged since the reserves were set aside—in private and in public, in Congress and in conventions, and finally in the courts up to the tribunal of last resort, which has said the final word. Two cases, one from Colorado and one from California, were decided against the appellants. The Colorado man was permanently enjoined from grazing on a forest reserve without paying the fees, and California men must answer to the indictment for grazing sheep without a permit.
This ends the discussion. The columns of this journal have voiced repeatedly the plaints of stockmen and their criticisms of the principle and

24. *Report of U.S. Supreme Court*, 220 U.S. 506 (1911).

policy of government control of its lands. The hearing has been fair and full and surely now space may be devoted to more profitable discussion.

An interesting addendum rounds out our knowledge of the events surrounding this historic episode. The official responsible for initiating these cases was Philip P. Wells, who in 1907 was law officer for the Forest Service. On June 9, 1911, he explained his actions in a letter to his friend Thornton T. Munger, then silviculturist with the Forest Service in Portland, Oregon.

I started them both—the Light case by agreement with the Colorado Cattle and Horse Growers Association at the Denver Public Lands Convention in May or June 1907; the Grimaud case by instruction to Greeley, then supervisor of the Sequoia (Sierra South) as soon as the Act of March 2, 1907 (giving the Gvt the right to appeal in certain criminal cases) passed, notifying him by wire of the passage. Both were put up as test cases. They happen to be grazing cases, but that is a detail. They establish beyond question the plenary authority of the Dept. to regulate the use of the Forests *for all purposes*. That is their true significance.[25]

In deciding for the government in the Grimaud–Inda case, as well as in the Light case, the Supreme Court affirmed the authority of Congress to provide for the administration of the national forests. The decisions, moreover, ruled that the secretary of agriculture had constitutional power to make and enforce regulations for the use and occupancy of the national forests. It supported the secretary in his determination to require those wishing to graze livestock on the national forests to obtain permits, which could be withheld for cause. Under the authority delegated to the secretary, the Forest Service could henceforth administer the national forests under scientific management in the public interest.

To be sure, controversies between permittees and the Forest Service and other federal bureaus would continue. Disputes about grazing fees would intensify. Attempts by federal agencies to apply restrictive management practices, when indicated as necessary by scientific research, would often be resisted by the livestock interests. But these crucial Supreme Court cases had far-reaching consequences. They resulted in the government's moving ahead to improve soil and watershed stability, increase forage yield, conduct revegetative programs, and otherwise restore and maintain the western range, a national natural resource without price.

Prior to 1900, there were few if any studies being made that could be considered as range research. For the most part, investigations were exploratory, directed toward the description of range plants and forage conditions. Subsequently, studies carried on by Arthur W. Sampson and James T. Jardine brought forth information on the habits of sheep and their grazing requirements. As a result of continued experimentation by the Forest Service and other agencies, improved practices of herding and of range mangement permit the pasturing of sheep on grasslands without destruction or overuse of the forage resource.

25. Munger Papers, Sterling Memorial Library, Yale University. When this letter was written, Wells was with the Reclamation Service in the Department of the Interior, having resigned from the Forest Service in 1910 when President Taft removed Pinchot from office (see chap. 5). The Act of March 2, 1907, to which Wells referred, was known as the Criminal Appeals Act (Public Law 223).

CHAPTER 7

The Development
of State Forestry

Although the legislatures of several states passed laws during the early part of the nineteenth century for the protection of woodlands, usually against fire and timber theft, the legislation was unrelated to scientific forestry. Since the word *forestry* was unknown in the United States in those days, legislative attempts to improve forest conditions were mostly directed toward reforestation and timber culture—a term often applied to the planting and cultivation of trees on open lands in the West.

The states, however, did take up the subject of forestry in advance of the federal government. Herbert A. Smith emphasized this fact in an article in 1938: "The Nation had never shown any substantial evidence in forest administration, but the States had given the subject a very considerable amount of attention. Their record was, in fact, striking." But he added that the concrete accomplishments of the states amounted to very little "prior to the time when the Federal Government took the leadership of a new, more vigorous, and better directed movement for forestry—the real thing, this time—following Gifford Pinchot's appointment as chief of the division of forestry in the United States Department of Agriculture on July 1, 1898."[1]

Shortly after the Civil War, several state legislatures, prodded by local citizens who had observed the rapidity of forest destruction, created committees of investigation. In Wisconsin in 1867, for example, three persons were appointed to investigate and report whether the forests were being destroyed and what efforts the state should make to preserve and encourage the extension of forest areas. This state action is of more than passing interest because it was taken just fifteen years after Congressman Ben Eastman of Wisconsin had proclaimed in Congress that the Lake States possessed "interminable forests of pine, sufficient to supply all the wants of the citizens in the coun-

1. "Early Forestry Movement in the United States," *Agricultural History*, vol. 12 (October 1938), p. 345.

try, from which this supply can be drawn for all time to come."[2] In 1868, following the committee's report, the legislature offered tax exemption and bounties for the preservation and planting of belts of trees.

During the early post–Civil War years, other states and territories passed laws intended to encourage tree planting by providing bounties, tax exemptions, or similar incentives. Among these were the Dakotas, Minnesota, Idaho, Iowa, Illinois, Kansas, Missouri, Nebraska, New Mexico, Nevada, Utah, Washington, and Wyoming. Some of their laws—Minnesota's, for example—resulted in considerable expenditures over long periods and were in effect for decades.

Although these laws generally failed to yield the results desired, they were both sensible and practical, considering the times and the conditions. States having thousands of square miles of treeless prairies or arid areas tried to encourage tree planting, because legislators realized the handicaps to agriculture in a country lacking supplies of wood for fuel, fenceposts, homes, barns, implements, and other necessities. Even such well-forested territories as Idaho and Washington had vast expanses lacking timber species. In a new country without railroads or even wagon roads for the transportation of wood from distant sources, forest trees added to the value of farms and ranches and to the efficiency of their operation.

Through a law passed in 1872, New York State laid the groundwork for its long-established state forest policy, and particularly for the creation of state forests. A commission was appointed to inquire into the advisability of creating a state park in the Adirondacks. One of the members was Franklin B. Hough, who four years later became the first federal agent to investigate and report on forest use and renewal in the United States. (See chapter 2.) With this commission's recommendations as a starting point, the New York State legislature in 1885 passed a law for the control of forest fire and created the famous Adirondack and Catskill forest preserves.

In its constitution of 1876, Colorado was the first state to authorize legislative enactment of a state forest policy, but the general assembly failed to pass such a law. Later, in 1881, the assembly directed the Board of Agriculture to compile information on forest culture and granted tax exemption for trees planted on irrigated lands. But laws of this kind had little influence on the advancement of forestry. The best that can be said for them, viewed from the perspective of the present, is that they may have assisted in arousing public opinion about the value of trees and forests.

The chronicles of all the states and territories record early and continuing legislation for the protection of woodland from fire. Taken state by state, this legislation is so varied, so frequently amended, and so dissimilar as to penalties, that to attempt to deal with it exhaustively is to penetrate a legislative thicket.[3] On the whole, these laws in their infinite variety prove legislators

2. *Congressional Globe*, 32 Cong., 1 sess. (1852), p. 851.
3. Experiments in forestry legislation are documented by J. P Kinney in *The Development of Forest Law in America*. Kinney compiled a comprehensive chronology up to World War I of "the multiplicity of laws in the various states and the bewildering rapidity with which one innovation after another has been introduced. . ." (pp. vii–viii).

were aware that firing the woods was an antisocial act, that wildfire destroyed not only the standing timber but damaged other property as well, that persons whose possessions were damaged were entitled to compensation, and that anyone willfully or carelessly setting the woods afire was guilty of at least a misdemeanor, if not a felony.

Maine was the first state in New England to set up a forestry office; in 1891, the legislature created the position of state forest commissioner. In 1908, the state suffered considerable loss from forest fires, and a year later the Maine Forestry District was created by law. This was an administrative district for forest protection. Woodland within the district was taxed at a uniform rate for the payment of expenses for protection. When put into operation, the system was unique among state forestry departments in that funds for protection were contributed by the timberland owners. For three-quarters of a century, relations between the Maine Forest Service and industrial and other private owners of timberland have been mutually helpful. It is believed that the first mountain lookout towers for fire detection were started in Maine by landowners and were privately maintained until taken over by the Maine Forest Service.

New Hampshire established a state forestry commission in 1893, but its first state forester was not employed until July 1909. He was Edgar C. Hirst, a Yale graduate.

As in other states, forestry in Vermont was aided during its formative period by a state forestry association. At the first meeting of the association in Burlington, January 5, 1904, Gifford Pinchot, Forester of the United States, gave an address and encouraged the group in its activities. In 1909, Austin F. Hawes was appointed the first state forester and served until 1916 when he went to Connecticut to become state forester there. The Forestry Association of Vermont held twelve annual meetings, the last in 1916, and was disbanded in 1922.[4]

In June 1904, the office of state forester was created in Massachusetts, and the law required that the appointee have a technical education. Over the years, administration of state forestry has been assigned to several agencies, including a Department of Conservation and a state forestry commission; it is now centered in a Division of Forests and Parks in the Department of Natural Resources.

The Rhode Island legislature authorized appointment of a commissioner of forestry in 1906. In time, the work became centered in the Division of Forests, Department of Agriculture and Conservation.

In an account of the start of professional forestry in New York, Gurth Whipple noted that as early as 1900 the state had employed some trained foresters. Among them was Ralph C. Bryant, an alumnus of Cornell and the first graduate of an American forestry school. However, although the need for professionally trained men had consistently increased from 1885, very few were available as late as 1908. "At that time," Whipple wrote, "it was necessary to comb the country for the group of forestry technicians who were

4. Perry H. Merrill, *History of Forestry in Vermont (1909-1959)*, Vermont State Board of Forests and Parks (Montpelier: 1959).

placed in charge of the Forest Reserve." Between 1908 and 1910, six technically trained foresters worked for the state and "from that time forward the supervision of practically all administrative work in forestry has been in the hands of professional foresters under civil service."[5]

The Movement for State Forests

A primary goal of the eastern states—the region where state forestry first became permanently established—was the acquisition of forest preserves and reserves, as they were variously designated. These publicly owned tracts were deemed necessary by the states, because they could be used as demonstration areas to show the benefits of scientific woodland management. Another reason for state forests was to enable foresters to test the results of various kinds of silvicultural practices. A third purpose, one that appealed strongly to citizens concerned about soil and water conservation, was the safeguarding of watersheds, particularly at the headwaters of streams. Apart from these considerations, the acquisition of forests by the states had popular support among citizens who used them for camping, fishing, hunting, and other forms of recreation.

New York State was the first in the nation to start a woodland purchase program; it began when the Adirondack Forest Preserve was established by law in 1885. A constitutional amendment in 1894 prohibited the cutting of trees in the preserve; hence management of the preserve has been wholly custodial and protective. Under prevailing policy, the practice of silviculture, which includes thinning and harvesting trees as well as growing them, is not possible. Other areas acquired by the state, however, have been managed for wood products in addition to water, wildlife, and recreation. For example, more than a quarter of a million acres of idle or abandoned farmland in thirty-four counties have been bought and reforested. These plantations are thinned and harvested as needed. In 1969, the wooded area owned by the state of New York and administered by the Division of Lands and Forests in the Conservation Department was in excess of 3.1 million acres.

Pennsylvania began land purchases for state forests under a law of 1897 that provided for the acquisition of three reservations of not less than 40,000 acres each on the watersheds of the Delaware, Ohio, and Susquehanna Rivers. The bill had been introduced in the legislature at the request of the Pennsylvania Forestry Association.

Joseph Trimble Rothrock, the first commissioner of forestry in Pennsylvania, served from 1895 to 1904. More than any other citizen, he was responsible for creating the Department of Forestry and the system of state forests. In an address delivered in 1915, he told how the state forests were managed.

Pennsylvania has now in Public Forest Reserve 1,001,227 acres, which she has acquired by purchase. It is especially worthy of note that from the date of the first purchase an effort has been made to place it under proper forestry conditions. In other words, we have no forest laws which retard or prohibit

5. New York State Department of Conservation and New York State College of Forestry, *A History of Half a Century of the Management of the Natural Resources of the Empire State* (Syracuse: 1935).

practice of forestry as a productive science. We have aimed at constructive rather than tentative forestry. That this policy has been successful is proved by the fact that land which fifteen years ago was purchased for $2.50 an acre now has an estimated stumpage value of $13 to $16 an acre. And it may be added that this statement applies to areas embracing thousands of acres.[6]

In 1969, the Commonwealth of Pennsylvania owned 3 million acres of the original Penn's Woods. Two million acres were in state forests and parks administered by the Department of Forests and Waters. Nearly 1 million acres were in state game lands, administered by the Game Commission. All the lands, with the exception of parks and reserved areas, were managed under multiple-use principles for wood, water, wildlife, and recreation.

As noted, in New York and Pennsylvania, as well as in other eastern states, much of the state-owned woodland is managed for water, wildlife, and recreation, as well as for forest products. Although timber cutting is restricted in some parks and scenic tracts, silviculture is generally practiced, from growing the seed to harvesting the mature tree. In the ten states usually considered as comprising this northeastern region, the area of managed state-owned woodland is in excess of 5 million acres, exclusive of single-purpose preserves, such as the Adirondacks and the Catskills.

Much of the acreage of state forests in the North Central region was acquired when private holdings became tax delinquent, mainly during the 1920s and 1930s. Hundreds of owners of cutover forest, as well as owners of unprofitable agricultural land, defaulted on their taxes. Then the states—and also many counties, in Wisconsin, for example—took possession. Thus, partly through tax forfeiture Michigan, Minnesota, and Wisconsin together own nearly 10 million acres in forest, game, and park lands.

Vast timbered holdings now owned by the western states were conveyed to them for the most part from the public domain. For this reason these states are often known as the public land states. The commercial forest acreage owned and operated by these states is about 8 million acres. On attaining statehood in 1959, Alaska was given the privilege of selecting 103 million acres from the 365 million acres of federal land in the territory. By 1969, the process of selection had been nearly completed, although the formal conveyance of the land to the state had not been made.

In the South, the forest holdings of the twelve states total in the aggregate less than 2.5 million acres. With few exceptions, state forestry in this region started developing only after the passage of the Clarke–McNary Act in 1924. Among other provisions, the act authorized funds to enable the secretary of agriculture to cooperate with the states in forest fire control and in the production of trees for planting by private landowners. In this development, the emphasis was on protection from forest fire, reforestation and improved management of private stands, and the production of forest crops for industry. Major policy objectives were directed toward these goals; forest acquisition was a minor one. Paradoxically, the relatively low acreage of state forests in the South may be considered a mark of progress; other pressing needs were

6. *Areas of Desolation in Pennsylvania* (Philadelphia: Privately printed by Herbert Welsh, 1915), pp. 80–81.

given higher priority than land acquisition and the limited funds available for forestry thus were used wisely on the whole.

The number of state forests in the fifty commonwealths is nearly 500. The exact figure is uncertain, because some state-owned woodlands, although under scientific management, have official designations other than state forests. In Idaho, for example, five large blocks of timber aggregating some 400,000 acres were consolidated into five state forests in 1950. But an acreage nearly as large, of state-owned timberland in scattered so-called school sections and smaller parcels, is not called a state forest. In short, not all state-owned woodland is state forest; it may be a park, game land, preserve, or simply state timberland. But practically all such areas, wherever situated and regardless of official designation, are administered by professional foresters under some form of multiple-use management.

The total area of state-owned commercial forest land was 20.8 million acres in 1963, according to the U.S. Forest Service.[7] This acreage is rising as the states acquire more woodland, especially near urban centers, for parks and for scenic and recreational purposes. Relatively little woodland has been acquired by the states during the past decade for forest production alone.

State Forestry Ascendant

Through the first decade of this century, twenty-five states had provided for forestry offices and personnel in their governmental structure. The forms that state forestry had taken and the laws on which they were based were notable for a lack of either uniformity or consistency. It is to be noted, however, that differences in the way in which the states have dealt with forestry are reflected in the differences shown by individual states in the efficiency of their performance. States with a history of strong, efficient administration generally have strong, efficient forestry programs, provided the forest resource is important enough to supply the incentive.

In some states, the enterprise started under the supervision of a forestry board (California) or a commission (Maine). In Pennsylvania, it began as a division in the Department of Agriculture, later acquiring separate departmental status. In Connecticut, the first state forester was assigned under law to the Agricultural Experiment Station; in Texas, he was put under the Board of Directors of the Agricultural and Mechanical College; and in Vermont, a member of the Board of Agriculture was designated the forest commissioner. In Tennessee and North Carolina, the first state forester was employed by the State Geological Survey; in Virginia, he was first put under the State Geological Commission. In reviewing the beginnings of forestry in the states, one can find other interesting examples of places in the government where forestry first took up its abode.

In 1969, state forestry administration could be found in the Department of Natural Resources in Alaska, Indiana, Massachusetts, Ohio, South Carolina, Utah, Washington, West Virginia, and Wisconsin. Forestry is a unit of the Department of Conservation in California, Illinois, Michigan, Minnesota, New

7. U.S. Forest Service, *Timber Trends in the United States*, Forest Resource Report no. 17 (February 1965).

York, and Tennessee. There are independent state forest services, as in Colorado and Maine, and independent state departments of forestry, as in Delaware, Florida, and Oregon. The State Park and Forest Commission houses forestry in Connecticut; in Maryland it is in the Department of Forests and Parks.

In Hawaii, forestry is under the Department of Land and Natural Resources; under the Department of Resources and Economic Development in New Hampshire; under the Department of Conservation and Economic Development in New Jersey; under the Department of Conservation and Development in North Carolina; and under the Conservation Commission in Missouri. The Department of Forests and Waters is the headquarters of forestry in Pennsylvania; the Department of Fish, Game, and Parks in South Dakota; and the School of Forestry in North Dakota.

Little consistency is to be noted in the titles given the first forestry officers in the states. In Pennsylvania, he was the commissioner of forestry. Wisconsin's first forestry law provided for the employment of a superintendent of forests who would be the state fire warden also. In North Carolina, the office of state forester was originally combined with that of fire warden. Whereas state forester is now the commonest title, we find others in use: director of forestry (Georgia); superintendent of forestry (Iowa); forest commissioner (Maine); chief forester (Massachusetts); chief, Division of Forestry (Michigan); deputy director of conservation, Division of Lands and Forests (Minnesota); director, lands and forests (New York); chief, Division of Forestry and Reclamation (Ohio); director, Bureau of Forestry (Pennsylvania); director, Forest Service (Texas); director of forests (Vermont); and supervisor (Washington). The foregoing list does not exhaust all the variations in the title of the ranking forestry official in each state.

Under pressure by state forestry associations and similar groups of citizens, state legislatures and governors found it necessary to do something about forestry. But they were often hard put to know what to do. Some states appointed commissions to study the matter. These commissions usually made recommendations as to how and where forestry should be integrated into the governmental infrastructure. But the recommendations might be ignored with the consequence that forestry might be disposed of politically. This happened in Louisiana when a law of 1910 specifically imposed fire protection responsibility on a forester, then designated as forester the register of the State Land Office, a political appointee.

Another expedient of legislatures was to provide for a state forestry office, then either neglect or refuse to provide funds for it. When the general assembly of Georgia, for example, passed the Forest Administrative Act of 1925, which provided for appointment of a state forester, the forester apparently was expected to function without funds. Let I. James Pikl, Jr. describe what happened:

> What followed is nearly unbelievable. The newly appointed state forester, Burley M. Lufburrow, accompanied by one of the board members, Bonnell Stone, visited the comptroller, auditor, treasurer, and the governor, in each case being politely but firmly told that no funds were available. . . . The board members, through Stone, signed a personal note in the sum of $1,000

at an Atlanta bank in order permit the work to get underway. An office was provided by the Atlanta Chamber of Commerce, since none could be found in a state building. The state forester, I might note, did not receive a salary check until eight months after he had been first employed.[8]

Georgia was not the only state to introduce a forestry policy into its government and then spend no money, or at best a pittance, to finance it. Earlier, in 1905, the legislature in the state of Washington, created the office of state fire warden and forester under a Board of Forestry Commissioners. To finance the new project, $7,500 was appropriated. This sum was barely sufficient to start the work, which included the appointment of county fire wardens. In the absence of state funds, the board authorized the state fire warden to solicit contributions from private citizens and companies. In 1905, contributions were received in the amount of $257. Although forest products made up the state's foremost industry, the legislature moved slowly in providing either funds or adequate laws for forest protection. Consequently, the lumber industry, which itself owned only a fraction of the timberland, bore the burden of financing much of the protective activity.[9]

With the enactment of the Weeks Law in 1911, a measure of uniformity was introduced into state activity in fire prevention and control. Under cooperative arrangements that provided federal money to the states, they had the strongest possible motive—which is to say, a financial reason—to improve their performance.

Among other things, the Weeks Law appropriated funds to enable the Forest Service, acting through the secretary of agriculture, to cooperate with those states that had legally established forest fire protection systems. The number of states that qualified for cooperative funds rose from eleven in 1911 to twenty-nine in 1924, when the Clarke–McNary Law superseded the Weeks Law.

Fostering further cooperative efforts between the states and the federal government, the Clarke–McNary Act was an unprecedented inducement to backward states to set up forestry organizations that would qualify for the federal grants. And, besides, it encouraged the more progressive states to raise their standards and financial commitments so as to participate fully in the federal grants for growing planting stock, for promoting farm woods management, and for controlling forest fires.

For the year 1949, the twenty-fifth anniversary of the Clarke–McNary Act, forty-four states budgeted $20.6 million for fire prevention and control. The federal allotment was $8.5 million. These amounts were further supplemented by private contributions, bringing the yearly total of all funds for fire prevention and control to $31.5 million. By 1969 the amount had more than tripled, to $95.5 million.

With the onset of the business depression of the 1930s, state appropriations for forestry were reduced in many states, or at best continued on a bare

8. "Pulp and Paper and Georgia: The Newsprint Paradox," *Forest History*, vol. 12 (October 1968), p. 10.
9. Ralph R. Widner (ed.), *Forests and Forestry in the American States* (Tallahassee: National Association of State Foresters, 1968), pp. 173–74.

maintenance level. Despite initial setbacks for state forestry in the early 1930s, the decade was notable for accomplishment in forestry, for it was the era of the Civilian Conservation Corps.

The CCC began in April 1933 and ended in 1942. At the peak of the program in 1935, more than a quarter of a million men were enrolled in 1,300 forestry camps. Many of the camps were on state forests and parks, where the men of the Corps built fire lookout towers and telephone lines; constructed firebreaks, roads, and trails; fought forest fires and combatted forest disease and insect infestations; collected tree seed and enlarged the output of the state nurseries; planted trees and improved timber stands; and engaged in other forestry projects too numerous to itemize. By any measure, the CCC program was a massive force that advanced state forestry in all its aspects on a nationwide front.

State Forestry Associations

The first state forestry association that was organized to promote tree planting as well as the general practice of forestry was the Minnesota Forestry Association, formed January 12, 1876. In March 1876, the legislature appropriated $2,500 to enable this unofficial organization to offer premiums for the planting of forest trees in certain counties to be determined by the association.

Following the formation of the Minnesota Forestry Association, citizens in other states organized similar forestry societies during the next half-century. Without exception, these state associations concerned themselves with the advancement of forestry by advocating needed legislation, by supporting the creation of forestry commissions and departments, and by undertaking public education to inform citizens of the benefits of forest conservation.

When the primary goals had been attained, or were likely to be, some of the associations lost their crusading zeal; membership, never large in any state, declined, and the associations either faded away or legally went into liquidation. The history of the conservation movement is cluttered with associations, now dead or moribund, that had a brief and promising existence only to languish for want of members, finances, or an object worthy of enlisting further support. A number of state forestry associations are among this sad company.

In New York State, a State Forestry Association was organized as early as 1885 but soon declined. Reorganized in 1913 by Hugh P. Baker, dean of the New York State College of Forestry at Syracuse, the association was active for several years thereafter in the advancement of state conservation but declined again.

Other state associations, having gained their initial forestry objectives, enlarged the scope of their interests; they embraced parks, recreational development, the preservation of scenic and natural beauty, and other aspects of resource conservation. In so doing, these associations undertook revitalization of their membership, programs, publications, and general activities. Because of their services to the public welfare and their continued usefulness, several state associations are noteworthy.

Formed in 1886, the Pennsylvania Forestry Association is the oldest one having continuous existence and still active. In July 1886, *Forest Leaves*, the association's official organ (now *Pennsylvania Forests*), began publication. Joseph Trimble Rothrock, the first president, carried on a campaign of public education for fire prevention and control, reforestation, and conservation in general. In 1895, the commonwealth created a Division of Forestry with Dr. Rothrock at its head in the Department of Agriculture. Six years later the division became a separate Department of Forestry, and in 1922, during the governorship of Gifford Pinchot, became the Department of Forests and Waters.

No state citizens' organization in the annals of American forestry has had a more useful record of public service than this association. Among the developments it promoted and brought to fruition were an adequate forest protection system for Penn's Woods; the first state-supported school founded solely to educate foresters for work on the state forests (the Forest Academy at Mont Alto); the acquisition of state forests; and a merit system for state forestry employees. A headquarters is maintained in Mechanicsburg.

Another venerable and still active body is the Connecticut Forest and Park Association, organized in 1895 as the Connecticut Forestry Association. Through its good works, including the organ *Connecticut Woodlands* and other publications, the association has helped bring about public forests and parks and has campaigned for reforestation, the planting of shade trees, and the preservation of natural beauty. The headquarters is in Hartford.

The Massachusetts Forest and Park Association (formerly the Massachusetts Forestry Association), founded in 1898, was organized "for the protection and improvement of parks and the preservation of natural scenery."[10] It procured the law creating the office of state forester, an office which is now in the Department of Natural Resources. It helped obtain state forests and parks and promoted community forests. In 1944, under the leadership of Harris A. Reynolds, long-term executive officer, the association created the New England Forestry Foundation to undertake consulting forestry and to provide forest management services to woodland owners. Through the association's efforts many scenic areas and beaches were preserved for public enjoyment. The headquarters is in Boston.

The Society of the Protection of New Hampshire Forests dates from 1901. For nearly seven decades this society has been a persistent force for good land use, for the preservation of forest and scenic resources against commercial exploitation, and for the encouragement of forestry practice by private owners. It has raised funds for state acquisition of superlative scenic areas, and has helped get appropriations for the acquisition of hundreds of forest tracts now owned by the state and by communities and towns. *Forest Notes*, a quarterly, is the official publication. Among the many dedicated foresters to whom New Hampshire and this society are indebted for outstanding service, three names stand out: Philip W. Ayers, Edgar C. Hirst, and Lawrance W. Rathbun. The headquarters is in Concord.

10. Erle Kauffman (ed.), *The Conservation Yearbook*, p. 73.

Dating from 1903, although not incorporated until 1952, the Ohio Forestry Association conducts resource activities in cooperation with other agencies, public and private. It publishes periodical bulletins and information about forestry, forest products, and related conservation needs and developments. Its interests extend beyond forestry, embracing parks and recreation, scenic preservation, flood-control soil conservation, and wildlife management. The headquarters is in Columbus.

Organized in 1907, the Georgia Forestry Association is the oldest in the South. It was largely responsible for the creation of the state's first Forestry Commission, and for the appointment of Georgia's first state forester in 1925. The association was long a moving force in the development of needed forestry legislation and promotes the protection, management, utilization, and marketing of Georgia's forest resources.[11] The headquarters is in Atlanta.

Second oldest in the South, the Louisiana Forestry Association was organized in 1909 with Henry E. Hardtner as president. For two decades the association was a major source of support for a state forestry program and the appointment of a nonpolitical state forester, a goal it achieved in 1917 when Reginald D. Forbes, a Yale graduate, became state forester. During the depression years of the 1930s, the association went into a decline and ceased to function. Reactivated in 1947 with Q. T. Hardtner as president, the association embarked on a course of promoting needed legislation. With the appointment in 1951 of James H. Kitchens, Jr. as executive secretary, the members advanced the state tree farm system and helped obtain funds for both state forestry administration and for federal forestry research. The publication is *Forests & People*, a quarterly; the headquarters, Alexandria.

Third oldest in the South, the North Carolina Forestry Association was formed in 1911. Although forestry is its main interest, it is also concerned with the protection and development of soil, water, and wildlife. *North Carolina Lands*, a comprehensive report published by The American Forestry Association in 1964, was prepared with advisory assistance from the state forestry association. Two special projects undertaken in recent years were a campaign to reduce accidents among woods workers and the production of a motion picture of the state's forest and related resources. The headquarters is in Raleigh.

The Texas Forestry Association, organized in 1914, was almost immediately successful in its first major undertaking. In 1915, largely through the association's efforts, the Texas State Forest Service was established as a unit in the Texas A&M University. Supported by industrial as well as by citizen memberships, the association has long had a full-time executive secretary. The official publication *Texas Forests* is issued bimonthly; the headquarters is in Lufkin.

The Mississippi Forestry Association (originally the Mississippi Forestry and Chemurgic Association) was organized in 1938. It helped obtain the adoption of needed legislation and has cooperated effectively with other organizations, public and private, in promoting youth education in resource management, fire prevention, wildlife protection, and soil conservation.

11. See chap. 17 for additional information about the Georgia Forestry Association.

During part of its existence the association has had paid executives. The headquarters is in Jackson.

The Florida Forestry Association, founded in 1923, sponsored legislation that in 1927 brought about the Florida Board of Forestry and the State Forest Service. It worked for laws for fire prevention and control and for the establishment of the Florida Park Board. The association has employed at times both an executive officer and a public relations director. Its headquarters is in Tallahassee.

Virginia Forests, Inc., the state forestry association, was formed in 1943. Its first major success was to induce the general assembly to provide statewide forest fire protection. It supported the law that provides a severance tax on forest products to provide funds for the Virginia Division of Forestry. It carries on educational programs in the schools. The magazine *Virginia Forests* is issued bimonthly from the Richmond headquarters.

In addition to the foregoing group of active citizens' associations, other state associations once carried on forest conservation programs but are now inactive or have gone out of existence. Among the states in which such associations were once active are Colorado, Maryland, Michigan, Montana, New York, Tennessee, Washington, and West Virginia.

The state forestry associations, together with several organizations known as state conservation councils, performed valuable functions during periods when initiative and leadership were essential to obtain legislation, appropriations, and other supports for forestry. During the formative years of state forestry when hard-won progress might be set back by the skulduggery or indifference of politicians, the associations kept watch on them. In short, many developments in state forestry were made possible by the pressure of the associations' contemporary invigilation. Politics has often been the antagonist—not the ally—of conservation.

One additional group of statewide associations has had a long history of support for state forestry, although their purpose is largely if not wholly the protection of privately owned timberlands from fire. One of the oldest of these is the Washington Forest Protection Association (formerly Washington Forest Fire Association), organized in 1908. For a quarter-century Charles S. Cowan, the executive officer, and the Association gave leadership to the advancement of forestry in the state. The California Forest Protective Association, formed in 1909, is another that has had a marked influence on the development of forestry.

Associations of timberland owners in a few states, especially in the Northeast, have been effective in obtaining needed legislation for forest protection, principally against fire but also against forest tree diseases and insects. The oldest of these is the New Hampshire Timberland Owners Association, which dates back to 1910. The Vermont Timberland Owners Association was organized in 1922, mainly for forest fire protection. A more recent entry into this group is the New York Forest Owners Association, founded in 1963.

The National Association of State Foresters

In recording the events that led to the formation of the National Association of State Foresters, Austin Hawes recalled that when an outbreak of white pine blister rust was discovered in New York State in 1909, a group of state foresters and pathologists met there to consider what action might be taken to limit the spread of the disease. Another conference on the rust was held in 1910, and a spin-off of this meeting was the formation of the Association of Eastern Foresters. Its territory included the New England states, New York, Pennsylvania, New Jersey, Delaware, and Maryland, not all of which had state foresters. Thus, membership in the association was not confined exclusively to state foresters. Indeed, according to Hawes, it "was organized to include State Forest officials and instructors in forestry." A constitution for the new association was ratified January 12, 1911, at another meeting in Washington, D.C. "There was more than just a touch of irony," wrote Hawes, "in the fact that we State Foresters were first brought together by forest diseases which ignored State boundaries."[12]

Although the Weeks Law of 1911 offered the states financial inducement to cooperate with the federal government and among themselves to reduce forest fire losses, state accomplishment was sporadic and inconsistent for another decade. Some states were making steady progress in state forest administration as well as in fire control; others were lagging. In the political traditions of the times, each state was apt to view its forestry problems from purely local consideration and to go its own way with little attention to what other, even adjacent, states were doing. Such counsel and guidance as the Forest Service could induce the states to accept had to be offered with utmost tact because the states were jealous of their rights and prestige.

A meeting of state foresters from sixteen states was held in Atlantic City, New Jersey, November 12–13, 1920. Less than half of the thirty-four states having forestry departments were represented. Present from the Forest Service were W. B. Greeley, E. E. Carter, and J. G. Peters, who worked closely with the states out of the Branch of Forest Management of the Eastern Division of the Forest Service.

Certain recommendations proposed by the Forest Service for increased federal-state cooperation in fire protection and forest renewal were approved. The state foresters recommended also that a federal appropriation of $1 million be made available for state cooperation in fire prevention and control, forest investigations, and timber production, including forest planting. One of the results of the conference was the unanimous decision to form a state foresters' association.

Thus, a month later, during a meeting on December 8–9, 1920, the Association of State Foresters (now the National Association of State Foresters) was formally organized in Harrisburg. The Pennsylvania Department of Forestry, of which Gifford Pinchot had recently been appointed commissioner, was host to the conference. William T. Cox of Minnesota was elected the association's first president. J. S. Holmes of North Carolina was elected secretary of the conference.[13]

During the half-century that the association has been in existence, it has functioned as an open channel of cooperation between the states and the

    12. Widner, *Forests and Forestry*, p. 105.
    13. Pennsylvania Department of Forestry, *Proceedings of State Foresters' Conference* (Harrisburg: 1922).

federal government. Its activities have strengthened forestry and related resource policies, not only of the federal and state agencies involved, but of private interests as well. As a clearinghouse of information, it has enabled state administrators to keep abreast of new developments everywhere in the nation, and thus to consider the progress in state forestry in the context of the national program. Through its annual meetings, the association has fostered high standards of professional employment, improvement in the compensation of state forestry employees, and a workable arrangement of cooperation in fire prevention and control. As the binding nexus between the federal government and the states, it has been the effective instrument for coordinating the often conflicting interests of the many bodies engaged in promoting forestry.

In 1948, for example, the Association of State Foresters developed a joint policy with the Association of Land Grant Colleges that resolved long-standing differences over the kinds of forestry services each should provide to the private owner. As a consequence, the extension services of the state agricultural colleges were acknowledged as having responsibility for educational assistance; the state forestry departments became responsible for providing technical assistance to landowners. The agreement had prompt benefits when these influential associations gave their united support to two vital pieces of legislation.

In 1949, an amendment to the Clarke–McNary Act authorized increased federal appropriations for expanded nursery production of forest-planting stock by the states. It also authorized increased federal appropriations for state extension services to farmers in the harvesting and marketing of forest products. A year later, the Cooperative Forest Management Act of 1950 provided for financial cooperation between the secretary of agriculture and the state foresters in making technical services available to private woodland owners and operators both in forest management and in the harvesting and marketing of forest products. A quick response to these federal laws resulted in state legislation and appropriations enabling the states to qualify for the funds Congress had provided. As evidence of the significance of these developments on the practice of forestry, one need only point to the 800 service foresters currently (1969) employed by the states in this useful work.[14]

The Regulation Controversy

In chapter 11, attention is centered on the protracted period of controversy among forestry administrators—federal, state, and private—over the proposal for public regulation of private timber cutting. The polemical nature of the proposal brought forth extreme viewpoints. Its more ardent adherents called for regulation by the federal government. Despite pressures by the proponents of regulation by federal law, Congress took no action.

---

14. In 1968, the National Association of State Foresters published *Forests and Forestry in the American States*, a reference anthology that had been in preparation for more than a decade. Brought to completion under the supervision of a publication committee made up of C. Huxley Coulter, state forester of Florida, and Ralph C. Wible, former state forester of Pennsylvania, the book was edited by Ralph Widner, sometime information officer in the Pennsylvania Department of Forests and Waters.

The regulation issue pervaded the consideration of forestry policy by the states during the 1940s. Almost without exception, the state foresters preferred state to federal regulation. Spokesmen for the forest products industry, who at first opposed any regulatory legislation whatever, were in time induced to compromise by accepting the principle of state regulation as the less objectionable of the two. But the forest industry's imprimatur of even state regulation was, for the most part, given grudgingly.

Industry's reluctant acceptance of the principle of state regulation as a means of advancing the practice of forestry on private lands was based on the plentiful evidence that industrial forestry was everywhere gaining ground. Industrial foresters could point to specific instances of progress that provided them with arguments against the need for laws to accomplish what was already being done voluntarily. Improvements in forest protection were removing the costly and uncertain risks from the long-term ownership of woodland. The increasingly popular tree farm movement, aggressively sponsored by the American Forest Products Industries, Inc. (now American Forest Institute) was bringing millions of acres annually under minimum standards of management.[15]

These voluntary efforts would be strengthened at the end of the decade by a new and greater public assistance program adopted by the federal government to enable the states to improve forest practices on private lands. The Cooperative Forest Management Act of 1950 brought about accelerated employment of foresters by the states to provide technical services to private woodland owners.

Nevertheless, during the period 1941–50, the legislatures of thirteen states passed laws[16] that provided for silvicultural standards calculated to maintain forest lands in productive condition. These states are California, Florida, Maryland, Massachusetts, Minnesota, Mississippi, Missouri, New Hampshire, New York, Oregon, Vermont, Virginia, and Washington. In phraseology, these laws are quite variable as are the definitions of forest practices they propose to regulate; moreover, the methods of enforcement and the violations subject to penalties differ from state to state.[17]

It has been remarked elsewhere but is worth repeating that as the practice of forestry became economically profitable thousands of private owners undertook to grow timber as a business. To be sure, some, including many small owners, failed for a variety of reasons. But others, particularly the industrial owners, put their stands under more intensive types of management than the regulatory laws required. It is interesting and deserving of emphasis

15. See chap. 20 for a discussion of tree farming.
16. The salient provisions of these state laws are analyzed in Society of American Foresters, *Forest Practices Developments in the United States: 1940-1955* (Washington: SAF, 1956).
17. A report, "Evaluation of California Forest Practice Act," by the Northern California Section of the Society of American Foresters, was published in the *Journal of Forestry*, February 1969. In this report, it was recommended that a determination be made of the effectiveness of the forest practice rules formulated by the Forest Practice Committee authorized by the act—information that apparently was not known after a quarter-century of experience with the act.

that since 1950 no state has passed a law regulating cutting practices. In retrospect, one could make a case for the presumption that the regulatory laws aided the advancement of forestry in the states to which they apply. But it is questionable whether they had influence in promoting the application of silviculture elsewhere. By 1955, as explained in chapter 11, the regulation controversy had run its course.

Registration and Licensure of Foresters

State registration and licensure of workers in the recognized professions is a long-established legal custom. It provides governmental recognition of a profession and protection for the public against inadequately educated and incompetent practitioners. Among the professions whose practitioners are registered and licensed by state law are accountancy, architecture, civil engineering and certain other engineering specialties, dentistry, law, medicine, pharmacy, and professional nursing.

A study of state registration and licensing for foresters was undertaken by the New York Section of the Society of American Foresters in 1937. By vote of the members, the section then decided not to seek a registration law in New York State. Elsewhere in the country, members of the society undertook studies of the possible benefits to the profession of state licensing.

Georgia was the first state, in 1951, to enact a law providing for a board of registration for foresters. This law simply provides for the protection of the public by improving the standards of professional forestry. Similar laws were passed in Michigan in 1955 and in Alabama in 1957. Since then five additional states have passed registration and licensing laws: Florida and South Carolina in 1961, Oklahoma and West Virginia in 1963, and New Hampshire in 1969. State laws generally require that an applicant to a board of registration for a license to practice forestry must be a graduate of a recognized school of forestry or must have gained by experience a knowledge of forestry substantially equivalent to that represented by a forestry degree.

The original Georgia law has been amended so that only a graduate of a school of forestry approved by the Board of Registration may be registered. Additional requirements are at least two years of experience in forestry work of a character satisfactory to the board and the recommendations of three registered foresters. A graduate of a school of forestry not approved by the board may be licensed provided he has had two years of qualifying experience and has passed a written examination. In either case, the applicant must be a graduate of a professional school of forestry.

The laws of some other states are less strict in their requirements. Qualifying forestry experience in lieu of full professional education is accepted as a condition for licensing, but a written examination must be passed.

The Society of American Foresters has long had a standing Committee on State Registration and Licensing of Foresters. It has maintained a historical record and a bibliography of the subject and has provided assistance to sections and chapters of the society working on legislation. Additionally, this committee has made information available to schools of forestry for use in classroom discussion of forestry policy.

Flaws in the Record

With one exception, the history of state forestry is a chronicle of ascending progress. In a few states the record is flawed by setbacks that originated, it should be noted, outside the forestry organization. In states where checks or reverses have occurred, they have almost never been the result of technical incompetence on the part of professional foresters. Not to put too fine a point on it, the recurrent blight on state forestry has been politics. And if the stultifying effect of politics is less apparent today than in earlier years, this is not to say that it has disappeared.

In too many states for too many years, all forestry employees, from the indispensable field ranger to the state forester himself, were appointed, continued in office, and were often removed subject to political patronage. No more debasing influence on the morale of a dedicated, ethical civil employee exists than the knowledge that, however competent his performance, his career and the welfare of his family are dependent on the favor of a political superior or a party boss. The effect has been to drive some good men out of state service, and to retain some less competent ones who were willing to obtain security and tenure through political favoritism rather than by professional merit. The worst effect of politics was the destruction of the enthusiasm that the forester normally feels toward his work. A forester who lost his job could get another. When he lost his élan, he lost his pride in accomplishment, a quality harder to recapture than a job.

If there have been foresters in state service disposed to acknowledge what they believed to be the authority of political imperatives, there have been others who put professional pride first. On occasion, their adherence to the ethical standards of the profession cost them preferment and even their jobs. This is not a pleasant aspect of the history of state forestry, but it is history nevertheless. The following examples could be extended, but perhaps they are sufficient to point up the problem that long existed and still exists.

An instance of how a politician may flout the laws he has sworn to uphold came to light in Georgia during the administration of Governor Eugene Talmadge. On March 4, 1936, H. H. Chapman, president of the Society of American Foresters, notified the governor that the society had investigated the recent appointment of one Elmer Dyal as state forester and found that the law had been ignored. Georgia's Forestry Administrative Act of 1925 required the state forester to be technically trained and to have at least two years of experience in technical and administrative work. Dyal was not in any sense a technically trained forester and had never had technical instruction in a school of forestry.

Chapman reminded the governor that the University of Georgia had maintained a School of Forestry since 1906 for the education of persons wishing to fill forestry positions. He pointed out that no effort had been made to give any of the graduates, educated at the state's expense, a chance to be considered for the position. Chapman then urged Talmadge and the Forestry Commission, which had approved the appointment, to reconsider in the interest of sound conservation and the reputation of the state.

The governor's reply of March 6, 1936, to Chapman is a bizarre illustration of political arrogance and ignorance:

My dear Mr. Chapman:
Your letter of the 4th has been received. I am sure you do not know Mr. Dyal. He is a born forester. A wood ranger right. He was born down in the Okefinoke Swamp.
With all good wishes, I am,
Very truly yours,
Eugene Talmadge, *Governor*[18]

Dyal's career as state forester was fairly brief, and he returned to the obscurity from which he had lately risen.

In 1936, W. S. Swingler, a district forester in the Pennsylvania Department of Forests and Waters, was suddenly dismissed by the politically appointed head of the department. The alleged reason for the dismissal was that it had been done to effect a reorganization; in point of fact, it had been done to make a place for another man with political influence. Swingler, whose technical ability and administrative competence were well regarded by professional colleagues, immediately obtained an appointment in the U.S. Department of Agriculture Soil Conservation Service and in time transferred to the Forest Service. During the next twenty-five years, he advanced to regional forester, thence to assistant chief of the Forest Service in charge of state and private cooperative forestry.

In April 1954, six members of the Society of American Foresters who were residents of Indiana filed charges of unprofessional conduct against Ralph F. Wilcox, state forester of Indiana, and Henry A. Beadell, assistant state forester. The charges alleged violation of the code of ethics of the forestry profession, canon 24 of which reads: "He [the professional forester] will not participate in soliciting or collecting financial contributions from subordinates or employees for political purposes."[19]

Evidence obtained through an investigation conducted by the society revealed that in June 1953 Wilcox and Beadell solicited financial contributions for a political campaign from subordinate employees in the Division of Forestry. In their defense, Wilcox and Beadell deposed that they had been compelled to write letters soliciting funds by their superiors holding political office in the state government. The council of the society instructed the society's president to write letters of censure to Wilcox and Beadell, urging them to use the code of ethics to resist a system which is clearly in violation of the ethical standards of the society. Both men dropped their membership in the society, though Beadell subsequently applied for reinstatement.

The manner in which partisan politics can jeopardize an honorable and productive career was illustrated by the dismissal on June 15, 1959, of Harrod B. Newland, associate director of the Kentucky Division of Forestry, by Laban P. Jackson, the commissioner of the state's Department of Conservation. The facts of this case show that Newland, a professional forester and a career employee in the state service for twenty-six years, was turned out of office, not because he engaged in politics, but because he tried to serve the

18. Letter quoted in "Appointment of Georgia State Forester Questioned,"*Journal of Forestry*, vol. 34 (April 1936), p. 431.
19. "Foresters' Code of Ethics," adopted November 12, 1948, by the Society of American Foresters.

forestry interests of Kentucky by tending strictly to forestry matters.[20] Because Newland stood apart from political activity, he was the victim of reprisal by those who would have used him for their political ends.

In June 1968, the Society of American Foresters protested to the governor of Mississippi the replacement of the professional state forester by an appointee without education in forestry and without professional qualifications.[21] This appointment was made despite the existence of a school of forestry at Mississippi State University which had been accredited by the society in 1967 for instruction in professional forestry.

In most states, the field foresters are secure in their positions and are relatively free of political interference either in the performance of their duties or in the employment of their subordinate personnel. Foresters in top positions, such as state forester or assistant state forester, are occasionally vulnerable to political importunities because they function in the decision-making arena and consequently can grant or withhold the kinds of favors that politicians seek. In general, however, the state forester who is a product of professional education and of the career system in his organization is respected in the state government and functions in the interest of the public and not of the political factions currently in office.

One reason that forestry has attained a measure of immunity from the machinations of politicians is the growth of civil service or merit systems of employment. In 1969, according to the National Association of State Foresters, thirty-six states had established merit systems for their forestry organizations.

Civil service systems are brought about in many ways, often by the efforts of professional employees. In Pennsylvania, for example, Gifford Pinchot, while secretary of forests and waters and twice governor, was unable or unwilling to obtain a civil service law for the protection of the commonwealth's professional and technical employees. Maurice K. Goddard, on becoming secretary, began to press for a merit system for the foresters. At first, the best that could be obtained was a merit system for foresters by authorization of the governor. From that base, Goddard pressed for a law to make permanent that which had been decreed by the governor. Pennsylvania's present enlightened personnel policy for its foresters is a monument to Goddard.

Three decades ago, in half the states that had state foresters, the incumbents were without professional education or degrees in forestry. In 1969, less than a half-dozen states had ranking forestry officers who lacked professional qualifications. This is a trustworthy measure of progress.

A Firm Foundation

In 1969, state forestry agencies employed approximately 2,500 professional foresters. The six leading states in numbers of foresters employed are

20. See "The Blight of Politics on a Career in Forestry," *Journal of Forestry*, vol. 57 (September 1959), pp. 687–88.

21. "Society Protests Mississippi Appointment," *Journal of Forestry*, vol. 66 (September 1968), pp. 735–36.

Washington with more than 200; Oregon and Pennsylvania with more than 150; and California, Wisconsin, Virginia, and New York with more than 100 each.

In addition to these forestry agencies, other departments and units of state government make use of the services of foresters: highway departments; water boards; parks and recreational services; departments of commerce or industry; departments of agriculture; game commissions, for which foresters manage game lands and refuges; and penal institutions, for which foresters supervise woods work by youth camps and similar correctional establishments. The author believes that by 1969 at least 250 foresters were so employed.

Other civil divisions of government employ foresters. These agencies include counties; townships; and municipalities, for which foresters manage parks, watersheds, street and highway tree planting and maintenance, community forests, school district forests, and miscellaneous types of municipal woodlands. Although the exact acreage of these various tracts is not known, it is estimated to be close to 4.5 million acres.[22] The number of foresters employed by all these agencies is not on record. The author believes that the total is at least 250.

In summary, by 1969 the total number of foresters employed by state governments and by other civil governments within the states is estimated to be approximately 3,000.

22. Kauffman, *The Conservation Yearbook*, p. 140.

CHAPTER 8

Forestry in the Department of the Interior

One of the earliest warnings that unregulated use of forests would lead to timber depletion in the United States appeared in a report issued by the Patent Office in 1849 (the year the Department of the Interior was created).

The waste of valuable timber in the United States, to say nothing of firewood, will hardly be appreciated until our population reaches 50,000,000. Then the folly and shortsightedness of this age will meet with a degree of censure not pleasant to contemplate.[1]

From time to time, similar warnings were issued by other government agencies, but they received scant attention from those in official positions who had the power to promote the forest conservation movement.

From the period of the Civil War through the 1880s, the main activity of the new Department of the Interior with respect to the public lands was to get rid of them. It was a policy enjoined by Congress—a policy which neither the secretary of the interior nor the commissioner of the General Land Office had authority to disregard even if he had been inclined to do so.

During these three decades, the disposal of the public lands was proceeding apace. "Doing a land office business" persists as an expression of brisk enterprise. It applied particularly to land distribution through homesteading and grants to railroads and the states. "No effective effort had ever been made to stop spoilation of the timberlands," Herbert A. Smith said of this period. "It was hopeless to attempt to stem the tide of disposal, and granted that this could have been done, the Government was wholly unequal to the task of administering the lands capably and too honeycombed with corruption to administer them honestly."[2]

Soon after it was created, the Department of the Interior did attempt to stem destruction and exploitation of the government's forests by appointing

1. Quoted in Samuel T. Dana, *Forest and Range Policy*, p. 76.
2. "Early Forestry Movement in the United States," *Agricultural History*, vol. 12 (October 1938), p. 4.

timber agents to police the public domain. (See chapter 1.) For the most part, however, the record of the agents was a sorry one, and in 1877, when Carl Schurz became secretary of the interior, he undertook to reorganize and enlarge the system of timber agents.

"I saw timber thieves, not stealing the single trees, but stealing whole forests," Schurz said later when recalling the conditions that faced him when he took office. "I saw dozens and scores and hundreds of lumber mills working at full blast without a single stick of timber being manufactured in them that did not come from the public lands."[3]

Schurz and a few other government officials knew that the nation's forests were not inexhaustible, although some members of Congress and some industrialists professed to believe that they were. During Schurz's administration (he served until 1881), he was the highest placed official in the federal hierarchy advocating a sound forest policy. Albeit his conservation recommendations received little favorable consideration by the Congress, the proposals made by him and by others in the Department of the Interior were eventually incorporated into departmental policy.

After Congress passed the Forest Reserve Act of 1891, the Department of the Interior had to wait until 1897 for Congressional authority to administer the reserves.[4] Still, authority without funds could accomplish little. Another year went by before an appropriation made possible the administration of the reserves and the protection and development of their resources.

But qualified personnel were hard to come by under the political patronage system then in vogue. It was not until 1900 that employees were selected by competitive examination. By that year, there were forty-one reserves covering a total area of more than 46 million acres. Under the field organization in effect, one or more reserves were assigned to a district with a superintendent in charge. A supervisor was responsible for each reserve; he in turn had a force of several forest rangers to patrol the reserve and to perform the necessary work. In 1901 the General Land Office gave responsibility for this work to a special forestry unit. Filibert Roth, who had been teaching forestry at Cornell University, was appointed head of it, and four experienced men were transferred from the Forest Service to assist him.

Nearly all of the few government employees who had technical experience or education in forestry were in the Bureau of Forestry, Department of Agriculture. Under an arrangement worked out by the secretary of the interior and the secretary of agriculture, the Bureau of Forestry, as official forestry advisor to Interior, prepared forest management plans for the reserves. One of the first of these plans, prepared in 1900, was for the Black Hills reserve in South Dakota. Although the Bureau of Forestry prepared the plans, the authority and responsibility for implementing them belonged to the General Land Office. There is scant evidence, however, that the Land Office acted on the technical advice provided by the bureau. Paul W. Gates of Cornell, historian of the public lands, observed that Congress "when it

3. "Remarks of Hon. Carl Schurz before the American Forestry Congress," *Forest Leaves*, vol. 11 (December 1889), pp. 120–21.
4. Forest reserves are discussed in chap. 2.

wanted professional advice, turned to Pinchot and the Bureau of Forestry in Agriculture. Administration of the forest reserves by the General Land Office under Commissioner Binger Hermann, with his sensitivity toward the views of western economic groups and disinclination to push forward along conservation lines, was making little progress."[5]

It was an unsatisfactory arrangement, and on a long-term basis doubtless an unworkable one. Pinchot detested Hermann, describing him as "a politician with a long beard, fat, smooth, slick, 'practical' in the worst sense of the word, with an eye to the main chance and a deep-rooted conviction that a public office is a private snap."[6] They disagreed on procedural matters and on the conditions of Pinchot's status in the Land Office. For example, Pinchot was to have been named a special agent and forester in the Department of the Interior without pay, but the plan never went through.[7]

The Binger Hermanns in public office care for little except the power and influence they possess. They react to new ideas by driving away or ignoring the individuals who would change old ways of doing things. In 1903, Filibert Roth left the Land Office. "It proved impossible," according to Gates, "for Roth to work with Hermann and he left to head the new School of Forestry at Michigan. Politics won out over professional forestry."[8]

To end the impasse that was blocking the development of a federal forestry policy and the application of technical management of the forest reserves, national organizations as well as individual citizens advocated the transfer of the reserves from Interior to Agriculture, where they would be under the direction of foresters. The American Forestry Association advocated the transfer. President Theodore Roosevelt was for it, as was Secretary of the Interior John Noble.

In 1905, the year the Bureau of Forestry was officially named the Forest Service, the transfer was made. The reserves then totaled 85.6 million acres, a forest heritage of incalculable wealth. Henceforth, the reserves, later to become the national forests, would be managed in the public interest by professional foresters and other civil servants with technical and scientific education.

During the half-century the Department of the Interior had custody of the public lands, it failed to give them the minimum protection from fire and trespass that even the most elementary standards of prudent administration required. Put bluntly, the department that might have been the conservation agency of the federal government, defaulted on its responsibilities and obligations.

It serves no useful purpose at this late date to speculate as to the number of years that would have passed before foresters might have been given the same opportunity to practice their skills on the forest reserves in the Department of the Interior that they were immediately given in Agriculture. As it happened, forestry as an art and a science did get recognition in Interior after the reserves were gone. In time, the quality of the forestry practiced on

5. *History of Public Land Law Development*, pp. 576–77.
6. *Breaking New Ground*, p. 194.
7. For Pinchot's version of this controversy see *Breaking New Ground*, chap. 34.
8. *History of Public Land Law*, p. 578.

Interior holdings would rank high in professional circles. In education, competence, and ethical standards, the foresters in Interior would rank with the best in America. The rest of this chapter describes briefly some of the forestry work performed by various bureaus of the department.

Forestry on Indian Lands

When Indian reservations were created by the federal government during the past century, many of them contained extensive forests of valuable species. Both the total area of Indian lands and the area of commercial forests thereon have been shrinking through sales, treaties, and other causes. Although the Indian lands are owned privately by the Indians themselves, the federal government acts as trustee. Ownership of the trust lands is of two kinds: individual and tribal.

Of the approximately 50 million acres owned by the Indians, tribally and individually, about 10 percent is in commercial timber. In the following account of forestry on Indian lands, it will be understood that the 5 million acres of commercial forest represent the estate under consideration. This commercial forest is spread over thirty-one states on forty-five reservations. Apart from this land, about 8 million acres of low-grade woodland and brush growth are not commercially operable for forest products.

Timber sales from Indian lands were first made under government supervision during the mid-1860s. Prior to 1888, timber cutting (trespass) on Indian lands was not specifically prohibited by law. Special legislative authority to sell reservation timber for the benefit of the tribes was granted the secretary of the interior in 1889, but it was limited to dead trees. A law of 1890 permitted the Menominee Indians in Wisconsin to cut their timber and sell it without restriction, up to the limit of the annual allowable harvest of 20 million board feet. Within a few years, extensive sales were made on reservations in Minnesota and Wisconsin, the logging operations being carried on under the supervision of the Indian Service (now the Bureau of Indian Affairs).

In 1902, a law was passed that had unusual significance, not only because it concerned the management of timber on the Chippewa Reservation in Minnesota and Wisconsin, but also because it prescribed the application of forestry knowledge and gave responsibility for this application to the Bureau of Forestry in Agriculture. This law strengthened the act of 1889; it prohibited wasteful cutting, required the abatement of fire hazards following logging, and provided that 5 percent of the standing pine trees on the Chippewa Reservation be left for forest renewal. Logging on the reservation was to be carried out in accordance with plans prescribed by the Bureau of Forestry, with the approval of the secretary of the interior. For the first time, the bureau was given a major opportunity for practical forest work on federal land.

During the first decade of the present century, Indian reservation timber in Minnesota and Wisconsin was either under the management of the Bureau of Forestry (renamed the Forest Service in 1905) or under management plans prepared by it. The Indian Service had no foresters of its own. In January 1908 an agreement between the Departments of Agriculture and the Interior provided for the management of 6 million acres of Indian timberlands at the expense of the Indian Service. This agreement, though in effect for only a year and a half, "marked the beginning of approved forestry principles on Indian forests."[9] It was abrogated by Interior in July 1909, ostensibly because of a decision that the secretary of the interior could not transfer his responsibility to the secretary of agriculture, but actually because of disagreement about the methods of management.

An act of June 25, 1910, enabled the Indian Service to start practicing forestry and brought about the employment of foresters. The secretary of the interior was authorized to sell mature, dead, and down timber from the unallotted lands of any reservation and to use the proceeds for the benefit of the tribe. This law made possible the conservative management of Indian forests.[10]

J. P Kinney, one of the first students to enroll in the forestry curriculum started by Cornell University in 1898, entered the Indian Service on February 25, 1910, with the title of assistant forester. Later, in recalling this period of his career, Kinney told of being interviewed by various officers in the Department of the Interior who explained "the purpose of establishing an administrative unit for the handling of forests on Indian lands." He noted, wryly:

I agreed to accept the position of Assistant Forester in the Indian Service with a rather definite indication that after a reasonable probationary period I could expect promotion to the position of Forester for the Indian Service at a salary approximately double that which I was to receive upon entrance to the Service. I then knew nothing about the rather normal incapacity of the Indian Service to meet its obligations in the matter of promotions. . . .[11]

In addition to Kinney, one other technically trained forester was employed by the service: George A. Gutches, a forestry graduate of the University of Michigan, who was district forester at Albuquerque, New Mexico. Subsequently, Kinney was named chief supervisor of forests; his small unit became known as the Indian Forest Service. Later, it was variously known as the Forestry Branch; the Division of Forestry; the Branch of Forest and Range Management when it was assigned range responsibilities; and currently it is the Forestry Program, Bureau of Indian Affairs.

Although the Indian lands held in trust by the federal government are subject to the control of Congress, which acts as trustee, they are administered for the benefit of the Indians themselves, not for the benefit of the general public. Since the beginning of the forestry program, the policy of management has been to obtain the maximum financial return from the timber harvests and at the same time to apply sound silvicultural practices that will maintain the lands in permanent production. Accordingly, the difficulties of applying sustained-yield management to the tribal woodlands have been economic rather than technical.

9. John Shanklin, *Forest Conservation*, U.S. Department of the Interior (1962), p. 11.

10. J. P Kinney, *The Development of Forest Law in America*, p. 253.

11. Kinney, *Indian Forest and Range*, p. 83.

At the request of Hubert Work, secretary of the interior, an objective, nongovernmental investigation of the economic and social conditions of the Indians was started in 1926 by the Institute for Government Research (now the Brookings Institution), under the direction of Lewis Meriam. Although the report was frequently critical of the government's aid programs for its wards, the Institute had only praise for the forestry work, as shown by the following excerpt:

> The survey staff wishes to record its impression that the Indian Service has many excellent men in its forest service. Their decision to practice selective logging on several of the jurisdictions seems specially worthy of commendation, especially because the land is at present of little value except for timber raising. The salaries of these able employees is comparatively low and consequently the turnover is high.[12]

In carrying out the intent of the government, the forestry staff has managed the Indian lands so that they might yield the highest financial return to the owners consistent with scientific forestry practice. But the foresters have had to perform their duties in accordance with defeasible Congressional policies and departmental regulations subject to change under the higher dictates of the owners' wishes. Frequently, Indians have demanded greater financial returns from harvests than the allowable cut for a given period would justify. As a result, overcutting (the removal of timber in excess of the periodic cutting budget) has occurred on occasion.

Under numerous acts of Congress, hundreds of thousands of acres of merchantable timberlands were allotted to individual Indians. The size of the tracts, generally not larger than 160 acres and often as small as 40 acres each, made supervision of their management difficult. Nevertheless, the foresters of the Bureau of Indian Affairs have been able to induce the owners of tracts unsuited to agricultural or range use to adopt conservative forestry practices. Their efforts were strengthened by the Indian Reorganization Act of 1934, which required the Department of the Interior to manage all Indian forests on a sustained-yield basis.

One of the objects of forest management on Indian lands has been a guiding prinicple for the foresters. It is predominantly a social objective—to develop Indian forests "for the purpose of promoting self-sustaining communities, to the end that the Indians may receive from their own property not only the stumpage value, but also the benefit of whatever profit it is capable of yielding. . . ."[13]

In accordance with this policy, over the years small sawmills were erected on timbered reservations to provide the Indians with employment and building materials. Generally, these mills were not commercial enterprises and most of them have ceased operating, since lumber for Indian needs could be purchased more cheaply from commercial producers. Three large commercial-type sawmills, however, are manufacturing lumber on Indian reservations: the

---

12. *The Problem of Indian Administration* (Johns Hopkins Press, 1928), p. 518.
13. Shanklin, *Forest Conservation*, p. 25.

Red Lake tribal mill at Redby, Minnesota; the Navajo tribal mill near Fort Defiance, Arizona; and the Fort Apache Reservation mill at Whiteriver, Arizona.

In reviewing the forestry work of the Bureau of Indian Affairs since 1910, one must understand that the commercial forests consisted almost entirely of overmature, old-growth stands. From a silvicultural standpoint, the requirement was to cut heavily in order to remove the timber that had reached or passed economic maturity or that had slowed in growth to the point of little or no net increment. Because of the need for heavy cutting, an initial depletion of the forest capital resulted. But this in turn was followed by marked acceleration of the second growth, permitting silvicultural practices that in 1968 were calculated to sustain an annual allowable harvest of at least 1 billion board feet. Although the area of commercial Indian forest decreased from 5.6 million acres in 1960 to 5 million acres in 1968, the timber resource is estimated by the Forestry Branch to have increased during the same period from approximately 36 billion to 40 billion board feet.[14] On most of the timberlands logged during the past five decades, residual stands are generally well stocked with second growth and are in productive condition.

In 1968, the commercial Indian forests yielded a harvest of 952 million board feet valued at $21 million. Timber harvest and other forestry-based projects provided 6,440 man-years of employment for workers in woods and mills and 4,000 man-years of indirect supporting employment. For these jobs, the Indians have preferential employment rights. In addition, hundreds of Indians are employed on seasonal projects such as fire fighting, tree planting, and insect and disease control.

In 1964, Indian possessions totaled 50 million acres of trust land held by tribes and individual owners. In 1968, the forestry personnel were responsible for the management of approximately 5 million acres of commercial forest having an inventory of 40 billion board feet, together with about 8 million acres of noncommercial woodlands owned by the Indians. The allowable annual cut was more than 1 billion board feet on a sustained-yield basis. The silvicultural, logging, and related forestry work of the Bureau of Indian Affairs was performed by 182 professional foresters. (The number of professional foresters was 50 in 1930.)

Since the establishment of the Forestry Program of the Bureau of Indian Affairs in 1910, approximately 29 billion board feet of saw timber and other products have been harvested from Indian lands under the supervision of the bureau's foresters. The value of the forest products was more than $267 million.

Orderly management of Indian forests which began with J. P Kinney[15] in 1910 has been carried on with ever greater participation by the Indians. Six decades ago, the Indians generally were insufficiently informed and insuffi-

14. In 1930, the timber stand was estimated to be 35 billion board feet.
15. J. P Kinney had charge of the forestry program from 1910 to 1933. His successors have been Robert Marshall (1933–37), Lee Muck (1937–39), LeRoy D. Arnold (1939–53), Percy E. Miles (1953–54), and George S. Kephart (1954–64). Perry E. Skarra has been director of the Forestry Program since 1964.

ciently interested in their timber resource to manage it themselves or to help guide technical personnel to do it. Conditions are now much improved. According to George S. Kephart, former head of the Forestry Branch:

Tribal participation has increased steadily in all phases of forest management planning, including the timing of timber sales, the prices to be received, the conditions of sale, etc. . . . Today, tribal officers discuss forest management problems regularly with federal government personnel, with the timber purchasers, with their Congressmen and others. They are advised in these deliberations by tribal attorneys. At least one tribe has retained a consulting forester from time to time. Today, no important action on timber matters is taken without consulting with tribal officers.[16]

The Bureau of Land Management

The long process of shaping a policy for the scientific management of the forested lands of the public domain—an effort that began with Carl Schurz in 1877—reached fulfillment nearly seventy years later with the creation of the Bureau of Land Management. In our republic, when the government finally becomes aware of a problem its reaction is to pass a law or set up a new bureau. In order to deal with the increasingly insistent problem of the public land resources, the government did both. The bureau came into existence in 1946 by merger of the General Land Office and the Grazing Service. Later, the bureau set up a Forestry Division, which was responsible for the management of the forested areas of the public domain.

In studying the development of public land policy and the history of governmental organizations dealing with land matters, one gropes through a thicket of laws and regulations of uncommon complexity.[17] The following paragraphs, delineating the events leading to the formation of the Bureau of Land Management (BLM), provide a condensed and simplified account of what would otherwise be an inordinately tedious chronicle.

The genesis of the Grazing Service was the Taylor Grazing Act of 1934. This act, as amended in 1936, provided for the segregation of 142 million acres of public grasslands to be parceled into grazing districts. A Division of Grazing, later named the Grazing Service, was created in the Department of the Interior to administer the districts.

Among the most valuable of the managed forest holdings under BLM jurisdiction are the so-called O & C lands in western Oregon. They were part of a grant made by Congress in 1866 to the Oregon and California Railroad Company, which proposed to build a railroad from Portland south to the California state line. The land grant was along the right-of-way and comprised about 3.7 million acres. Three years later, another grant of 105,000 acres was made to the state of Oregon to encourage the construction of a wagon road between Coos Bay and Roseburg, Oregon.

The laudable object of these grants was to promote agriculture and settlement; in short, to open up the country. The two grants specified that the

16. "The Truth about Indian Timber," *American Forests*, vol. 74 (October 1968), p. 54.

17. For a comprehensive and scholarly exegesis of the legal aspects of the government's handling of its lands, see Gates, *History of Public Land Law.*

lands should be sold to bona fide settlers only (not to land speculators) and that no settler should have the right to purchase more than 160 acres (a quarter section). Considering the instances of land frauds against the government, one need not add that these restrictions were violated.

About the turn of the century, public criticism of the successor company (Southern Pacific) arose because of an alleged breach of the terms of the grant. Petitioned to cancel the grant, Congress in 1908 directed the attorney general to sue to reclaim the lands. Seven years later, the suit having reached the Supreme Court, the justices decided for the government and forfeited the grant. In 1916, Congress revested title of the lands (2.9 million acres) to the United States, specifically to the jurisdiction of the Department of the Interior. In 1919, Congress decreed that the lands still unsold (93,000 acres) that had been granted to the Coos Bay Wagon Road Company also must be reconveyed to the federal government.

In the Revestment Act of 1916, Congress inserted a provision for liquidation of the land and timber and for revision of the whole estate to private ownership. This policy proved to be another failure of Congress to heed the lessons of history. The profound need for a change in resource policy got little response from Congress. The phenomenon was not wholly political; most Congressmen either lacked the knowledge to deal with the problem or were disinterested. The mental attitudes of 1866 were brought to bear on the problems of 1916. Some Congressmen may have cherished the illusion that they were doing the right thing for the forest resource. It is clear, however, that the objective of others was to bestow on new settlers the same freedom to exploit the resource that western pioneers had traditionally possessed under land laws passed by the Congress. Resource laws were still being made by men who were influenced in their ideas by the earlier availability of cheap land and abundant timber and who were unable to understand and cope with the contemporary need for management of this immensely valuable resource.

Predictably, forest destruction and losses followed. Much timber was wastefully logged. Most of the resulting cutover land was found to be unsuited to agriculture, and when homesteaded was often abandoned. The national interest, as well as the economic exigency of the Douglas-fir region, was entitled to a better administrative setup for these rich and productive stands. Although the O & C revested lands had not been intensively inventoried at that time, they then comprised 2.5 million acres, mostly of old growth Douglas-fir and associated species, such as western hemlock, western red cedar, grand fir, silver fir, noble fir, and Sitka spruce. Fortunately, the failure of Congress to safeguard this magnificent resource did not stop the efforts of conservationists, both inside and outside the government, to press for an enlightened solution. The criticism of Congress that ensued was amply justified.

Furthermore, within a decade the Revestment Act was found to be inefficient and inoperable. Income from the sale of timber was insufficient to pay the various beneficiaries—the State of Oregon, the counties in which the lands were situated, the federal government itself, and other funds into which the law required receipts to be distributed. Additional legislation (the Stanfield Act of 1926) to reimburse the counties for their losses in taxes failed to solve the dilemma. At the end of another decade, the federal government had incurred a deficit of more than $10 million in the administration of the O & C lands. Moreover, the deficit was certain to grow under the unworkable fiscal and administrative policies handed down by Congress. Public criticism was directed both at Congress and at the Department of the Interior. Another source of criticism was conservation-minded citizens, both inside and outside government, who condemned Congress, which, in decreeing the disposal of the O & C lands, had made no provision for conservative management of the lands while they were in government ownership or in transition to private ownership.

Belatedly, Congress was persuaded that the logical way out of the impasse into which it had delivered this enormously valuable resource was through the practice of sustained-yield forestry. The O & C Act of August 28, 1937, stipulated that the administration of these lands, together with the Coos Bay Wagon Road Company lands—a total of 2.6 million acres—would be under a system providing for continuous sustained-yield production. Gates's comment on this law is pertinent.

The Act of 1937 was a landmark in the development of forestry in the Department of the Interior. Though Interior was given primary management responsibility for the O & C lands, it was authorized to arrange with Federal, state, or private forest owners for coordination of fire protection and other aspects of control. It was also authorized to reclassify "agricultural," that is cutover land, if it was found such land was more suitable for growing timber than farming. Most important, the Secretary of the Interior was required to manage the lands on a sustained yield basis, providing for the cutting of no more timber than the lands were reproducing to assure a constant source of supply for dependent industries.[18]

Administration of sustained-yield forestry on the O & C lands was assigned to the General Land Office. Headquarters for the O&C Revested Lands Administration was set up in Portland, Oregon, in 1938. Walter H. Horning, a professional forester, was appointed administrator and chief forester and was charged with setting up a management program for the lands.

In 1940, Horning reported that the lands totaled 2.6 million acres, of which about 2 million acres were timbered. The remainder was cutover, burned over, and nonforest acreage. The O & C lands then contained about 16 percent of the sawtimber in the Douglas-fir region and about 3 percent of the remaining supply of sawtimber in the United States. Douglas-fir was the principal species, comprising 85 percent of the stand, which had an estimated value of $50 million, a value based on depression-era standards. As determined by the foresters, the annual allowable cut was 500 million board feet, and at this cutting rate the stand of mature timber was estimated to last 100 years.[19]

Horning emphasized that the lands were managed for permanent forest production, as required by law. Timber sales were on the basis of clearcutting. The principal purpose of the Revested Land Administration was to contribute

18. Ibid., pp. 603–4.
19. W. H. Horning, "The O. & C. Lands: Their Role in Forest Conservation," *Journal of Forestry*, vol. 38 (May 1940), pp. 379–83.

"to the economic stability of local communities and industries." He added that the cost of sales and management during 1939, based on the volume of timber sold, averaged 16 cents per 1,000 board feet.[20]

Two years later, Horning outlined in detail "one of the most comprehensive planning projects in forest resource management in the United States."[21] A land-use classification had been undertaken for the area, the major portion of which was still clothed with primeval forest. Under the system of clearcutting, sales were being made first in overmature and deteriorating timber. A fire protection system was in force with controlled burning of logging waste to reduce the fire hazard. Reforestation work had been started on areas lacking sufficient young growth. Finally, an economic study of local marketing areas was being made.

In a paper presented at a meeting of the Society of American Foresters held in Minneapolis in December 1946, Horning was optimistic about the constructive possibilities of sustained-yield forestry on the O & C lands.[22] He proposed a way in which public forests could be used to influence industrial stabilization through cooperative agreements with private owners of timber under the terms of the Sustained Yield Unit Law of 1944.[23] Technically, under sustained yield a given forest unit is managed with the object of achieving an approximate balance between net growth and harvest so that the annual or periodic yield of forest products can be maintained in perpetuity.

Notwithstanding the fact that the O & C lands were required to be managed under the principle of sustained-yield forestry, Horning and his staff of foresters were under great pressure from interests that would circumvent their long-range plans for cooperative sustained-yield units. These interests were mainly timber operators in the region who either owned no timber or who owned an insufficient volume to sustain their operations. Horning's comments on these operators who "avoid the responsibility of growing timber" illuminated the difficulties.

As exploiters of mature timber their sole interest is in having unrestricted supplies to use. They are not in sympathy with any program, however meritorious, or however much in the interest of community welfare, if it includes anything that looks like effective control over the rate of timber cutting. Now that such a plan has been adopted and is in the process of being carried out they seek to block it by creating confusion in the public mind. They indiscriminately hurl charges of monopoly, communism, and new-dealism.[24]

Opponents of the cooperative sustained-yield units were mainly small operators who allegedly feared that the large land-owning companies would obtain preferential access to government timber and would reduce or cut off their log supply. They not only expressed their opposition at public hearings but solicited the support of their Congressmen. The result was that no co-

20. Ibid.
21. "Planning Sustained Yield Forest Management on the O. & C. Lands," *Journal of Forestry*, vol. 40 (June 1942), pp. 474–76.
22. "The Promised Land of Managed Forests," *Journal of Forestry*, vol. 45 (October 1947), pp. 741–45.
23. For an account of this act and its effect on private forestry, see chap. 19.
24. W. H. Horning, "The Promised Land."

operative sustained-yield units were ever started by the Department of the Interior on BLM lands. Similar attempts to circumvent other aspects of the forestry program of the O & C lands would be made from time to time, but none successfully.

The western Oregon timber stand, estimated by Horning to be worth $50 million in 1940 and capable of supporting an annual allowable cut of 500 million board feet, has been managed so well that its productive capacity has increased manyfold. The volume of timber harvested in 1967 amounted to 1.3 billion board feet valued at $51 million.

It will be recalled that the General Land Office created a forestry unit in 1901 with Filibert Roth in charge. When the forest reserves were transferred from Interior to Agriculture in 1905, this forestry unit ceased to exist. Notwithstanding the Land Office's responsibilities for the millions of acres of timbered public domain still under its jurisdiction, it did not reestablish a specific forestry unit until March 1946. Then, at the urging of Lee Muck in the Office of Land Utilization, a Forestry Division was created and charged with the management of public domain forests as well as with the Alaska Fire Control Service.

During 1939, the department created the Alaskan Fire Control Service for the territory's public domain lands. Roger R. Robinson, an able forestry administrator, was named director of this organization. It functioned primarily as a protection force until 1944 when it was expanded to include the management, as well as the protection, of the commercial timber on the public lands of Alaska. Robinson was given charge of this enlarged forestry responsibility.

Meanwhile, in July 1943, Alf Z. Nelson, formerly with the Forest Service and more recently on the staff of the National Resources Planning Board, had been appointed to the General Land Office to oversee the forestry operations on the O & C lands and the public domain. As no forestry was being practiced on the public domain, Nelson worked mostly on the O & C program. When the Division of Forestry was created in the Land Office, he was made acting chief. For the first time in over forty years there was an opportunity to provide intensive forest management on the unreserved and unappropriated public domain.

When the Grazing Service and the Land Office merged in July 1946 to form the Bureau of Land Management, a branch of Timber and Resource Management, with Nelson as acting chief, was set up in the bureau to handle forestry, timber sales, and fire protection on the public lands, including those in Alaska. In January 1948, BLM established a new Division of Forestry; Nelson was again appointed acting chief, continuing in this position until mid-1949 when he left federal service.

In late 1948, Horning was transferred to Washington, D.C., and assigned to the Division of Forestry. He became chief of the division on Nelson's departure and served until May 1961 when he was reassigned to Portland, Oregon, to compile a history of the O & C lands. He died before this project was completed.

Horning's successor was Eugene V. Zumwalt, a forester who had joined BLM in Alaska in mid-1953 as assistant regional forester, becoming assistant to the area administrator in 1959. Later, Zumwalt became assistant director for resources, with responsibility for lands, minerals, range, and other resources, as well as for forestry.

A cardinal object of sustained-yield management of BLM forests is to help maintain the economic stability of the communities dependent on the timber for their industries. Assurance of a permanent supply of raw material is essential to justify the considerable financial investments in sawmills and other types of manufacturing plants without which full utilization of the resources cannot be made.

Although the principle of sustained-yield management has been explained elsewhere, it is worth defining again as the operation of a forest for continuous production in order to maintain a balance between net growth and drain. By drain is meant the annual or periodic losses resulting from wood harvesting, fire, insects, and disease. Sustained-yield management is a form of multiple-use forestry, the practice which combines two or more objectives, such as timber production and water, or forage production for livestock, or browse for deer, or soil erosion prevention, or recreation.

No single bureau of the federal government has custodial responsibility for as large an acreage of the nation's real estate as BLM. It manages the resources on 458 million acres, which comprise about 20 percent of the country's total land area. The form of management is under the principle of multiple use, in accordance with the Classification and Multiple Use Act of 1964.

The total area of forest and woodland under BLM jurisdiction is 145 million acres. Of this area, 37 million acres are commercial forest. The volume of commercial timber, as estimated by the bureau's foresters, is an impressive 177 billion board feet with an annual producing capacity of 1.6 billion board feet.[25]

Although the noncommercial timberland is not subject to the same intensive management as the commercial stands, it is nevertheless given full protection and is managed for products and services, other than timber, such as forage, water, wildlife, and recreation.

BLM has offices in all the western states, including Alaska. In all offices where forestry is a major function, foresters are on duty. In 1969, the bureau employed nearly 900 career foresters.

Since its inception in 1946, BLM has had five directors. Two have been foresters: Charles H. Stoddard (June 1963–June 1966) and Boyd Rasmussen (since July 1966).

Wildlife Refuges

In 1903, the Pelican Island Reservation was created in Florida by proclamation of President Theodore Roosevelt. A sanctuary for marine birdlife, it was the first of the national wildlife refuges. Additional refuges established during the following two decades were mainly for migratory birds, although big-game refuges, such as the National Bison Range in Montana, were acquired also.

25. U.S. Bureau of Land Management, *Public Land Statistics: 1967* (1968).

Wooded lands were not specifically sought, although some refuges contained extensive areas of tree growth. As the art of wildlife management developed, manipulation of the woody vegetation to improve cover, food, and nesting conditions was undertaken. But such manipulation was not forest management in the technical sense. In time, however, scientific forest management would be applied to the wooded refuges with conspicuous success.

For some thirty-six years, the national wildlife refuge system was under the jurisdiction of the Bureau of Biological Survey in the Department of Agriculture. When the Resettlement Administration was established in April 1935, it began a federal program of purchasing submarginal agricultural lands and retiring them from crop production. Some of the lands acquired were partially wooded and were adapted to wildlife production. In June 1935, an act of Congress authorized a fund of $6 million for the purchase of additional lands for waterfowl and wildlife refuges. Together, these two programs added about 1 million acres to the refuge system.

As the result of a recommendation by President Franklin D. Roosevelt in May 1939, the Bureau of the Biological Survey was transferred from Agriculture to the Department of the Interior. Concurrently, the Bureau of Fisheries was transferred from the Department of Commerce to Interior. On June 30, 1940, these two bureaus were combined to become the Fish and Wildlife Service. At that time, there were 263 refuges containing 13.6 million acres. Since then, the refuge system has been under the administration of the service. Refuge management is a responsibility of the Bureau of Sport Fisheries and Wildlife.

Where compatible, multiple-use management is practiced on the refuges, with management for waterfowl and game species being, of course, the dominant purpose. Since the object of management is to provide optimum habitat for wildlife, the practice of silviculture is of secondary importance, as is the financial revenue from forest products. Sustained-yield forestry is quite compatible with long-term wildlife management in most forest types naturally occurring on the refuges. Where the silvical characteristics of the stands permit, harvesting is by a light selection system whereby economically mature trees are removed in groups or blocks to open the forest canopy sufficiently to produce ground cover and an understory of plant foods.

Under modern silvicultural practices, the sustained harvest of forest products promotes healthy stands, which in turn provide the essential food and cover for optimum wildlife populations. Without some degree of management, a forested refuge is unable to attain its full resource potential. For example, it is pointed out in a 1962 report that officials in the Division of Wildlife Refuges "have seen refuge turkey populations decline and excessive deer populations destroy their own range due to the lack of adequate forest management programs."[26]

One of the objectives of management is to maintain the natural ecological balance in the various forest types in order to produce a sustained yield of the

26. "Forests for Wildlife on the National Wildlife Refuges," U.S. Fish and Wildlife Service, Leaflet 404 (May 1962, mimeo.).

native wildlife species. Since Aldo Leopold wrote his classic text *Game Management* in 1933, a great deal has been learned by foresters and wildlife biologists, working together, about the relation of forest types to wildlife species. The quality of silviculture practiced on refuges is not diminished because the resulting product happens to be wildlife rather than sawlogs or pulpwood. On many forested refuges, wildlife may be the primary crop; the harvesting of wood products, however, not only returns revenues from the operations but makes the maintenance of optimum wildlife populations possible. Intensive forestry has a place in wildlife management, a truth recognized by the Bureau of Sport Fisheries and Wildlife, which employs professional foresters to work with game biologists in the furtherance of the bureau's objectives. All the foresters in the bureau have had training and experience in wildlife management.

A well-known example of intensive integrated management for wildlife and timber is the 33,000-acre Piedmont National Wildlife Refuge in central Georgia, north of Macon. Acquired during the late 1930s, the area, which formerly supported hardwoods and pines, had much-depleted populations of wildlife, was badly eroded, and had little commercial timber. Under government ownership, the land was restocked with deer and wild turkey. Unproductive areas were reforested. New management practices improved the habitat so that ducks and other migratory birds were attracted, and their populations expanded. The numbers of quail, rabbits, and squirrels likewise increased.

As a result of three decades of sustained-yield management, by the 1960s the deer-carrying capacity of the refuge averaged one deer for each 25 acres. The timber stand averaged 8,000 board feet per acre. Approximately 380 deer and 7 million board feet of wood products were being harvested yearly. The growing stock, both of wildlife and of timber, was being increased under a plan that retained 20 percent of the acreage in hardwoods, 75 percent in pine types, and 5 percent nonforested. The harvesting cycle is planned so that at least 75 percent of the woodland remains relatively open. An understory of mostly low-growing shrubby and herbaceous vegetation provides food for deer, nesting sites for turkey, and good habitat for other species.

In summary, a management system for the refuge has been developed by professional foresters for growing and harvesting the timber under the principle of multiple use. The principle recognizes that wildlife production, together with recreational and educational use of the area, is the main goal of the system. This demonstration of multiple-resource management has been so successful that it has been extended to other forest lands, both public and private, in the Piedmont region.[27]

By July 1969, there were 321 national wildlife refuges with an aggregate area of 28.6 million acres, of which some 18 million acres are in Alaska. Of the approximately 2.5 million acres that are forested, about 1 million acres are suitable for intensive management for integrated timber production and wildlife. Income from forest products harvested in connection with wildlife

27. U.S. Fish and Wildlife Service, *Piedmont National Wildlife Refuge* (Atlanta [circa late 1960s]).

habitat improvement operations amounted to $1.2 million in 1967; the volume cut was 43 million board feet.

The National Park Service

In Arkansas, a group of mineral hot springs, believed to be helpful in the relief of certain human ailments, was withdrawn from the public domain in 1832 for the use of the public at large. Although this tract did not become the Hot Springs National Park until 1921, chronologically it was the first such reservation ever made by the federal government.

The next withdrawal of public land destined to become a national park occurred in 1864 when Congress granted Yosemite Valley and the Mariposa grove of big trees (giant sequoias) to the state of California "to be held inviolate for all time for public use, resort, and recreation."[28] Lands surrounding these areas were set aside as a national park in 1890, and in 1905 California receded Yosemite Valley and the grove of big trees to the federal government so that they could become part of spectacular Yosemite National Park.

With the creation of Yellowstone National Park in Wyoming (then Montana Territory) in 1872, Congress for the first time authorized the establishment of an area "dedicated and set apart as a public park or pleasuring-ground for the benefit and enjoyment of the people."[29] The control of the park was assigned to the Department of the Interior, and the secretary was directed to preserve the timber, mineral deposits, and natural wonders, and to prevent the destruction of fish and game, particularly for merchandise or profit. But Congress appropriated no money for administration in the expectation that the park would be self-supporting. Consequently, regulations against trespassing, the killing of game for the market, and the cutting of timber were poorly enforced. Vandalism was rife, geyser formations were defaced, and wildlife poaching was widespread. Handicapped by lack of funds and by politically appointed assistants who were incompetent, if not venal, the several superintendents were unable to provide the park with proper administration or even suitable protection.

By 1886, numerous Congressmen were ready to surrender the nation's first national park to commercial exploiters. As a temporary measure, Secretary of the Interior L. Q. C. Lamar, acting under a law of 1883, turned the park over to the protection of the War Department. It remained under military control for thirty-two years.[30]

Sequoia National Park was established in 1890 to preserve "timber and ornamental trees . . . some of which are the wonders of the world on account of their size and the limited number growing. . . ."[31] Mount Rainier National Park in Washington, established in 1899, was the sixth area so preserved prior to 1900.

28. *Act of June 30, 1864* (13 Stat. 325).
29. *Act of March 1, 1872* (17 Stat. 32).
30. For a detailed account of this period see H. Duane Hampton, "The Army and the National Parks," *Forest History*, vol. 10 (October 1966).
31. *Act of September 25, 1890* (26 Stat. 478).

During the first decade and a half of the present century, additional parks were created: Crater Lake, Glacier, Grand Canyon, Olympic, Rocky Mountain, and others. Civic organizations, conservation associations, and private citizens began urging the government to create a special bureau for park administration. Gifford Pinchot was not among them.

In 1915, Stephen T. Mather was employed as an assistant to the secretary of the interior to administer the thirteen parks then existing, although Congress had not as yet provided legislative policies specifically for their administration. Mather's appointment was made in anticipation of such legislation, and on August 15, 1916, the law was passed creating the National Park Service in the Department of the Interior. Mather was named as its first director.

A contretemps at a parks conference in Des Moines in January 1921 was symptomatic of the tensions between bureaus in the development of parks and recreation policy. During one of the meetings, Arthur H. Carhart, recreation engineer in the Denver office of the Forest Service, told the audience about the vast acreage of the national forests and the manifold opportunities available for recreational use by the public. He emphasized that the national forests were open for use by all the people and that every one was welcome. Apparently thinking that Carhart was promoting the concept that the national forests were the people's playgrounds, whereas the national parks were for the wealthy, Mather objected to such "advertising" and argued that the national forests should not develop recreation, that it was not their business to do so, and that they were duplicating the work of the Park Service.[32]

Newspapers in Denver and Des Moines played up the "clash" between the two officials and added to the controversy by misstating both the basis of the disagreement and the comments of the two spokesmen. Then a resolution offered by Harris A. Reynolds of the Massachusetts Forests and Parks Association was opposed by the Park Service representatives on the basis that "the recreational use of national forests was insignificant,"[33] which it clearly was not. However, when the resolution was adopted, it had a certain timeliness in that it recognized that public forest lands, wherever located and regardless of ownership, offered opportunities for recreation without impairment of economic values, and that millions of people were already enjoying recreation in national, state, county, and municipal forests as well as in parks.

One purpose of the meeting was to urge state, county, and local governments to acquire land and water areas suitable for recreation. But what displeased Mather was the practical and outspoken suggestion by an officer of the Forest Service, supported by state foresters, that public funds should be appropriated for recreational development in national forests.

Out of the meeting came a constructive and lasting action, the formation of the National Conference on State Parks. Since 1921, this organization has promoted research and planning for the acquisition and development of state and local parks and open spaces for public recreation.

32. Donald Nicholas Baldwin, "An Historical Study of Western Origin, Application and Development of the Wilderness Concept, 1919 to 1933" (Ph.D. thesis, University of Denver, June 1965).
33. Ibid.

Still, the bickering between the Forest Service and the Park Service continued intermittently until recent years when cooperative activities and attitudes became well established. Robert Shankland doubtless stated the issue correctly when he wrote that the Forest Service "worried constantly over Park Service aims. Mather, the foresters maintained, had cost them more of their potential domain than Paul Bunyan."[34] Shankland gave an example of proposals that caused the trouble.

In promoting his two chief park-extension projects, Mather, as noted, had the Forest Service of the Department of Agriculture to contend with. The Yellowstone enlargement would lighten the Teton National Forest by 850,000 acres, and the Greater Sequoia scheme would do even worse to the California national forests, but not if the Forest Service could help it. The presence or threat of anguished protest from that corner of the bureaucracy kept Mather well curbed. The trouble was that the relationship between the two bureaus tended to resemble the relationship between the two ends of an hourglass: what augmented one depleted the other. But, plainly, all the movement was one way. With the Park Service trying to advance it and the Forest Service to hold it up, unpleasantness was hard to avoid.[35]

The conflicts between the Forest Service and the National Park Service over the latter's ambitions to establish national parks out of national forest lands were compounded by politicians and local promoters who sought to carve parks out of forests for commercial purposes. Robert Sterling Yard, executive officer of the National Parks Association, reported such a movement in a letter to members on February 2, 1928.

Yard related how Congressman Otis T. Wingo of DeQueen, Arkansas, had introduced a bill in Congress to designate the Mena National Forest in western Arkansas the Ouachita National Park. William B. Greeley, chief of the Forest Service, and A. B. Cammerer, then assistant director of the Park Service, had examined the area in 1926 and together declared it to be below national park standards. Mr. Wingo, at a hearing on February 2, 1928, before the House Committee on Public Lands, "vigorously challenged the authority of national policy when opposed to local wants." He claimed that the secretary of the interior and the director of the Park Service "took too lofty a view of National Parks, and that the people of his district in Arkansas had as much right as any one else to have a national park." He further claimed that "if advertised by the name 'national park' and opened up by motor roads, the area would be patronized from adjoining states. He expressed his determination that his district should have 'its rights.' "[36]

Rivalry between the two services continued. In a memorandum to the directors of The American Forestry Association, January 20, 1939, Henry S. Graves, chairman of the Committee on Coordination of National Park and National Forest Policies, wrote: "Controversies over specific projects have hardened opinions in both bureaus; hence reconciliation of policy by the usual means of conference and agreement seems out of the question." He also noted that the conflict was becoming a public one. "Since Congressional

---

34. *Steve Mather of the National Parks*, p. 172.
35. Ibid., pp. 176–77.
36. Graves Collection.

action is required for additions to the national park system, the general public is brought into discussions of individual projects for new parks, causing sharp alignment among conservation organizations which have interests in both national forest and national park development."[37]

That this situation caused, and still causes, confusion in the ranks of the conservation movement, as well as confusion among the general public, is proved by numerous references in newspapers, conservation magazines, and technical journals. Because the early national parks were areas of outstanding distinction, their popularity resulted in public demand for more parks with more roads and more facilities to accommodate visitors. In order to expand the number and area of the parks, officials and park organizations searched for suitable new sites. Thus, the National Park Service looked to the national forests with their impressive mountain scenery and other attractions.

But recreation is just as important in the national forests as in the national parks. It is an integral part of the Forest Service's long-range plans for multiple-use management. Accordingly, the Forest Service objected to the disruption of these plans through segregation of portions of national forests for transfer to national park status and single use. Moreover, the elimination of large segments of national forest that had long been under good management for wood, water, wildlife, and forage, as well as for recreation, was, and is, disruptive of stability of policy and administration.

Nevertheless, the annals of the park movement show that its tendency has been to create a park system without reference to the effect on the national forests from which the additions are derived. The federal government has never corrected the basic defects in this land policy, which invites competition and controversy, often carried on in the public arena. Efforts by the government, as well as by conservation organizations, to define national park standards have helped defeat proposals for the acquisition of parks of substandard quality, but such definitions have not prevented conflict between the Park Service and the Forest Service.

Stephen Mather was an able and dedicated director who fought for increased appropriations that would make the parks more accessible to the public and would enable the employment of qualified personnel to protect and supervise them. In their zeal to enlarge the park system, Mather and several of his successors tried, and in some cases succeeded, to carve huge acreages from the national forests for new parks or for additions to old ones. In 1968, pressures on Congress by the preservationist elements in conservation, led by the Sierra Club, resulted in legislation creating the Cascades National Park out of national forest lands in the State of Washington. The Redwood National Park in California, also authorized in 1968, was partially at the expense of a national forest unit taken out of government ownership in order to exchange federal land for redwood timber in private ownership.

Forestry in the Park Service

Ansel Franklin Hall, a forestry graduate of the University of California, was chief of the Division of Education and Forestry in the Park Service. In

37. Ibid.

1927 his duties were enlarged to include planning and administering the protection of the system's forests from fire. In March 1928, he was given the added title of chief forester and in July was assigned an assistant, John D. Coffman—a forestry graduate of Yale and supervisor of a California national forest—who was appointed fire control expert. Both officers had their headquarters at the University of California at Berkeley.

It was not until 1928 that Congress made the first general appropriation ($10,000) for protection of the parks from forest fire. Formerly, the custom had been to make separate appropriations for specific parks. The difficulty encountered by the Park Service to provide the parks with protection can be judged by the manner in which Congress doled out the funds. In 1921, an appropriation carried the proviso that the secretary of the interior "make a detailed report to Congress on every fire. A foolish provision was added in 1922 that none of the money was to be used for any precautionary fire protection or patrol work. Fire lookouts were not authorized until 1931."[38]

In April 1933, Coffman was transferred to the Washington, D.C., headquarters to take charge of the Emergency Conservation Work Program for the service. When a Branch of Forestry was created in the service in November of that year, Coffman was named chief forester and held this position until his retirement in 1952. His job was to organize all the forestry work of the service. A regional forester was designated for each of the four (later five) regional offices.

Coffman has the distinction of having been the first professional forester employed by the National Park Service to devote full time to the forestry aspects of Park Service administration. In recognition of his outstanding contributions to forest management for park and recreational purposes, he was elected a Fellow of the Society of American Foresters in 1946.

With the influx of visitors into the national park system during the months when the woods are most inflammable, fire is a constant hazard. Lightning is another fire starter, especially in the mountainous West. In 1937, the Heavens Peak fire in Glacier National Park spread destruction over more than 7,000 acres. In October 1946, a fire which started outside the boundary of Acadia National Park in Maine destroyed vegetation on 8,000 acres inside the park and 17,000 acres outside. A congressional appropriation of $400,000 was voted to reforest the burn and repair the ravages of the conflagration.

In view of the ever-present fire danger, the duties of the regional foresters were mostly protective. They organized park personnel for fire prevention and control. When forest diseases and injurious insects threatened the destruction of woody vegetation, they undertook control operations. For example, for many years the foresters worked on the control of the pine blister rust, a serious disease affecting both eastern and western white pines.

In addition to protective functions, the foresters mapped forest types; engaged in research, often cooperatively with scientists both inside and outside government; and undertook tree cutting projects where such cuttings were necessary for human safety, fire hazard reduction, or for disease or

38. John Ise, *Our National Park Policy*, p. 206.

insect control. Current research includes studies of fire ecology and the effects of fire on the reproduction of such rare species as *Sequoia gigantea*.

In 1952, John D. Coffman was succeeded by his assistant Lawrence F. Cook. Subsequently, Cook had the title of chief of ranger activities, and Sture T. Carlson, another forester, was brought into the Washington office from Santa Fe as chief of forest park and wildlife protection. Forestry became part of the Division of Resource Management.

Over the years, many professional foresters have entered the Park Service as rangers. Some have risen to become superintendents of national parks and monuments as well as regional directors. In 1969, the deputy director of the Park Service was Harthon L. Bill, a forester, and the assistant director for operations was Robert B. Moore, also a forester.

CHAPTER 9

Education for the Profession

Instruction in forestry was available at a few universities in western Europe for a century before the first school of forestry was established in the United States. Although lectures in forestry and tree culture were given in twenty or more land-grant colleges in the United States during the last quarter of the nineteenth century, this instruction was not professional in character. Generally, the lectures were given by teachers of botany or horticulture and emphasized tree planting, farm woodland care, and the influence of forests on climate and streamflow.

Franklin B. Hough, special forestry agent in the Department of Agriculture and probably the most influential individual in inducing the federal government to undertake forestry work, had not been an advocate of technical training in forestry. In a paper written in 1883, he questioned the need for such instruction and doubted that graduates would find employment. Pointing out that neither the federal nor the state governments had systems of forest management requiring the services of foresters, he added that, even if a few railroad companies might employ foresters, he knew of no private estates where they might find engagements. In his opinion, the United States did not "for the present, and perhaps for many years to come, require a class of persons who have been specially trained to the degree that is deemed necessary in the better class of forest schools in Europe, because such persons could not find employment either in charge of public or private forests at the present time. . . ."[1]

Bernhard E. Fernow, who became head of the Division of Forestry in the Department of Agriculture in 1886, noted in his report for that year that there were no schools of forestry in the nation nor any regularly appointed chairs of forestry in any of the colleges and universities. Such instruction as was being given was only incidental to other courses in farm economics or horticulture.

1. "Forestry Education," paper presented at the American Forestry Congress, 1883.

But in the division's report for the following year, more definite information was given about the extent of forestry education being offered. Indeed, for that period, the number of institutions listed as providing instruction in forestry is impressive. They included the agricultural colleges at Cornell, Iowa, Massachusetts, Michigan, Missouri, and New Hampshire; the universities of North Carolina and Pennsylvania, and Yale. As early as 1873, Professor William Henry Brewer of the Yale Scientific School was giving lectures on forests and forestry, probably the first instruction of its kind to be offered in an American university. No mention was made in the report of the courses given at the University of Michigan as early as 1881.

These lecture courses were exemplified by one offered at the Pennsylvania State College starting in 1889. Given by William A. Buckhout, a professor of botany, the course was described in the following manner in the college catalog:

The instruction in forestry consists of lectures in connection with Hough's *Elements of Forestry*, during the spring semester of the senior year. At this time during the end of the course of a study the students are by their maturity and previous training fitted to consider profitably one of the scientific and economic subjects of the day. The value of forests for both climatic and economic considerations is treated of together with the best available methods for their consideration and conservation and replacement.

Although the availability of such lectures indicated a growing interest in forestry education, no curriculums were offered anywhere in the United States to prepare men for careers in forestry. Dr. Buckhout's pioneering instruction ended in 1906, when a Department of Forestry was set up at Penn State with Hugh P. Baker, a forestry graduate of Yale, as professor of forestry.

Viewed in the light of the present development of professional forestry education, one of the most singular proposals of the 1890s was Fernow's suggestion that forestry be taught at the Military Academy at West Point. In addition, he proposed that Congress authorize obligatory courses at the agricultural colleges and a postgraduate course in the Department of Agriculture. Commenting on this proposal years later, Herbert A. Smith wrote:

Fortunately, however, Congress did not find acceptable the recommendation for making West Point a forestry as well as a military academy and making national-forest administration an army job. On the other hand, neither did Fernow's plan make headway; and his acceptance in 1898 of the call to develop a professional school of forestry at Cornell, followed by the opening of the Yale School of Forestry two years later, started technical forestry education in the United States on the path which it has ever since pursued.[2]

First Professional Curriculum

Cornell University was the first institution of collegiate rank to offer a curriculum of professional education in forestry. Headed by Bernhard E. Fernow, the four-year curriculum led to the degree of Bachelor of Science in

2. "Forest Education before 1898," *Journal of Forestry*, vol. 32 (October 1934), p. 689.

Forestry (changed to Forest Engineer in 1902); it was centered in the New York State College of Forestry, which had been authorized by the state legislature in 1898.[3] The promising educational venture was short-lived, however, because the governor vetoed funds for the college in June 1903, and professional forestry education at Cornell abruptly ceased.

In 1900, Yale opened its renowned School of Forestry, which enjoys the distinction of being the oldest forestry school in continuous operation in the Western Hemisphere. Set up as a graduate school, it accepted only students with a bachelor's or comparable degree. The two-year curriculum led to the degree of Master of Forestry.

Henry S. Graves, first dean of the Yale University School of Forestry, wrote his personal recollections of the genesis of the school for an informal address that he gave in New Haven, probably late in 1942 or early 1943.

In 1898 Pinchot was appointed Chief of the Division of Forestry in the U.S. Department of Agriculture. In a few months I followed as Assistant Chief. He rented a house on Rhode Island Avenue. We lived together for two years. It was there that the idea of a Forest School at Yale was conceived. One of our greatest handicaps was the lack of trained foresters. A forest school had been started at Cornell in '98, but its Director was a German whose methods we did not like. We had our own ideas about training foresters, and the thought of associating Yale with the new undertaking appealed to us. George Seymour used to call on us from time to time. He was greatly interested and urged Pinchot to provide the funds for an endowment for the proposed forest school at Yale. I recall saying one evening to Pinchot: "If you and your family will give an endowment for a Forest School at Yale, I will go up and run it." This was in line with my usual modesty in suggesting my own name for positions. Little did I know then about procedures in appointing professors and Deans. In point of fact, however, the University had to take me because there was no one else in the country except a couple of Germans who were in our judgment impossible.[4]

The enthusiasm of Pinchot and Graves in this new venture in professional education apparently was not shared by President Arthur T. Hadley of Yale. In his address at the White House Conference of Governors in 1908, he reported: "When we first started our forestry school at Yale, eight years ago, things looked darker than they look now. It did not seem as though there was any interest in forestry at all. . . . Our fear in the establishment of that school was that there would not be demand enough for the graduates. . . ."[5]

In 1903, the University of Michigan and Michigan State College established forestry curriculums, as did the University of Maine, the University of Minnesota, and the Pennsylvania State Forest Academy at Mont Alto. The latter institution was different from the others in that it was created by the

3. In this same year, Carl A. Schenck began offering instruction in his Biltmore Forest School, which is discussed in detail in chap. 3.

4. Paper prepared for a meeting of The Dissenters, a literary group in New Haven (Graves Collection, Sterling Memorial Library, Yale University). The German director of the Cornell forestry school referred to by Graves was, of course, Bernhard Fernow. George Seymour was a patent attorney.

5. *Proceedings of a Conference of Governors in the White House, Washington, D.C., May 13-15, 1908* (1909), pp. 117-18.

state legislature especially to train foresters for the management of the commonwealth's forest reserves.

Three additional institutions started teaching forestry in 1904: Iowa State College, Harvard University, and the University of Nebraska, which offered forestry instruction in connection with horticulture, then later dropped it. In 1905, Colorado College started a course, but in 1934 it too was discontinued.

In 1906, Oregon State College and the University of Georgia began programs in forestry, and a year later, Pennsylvania State College, the University of Washington, and Washington State College. In 1909, the University of Idaho set up its forestry work.

By 1910, seventeen institutions of collegiate rank, together with the Biltmore "master" school, had started technical programs in forestry. Some curriculums were begun before a well-defined need for foresters actually existed. In truth, the development of forestry education was largely unplanned; colleges and universities entered the field in anticipation of needs that did not materialize until later. The fortuitous nature of the development is indicated by the establishment of two schools in Michigan, two in Pennsylvania, and two in Washington, whereas in other densely forested states, where foresters were already at work and more were needed, no educational facilities would be provided for years to come.

As one consequence of the precipitate increase in the number of schools, funds to sustain them were often less than adequate. Because of handicaps in finances, facilities, and teaching staff, forestry leaders were concerned about the ability of the schools to maintain, much less raise, the educational standards necessary for this new and expanding profession.

Conferences of Forestry Educators

In December 1909, Gifford Pinchot, then chief of the Forest Service, called the first national conference on forestry education, in Washington, D.C. A committee of five was appointed to study the kind of technical education and the standards of instruction needed to provide competent practitioners. At a supplementary conference in December 1911, delegates from sixteen Canadian and U.S. schools considered the provisional plan submitted by the committee, which was then requested to prepare a final report.

Henry S. Graves was chairman of this group whose report emphasized the need for high standards of "advanced professional training, to include not only a substantial general education but also a well rounded course in all branches of technical forestry." The report went on:

Upon the forest schools rests the responsibility not only of training men in technical forestry, but of creating a body of professional men who can formulate the principles and do the constructive work required by our conditions. The rapidity with which the science and practice of forestry develops, and the quality of the work done, will depend on how the forest schools meet their responsibility.[6]

Submitted in 1912, the report of the Graves committee made a notable contribution in that it set forth a standardized forestry curriculum. The tech-

6. "Standardization of Instruction in Forestry," report of the Committee of the Conference of Forest Schools, *Forestry Quarterly*, vol. 10 (1912), pp. 341-94.

nical courses basic to an education for the profession were specified. Of the total instructional time to be devoted to each, nearly half was to be centered on silvics, silviculture, management, and mensuration; more than a quarter of the time to forest utilization and products; and the balance to forest protection from fire, insects, and disease. Such "practical" subjects as the use of axe and saw, horsemanship, and camping and woods skills were deemphasized as part of a regular curriculum. Although the importance of practical field work was recognized, the committee assigned first priority to scientific, mathematical, and economic subjects as essential knowledge needed by the competent forester.

Advocated were courses in history, economics, English, and foreign languages, as well as in botany, geology, and adjunctive scientific subjects. "The educational requirements for training in professional forestry," the committee said, "should be at least equal to those for the other learned professions, such as civil and mechanical engineering, law, medicine, etc."[7]

Up to the period of World War I, twenty-four forestry schools had been established in the United States and twenty were still in operation. Most were in land-grant colleges and offered four-year undergraduate curriculums. Harvard and Yale had the only wholly graduate schools. Increasing employment opportunities in federal and state forestry work, coupled with the attraction of forestry to young men as a career, were creating demands for professional education that the colleges and universities were eager to fill.

Although the first two schools (Cornell and Biltmore, both of short life) were headed by German foresters, professional forestry education in the United States was characterized from the start by a fresh and independent spirit little influenced by the subject matter, teaching methods, and educational customs of western Europe. With the urgent need for training men for a profession just coming into existence and lacking educational traditions of its own, the early schools were quite different from their European prototypes. Forestry education, like the whole forest conservation movement, was markedly influenced by the crusading fervor of Gifford Pinchot. An essential goal of that crusade was to reverse the trend of timber destruction and to bring about the management of millions of acres of publicly owned woodland acquired and being acquired by the federal government and the states. Forestry educators entered into this program with a zeal that persists even seven decades later.

Moreover, during the first three decades of professional education, there was concentration on those subjects that best served American needs. For example, a major influence on all schools was the written examination given by the U.S. Civil Service Commission to recruit junior foresters for positions in the federal government. On approaching their graduation, students were encouraged to take the examinations, whether or not they aspired to careers in federal service, and many schools kept detailed records of the examination ratings of their graduates. A controlling, if unacknowledged, force in subject matter teaching was its contribution to the ability of students to pass examinations. The prestige of some schools was based on this factor.

7. Ibid., pp. 343–44.

A second national conference on forestry education was held December 1920 at New Haven under the auspices of the Yale University School of Forestry. James W. Toumey, chairman of the conference and dean of the Yale School of Forestry, pointed out certain educational weaknesses that had developed in some schools. Local needs had resulted in extended training in some subjects at the expense of others necessary to a well-rounded curriculum. Some basic preforestry courses were restricted or eliminated, and Toumey remarked that foresters were graduated lacking sufficient background in general educational subjects.

In general, the forestry educators believed that the schools should endorse standard requirements for graduation with a degree in forestry. Some went on record as convinced that the four-year undergraduate program was not enough; and representatives of the eastern schools were of the opinion that five years should be the minimum for professional forestry education. Specific recommendations were made for subjects and semester hours of credits for the Master of Forestry degree.

Education in Forestry, the proceedings of the conference, was published in 1922 as a bulletin of the Bureau of Education, then in the Department of the Interior. Although the conference was not notable for specific results, it kept the topic of education alive within the profession and resulted in a series of reports presented to the Society of American Foresters and published in the *Journal of Forestry*.

The Forestry Education Inquiry

In 1929, through the generosity of the Carnegie Corporation of New York, a grant of $30,000 enabled the Society of American Foresters to make a study of forestry education then being offered by twenty-five colleges and universities in the United States. Henry Graves was made director of the inquiry and Cedric Guise of Cornell, assistant director.

After three years of study, Graves and Guise presented the results of their investigations in the book *Forest Education*, published in 1932 by Yale University Press. The most thorough appraisal of the subject ever made in America, it brought together a wealth of information about employment, the kind of instruction required for a career, teaching staffs, facilities, finances, and the policies of the various schools. It described also the methods of instruction in foreign schools of forestry. Predictably, the bad consequences of the competitive and unplanned proliferation of new schools during the first three decades of the century showed up in deficient finances and unsatisfactory teaching staffs at many institutions. Funds and personnel, the investigators found, "were wholly inadequate to build up a first class preparation in forestry of professional grade. Apparently the colleges with which the schools are associated have no realization of what is involved in the preparation for a profession so broad and diversified as forestry."[8]

At a majority of the schools (as of 1931–32), the total annual budgets were under $50,000 each with less than ten teachers on the staff. Incredibly, the budgets were less than $10,000 each at eight of them, and twelve schools

8. P. 247.

had fewer than five teachers on their staffs. As Graves and Guise pointed out, "a much smaller number of schools, if well equipped, would be able to take care of the real demand for professional foresters."[9]

During their study, Graves and Guise declined to rate or grade the forestry schools as a measure of adequacy in meeting the requisites for educational preparation for the profession. They centered their efforts on identifying the essential requirements of forestry education and on setting forth the standards that should constitute the objectives of the professional school. Although ratings had been applied to education in other professions, Graves and Guise claimed that forestry was "not yet stabilized like medicine, law, and engineering."[10]

Nevertheless, some leaders in the profession disagreed with this viewpoint, believing that the inadequate schools were lowering the general level of forestry education, which, in any case, was of indifferent quality. Raphael Zon, outspoken editor-in-chief of the *Journal of Forestry*, was censorious of the schools, especially of the intellectual standing of their faculties. In 1927, he had proposed a grading of the schools as a stratagem (he called it a weapon) "to weed out the weak, encourage the strong, and raise the average level of all."[11] Another proponent of grading the schools was H. H. Chapman of Yale, who in 1934 undertook to do it.

The Rise of Accreditation

In December 1933, the Society of American Foresters embarked on its most momentous educational project to date. The society's Executive Council decided to classify the institutions offering professional instruction. For this purpose, a special study was undertaken by Chapman to provide the basis for adopting a list of approved schools and was completed in September 1935. Using the data provided by Chapman in *Professional Forestry Schools Report* published by the Society in 1935, the Council approved 14 institutions whose graduates were immediately eligible for admission into the society as junior members, the entering professional grade. Six additional institutions were listed as covering "the general field of professional forestry, but full approval was withheld because they did not meet fully the standards required for such approval."[12]

Accrediting for professional forestry education was thus applied for the first time in the United States. Chapman, who had been elected president of the Society of American Foresters, was made chairman of the Committee on Accrediting in 1936, and the periodic examination of forestry curriculums for the purpose of accreditation became a permanent function of the society. This activity is now carried on by the Committee for the Advancement of Forestry Education.

In 1933, the advent of the Civilian Conservation Corps created new and unprecedented needs for foresters. Whereas unemployment was then wide-

9. P. 246.
10. P. 248.
11. "Our Forest Schools," *Journal of Forestry*, vol. 25 (March 1927), pp. 252–56.
12. Pp. v–vi.

spread in some other professions—for example, in the several engineering specialties—in forestry the demand exceeded the supply, a condition brought about by the sudden requirement for foresters to supervise the expanding conservation work of the CCC and other government agencies. Schools of forestry, swamped with applications for admission, were quickly filled to capacity. Inevitably, new forestry curriculums were started—five during the 1930s. The number of undergraduate forestry degrees rose from 355 in 1933 to 502 in 1936 to 1,102 in 1939.

In the Society of American Foresters, the Division of Education, organized in 1935, viewed this increase in schools and enrollment with misgiving. As the government's emergency conservation work, which had stimulated the expansion, was intended to be a temporary expedient to provide public employment, the hiring of foresters was certain to slack off. Moreover, the twenty-four existing schools were deemed adequate to take care of the normal demand for foresters. Accordingly, the Division of Education deplored the establishment of new schools except where the need was clearly demonstrated and then only when the standards of professional instruction set by the society could be maintained.

Predictably, with the phasing out of the CCC camps and the onset of World War II, attendance in the schools dropped. Fall enrollment of undergraduates, which had reached a high mark of 6,067 in 1937, fell to a nadir of 503 in 1943.

In the intervening time, the society's work in accrediting forestry education, begun in 1935, continued with seven more institutions having been granted accreditation by 1939. During the previous year, a body known as the Joint Committee on Accrediting was created by the American Association of Land-Grant Colleges and State Universities and the National Association of State Universities. This Committee undertook to exercise a measure of control over the expanding practice of accrediting programs by the professional societies. One major criticism directed at some professional societies was their requirement of advance payment of fees before making institutional examinations. As the Society of American Foresters neither requested nor accepted payment for its accrediting work, having decided to finance such activities out of its own funds, the society did not come in for this particular criticism.

In 1942 and again in 1948, the society's Committee on Accrediting reexamined the curriculums at all forestry schools. Plans for the 1948 survey were set up in consultation with the Joint Committee on Accrediting. Twenty-five institutions were accredited.

In 1949, the functions of the Joint Committee on Accrediting were taken over by the National Commission on Accrediting. When, three years later, the National Commission asked all professional societies to perform their accrediting work cooperatively with the six regional educational associations, the Society of American Foresters with irenic promptness agreed to cooperate. As a consequence, relations between the society and the National Commission were cordial.

In 1969, the National Commission recognized thirty-four professional societies, including the Society of American Foresters, as accrediting bodies. In addition, the U.S. Office of Education recognizes the society as the sole accrediting agency for professional forestry education.

Post-World War II Adjustments

Immediately following World War II, attendance in the schools of forestry rose again. Fall enrollment of undergraduates was 571 in 1944; in 1948 it totaled 8,212. A major stimulus of the increase was the so-called G.I. Bill of Rights, which provided military veterans with educational benefits.

Because forestry had a popular appeal for the ex-service man, the schools were once more flooded with applications. Temporarily, their physical plants were barely able to meet the influx and their teaching staffs were barely adequate to maintain the necessary educational standards.

Four new schools were started soon after the end of the war, and more were in prospect. Again the Society of American Foresters attempted to put some reasonable restraint on the anticipated proliferation of forestry curriculums. In 1946, a resolution was adopted; as reaffirmed in 1957 it stated:

> In view of the capacity of existing schools of forestry in the United States to supply the demand for professional foresters, the Council of the Society of American Foresters recommends against the establishment of new schools or departments for professional training in forestry, unless there is a need not adequately met by the existing schools and unless such new schools or departments are effectively staffed, properly financed, and possessed of adequate facilities for professional education.[13]

Career opportunities rose and fell during the 1940s and 1950s, but generally they continued to be good. State forestry agencies as well as the federal government were recruiting forestry graduates in unprecedented numbers. In addition, industrial employment provided new and inviting careers, and hundreds of young foresters took jobs with the expanding pulp and paper companies. As more jobs opened in forestry, more high school graduates looked on the profession as likely to offer a challenging career, and applications for admission to the schools rose again. Undergraduate enrollment, which reached 8,212 in 1948, dropped to 4,909 four years later, then steadily climbed to 8,612 in 1961.

Seeking to capitalize on this burst of interest in forestry, some college administrators started new curriculums that in several instances were poorly planned, poorly financed, and poorly staffed. A few university executives took the precaution of inquiring of the Society of American Foresters as to the requirements in personnel and physical plant for a soundly based curriculum, and some declared that their institutions would strive for programs of high quality. But their main preoccupation appeared to be setting up programs cheaply with minimal concern for quality. When informed about the standards for accreditation, they usually did only those things required to meet the minimum criteria, conveniently postponing until an indefinite later time the implementation of their professed goals of excellence.

In more than one state, the procedure of orderly planning was bypassed when politicians rushed to endorse a new curriculum in a state-supported institution where a forestry curriculum was already being offered in another state-supported college. In a number of states where new schools were pro-

13. "SAF Policy Statement on New Forestry Schools," *Journal of Forestry*, vol. 55 (August 1957), pp. 609-10.

posed, existing schools with unused plant capacity or with facilities capable of expansion could have accommodated the additional students with less expense to the taxpayers than that of setting up new and competing curriculums. Fortunately, not all the proposals for new schools materialized, but enough of them did to create duplication of curriculums and competition for students, a condition hardly conducive to the systematic development of higher education or the growth of the profession.

Despite the policy on new schools adopted by the Society of American Foresters in 1946—a policy that was set only after careful consideration—fourteen new schools have since been established. Although the statement of policy was made available to university administrators known to be contemplating new schools, it had little effect, if any, on their decisions. In one case, it deterred a teachers college and in another case a small liberal arts college from starting degree programs in forestry. But why such colleges should ever have considered themselves qualified to inaugurate a degree program in a profession so soundly based on science and technology is difficult to understand, except perhaps by the minds of the academic executives concerned.

To be sure, in a few states where regional needs warranted them, new schools were justified. With these exceptions, the historical record of forestry education in America shows that the organization of curriculums has been a haphazard business. It shows further that in certain states decisions to start forestry programs were based less on demonstrated professional need than on local institutional rivalries. As a result of this system, or lack of it, forestry education suffers from a group of weak schools in institutions whose executives refuse to recognize weaknesses, or seeing them, are unable to do anything about them.

Of the fourteen new curriculums started in forestry since the close of World War II, only seven have qualified for accreditation.

In 1969, California had two state-supported programs in professional forestry; Illinois, two; Louisiana, three; Michigan, three; Texas, two; and Washington, two. Connecticut, Massachusetts, North Carolina, and Tennessee each had two professional schools also, though one was in a state-supported institution and one in a privately endowed university.

Forestry Education Reappraised

A conference of the heads of forestry schools was held at the University of Michigan in 1945. Its purpose was to discuss post–World War II developments in curriculums, degrees, and related problems faced by the schools. From this meeting arose the Council of Forestry School Executives, which has been an influence in advising and guiding the Society of American Foresters with respect to matters affecting education for the profession. This council proposed that the society make a study of forestry education similar to the one made by Graves and Guise in 1932.

In 1957, the Society of American Foresters received a grant of $39,500 from the Old Dominion Foundation in support of a new appraisal of professional education. This grant was supplemented by $17,000 contributed by the society, together with quarters, services, and facilities made available by the State University of New York College of Forestry at Syracuse University.

The objective of the project was to review the development of professional forestry education during the previous six decades, to analyze its current status, and to set goals for the future.

Samuel T. Dana, dean emeritus of the University of Michigan School of Natural Resources, was director of the project. He was assisted by Evert W. Johnson of the Auburn University School of Forestry. Their report, *Forestry Education in America—Today and Tomorrow*, was published in 1963 by the Society of American Foresters. Among the authors' conclusions and recommendations, the following are significant to this chapter:

- —Five years of college work are desirable for full professional undergraduate education in forestry.
- —Graduate work in forestry should follow after the student has received the first professional forestry degree.
- —Technical (subprofessional) training should be expanded. To be adequate, such programs should be not less than two academic years in duration, leading to the associate's degree.

Additional proposals were put forth for strengthening the accrediting procedure and for the advancement of forestry education generally.

Technical or subprofessional instruction in forestry was offered at several institutions during the first decade of the present century. Usually called ranger courses, their length varied from a few weeks to two years. They did not lead to a degree. Most were short-lived; none of the pioneer courses or schools exists today.[14]

It was not until 1912 that a technical school was founded that attained permanence. In that year, largely through the efforts of Dean Hugh P. Baker, the New York State College of Forestry at Syracuse established the New York State Ranger School at Wanakena. A subsidiary unit of the college, the school has continuously offered a one-year course and is the oldest institution for technician training in America.

In 1969, the Society of American Foresters listed nine schools that offered technical training for subprofessional work as forestry aide or forestry technician. Seven were two-year schools; two offered one-year courses.[15]

Professional Education Today

From 1900, when the first forestry degree was conferred (by Cornell), through 1968, a total of 42,560 undergraduate degrees was granted by American schools of forestry. In addition, 8,466 master's degrees and 1,285 doctorates were awarded.

In December 1969, fifty-four U.S. colleges and universities offered instruction in forestry and adjunctive curriculums leading to the bachelor's or master's degree. Of these, thirty-five were accredited by the Society of American Foresters. Of the remaining nineteen nonaccredited institutions, nine had been in existence for ten years or longer, during which period they had been

14. For an account of these early experiments in practical forestry education, see Samuel T. Dana and Evert W. Johnson, *Forestry Education in America*, chap. 7.

15. "Colleges and Universities in the United States Offering Instruction in Forestry," *Journal of Forestry*, vol. 67 (January 1969), pp. 79–80.

unable or unwilling to strengthen their programs in order in meet the accrediting criteria.

Five major curriculums were offered: general forestry, wood technology and utilization, range management, wildlife management, and forest recreation. One-half the number of students enrolled and one-half the degrees granted were in general forestry.

Undergraduate enrollment reached its peak in the fall of 1968, a total of 13,137, according to the Society of American Foresters. During that year, the number of degrees was the highest on record: bachelor's degrees, 1,963; master's degrees, 482; and doctorates, 129.

CHAPTER 10

Timber Famine Warnings: Prelude to Regulation

The identity of the person who first predicted a timber famine in the United States is unknown, but one of the earliest to do so was the Reverend Frederick Starr of St. Louis. In the report of the commissioner of agriculture for 1865, Starr's article, "American Forests, Their Destruction and Preservation," helped launch the forest conservation movement. Even if the country undertook a program of forest preservation, he believed that a full century might be required to raise an adequate supply of wood for all our wants. Among other things, he advocated research on how to manage forests and how to establish plantations, proposing that the experiments be undertaken by a government-endowed private corporation to avoid political interference and corruption. According to William N. Sparhawk, "That, more than likely, was the start of the movement for better forest management."[1]

In 1868, Joseph M. Wilson, commissioner of the General Land Office, predicted "that in forty or fifty years our own forests would have disappeared and those of Canada would be approaching exhaustion."[2]

In October 1889, at a combined meeting of The American Forestry Association and the Pennsylvania Forestry Association held in Philadelphia, Carl Schurz was a featured speaker. Lawyer, writer, newspaper editor, former senator, and former secretary of the interior, Schurz in his time was one of the best informed men in America. His widely publicized address carried this warning: "If the present destruction of forests goes on for twenty-five years longer, the United States will be as completely stripped of their forests as Asia Minor is today."[3]

Similar doomsayings had been voiced by other spokesmen during the last two decades of the nineteenth century and would be heard with increasing

1. "The History of Forestry in America," in U.S. Department of Agriculture, *Trees: The Yearbook of Agriculture*, p. 704.
2. General Land Office, *Report* (1868).
3. "Remarks of Hon. Carl Schurz before the American Forestry Congress," *Forest Leaves*, vol. 11 (December 1889), p. 121.

frequency during the early decades of the twentieth. President Theodore Roosevelt startled the White House Conference of Governors in 1908 by declaring: "We are over the verge of a timber famine in this country, and it is unpardonable for the Nation or the States to permit any further cutting of our timber save in accordance with a system which will provide that the next generation shall see the timber increased instead of diminished."[4]

President Roosevelt's warning carried weight because it was reinforced by the prestige of his high office. But the voice that was heard most often throughout the land was that of Chief Forester Gifford Pinchot. In 1910, he asserted that "the United States has already crossed the verge of a timber famine so severe that its blighting effects will be felt in every household in the land. The rise in the price of lumber which marked the opening of the present century is the beginning of a vastly greater and more rapid rise which is to come. We must necessarily begin to suffer from the scarcity of timber long before our supplies are completely exhausted."[5]

In *Forests and Men*, William B. Greeley credits Pinchot with having introduced the phrase "timber famine." Whether Pinchot actually coined the term is uncertain, but he was capable of it, for he ever sought the colorful, vigorous expression. Whenever he had a choice between a weak or a strong word, strength had it. He made a point of deliberately inserting what he called "force" words into his writings, especially his speeches. And his way of using such words was dramatic. At a crucial place in a speech, he would extend his long left arm; then, raising his right fist high, shaking it for emphasis, he would bring it smashing down into his left palm. He was always conscious of the effective gesture, and had a natural gift for vivid speech and sinewy writing.

Regulation: The Hoped-for Solution

Numerous and imaginative were the proposals made over the years for solving the problem of forest devastation. But one gained early support and persisted until well past the time when the problem it was designed to solve no longer existed. This proposed solution was public regulation[6] of private forest management, or, in other words, silviculture by law.

In a paper published in 1909,[7] Pinchot listed five obstacles to private forestry, which are summarized below:

1. Low stumpage prices hold down forest values and create indifference to them. (Pointing out that the then prevailing cheap stumpage discouraged expenditures for protection and management, Pinchot admitted that while higher stumpage prices would not guarantee the

4. *Proceedings of a Conference of Governors in the White House, Washington, D.C., May 13-15, 1908*, p. 9.

5. *The Fight for Conservation*, p. 15.

6. Regulation, as used throughout this chapter, means the control of forest management by the exercise of public authority. It is not intended to connote that branch of forestry concerned with the technical (as opposed to the business and administrative) aspects of organizing a forest for sustained yield.

7. "Forestry on Private Lands," *Conservation of Natural Resources, The Annals of the American Academy of Political and Social Science*, vol. 33 (May 1909), p. 8.

practice of forestry, they would justify the outlay without which forestry is not practicable. Stating a basic tenet of forest economics, he added, "Ultimately a tree must sell for what it costs to grow plus the grower's profit.")

2. The profits of forestry are lower than those offered by most investments in the United States.

3. A desire for quick returns rather than long-time investments is another bar to the practice of forestry in the United States.

4. The great danger of destructive forest fires often forces private forest owners to rush their timber to market.

5. In the minds of most large stumpage holders the most serious obstacle to conservative lumbering lies in a faulty system of forest taxation.

Within four decades, these five obstacles to private forestry had largely been hurdled. But during the early years of the twentieth century, they were hindrances to private forestry of such magnitude that Pinchot's proposed solution was, characteristically, direct legislative action. He proposed that forestry be promoted on private lands by two kinds of legislation—laws that would encourage and laws that would control.

Under legislation that would encourage, he called for state laws for improved fire control and for a reduction of excessive taxation. Forest fires were allowed to burn long after the people had means to stop them, he explained.

Under legislation that would regulate, he called for state laws (at this date he did not advocate federal law) that, while not depriving a forest owner of his property, would restrict him in the use of it, if such use would impair or destroy "the efficiency of forests needed to protect the land or water resources." He went on: "If the public interest requires that forests should be maintained without the possibility of beneficial use by the private owner, the state itself should take the property over, of course with due compensation."[8]

This was the proposal around which controversy would swirl for the next half-century.

In a companion paper, Henry S. Graves supported Pinchot's prescription of a dose of legal medicine for curing the ills of forestry. Graves's opinion was that "state regulation of private forests should be confined to restricting the use of fire and to requiring a reasonable organization of the forests for protection, and should not be extended to governing the methods of cutting; that the protection of watersheds should be accomplished by the establishment of public forests; and that the problem of the future timber supply may be solved effectively by means of the public forests supplemented by forestry practiced on private lands under state encouragement and co-operation."[9]

In 1919, Frederick E. Olmsted, president of the Society of American Foresters, appointed a Committee for the Application of Forestry. Pinchot was named chairman of the committee, which was instructed "to recommend

---

8. Ibid., p. 11.
9. "Public Regulation of Private Forests," *Conservation of Natural Resources*, p. 2.

action for the prevention of forest devastation of privately owned timber-lands in the United States."[10]

In its report, the committee declared that "within less than fifty years, our present timber shortage will have become a blighting timber famine." One of the report's key recommendations was that the federal government should be authorized "to fix standards and promulgate rules to prevent the devasta-tion and to provide for the perpetuation of forest growth and the production of forest crops on privately owned timberlands for commercial purposes." In short, the committee came out for direct federal control of cutting practices on private woodlands to be administered by the Forest Service. (Farm woods were exempted.)[11]

It was hardly surprising that this would be the committee's recommenda-tion, since Pinchot's views were well known in advance. President Olmsted, a Forest Service official, was himself a strong advocate of direct federal regula-tion.

A group of society members opposed the proposal for mandatory regula-tion to be enforced by the federal government. They held the opinion that regulation, if necessary (and they thought it probably was), could be better achieved through cooperation under the auspices of the states. This, in general, was the opinion also of William Greeley, soon to succeed Henry Graves as chief of the Forest Service. Within the forestry profession, as repre-sented by the Society of American Foresters, the members were divided.

In 1920, the membership of the society totaled only 500. So small an organization could hardly be strong in a political sense or effective in swaying public opinion. But forestry was gaining recognition as a profession and the society had some standing as the voice of professional opinion. Understand-ably then, Chairman Pinchot, supported by President Olmsted, hoped that his committee's recommendations would be adopted as the society's policy. If so adopted, Pinchot had outside publicity facilities, notably the National Con-servation Association, to bring them to the attention of the public.

But the members were in no mood to accept the committee's recom-mendations, which were submitted in January 1920 at the society's annual meeting in New York City. Although the membership at large was opposed to devastation of private forest lands, the proposed method of preventing devas-tation precipitated controversy. And however much members of the Society respected Pinchot as its founder and first president, some were critical of his having distributed reprints of the report to newspapers and the general public before the members saw it. He himself later in life conceded that he had a tendency to act impetuously, that he sometimes hurt the feelings of his friends by taking "a bullheaded course." This was one of those times.

Among Pinchot's friends in Congress was Senator Arthur Capper of Kansas, a newspaper and farm journal publisher with a sincere concern about the nation's natural resources. In May 1920, he introduced a Senate bill that included the recommendations of the Pinchot Committee for the Application

10. "Report of the Committee for the Application of Forestry, Society of American Foresters," *Journal of Forestry*, vol. 17 (December 1919), p. 899.
11. "Forest Devastation: A National Danger and Plan to Meet It," *Journal of Forestry*, vol. 17 (December 1919), p. 899.

of Forestry. A salient provision of the bill called for the formation of a federal forest commission that would supervise timber cutting on private holdings. This bill had the immediate backing of Pinchot and of the National Conservation Association.

A brief digression is in order to identify the National Conservation Association. It was organized by Pinchot in 1909 as a medium for influencing public opinion to put into practical effect the conservation principles declared by the Conference of Governors at the White House in May 1908. He hoped that it would attract a membership of from 50,000 to 100,000. Charles W. Eliot, retiring president of Harvard, was the first president, to be succeeded by Pinchot himself within a few months when he was discharged as chief of the Forest Service by President Taft in 1910. Largely a one-man organization, the association had a board of directors selected by Pinchot. Among them were James R. Garfield, Roosevelt's secretary of the interior, and Henry L. Stimson, later to be appointed secretary of state and still later of war. Harry Slattery, a former private secretary to Pinchot, served as secretary of the board until the association ceased operations in June 1923 when it was consolidated with The American Forestry Association.

Membership never reached the numbers expected by Pinchot. Indeed, the maximum seems to have been less than 2,500. Its magazine, *American Conservation*, went through six issues and then stopped publication. Financial support came mostly from Pinchot's personal funds, with some assistance from his brother Amos and a few well-to-do friends. This, then, was the National Conservation Association that got behind the Capper bill with salvos of publicity.

Graves, then chief of the Forest Service, had been an early and consistent proponent of public regulation of private forest management, but with an important qualification. He favored regulation by the states, not by the federal government, the position originally taken by Pinchot when he first began public discussion of the need for such control in the public interest. In the *Journal of Forestry* (December 1919), Graves described the problem as one in which the federal government should provide leadership by working "through and in cooperation with the States. The legislation affecting the private owner in the matter of protection and continuance of forests should be by the States." That was certainly plain enough.

In 1920, Graves resigned as chief of the Forest Service to return to Yale University as dean of forestry. He was succeeded by Greeley, a Yale graduate and career forest officer, who had entered the Forest Service in 1904, had served in national forests in the West, and had performed distinguished duty as a lieutenant colonel in the Forestry Division of the American Service of Supply during World War I.

Who Shall Do the Regulating?

Greeley had hardly warmed his predecessor's chair before requests began to come in for a clarification of the government's regulation program. His annual report for 1920 outlined the policy of the Forest Service. He made plain his conviction "that the problem of halting forest devastation is fundamentally a national, not a local, problem, and must be faced and handled as such." But it was his belief also "that the speediest, surest, and most equitable action can be secured through dependence on the police powers of the States for the enforcement of such reasonable requirements as should be made of private owners and on the State governments for providing organized protection of private lands against fire." Recognizing that federal leadership and federal aid would be needed, he said, "It should be obligatory upon private owners to apply the safeguards necessary to prevent devastation." Finally, he got to the heart of the matter as he saw it by declaring that the first and most essential step was nationwide protection from forest fires.[12]

We must remember that most people who thought about the forest problem realized the urgency for improvement in the management of all private woodlands, including industrial holdings. Clearly, there was need for improvement in the prevention and control of fire, insects, and disease losses, in taxation, and in research. Conservation organizations, such as The American Forestry Association and state forestry associations, also advocated substantial increases in the acreage of publicly owned forests. Another need, frequently voiced in forestry meetings, was for more energetic cooperation between federal, state, and private agencies.

It must be remembered also that, by 1920, advances had been made in forestry technology so that elementary protection, management, and silvicultural practices could be undertaken with confidence. Foresters were ready and able to apply the research findings of the federal forest experiment stations, the state agricultural experiment stations, the forestry schools, and industry. But there was need for a comprehensive government policy, adequately financed, to stimulate the application of forestry in its many and varied aspects. Thus, the regulation approach was only one of the several currently put forward as solutions to the national forest problem. But it was the most controversial.

To return to the Capper bill—a key provision of the bill would have put timber cutting on private land under the supervision of the federal government. Later versions varied in the methods by which the federal authorities would exercise control, but the principle of direct government administration remained in them.

To combat this proposed legislation, which was unacceptable to industry and which some corporation lawyers believed to be unconstitutional in any case, a new task force entered the arena. This was a group of individuals who late in 1920 organized the National Forestry Program Committee. The committee's object was to promote legislation that would coordinate the several plans to assure an adequate and permanent timber supply.

A bill drawn up by this committee emphasized the responsibility of the federal government in general, as well as in specific terms. Greeley said that it "put Uncle Sam in the role of educator and co-operator rather than that of police officer."[13] While avoiding federal regulation, the bill authorized federal funds to assist states that passed laws requiring private owners to manage their woodlands so as to keep them permanently productive. Introduced by

12. U.S. Forest Service, *Report of the Forester* (1920), p. 1.
13. *Forests and Men*, p. 103.

Congressman Bertrand H. Snell of New York in December 1920, the bill was supported by Chief Forester Greeley.

Greeley's deep-seated opposition to the use of federal police powers to force private landowners, especially industrial owners, to comply with governmental standards of forest practices is nowhere better illustrated than in his letter of November 20, 1920, to the president of the Western Forestry and Conservation Association.

I take it as unnecessary to further emphasize the general position of the Forest Service—that the task of keeping our forest lands productive should not be attempted by federal control of forest industries or of the use of private property, but rather through the encouragement of local initiative; that the prevention of forest fires, the disposal of slashings, and the control of cuttings where necessary to keep timberland productive should be dealt with by state agencies and under the police powers of the states; and that the function of the federal government should be to cooperate with money and with brains as far as it can command either, to work out the standard and necessary requirements applicable to each forest region, and to bring about their adoption as far as it can through its cooperative relationship.[14]

Pinchot opposed the Snell bill. He was convinced that even if the federal government assisted the states financially to keep private lands productive, state laws would be weak, either in language or execution, because powerful lumber interests would control the legislatures. The Snell bill failed to pass. The Capper bills failed even to reach the floor of the Senate for vote.

In March 1920, Pinchot accepted appointment as commissioner of forestry for the Commonwealth of Pennsylvania. Two years later he successfully campaigned for the governorship, and served from 1923 to 1927. Thus, for a period of seven years he was occupied largely with political affairs, for the most part on the state level, and his conservation interests were subordinated to them. While he was still adamant in his belief in the necessity for federal regulation of the forest products industry, he had little time to promote his views on the national scene or to lobby for the cause.[15]

Meanwhile, in 1923, at the motivation of Greeley, Senator Charles L. McNary of Oregon sponsored a Senate resolution for the appointment of a Select Committee on Reforestation to investigate problems relating to reforestation for the purpose of establishing a comprehensive national policy for lands chiefly suited for timber production. This policy would be designed to insure a perpetual supply of timber for the citizens of the United States. Under the senator's chairmanship, the committee held twenty-four hearings all over the country and accumulated a mass of testimony. A native of the Douglas-fir region and a tree planter, he had more than a casual interest in forestry, because forest products constituted the most valuable industry in his state's economy.

14. Western Forestry and Conservation Association Papers (Oregon Historical Society Library, Portland).

15. During Pinchot's two terms as governor of Pennsylvania (1923–27 and 1931–35), he proposed that the General Assembly regulate public utilities and the liquor industry but made no fight for forest regulation in the Commonwealth. For a well-documented account of his political career, see Nelson M. McGeary, *Gifford Pinchot*.

Greeley saw to it that the committee, everywhere it went, heard a succession of landowners who emphasized that the universal risk to growing trees was fire. Witnesses testified that after fire, the worst handicap was the tax burden.

When the committee submitted its report in 1924, it avoided the controversial issue of regulation and proposed a two-pronged attack on the problems it was set up to investigate. It recommended that public forest ownership be extended where special public interests required it, and that commercial reforestation be encouraged by the removal of risks such as fire.

But even before the report had been submitted to Congress, Senator McNary introduced a bill incorporating its recommendations. A similar bill having been introduced in the House of Representatives by Congressman John Davenport Clarke of New York, the two became the Clarke–McNary Act of June 1924. Recognizing that protection from fire is the basis of forestry, the law established a three-way cooperative approach by the federal government, the state governments, and private woodland owners.

"The diversion of Gifford Pinchot's interest to a new arena in Pennsylvania politics left the supporters of forest regulation without a leader," Greeley commented later. "They made no fight against the new and popular proposal from the West. It was ten years before federal control of logging practices was heard from again."[16]

The Attack Renewed

But Greeley was dead wrong in saying that ten years would elapse before federal control of logging practices would be heard from again. When Pinchot finished his term as governor of Pennsylvania in January 1927, he promptly resumed active participation in conservation, including vigorous agitation for federal regulation. In this renewed crusade, he had a new ally.

Lt. Colonel George P. Ahern, a career army officer, developed an interest in forestry early in life. As a young lieutenant in Montana in 1894, he gave lectures on forestry at the State College at Bozeman. During the first decade of the present century, he set up the administration for forestry in the Philippines. Appointed head of the Philippine Bureau of Forestry in 1900, he obtained advice from Pinchot, who visited Ahern in the Islands in 1902, and together they inspected the forests. Although Ahern had no professional education in forestry, he was a seasoned administrator who respected technical competence and who in turn was respected by the foresters who knew him and his work in the Philippines.

On returning to the United States in the 1920s following his retirement from the army, he delved into forest conditions resulting from the operations of the forest products industry. What he saw shocked him. In 1928, he published a bulletin entitled *Deforested America* with a foreword by Pinchot, who had provided Ahern with information and ideas. Ahern denounced the lumber companies for "ghastly forest devastation" but also accused the Forest Service and Greeley, its chief, with complacency while destructive logging went on unabated.

16. *Forests and Men*, p. 109.

With Pinchot's help, financial and otherwise, *Deforested America* was mailed by the thousands to newspapers, schools, legislators, foresters, and the general public. Senator Capper arranged for 10,000 copies to be printed as a Senate document; many were mailed at government expense under the senator's frank.

Since the Committee for the Application of Forestry had failed to achieve its goal, the Society of American Foresters tried again in 1928 by appointing a carefully selected Committee on Forest Policy under the chairmanship of Barrington Moore, a highly regarded forester and ecologist. Preliminary drafts of the committee's report were discussed at society gatherings, and comments on it were published in the *Journal of Forestry*. Dissatisfied with some of the proposals in the report, Pinchot and Ahern drafted a dissenting minority report for presentation at a meeting of the society in Des Moines in December 1929, and at the same time released it to the press.

In their minority report, "The Cure for Forest Devastation," Pinchot and Ahern charged that the majority report was not vigorous in opposing forest devastation and in demanding that it be stopped.

H. H. Chapman, professor of forest management at Yale, later to become president of the Society of American Foresters, was one of the best known and most articulate foresters in America. His comment on the forest policy proposed by Ahern and Pinchot was forthright and pragmatic: "In thirty years I have failed to discover any really effective plans by which private devastation could be stopped by the passage of laws, except as economic conditions and public cooperation combined to secure fire protection and tax reform."[17]

Then, in a typical Chapman affirmation, labyrinthian and prophetic, he added:

I will stake my entire professional experience, judgement, and reputation on the statement that I consider the substitution of an attack on large forest owners and a drive for a national law to stop devastation by force, in place of a drive to consolidate and save the integrity and efficiency of the Forest Service, the keystone of the arch of forestry in this country, to be a cardinal error of strategy which will defeat the very ends for which it may ostensibly be striving.[18]

The annoyance of some society members at the public release of the Pinchot-Ahern opinions before the society's official report was completed was nothing compared with the wrath of the lumbermen, who promptly challenged the dissenters. Wilson Compton, secretary of the National Lumber Manufacturers Association, an economist, and an articulate spokesman for the industry, wrote a pamphlet in rebuttal entitled *Reforested America*.[19] Compton defended the industry's expanding practice of forestry, asserting that the Clarke–McNary policy of cooperation between the federal and state governments and private owners was advancing the application of good forest

17. Manuscript, December 12, 1929 (Henry S. Graves Collection, Sterling Memorial Library, Yale University).
18. Ibid.
19. Published by the National Lumber Manufacturers Association, 1929.

management. He protested that the Ahern publication was deceptive propaganda and that Pinchot's proposal for direct federal regulation would substitute compulsion by law for the voluntary cooperation that was producing results.

But the controversy really became heated when *American Forests* magazine, published by The American Forestry Association, ran an advertisement in its February 1929 issue. Through this ad, the National Lumber Manufacturers Association offered free copies of Compton's *Reforested America* to readers who would write for them. Pinchot dispatched an angry letter to Ovid Butler, the editor, protesting the use of the magazine "for the dissemination of propaganda intended to facilitate the continued destruction of American forests."[20] Privately, he complained that the association was controlled by lumbermen.

Wilson Compton, with whom the author had numerous conversations on forestry matters over a period of two decades, was sincere enough in his advocacy of increased application of silviculture by industry. But in defending its expanding practice, he was defending what he hoped would occur, not a contemporary happening. Actually, little industrial forestry other than fire control and reforestation was practiced during the 1920s. Proponents of regulation had ample justification for their belief that public control of private cutting practices would be needed in addition to protection against fire, the first essential. In April 1944, the National Lumber Manufacturers Association would adopt a declaration that recommended:

Timber cutting and forest practice rules for continuous forest production, based on the tested experience of forest owners, adapted to conditions in the state and suitable for incorporation into a forestry code to be administered under appropriate state laws; and
Where necessary, the establishment or further strengthening of an agency under state law, qualified to administer and enforce the above fire laws and forestry code.[21]

In an open "Letter to Foresters" in the *Journal of Forestry* (April 1930) seven proponents[22] of the regulation movement called on the profession to face squarely the problem of forest devastation. "The forests of America were never in more peril than at this moment. We are headed toward forest bankruptcy. What forestry there is on private lands is too little to exert the slightest effect on the problem of our future forests." Rejecting any form of public control other than federal, the group asserted: "The forest problem is a national problem. It cannot be solved without federal regulation. There is a wide and unquestioned field for state regulation, but it is idle to rely on independent action by forty or more states in time to save our forests."

Four prominent spokesmen for private forest enterprise, all former Forest Service officers, took issue with Pinchot and the others. R. C. Hall, a forester

    20. "Pinchot Protests Lumbermen's Advertisement," *American Forests*, vol. 35 (April 1929), pp. 240–42.
    21. Clarence Korstian, *Forestry on Private Lands in the United States*, p. vi.
    22. George P. Ahern, Robert Marshall, E. N. Munns, Gifford Pinchot, Ward Shepard, W. N. Sparhawk, and Raphael Zon.

with special competence in timber valuation, claimed that "since in most regions fire prevention alone will stop forest destruction, let foresters keep up the fight on that line until forest property is insurable at reasonable rates."[23] Royal S. Kellogg, the forest industry association executive, objected to the Pinchot supporters using the Society of American Foresters as an institution for propaganda and the advancement of personal theories of public policy. Others also registered objections.

Within the Society of American Foresters, a group of members loyally supported Pinchot's views on the necessity of federal regulation to prevent nationwide forest depletion. And there was another group that did not. Henry Graves, for example, who two decades earlier had proposed regulation by the states, was of that opinion still and did not associate himself with the Pinchot-Ahern minority report. Likewise, Pinchot's close friend and old Forest Service colleague, Herbert A. Smith, declined to subscribe to it.

In seeking to analyze the motives of those who took a stand against federal regulation, one risks the hazard of oversimplification. If most of the foresters were opposed to federal control, they were not, per contra, condoning the destruction resulting from wasteful logging that had been traditional with the lumber industry, and by and large still was. Only a few lumber companies were attempting to harvest their timber in accordance with minimum silvicultural standards. Their transition from the practice of timber mining to forest cropping was proceeding with discouraging slowness. But progress, however gradual, was indeed being made.

The trouble with the rate of progress, as Pinchot saw it, was that it was too gradual to ward off the coming timber famine. But the bogey of timber famine was ceasing to be a pivotal issue and was even becoming an embarrassment. Some of the most zealous advocates of federal regulation—Robert Marshall and Raphael Zon, for example—had dropped it from their arguments. They continued to defend federal rather than state control because of their conviction that federal rules would be enforced more strictly and impartially than state rules, which they believed would be dictated in any case by the industry operators.

In 1931, three years after the Society of American Foresters had set up the Committee on Forest Policy, the committee's report was submitted to the members, who approved it by letter ballot. One feature of the report was a provision for public control of private forest exploitation. A majority of those voting endorsed public control, but favored state rather than federal supervision.

A New Plan for Forestry

When William Greeley resigned as chief of the Forest Service in 1928, Herbert A. Smith wrote "an appreciation and interpretation" of Greeley's eight years in office. In commenting on Greeley's attitude on the regulation issue, he wrote that "at the present time the idea of compulsion has been almost completely superseded by that of persuasion, education, and depen-

23. "Observations on the Letter," *Journal of Forestry*, vol. 28 (April 1930), p. 461.

dence on economic conditions plus a voluntary acceptance by the lumber industry of public responsibilities for maintaining productiveness."[24]

Robert Y. Stuart, another career forest officer, succeeded Greeley in May 1928. During the forepart of Stuart's five years in office the regulation issue was quiescent. His administration was notable for the publication of the most important document on forestry policy up to that time. This was the monumental report *A National Plan for American Forestry*, submitted in March 1933 by Henry A. Wallace, secretary of agriculture. It was compiled in response to a senate resolution of the previous year by Senator Royal S. Copeland of New York, a physician turned politician with interests in parks and education.

According to Stuart, the Copeland report was the most comprehensive and exhaustive survey yet made of the forestry situation. Among its many recommendations, two were salient: a huge increase in public ownership of forests and more intensive management of public woodlands. The report had been prepared by the Forest Service, largely under Earle H. Clapp's direction. Significantly, public regulation was mentioned in the report, but not as one of Secretary Wallace's recommendations. Under Stuart, as under Graves and Greeley, Forest Service policy supported the principle of encouraging the states to pass laws to control devastation on private lands.

Franklin D. Roosevelt was elected president in November 1932. In January 1933, prior to the presidential inauguration, Governor Pinchot went to Hyde Park to discuss a national forestry program that Roosevelt had asked Pinchot to develop. Because he had been out of direct touch with national conservation matters since his second governorship campaign (that is, for a couple of years), Pinchot sought assistance from Robert Marshall.

Marshall had helped the Forest Service write *A National Plan for American Forestry*. No member of the forestry profession more zealously advocated public control of sufficient forest area to safeguard the public interest in the forest products industries' raw material supply. In a pamphlet, *Social Management of American Forests*, published in 1930 by the League for Industrial Democracy, Marshall urged complete public ownership of all forest lands except farm woodlots, plus rigorous federal regulation pending the consummation of this program. A membership society in New York City, the league engaged in education toward a social order based on production for use, not for profit. Among other activities, it conducted research, sponsored lectures and conferences, and in general promoted sentiment for increasing social control of natural resources. Noman Thomas, Stuart Chase, and H. S. Raushenbush were among its pamphleteers. Marshall was in sympathy with its aims and quite at home among its followers.

Interestingly enough, the program proposed to Pinchot by Marshall was not original with him. It originated with Raphael Zon, director of the Lake States Forest Experiment Station at St. Paul. A Russian immigrant, Zon had taken a forestry degree at Cornell in 1904 and had since been in the Forest

24. "William B. Greeley: An Appreciation and Interpretation," *Journal of Forestry*, vol. 26 (April 1928), p. 428.

Service, mainly in research. A member of the Pinchot coterie, he and Marshall had similar liberal economic and social views.

Marshall called on Governor Pinchot in Harrisburg on January 12, 1933, returned with a draft of a recommended program on January 19, and described the results of his meeting in a letter to Zon on January 23. This letter contained a paragraph that reveals how national policies are sometimes influenced.

I discussed with Pinchot some of the things which you and I have been talking about, mentioned your four point program, and gave him my viewpoint that it seemed to me the two things we should stress were public ownership and forestry through unemployment work. I tried to emphasize that we weren't concerned only with devastation, which does not apply to more than fifty-five million acres of private lands, but deterioration which affects at least twice that area. I also argued him out of regulation with surprising ease.[25]

Pinchot sent Roosevelt "facts and suggestions concerning the forest problem" on January 20, 1933. With minor alterations and deletions, the statement was substantially as prepared for him by Marshall. This was his comment on regulation:

Federal regulation would be difficult to apply when the majority of timberland owners are bankrupt, or verging on it. If they ever become rich and powerful again it would be equally difficult to keep them from controlling the agency which regulates them.
Private forestry in America, as a solution of the problem, is no longer even a hope. Neither the crutch of subsidy nor the whip of regulation can restore it. The solution of the private forest problem lies chiefly in large-scale public acquisition of private forest lands.[26]

The New Deal Approach

On May 29, 1933, while the National Industrial Recovery Bill was pending in Congress, a memorandum, "Ending Forest Devastation Through Industrial Control," was sent to President Roosevelt by Ward Shepard, then a fellow of the Carl Schurz Foundation of Philadelphia. Shepard was a former assistant chief of research in the Forest Service who had recently made a study of the administration of forest regulatory laws in Austria, Czechoslovakia, and Germany. Contending that public regulation to prevent devastation was feasible, he cited the successful experience of certain western European nations as promising for similar application in America. He wrote:

It is claimed that the lumbermen will capture the regulatory machinery, but the same can be said of railroad, public utility, or other forms of regulation. If this claim were true, the Government should renounce every effort to regulate industry and could not possibly justify the Industrial Recovery Act. But the claim is untrue and a negation of government.
The Federal Government has constitutional power to prevent the devastation of forests needed to protect the flow of navigable streams. The states

25. Edgar B. Nixon (ed.), *Franklin D. Roosevelt and Conservation, 1911-1945*, vol. 1, p. 132.
26. Ibid., p. 130.

have legal authority to prevent the waste or destruction of natural resources, including forests, as confirmed by court decision and as carried out in laws, for example, to prevent the waste of oil and gas. Still more direct, the Government has the power to enforce forest management as a condition to the granting of licenses to operate under the Industrial Control Bill.[27]

The Shepard memorandum was referred to Secretary of Agriculture Henry Wallace, who replied on June 15, 1933. Wallace asked for the president's sanction of two policies:

1. Approval of the principle of regulation of privately-owned forest lands in connection with the administration of the Industrial Bill and the Agricultural Adjustment Act. . . .
2. The delegation to the Secretary of Agriculture of the necessary authority to administer for the lumber and other forest industries the provisions of the Industrial Bill relating to or closely allied to the treatment of forest lands.[28]

Secretary Wallace's memorandum to the president was accompanied by a supporting statement containing the department's opinions on the proposals for public regulation and its administration. This memorandum had been prepared following a discussion between Shepard and Chief Robert Y. Stuart of the Forest Service. It contained this conclusion: "In the judgment of the Department, no additional legislation on the regulatory phase is required at the present time. It will be better first to try out administration under the Industrial Relief Bill [sic] and the Agricultural Act and be guided accordingly."[29]

Anticipating the enactment of the National Industrial Recovery Bill, Secretary Wallace on June 16 sent another message to the president. He repeated his request of the previous day that he be delegated authority, under the act when passed, to deal with the lumber and other forest industries through agreements and licenses and also through codes of practice and agreements. His argument was that, since the act made provision for the conservation of natural resources, the government should insist on "the principle of preventing forest destruction on private lands and keeping them productive by requiring sustained yield management and satisfactory silviculture and protection as a quid pro quo for the curtailment of output, etc."[30]

The National Industrial Recovery Act of June 16, 1933, was passed by Congress to speed up economic recovery from the effects of the Great Depression. Through the National Recovery Administration, all industry was to be ruled by codes. Under the act's aegis a Code of Fair Competition for the Lumber and Timber Products Industries was written by industry representatives and approved by the government. This Code contained ten articles covering such items as labor, production controls, prices, and conservation. One, commonly referred to as Article X of the Lumber Code, provided for the conservation and sustained production of forest resources. As encouraged

27. Ibid., p. 166.
28. Ibid., p. 172.
29. Ibid., p. 180.
30. Ibid., p. 181.

by Article X, rules of forest practice drawn up by a joint committee of public and private representatives were adopted by the industry.

The purpose of Article X was to secure the practice of forestry on private lands. Accordingly, the rules of forest practice as developed jointly by representatives of public and private agencies established minimum standards of management. These standards were devised to change the pattern of operation from one of wasteful, destructive cutting of timber to one of harvesting under permanent sustained-yield management. Under the Lumber Code Authority, the rules formulated for each forest region were to be binding on the operators in that region. Some operators submitted to the regional enforcement agencies plans that provided for a higher degree of management than required by the standard rules. Others agreed to follow the standard rules, but some made no declaration of intent at all. After June 1934, violators were to be subject to fines and even imprisonment. However, in May 1935, the Supreme Court declared the National Industrial Recovery Act unconstitutional.

Since such rules as had been adopted were in force less than a year, self-regulation by the industry under the Lumber Code never had a fair trial. But the educational benefits of the experiment continued. Several regional lumber trade associations expanded their efforts to improve the management of their members' lands. For example, foresters were hired by the Southern Pine Association, the West Coast Lumbermen's Association, and the Western Pine Association.

Through the influence of Greeley, then secretary-manager of the West Coast Lumbermen's Association, and other leaders in the Douglas-fir region, the Pacific Northwest Forest Industries created a permanent Forest Conservation Committee with professional foresters on its staff. Later, this committee was reorganized as the Industrial Forestry Association; its primary object is to promote private forestry in Oregon and Washington by stimulating improved protection and timber harvesting methods.

Stuart died in October 1933 and was succeeded in November by Ferdinand A. Silcox, a former Forest Service officer who left forestry after World War I to enter labor-industry counseling. As this was the first year of the New Deal, a political movement to which Silcox was dedicated, he promptly stepped up Forest Service action in regulation. His proposal was for a three-point program: (1) increased public ownership and management, (2) public cooperation with private owners, and (3) public regulation. Under the third point he advocated state regulation with federal participation, with a proviso for direct federal control if the states failed to pass and enforce adequate laws.

At the thirty-fourth annual meeting of the Society of American Foresters held in January 1935 in Washington, D.C., Chief Forester Silcox read a keynote paper, "Foresters Must Choose"—an address directed at a larger audience than those present. Claiming to represent the public point of view, he propounded the social theories of the New Deal in terms of employment, stable communities, and balanced land resources, all related to forestry and the forest industries.

Handsome, personable, articulate, and withal a forester's forester who had come up through the ranks, Silcox personified for that heady era the new and satisfying status of the professional forester as a man of action in a revolutionary movement. His was both a statement of principles and a call to foresters to adopt the "aggressive, crusading spirit" of the profession's youth. He urged his colleagues to join him "on the thrilling frontier where men battle for yet disputed principles."[31]

In his address, Silcox offered a "few basic principles as the creed of the new frontier to be conquered by our profession." The following brief quotations from these principles provided the essentials of the Forest Service's policy for almost two decades to come:

1. The primary objective of forestry is to keep forest land continuously productive. This must take precedence over private profit.
2. Forest devastation must stop, and forest practice must begin now, not in the nebulous future.
3. Public control over the use of private forest lands which will insure sustained yield is essential to stabilize forest industries and forest communities. The application of the required practices on private lands must be supervised by public agencies and not left to the industry.[32]

Moreover, he proposed two radical departures in previous Forest Service policy. He called for increased acquisition of federal and state forests to include merchantable timber with which to create sustained-yield units suitable for immediate utilization. He also recommended that the federal government and the states should enter the business of logging their own timber and manufacturing their own products, where necessary to maintain existing communities and permanent employment, or to produce cheap lumber for local needs.

Silcox devoted much of his official time to promoting public regulation. Greeley, a long-time friend, writing about this period in later years, said Silcox was disposed "to trade government aids in forestry for New Deal social and industrial aims." He added that "Silcox never offered specific legislation on forest regulation. His proposals were general and vague."[33] Whether Silcox would have eventually proposed specific legislation on this controversial issue will never be known.

When Silcox died suddenly in December 1939, there was considerable speculation about his probable successor. As Silcox had been an ardent New Dealer, it was understandable that no forester, however well-qualified professionally, would be acceptable unless he too was prepared to use the position to advance the Roosevelt social program.

Gardner Jackson, a Washington newspaperman specializing in labor and social welfare news, was a guest at a White House function shortly after Silcox's death. On December 19, 1939, he wrote to Mrs. Roosevelt, presumably at her request, reminding her of their recent conversation at the

31. *Journal of Forestry*, vol. 33 (March 1935), pp. 198–204.
32. Ibid.
33. *Forests and Men*, pp. 210, 212.

White House and proposing the names of four Forest Service officers for the position of chief. These, in the order of their listing, were Robert Marshall, Lyle F. Watts, Christopher M. Granger, and E. N. Munns.[34]

In his letter, Jackson quotes Raphael Zon as being opposed to Richard Rutledge, regional forester of the Intermountain Region at Ogden, Utah; Nelson C. Brown of the New York State College of Forestry, who was President Roosevelt's advisor on forestry at the Hyde Park estate; and E. W. Tinker, an assistant chief. Zon is quoted by Jackson as writing, "I need not tell you that the appointment of any of these three would be a calamity."

No one was appointed as Silcox's successor until January 1943, when Lyle F. Watts was selected. During the interim Earle H. Clapp, associate chief of the Forest Service since 1935, served as acting chief.

34. This letter is in the Conservation Library Center, Denver Public Library.

CHAPTER 11

The Continuing Battle for Regulation

Earle H. Clapp's demand for public regulation was, if anything, more vigorous than that of Silcox. "He organized all the resources of the Forest Service behind an unequivocal program," according to Greeley, "attempting even to command the personal support of service men in their local public relations."[1]

As if this program were not ambitious enough, Clapp proposed to increase the area of public forests by 224 million acres: 134 million acres of additional federal forests and 90 million acres of state forests. Thus, with some 88 million acres of commercial timber in state forests, his proposal would have resulted in putting into government ownership nearly half of the nation's commercial forests. This, he alleged, was necessary to safeguard the forest economy. It was also calculated to give government agencies economic control of the forest products industry, for, in controlling stumpage, the raw material, the government could effectively control logging and manufacturing.

In testimony before the Joint Congressional Committee on Forestry at several hearings during the early months of 1940, Clapp outlined a program that was as comprehensive as any that had been laid before the Congress and the American people up to that time. The program included public and private cooperation in every conceivable aspect of forestry, including financial credits. But its keynote was regulation, and on that controversial basis it never won complete acceptance.

Created in response to a special message to Congress in March 1938 from President Roosevelt, the Joint Congressional Committee on Forestry was pointedly directed to inquire into, among other things, "the need for such regulatory controls as will adequately protect private as well as the broad public interests in all forest lands." It was authorized in June 1938, with

1. *Forests and Men*, p. 212.

Senator John H. Bankhead II of Alabama as chairman. As was usual with such committees, this one was given a broad charter. It was asked to look into forest ownership and management, timber production and consumption, watershed protection and flood control, together with the "social benefits which may be derived from such lands."[2]

After extensive public hearings throughout the country, with hundreds of witnesses presenting testimony on all aspects of forest and related conservation, the committee submitted its report[3] to Congress in March 1941. Of fifteen recommendations, only one dealt with regulation. And it dealt with regulation in a peculiar way.

The committee recommended more federal aid to the states in fire prevention and control, provided the states would enact legislation "for proper State, county, and district fire protection and regulations governing minimum forestry practices to be administered as approved by the Secretary of Agriculture."[4] If any state subsequently failed to enforce standards of forestry practice deemed necessary by the secretary, its federal fire control funds would be withdrawn.

To be sure, private woodland owners would participate in determining the regulations of forestry practice and would have rights of appeal through regional boards or review agencies that would be established. Finally, the states were to have a period of from three to five years to enact legislation that would be satisfactory to the secretary.

On March 27, 1941, Ward Shepard, who was now a planning specialist with the Indian Field Service in the Department of the Interior, sent a memorandum to Secretary Ickes in which he called the committee's report "a weak compromise between sharply conflicting views of the Committee." He criticized it as "far short of what ought to be expected of this Administration," and mentioned two main defects, one of which was regulation.

The Committee fails to make an effective proposal on the all-important subject of public regulation of private forests. It recommends that the States adopt *minimum* regulations, and that if they fail to do so within five years, the Secretary of Agriculture *may* withdraw funds for fire protection and other forestry cooperation. . . . This proposal closely fits the strategy of the lumbermen in opposing effective Federal intervention against forest devastation, for they can hamstring effective State legislation.[5]

In April 1941, President Roosevelt asked Secretary of Agriculture Claude R. Wickard for his opinion on the Joint Congressional Committee's report. Wickard replied on May 12 that he also found the report defective.

Only two forms of attack on the private forest land problem afford positive assurance that the public interest in these forests will be safeguarded. The *first* of these forms is public regulation of forest practices. This is the most difficult job that has ever been faced in American forestry, and will

2. *Concurrent Resolution of March 14, 1938*, S. Con. Res. 31, 75 Cong., 3 sess., 1938.
3. *Forest Lands of the United States*.
4. Ibid., p. 29.
5. Edgar B. Nixon (ed.), *Franklin D. Roosevelt and Conservation, 1911-1945*, vol. 2, p. 495.

require for successful consummation the full backing and, I believe, the full strength and authority of the Federal government.

While the Committee, for the first time in the history of Congress, recognizes—and unanimously—the necessity to apply the principle of public regulation to forests, the plan proposed has serious structural weaknesses which in my judgement will jeopardize its success, and which are as likely to set the forestry movement back as to insure its progress.

For example: The plan turns the job of regulation over to the States, with Federal financial cooperation and approval of standards. The chief Federal penalty for failure of the States to act is mandatory withdrawal of funds for regulation and for fire protection. In some States strong industrial interests control the State machinery, and these are ordinarily hostile to regulation of forest practices. Control by industrialists is most likely to be exercised adversely in heavily forested States where the need for regulation is greatest, and in such States the result in the end might well be neither fire protection nor regulation.[6]

Replying to this memorandum on May 14, the president suggested that the secretaries of agriculture and interior "each appoint one representative from the outside—not a professional forester—to go into this whole subject and make a report to both of you within two or three months."[7]

Wickard wrote back on June 18, pointing out that finding the right man would not be easy. He suggested three names but said that he believed the problem was "one of political judgement," and asked, "How can we get the most favorable legislation when prevailing sentiment on the Hill is against public regulation?" His department favored "straight Federal regulation" and had tried to persuade the committee to back regulation. "For strategical reasons," he said, "we suggested a program under which the States would be given a chance to do the job with Federal aid, with the Department of Agriculture authorized to take over if any State failed to tackle it. Even this was too much for the committee. What course shall we now pursue?"[8]

For several reasons, this choice was a difficult one, as Wickard went on to explain in his memo:

Shall we ask Congress for straight Federal regulation; or shall we, from consideration of States' relations and the sentiment on the Hill, stick with the present plan of asking for Federal regulation only on condition that the States fail to do the job? We have bills of both types prepared. One complicating factor is that Senator Bankhead has asked me to help him prepare a bill that hews to the line laid down by the Committee.

If we go directly after straight Federal regulation, what will be the effect on the Congress? If we ignore the Joint Committee's report I fear the reaction may be decidedly adverse. Somehow we must induce the Congress to modify and strengthen the report of its own committee, so we can count on help within the Committee itself. Several members, Pierce for example, are eager to take stronger action than their signatures on the report would indicate.[9]

6. Ibid., pp. 506-7.
7. Ibid., p. 510.
8. Ibid., pp. 518-19.
9. Ibid. The reference is to Congressman Walter M. Pierce of Oregon, who introduced a bill in 1941 that provided for direct federal control if a state failed to act.

Secretary Wickard sent another memorandum, dated August 11, to the president. "I have become convinced," he wrote, "that much will be lost unless we get an Administration measure on forestry—particularly on public regulation of present destructive cutting—introduced into Congress and enacted in the immediate future."[10] Considerations of national defense, preparations for possible war, and urgent foreign policy matters took precedence over this controversial domestic issue, and no action or guidance from the White House was forthcoming.

Moreover, an official in another powerful agency of government took an antiregulation stand. In 1941, James E. Scott was an officer of the Bureau of the Budget dealing with agriculture and natural resources. Formerly, he had been in administrative and financial management in the Forest Service. One of his duties was to see that agency legislative proposals were cleared through the Bureau of the Budget in accordance with an executive order for compliance with presidential policy. Thus, when the bill drafted by the Forest Service became public and there was no record of its referral to the bureau, Scott sent the following memorandum to the director of the bureau:

Reference is made to my memorandum of October 22. On or about the above date, I asked Mr. Shields, Special Assistant to Secretary Wickard, to look into the action of the Forest Service in drafting an omnibus bill for forestry legislation. I now learn that the Forest Service has done this job ostensibly at the request of Senator Bankhead, who is Chairman of the Congressional Joint Committee on Forestry. Under date of October 10, 1941, the Acting Chief of the Forest Service, Mr. L. [sic] H. Clapp, addressed a letter to Senator Bankhead and transmitted to him the draft of the new omnibus bill. Mr. Clapp in a way cleared his action with the Secretary's office; that is, he presented the letter and draft of bill to Mr. Carl Hamilton, one of the younger assistants to the Secretary, who is as yet quite inexperienced in policy matters, and on the basis of his initial forwarded the material to Senator Bankhead. The Secretary, Mr. Shields, Mr. Jump, or any of the other key men so far as I have been able to discover, knew nothing about this action or had opportunity to view the material. In both the letter and the language of the bill, the position of the present leadership of the Forest Service is quite forcibly set forth and the language of the bill is replete with propaganda as well as strictly legislative proposals.

In brief, it provides for public regulation of practice on private forest lands pointing quite definitely toward ultimate Federal regulation although in the beginning States would be given a trial period within which to work out a satisfactory plan. . . .[11]

Scott patently believed that Clapp, intent on getting his own brand of regulatory legislation, was deviously bypassing his own superior, Secretary Wickard, and dealing directly with Senator Bankhead. This episode illustrates the nature of some of the internal stresses and strains caused by the regulation issue.

In November 1941, a month before the United States entered World War II, Senator Bankhead introduced the Cooperative Forest Restoration Bill, also

10. Ibid., p. 523.
11. Scott to Harold D. Smith, October 31, 1941 (National Archives).

known as the Omnibus Forestry Bill, which included the recommendations of the Joint Congressional Committee. The bill prescribed the specific procedure whereby regulation of private forestry practices would be enforced in the states.[12]

Congress never held hearings on the Bankhead bill, probably because of its preoccupation with more urgent war legislation. But other regulatory bills would be introduced during the war years; for example, a bill in 1942 by Senator M. C. Wallgren of Washington and another in 1945 by Congressman F. E. Hook of Michigan. These bills provided for direct federal control of private forest cutting under the administration of the secretary of agriculture, bypassing the states. Nothing came of them.

The War Years

The nation having declared war, on December 26, 1941, Secretary Wickard again wrote the president, saying:

I feel that I can no longer delay bringing to your attention the fact that we urgently need war legislation on some phases of forestry.

Our need is for Federal regulation to stop the destructive cutting of privately owned forests. Thus increased war demands for timber could be met without impairing the productivity of the forests. Another is authority to extend and intensify fire protection, without which regulation cannot be effective.[13]

Wickard suggested that the best way to get the legislation he proposed was to capitalize on the recommendations of the Joint Congressional Committee, strengthening the law to meet war needs and provide for direct federal action wherever feasible. He urged Roosevelt to authorize him to work with Congress along these lines, which the president did.

Wickard's proposal of December 26 was referred to the Bureau of the Budget, which did not get around to commenting on it until May 16, 1942. On that date, Wayne Coy, assistant director of the bureau, sent a long memorandum to Roosevelt. In it, he analyzed the proposals for legislation "covering the whole field of needs in forestry as envisioned by the Forest Service." Coy reported that this proposed legislation had been "thoroughly and jointly studied by representatives of Secretary Wickard and the Forest Service with members of my staff whose experience in and intimate familiarity with the forestry movement of this country extends back over 30 years."[14]

He noted that under the Department of Agriculture's proposed legislation, federal regulation would be administered by the secretary who would classify all privately owned land in each state as either forest or nonforest. Then, through a system of national and local advisory boards, the Forest

---

12. For details of the proposals, see Samuel T. Dana, *Forest and Range Policy*; and Lawrence S. Hamilton, "The Federal Forest Regulation Issue," *Forest History*, April 1965.

13. Nixon, *Franklin D. Roosevelt and Conservation*, vol. 2, p. 543.

14. Ibid., p. 549. The staff members to whom Coy referred were Sam R. Broadbent and James E. Scott, both former career officers in the Forest Service.

Service, as the action agency, would determine the area of woodland on which forest operations would be regulated. For these lands, the Forest Service would next formulate rules of practice, put them into effect, and enforce them.

In his analysis, Coy pointed out that the opinions of foresters and other qualified persons regarding the necessity for public regulation were widely divergent. In his summary of the situation, he noted that the state foresters generally opposed federal regulation; that The American Forestry Association favored state regulation rather than federal and urged that the entire issue be set aside until after the war; and that the Society of American Foresters endorsed public regulation when necessary in specific localities but seemed to prefer state to federal control. Industry, on the other hand, would fight regulation. Then, Coy presented the stand the Budget Bureau had taken:

This office believes that the need for public regulation and particularly Federal regulation of private forest practices has not been convincingly demonstrated. . . . The introduction of legislation providing for Federal regulation in this field will certainly arouse a major controversy and would be particularly untimely now when unity of effort is so essential. The cost of a regulatory system such as is now proposed cannot be exactly determined but first year cost would probably not be less than $3,000,000 and this figure would undoubtedly increase year by year.[15]

This appears to be the first time any government official or agency tied a specific price tag to regulation. Thus, the Budget Bureau made a signal contribution to the basic considerations underlying this issue by putting costs into the record.

Coy concluded this portion of the bureau's analysis with this unequivocal and emphatic declaration: "I recommend that the proposal for Federal regulation of forest practices on private lands be held as not at this time in accord with your program." During a review of the memorandum with Roosevelt at the White House on May 13, Budget Director Harold Smith wrote "O.K." beside the recommendation, meaning that the president concurred.

The presidential OK was confirmed by Roosevelt in a memorandum to Smith and Coy on May 19, 1942:

In regard to the forestry legislation, I think that at this time, and until the war is over, the following policy should be followed without any further action on the part of the Federal Government;
1. There shall be no Federal legislation providing for Federal regulation of forestry practices on private lands.[16]

This decision shows that both the White House and the Bureau of the Budget were responsive to the voice of public opinion. An instance of that voice was a guest editorial in *American Forests* (April 1942) in which W. B. Greeley pointed out that the nation's forests, particularly the dense and flammable stands of the West Coast, were vulnerable to enemy incendiarism. He called on foresters and forestry agencies to be alert to attacks that could disrupt communications and transportation facilities and otherwise cause

15. Ibid., pp. 550–51.
16. Ibid., p. 554.

emergencies injurious to the war effort. In point of fact, such attacks occurred later when the Japanese sent fire balloons across the Pacific intending to cause fire storms. Some forest fires resulted, none of them severe, fortunately.

"We should all have learned by now that we cannot win this war and at the same time continue 'business as usual' or politics as usual or controversies over peacetime concerns as usual," Greeley wrote. "Whether a policy of Federal forest regulation is right or wrong is beside the point. We have a far more urgent task on our hands, *right now*. The most perfect scheme of totalitarian forestry ever devised will avail little if the forests are burnt out by war. . . . Let us first carry American forests through their critical hazard by the most unified cooperation of which we are capable. And then settle the questions of their future."[17]

Despite Roosevelt's order to Smith, during 1942, while the United States was totally absorbed in the war effort, Clapp tried to induce the president to force compliance with regulations on timber cutting that the Forest Service would set up for the Department of Agriculture under the emergency war powers granted the president by Congress. The alleged justification was that this expedient would increase the volume of forest products needed for the war. But a group of foresters and industry leaders advised Donald Nelson, director of the War Production Board, that it would have precisely the opposite effect. Nothing came of this proposal. Some officials in the War Production Board, which was responsible for the output of forest products for war needs, believed the proposal to be a subterfuge to get the president to assign to the Forest Service control over the nation's forest economy under the pretext of war necessity.

In a querulous display of disapproval, Pinchot resigned his membership in the American Forestry Association because of alleged "editorial attacks" on Clapp and the Forest Service in *American Forests* (January 1943). From his letter of resignation, it is apparent that Pinchot was provoked because of the association's failure to support the principle of federal control of private timber cutting. There had been a time, he said, when the association had effectively promoted the progress of forestry in the United States. But the association had taken up "the feeble habit of advocating anything that everybody was for, and nothing that anybody was against," and "had fallen under the influence of the lumber interests."[18]

Pinchot went on to say that he had never expected to see the association "actively working to hinder the spread of forestry by fighting the Government's efforts to reduce forest destruction by control of lumbering, and advocating instead State control, as it is doing, happily with small effect, today." Clapp and the Forest Service had been attacked in *American Forests*, Pinchot charged, because they stood for federal control of cutting on private lands. He concluded:

17. "The War Job for Foresters," *American Forests*, vol. 48 (April 1942), p. 175.
18. Pinchot to W. S. Rosecrans, president of the association, April 8, 1943 (Henry S. Graves Collection, Sterling Memorial Library, Yale University).

Because Clapp supports this policy, which was supported with a single exception, by every Chief of the United States Forest Service since its foundation, Ovid Butler and the Association go out of their way to attack him.

Nearly ten years ago I was elected an honorary member of the American Forestry Association. For the reasons given above, and because I have lost confidence in the Association, I can no longer continue my membership, and I hereby resign.[19]

At this stage in his career, which was drawing to a close, Pinchot was suffering from the infirmities of advanced age (he was nearly seventy-eight) and from a sense that the forestry movement had passed him by.[20] His counsel on forestry policy was no longer sought as of old, though he kept up a running fight with Harold L. Ickes, secretary of the interior, to prevent the transfer of the Forest Service from the Department of Agriculture to the Department of the Interior. Pinchot died October 4, 1946, respected and full of honors, but he had long ceased to be an effective voice in the movement for federal regulation of private forest management.

On January 8, 1943, two months before Pinchot had come to the defense of Clapp, Lyle F. Watts was appointed chief of the Forest Service. Watts spent a large part of the next six months traveling and investigating the forest situation in all parts of the United States. At a meeting of the Wisconsin–Upper Michigan Section of the Society of American Foresters in Milwaukee on September 20, he went all out before his fellow professionals for federal regulation.

The most urgent need is to stop destructive cutting so that the productivity of every acre now bearing merchantable timber may be retained. I want to say with all the force I have that nation-wide regulation of cutting practices on private forest land under strong federal leadership is absolutely essential if needless destruction of productive growing stock is to be stopped. . . . Federal legislation is needed to take direct action where suitable state legislation is not enacted and where enforcement or the practices established are not adequate.[21]

As long as the nation was fighting World War II, Forest Service activities were directed toward the war effort. The service's long-range goals still included regulation, but public agitation for it was de-emphasized. Nevertheless, Watts kept stressing the warnings issued by his predecessors Silcox and Clapp. In his first annual report (for 1943), he said: "After 50 years of educational effort, the people are generally unaware of how critical the forest situation is."[22]

When war pressures ceased, however, Chief Watts and the higher Forest Service officials resumed the campaign for regulation. Although his personal relations with many forest industry executives were cordial, Watts was critical

19. Ibid.
20. Pinchot's posthumous book *Breaking New Ground* reveals none of this, because the book stops chronologically with the year 1910.
21. "Comprehensive Forest Policy Indispensable," *Journal of Forestry*, vol. 41 (November 1943), p. 787.
22. U.S. Forest Service, *Report of the Chief of the Forest Service, 1943* (1943), p. 14.

of the industrialists' performance in forest management and doubtful of their sincerity—opinions he voiced in private conversations. He and others of like viewpoint believed that industrial holdings would not be maintained in reasonably productive condition (his favorite expression) without federal-state compulsion.

Throughout the early 1940s, the need for public regulation was being accepted, however reluctantly, by an increasing number of lumbermen and professional foresters outside the Forest Service. Typical of the foresters who were persuaded was Clarence F. Korstian, dean of the Duke University School of Forestry, who undertook a countrywide study of the application of forestry on private lands at the invitation of the National Lumber Manufacturers Association. As defined in the foreword by Wilson Compton, secretary-manager of the association, the study was to be an impartial survey "to help resolve the cross currents of opinion concerning the status, problems, and prospects of private forestry in this country."[23] *Forestry on Private Lands in the United States*, Korstian's book on the results of his study, was a searching summarization of the condition of private forest administration, both on a regional basis and on the basis of accomplishment in protection, management, and research.

Korstian asserted flatly: "Public control of forest cutting practices on private lands in the United States now appears inevitable. . . . In almost every country in the world where forests are important it has been found necessary to apply some sort of public control over their exploitation. The United States will not long remain an outstanding exception."[24] Moreover, he recommended that private properties that could not be managed economically should be sold at a fair price to public agencies that would keep them productive.

In his survey, Korstian interviewed numerous individuals representing industry, government, and the general public, and collected data on forest conditions from companies, government agencies, and trade associations. In summing up, he presented what probably was as valid a consensus as could be obtained during the war period:

> The American public and industry itself will not long tolerate the mistreatment of forest lands even by any minority of owners and operators, notwithstanding the progress in the application of sound forestry practices on the majority of commercial forest lands. In dealing with a serious national problem, such as the present one, it is contrary to the principles of democracy to permit a minority to go its way, especially where it is distinctly inimical to the interests of the public.[25]

Korstian also included two model patterns for state regulation in his book. The first, "Draft of a Model Bill for State Control of Cutting on Private Lands," was prepared by the Regional Committee on Forestry Problems of the Eastern States Council of State Governments. The attorneys general of five northeastern states assisted in its preparation.

23. Korstian, *Forestry on Private Lands*, p. v.
24. Ibid., p. 183.
25. Ibid., p. 184.

Korstian endorsed the model bill because it provided that the minimum cutting-practice rules adopted by a state forestry board or comparable state agency would be based on studies of rates of growth and techniques of cutting applicable to the different forest types. Korstian was a silviculturist—a research forester as well as a teacher—who had visited the major forest types of the United States, Canada, and western Europe. He understood what most lay advocates of regulation did not—that local forest conditions and the forestry practices applicable to them are so diverse that rules of practice cannot adequately be written into laws.

The second model—"Draft of a State Bill to Regulate Cutting on Private Forest Lands through a System of Licensing Operators"—was drawn up in the Legal Aid Clinic of Duke University with assistance from the Eastern States Council of State Governments. Under a modified plan of state regulation, a board would establish minimum cutting practice rules and would license timber operators who would be required to comply with the board's standards. Neither model bill was ever enacted into law in precisely the form suggested.

Then, in 1945, the Forest Service made a national reappraisal of forest conditions. Basic knowledge of the timber resource was updated and expanded. The data were evaluated in terms of the general economy to determine the next steps necessary for forestry progress. A startling fact came to light. There was a forestry problem on private land, all right. But the heart of the problem was in farm woodlots and similar small woodland holdings and not in the large tracts owned by industries.

This finding required a quiet reappraisal also of Forest Service policy toward regulation. Heretofore, it had been politically safe to criticize private ownership for its alleged failure to practice forestry, because private owners were equated with industrial owners. But it was politically inexpedient to criticize and threaten to regulate three million small forest owners, because most of them were farmers, and Congress was traditionally sensitive and responsive to the interests of farmers.

In 1949, Chief Watts outlined the elements deemed necessary to bring about good management on all woodlands. "Our national forests and most other public forests are or will be managed for sustained yield," he said. "The crux of the problem is the forest lands in private ownership; to them we must look for the bulk of our supply of forest products." He then proposed: "Regulate timber cutting and related forest practices." According to a control plan advanced by the Department of Agriculture, the regulation would be by a combination of federal-state enforcement. But Watts's proposal to regulate was to be supplemented, in his own italicized words, by certain *"public aids to private forest-land owners, especially the small owners."*[26]

To support his argument, Watts raised up the specter of wood deficit propounded some four decades earlier by Pinchot.

Deterioration of forest resources in the United States already has gone so far that we face a period of timber shortage before timber growth can be built

26. "A National Program for Forestry," in U.S. Department of Agriculture, *Trees: The Yearbook of Agriculture*, p. 758.

up to the point of sustained abundance. . . . The longer action to build up the timber resource is delayed, the longer and more acute the period of short supply will be.[27]

The Regulation Movement Grinds to a Halt

For nearly two decades, during the administrations of Silcox, Clapp, and Watts, the Forest Service hierarchy devoted much time to promoting federal regulation. But not all the rank and file personnel talked regulation with the fervor of the higher staff, and some became heartily sick of hearing the recurring theme.

The 1940s were notable for truly momentous advances in industrial forestry. Leading the industry were the paper companies, which were buying cutover as well as stocked woodland by the millions of acres and hiring professional foresters by the thousands to manage it. The intensity of silviculture practiced on much of this land within a decade became equal to, or better than, the quality of that on some national or state forests. It could truthfully be said that at last industrial forestry was a reality.

Yet, during the late 1940s and into the 1950s, Watts and his followers continued to find fault with industry for alleged failure to maintain its lands in "reasonably productive condition." To more than one contemporary observer it appeared strange that, as industrial forestry became better, the attitude of the regulationists became more critical.

On January 22, 1951, President Harry S. Truman appointed the President's Materials Policy Commission "to study the broader and longer range aspects of the nation's materials problem as distinct from immediate defense needs."[28] He asked William S. Paley, chairman of the commission, to make recommendations to bring supplies and requirements of essential materials into balance.

The commission's report, submitted to the president on June 2, 1952, contained thirteen recommendations dealing with timber resources. In regard to public regulation, the commission recommended that the federal government's chief role in prohibiting destructive cutting should be to lend assistance to the states in setting up systems of compulsory regulation. Control by the federal government itself was neither proposed nor even mentioned.

With respect to timber stand improvement on federal forest lands the commission made an astonishing recommendation, one in which for the first time a high governmental authority officially acknowledged the superior quality of silviculture practiced on industrial holdings:

That the Federal Government raise the level of silvicultural work on its commercial timber land at least to the level maintained on intensively managed private forest lands of comparable value.[29]

Following receipt of the commission's report, the president in July 1952 directed the National Securities Board to review it and advise him with

27. Ibid., p. 760.
28. President's Materials Policy Commission, *Resources for Freedom*, vol. 1, *Foundation for Growth and Security* (1952), p. iv.
29. Ibid., p. 44.

respect to its recommendations. In a report to the president on December 10, 1952, the board supported the recommendation of the Paley Commission and made the following proposal:

That the President direct the Department of Agriculture and the Department of the Interior to develop programs for raising the level of silvicultural work on their commercial timber land to a level equal to that maintained on intensively managed private forest lands of comparable value and to include such programs in their respective requests for appropriations.[30]

In the discussion section on this particular recommendation, the report laconically noted the position taken by each department: "Concurs."

The regulationists had bred dissension in the ranks of the Forest Service, as well as in the profession, and had caused confusion among the public. However sincere their motives, they jeopardized the accomplishments of a half-century by driving ahead to attempt the impossible. Fortunately, a man of perception and judgment now entered the sphere of action—Richard E. McArdle, who became chief of the Forest Service when Lyle Watts retired on June 30, 1952. In his last annual report (for 1951), Watts was still advocating public regulation. McArdle's first annual report did not even mention regulation, nor did any of his subsequent reports as chief.

McArdle was not ambitious to dominate the forest industries. Like his predecessor W. B. Greeley, he wished to give the national forests efficient and honest administration and to perpetuate the general forestry progress won through cooperation with the states and with private owners. It was a good time for consolidating the gains already made, and he sensed that fact. Moreover, while aware of the hopes and struggles of the early years of the conservation movement and of the necessity to maintain continuity with the past, he wished now to use his office to endow American forestry with stability and permanence.

Controversy Yields Constructive Results

Looking back on the Forest Service's long record of regulatory propaganda, we see certain indirect benefits resulting from it. In 1941, a confidential public-opinion survey was conducted for the American Forest Products Industries, then a subsidiary of the National Lumber Manufacturers Association. More than half the American people queried believed that the industry was depleting the nation's timber supply at an alarming rate. School teachers, in particular, were found to be highly critical of the industry. In short, the public had a poor opinion of the lumbermen, who were held to be forest butchers with profit as their sole motive. Industry, under attack as a despoiler and devastator, began to gather, then present, public information on progress in private timber growing. Trade associations and industrial committees combated federal regulation on the one basis most likely to succeed; that is, through facts and figures and on-the-ground demonstrations that such regulation was unnecessary.

30. *The Objectives of the United States Materials Resources Policy and Suggested Initial Steps in Their Accomplishment*, p. 60.

American Forest Products Industries (AFPI) began a campaign of public information designed to show that industry was growing and protecting timber for permanent yield. All statements issued by AFPI were to be "conservative and truthful." Within a year the organization had sponsored hundreds of magazine articles, nationwide newspaper coverage, syndicated features, motion pictures, and booklets for school children.

But good forest practice has to start and end in the woods, and that is where its accomplishments must be measured. Thus, the Tree Farm Program, started in the state of Washington in 1941, is a concrete example of AFPI's results. In twenty-five years the number of tree farms increased to more than 32,000 in forty-eight states and covered a total area of 72 million acres.

Progress in state forestry was spurred by the pressures for regulation. As noted earlier, the Clarke-McNary Act of 1924 was a compromise law between the regulationists on the one hand and industry and the states opposing regulation on the other. This act set a pattern for cooperation between the federal government, state governments, and private forest interests in forest protection and in reforestation that has endured to this day. But its immediate effect was even more notable; it influenced those states that lacked competent forestry agencies to set them up.

Thus, by the start of World War II, forty-four states had forestry departments or similar units of government. For example, the acceleration of southern state forestry was spectacular. Whereas only four southern states had commissions or departments of forestry in 1920, within two decades all had established them.

The National Association of State Foresters, organized in 1920, increasingly influenced the public attitude on local forestry matters, including regulation. By exchanging views at annual meetings and passing around information throughout the year, the association developed for its members stronger ties of cooperation with the federal government, while at the same time developing a stronger sense of independence from federal domination. It is no exaggeration to affirm that when the state foresters opposed federal control of private forestry, they were forced to improve their own professional competence and their own administration of the state forest resources.

That the pressure for federal regulation influenced the states to become more progressive and responsible in their handling of the forest resource can be seen in the action of the Council of State Governments. Early in 1942, the council had a Forestry Committee that recommended the enactment of regulatory legislation, predicting that if the states did not enact it, the federal government would. In 1945, the council distributed the draft of a model forest practice bill to the states.

Although the states, with industry backing, never ceased to oppose federal regulation, the concept of private forest practice under state control became in time an acceptable alternative, at least to some states. True, those states that enacted regulatory laws generally required forms of forest management less stringent than that proposed by the several federal bills introduced. As pointed out by C. Raymond Clar of the California State Division of Forestry: "The state laws that were enacted have required, for the most part, entirely sensible good practices from timber operators in their harvesting methods."[31]

Statutes regulating cutting practices were adopted by thirteen states during the period 1941–50, none since then. These laws were searchingly analyzed by a Committee on Forest Practices set up within the Division of Silviculture, Society of American Foresters. The committee's report indicated that the laws were difficult to enforce and not particularly effective. Inspection of logging operations was expensive. The low penalties provided were not a deterrent for violations. Nevertheless, the committee concluded that "by and large, the regulations are well accepted and compliance is generally good."[32]

In the first half of his conservation career, by any measure Gifford Pinchot was an outsize man who correctly read the signs of his times and who became the spokesman for a movement that attracted some of the best and most influential minds of his age. By dedicating himself to the service of society, he hastened the course of events leading to the management of all natural resources in the public interest. But the sincerity of his beliefs did not prevent him from errors of judgment, and his obdurate insistence on federal control of private forestry was one of them. In the end, Pinchot was the leader of a lost cause who may not have realized that he had outlived the cause itself.

If it is possible to prove the rightness or wrongness of a cause from its historical antecedents, then federal regulation as a cause was a mistake. No other proposal in forestry rivaled regulation in the amount of public confusion and professional controversy it provoked. And yet, out of it came notable advances in forestry.

31. "State Forestry," in Henry Clepper and Arthur B. Meyer (eds.), *American Forestry: Six Decades of Growth*, p. 214.

32. Society of American Foresters, *Forest Practices Development in the United States, 1940 to 1955* (Washington: SAF, 1956).

CHAPTER 12

Wings over the Forest

During the decade following the first successful flight of the Wright brothers in 1903, forestry officials in several parts of the United States and Canada proposed investigating the possible use of aircraft in forestry, particularly in patrolling woodland to detect fires. As early as 1911, forest supervisors meeting in El Paso, Texas, passed a resolution "that the use of aeroplanes for fire patrol be given consideration, since it appears that they will soon be of value in that work."[1]

Two years later, the Western Forestry and Conservation Association went so far as to draft a contract with the Curtiss Company for experimental flights but dropped the plan because its practicability was questioned. In his 1916 annual report, the state forester of Washington mentioned that the state had studied the possible utilization of the airplane for patrol, as well as for transportation of men and equipment for fire fighting, but had decided against it because of the expense.

In Wisconsin, Frank Moody of the State Conservation Commission proposed in 1916 that aircraft could be used not only for spotting fires but for carrying mail, supplies, and personnel to remote forest areas. According to the Wisconsin Historical Society, the first forest patrol flight was made June 29, 1915, by L. A. Vilas in a Curtiss flying boat. Edward M. Griffith, state forester, made an ascent with Vilas on June 22 and apparently was impressed with the possibilities of aerial fire observation. A marker erected by the Historical Society near Big Trout Lake records that Vilas made patrol flights almost daily during July and August 1915. It was, reads the marker, "the first time anywhere that an aircraft was used in detecting and locating forest fires and patrolling large forest areas." Vilas received no salary from the state; as a sort of honorary forest warden he flew the patrols as a hobby.

---

1. "First Annual Meeting of Supervisors of Forest Service, District III (Southwest), November 9-14, 1911, in El Paso, Texas" (U.S. Forest Service Records, National Archives).

In 1909, William T. Cox, then with the Forest Service, saw a flight by the Wright brothers at Fort Myer near Washington, D.C.[2] Remembering it when he became state forester of Minnesota, he worked up a plan whereby the U.S. Navy would assign flying boats and personnel to a forest patrol unit based at its Naval Militia Station at Duluth. Cox estimated that 5 million acres of northeastern Minnesota wilderness could be protected at an annual cost of $60,000. He mentioned that the proposal had been discussed with naval authorities in Washington, D.C., and that "Secretary Daniels seems favorable."[3]

Nothing came of this proposal, but it was revived after World War I when the Air Service began its aerial patrol in California in 1919. In a letter of January 2, 1920, to Senator Frank B. Kellogg of Minnesota, Colonel O. Westover of the Air Service reported that funds and personnel were not available to establish a hydroplane station at Duluth to assist the State Forest Service, although the colonel said that the Air Service was in hearty sympathy with the project.

Similar suggestions for the use of aircraft were being made by forestry officials in Canada. Articles and notes on the subject were published in the *Canadian Forestry Journal* as early as 1915. An account of the British Columbia Forest Service buying a flying boat for fire patrol was published in the issue of August 1918, and a report on the use of the flying boat for fire detection in the province appeared in the issue of October 1919.[4]

The highly publicized use of airplanes during World War I stimulated the imagination of civilians as well as the military. Flying became a popular field of experimentation by civil governmental agencies and soon by industry.

That the Forest Service had been considering the use of aircraft in forestry prior to 1919, particularly in fire detection and control, is proved by the writings of certain forest officers. On December 3, 1918, Chief Forester Henry S. Graves wrote a seven-page letter to L. D'Orcy, associate editor of the magazine *Aviation and Aeronautical Engineering*; the letter was published as an article in the issue of January 15, 1919. Graves predicted that fire protection would offer a useful field for aircraft and cited what he believed to be its possibilities.

In February 1919, the *Air Service Journal* quoted a letter by John [sic] L. Hall, acting forester, U.S. Forest Service, to the Standard Aircraft Corporation of New Jersey.[5] Hall asserted that the Forest Service believed aircraft could be used to advantage in fire patrol of the national forests. He said, "It has been estimated that thousands of dollars worth of valuable timber would be saved annually if flying machines were used for the detection of forest fires and the transportation of fire-fighting crews to the scenes of conflagrations." But, he added, the service was not prepared to purchase and operate the number of aircraft sufficient for the purpose. Forest Service appro-

2. The U.S. Government acquired its first military airplane on July 30, 1909.
3. "Aerial Forest Patrol," *American Forests*, February 1917.
4. For these and other references to the use of airplanes in fire detection, see Malcolm Edward Hardy, "The Use of Aircraft in Forest Fire Control" (master's thesis, University of Washington College of Forestry, Seattle, 1946).
5. "Airplane Patrol for the Forest." The *Journal* doubtless meant William L. Hall.

priations were too limited for a project of such magnitude. Moreover, the Forest Service did not want to ask Congress for the funds when the Air Service had both the planes and the trained officers.

Aerial Fire Patrol Begins

The action that finally initiated the first organized aerial fire patrol in the United States resulted from a letter of March 7, 1919, from Secretary of Agriculture D. F. Houston to Secretary of War Newton D. Baker. It is not known whether this letter was prepared in the Forest Service for Secretary Houston's signature, but all available evidence suggests that it was. It read, in part:

One of the most difficult problems in the administration of the National Forests is the prevention of forest fire. It is believed that aircraft could be used to great advantage in the work of fire patrol, as well as in the making of forest maps. It is very desirable to make some experiments and demonstrations in the use of both airplanes and balloons in forest work. The public values involved justify a considerable undertaking, if the means can be found. I hesitate, however, to take up any work involving the use of aircraft if it is possible for the War Department to handle it for us under a plan of cooperation. . . .[6]

Secretary Houston then suggested that the Air Service combine air patrol of the national forests with the training of its aviators. He mentioned that Chief Forester Graves had discussed the suggestion with General William L. Kenly, director of military aeronautics, and that the general believed the plan was entirely feasible. He went on:

I am, therefore, presenting the matter to you with the request that, if possible, experiments in forest fire patrol be undertaken by the Air Service during the coming season at certain points in the National Forests. It is suggested that experiments could be undertaken at one or more points in California at the existing training camps. It is suggested that these experiments include the use of both airplanes and captive balloons for forest fire detection.

Graves pointed out that favorable conditions existed for such experiments in the central Sierras not far from Sacramento, in Washington near Tacoma, and near Portland, Oregon. In addition, he suggested the possibility of experiments in the East, for example, in the White Mountains and the southern Appalachians.

On March 24, 1919, the adjutant general, by order of the secretary of war, wrote the director of the Air Service: "In compliance with the request of the Secretary of Agriculture, you will undertake to the extent that equipment, personnel, and other necessary facilities are available, such experiments in cooperation with the Department of Agriculture as will serve to adequately demonstrate the value of such patrol."[7]

Major General Charles T. Menoher was the director of the Air Service. Graves discussed the details with him, and asked specifically that the Air Service conduct patrols during the coming summer over the Angeles, Cleve-

6. War Department Records, National Archives.
7. Ibid.

land, and Santa Barbara National Forests in southern California and the White Mountain National Forest in New Hampshire. General Menoher notified Graves on April 3, 1919, that his forest officers could communicate direct with the commanding officers of Rockwell Field near San Diego, March Field at Riverside, and Mather Field at Sacramento.

In his personal memoirs, Coert duBois, one of the early officers of the Forest Service, told of his enthusiastic participation in the events leading up to the operational use of aircraft in American forestry.[8] An 1899 graduate of the Biltmore Forest School, he entered the Forest Service in 1900, and by the period of World War I had become district forester of the California District (now Region 5).

DuBois was one of the first American foresters to analyze the factors that made forest fires possible. He attempted to define fire ratings as guides to needed finances, personnel, equipment, and policy, as well as to public education, legislation, law enforcement, organization of control forces, detection, communication, and reduction of hazards. In a 1914 document, "Systematic Fire Protection in the California Forests," he had prepared a guide for the use of forest officers. DuBois wrote: "A way must be devised of reducing all of these factors to concrete terms so that any forest area after careful study can be given a rating which will convey to our minds something of an exact measure of its total fire danger."[9]

In San Francisco early in 1919, duBois, a World War I lieutenant colonel recently discharged from the Corps of Engineers, met a young Air Service officer named Henry H. Arnold, later to become famous as the World War II commanding general of the U.S. Air Force. DuBois explained to Arnold the problem of forest fire detection and control on the national forests and told how Air Service planes could supplement the Forest Service lookout system by patrol flights to detect and report fires promptly. Arnold was interested because of his desire to find stimulating peacetime duty for his flyers and planes. Although the cooperative agreement that resulted between the Air Service and the Forest Service was authorized by higher authorities in Washington, D.C., the personal cooperation that developed between Arnold and duBois apparently had much to do with the initial success of the first aerial patrol of the west slope of the Sierras.

In his autobiography, Arnold tells that in June 1919 he was ordered from Rockwell Field near San Diego, where he was district supervisor, Western District of the Air Service, to San Francisco, where he was "given charge of all aviation in the western part of the United States." He goes on:

8. "Autobiography of Coert duBois," *The Biltmore Immortals* (Germany: privately printed by C. A. Schenck, 1953–57), vol. 1, pp. 149–89, and vol. 2, pp. 53–85.
9. Harry T. Gisborne, a forester who specialized in the application of scientific research techniques to studies of fire, wrote an article, "Mileposts of Progress in Fire Control and Fire Research," for the *Journal of Forestry* (August 1942). In it, he said: "In 1914, Coert duBois' 'Systematic Fire Protection in the California Forests,' an unnumbered publication that is not labeled as either a bulletin or a circular and is marked 'Not for public distribution,' was very definitely a national milepost in progressive thinking on methods. . . ." In September 1919, duBois resigned from the Forest Service to enter the Consular Service.

We were trying to find ourselves during this period—trying to find out how the airplane could be used and what value it might be to the public. Out on the West Coast we carried on an innovation strictly on our own. That was the aerial Forest Fire Patrol. I set it up in June, 1919, and it was continued by the Army Air Service for some years until the Forest Service was able to take it over with planes rented from civilians. We made air patrols over the forests of the West from the Cascade and Olympic Mountains, along the Sierra Nevada and Coast ranges down to the Sierra Madre. Our purpose was to find out if the airplane could detect and locate fires and direct the fire fighters in their suppression work. The Forest Fire Patrols operated from bases in the valleys and flew over mountain peaks and high points in the ranges. This service not only reduced the actual fire damage in the timberland to a marked degree and thus saved millions of dollars in timber, but it also accustomed our pilots to some of the most difficult cross-country flying in the world.[10]

An account of the first three years of the operation was written for the War Department by Lester Draper Seymour.[11] Much of the following information was gleaned from it.

The Season of 1919

In California, patrol flights began twice daily on June 1 from Rockwell, March, and Mather Fields. DuBois had visited each of these fields and had worked up plans with the officers in charge. Later in the summer additional flights were made from Redding, Red Bluff, and Fresno. They continued until September 15. Curtiss JN planes ("Jennies") were used.

In Oregon, the forest patrol started August 2, 1919, and continued until August 22. Seven Curtiss-type planes were used. They flew at 60 miles per hour; 20,160 miles were flown during the twenty-one-day period. On August 23, the Curtiss planes were replaced by larger De Haviland ships that were more efficient. These continued the patrol until October 7. During the thirty-five days of flying, these planes flew six hours daily, 95 miles per hour, for a total of 39,900 miles. There were six forced landings, and one plane was wrecked, a total loss. Since the aircraft were not equipped with wireless sets, as they were then called, fires were reported by the use of message-dropping cans.[12]

Summarizing the 1919 results, Seymour noted that the patrols started too late in the season to equip the planes with radio. Reports of fires also were dropped by small parachutes to various lookouts and relayed by telephone. Carrier pigeons were tried but were found less satisfactory than dropping messages by parachute.

During the season, an impressive total of 236,665 miles was flown for a total of 2,871 flying hours. The area covered was 18 million acres. Of the 570 fires discovered, 128 were detected by the Oregon flights. There was one fatality, in Oregon.

---

10. *Global Mission* (Harper and Brothers, 1949), p. 92.
11. "Aerial Forest Fire Patrol Service—1919, 1920 and 1921" (War Department Records, National Archives).
12. F. A. Elliott, "Airplane Patrol of the Forests," *American Forests*, April 1920.

On December 3, 1919, General Menoher sent a letter of commendation to all Air Service personnel who had participated in the pioneer work of the forest patrol. He wrote that theirs was "a very trying and exacting duty and the fact that they acquitted themselves in such splendid manner reflects a glowing tribute to the initiative and perseverance of those who undertook so hazardous a work as patrolling the forest areas where the scarcity of landing fields necessitated a daring of first order."[13]

In an Air Service memorandum of December 12, 1919, it was noted that "as a result of the success of this patrol protection agencies have asked that it be extended in 1920 to cover the states of Montana, Idaho, Washington, Oregon, California, and western Wyoming."[14] Secretary of War Baker wrote the secretary of agriculture on December 27, 1919, that Colonel Arnold recommended continuance and enlargement of the work, and that plans were being considered.

No event in American conservation since the Ballinger-Pinchot controversy stimulated as much public interest as the aerial forest patrols of 1919. Newspapers and magazines of general circulation, as well as those directed to technical and scientific readers, published feature articles about the project. Employment of the fixed-wing aircraft, a form of transportation less than two decades old and only brought to a stage of practical everyday use by improvements during World War I, attracted the attention of people everywhere. The use of military equipment for civilian benefits was also generally applauded.

Reporting on the Forest Service's experiences in *Scientific Monthly*, Richard F. Hammatt mentioned one fire in southern California near the end of the season when the airplane was used to help guide the work of actual fire suppression. He told how "as a result of short daily flights the Forest Supervisor was able to direct the movements of more than 2,000 fire fighters, pick locations for new camps, determine where the new fire lines should be built, and keep his crews informed at all times of the progress of fires which ultimately burned over some 160,000 acres of rough brushy country absolutely inaccessible except to men on foot."[15]

The Season of 1920

Congress made an appropriation of $50,000 to the Forest Service for its participation during the second season. An agreement signed April 14, 1920, between Colonel Arnold for the Air Service and Paul G. Reddington for the Forest Service set forth the terms of the cooperative program, which again was to include both California and Oregon. The Air Service would have 35 officers and 148 enlisted men and flying cadets on duty. For the Oregon flights the observers would be Forest Service civilian personnel. During April, the Air Service gave a course of instruction for twenty-two Forest Service

13. War Department Records, National Archives.
14. Ibid.
15. "Winged Patrols over Expansive Forests," *Scientific Monthly*, vol. 122 (April 10, 1920).

personnel at March Field. They were given training in aerial observation and instruction in communication so they could act as observers.

The planes were to be equipped with radio transmitting sets. Receiving stations equipped with Army Signal Corps sets were established at nine localities in California and at three in Oregon.

For the second year, the Forest Service designated Charles W. Boyce as observer in charge of the Oregon patrol. Reporting on the assignment in the *Journal of Forestry*,[16] he gave details of the personnel and equipment employed. The pilots were army personnel, but the observers were provided by the Forest Service. De Haviland airplanes were used; they had been rebuilt and powered with 400 horsepower Liberty motors. Each plane was equipped with a radio-sending set operated by a small, wind-driven generator on the landing gear, with sending keys and attachments on the fuselage. A wire, 250 feet long, dragged behind the plane, served as the antenna. Each plane carried a pilot and an observer. It flew at an average speed of 100 miles per hour at 9,000 feet elevation.

Flights were made from four Air Service fields in California and from two in Oregon. The total mileage flown was 476,085 on 1,301 patrols; 16 million acres were covered. The number of fires discovered was 1,632; of these, 818 were reported first by the patrol. On the average, thirty-seven planes were in daily use. There were forty-one forced landings and three fatalities.

At a meeting of the California State Board of Forestry in 1920, Colonel Arnold was thanked for the valuable protection service rendered by the air patrol. A resolution was addressed to the War Department, and the California Congressional delegation requested a special appropriation of $60,000 to enable the Forest Service to cooperate in the fire detection project in the western states.

The initial success of the air patrol stimulated interested citizens, communities, and organizations to press for its continuation. On March 21, 1921, C. S. Chapman, on behalf of the Oregon Forest Fire Association, an organization representing the bulk of the privately owned timber in the state, sent a special resolution to the secretary of war. The association urged Congress and the War Department to maintain the air patrol over the forested areas of the West and pointed out that considerable expense had been incurred by cities and protection agencies with the understanding that the patrol was an established institution.

Extension of the aerial patrol to cover forests in Oregon was advocated by, among others, Governor Benjamin W. Olcott, an ardent conservationist. He made special trips to Sacramento and San Francisco to discuss with Colonel Arnold the feasibility of Army Air Service patrols in Oregon similar to those planned for California. Moreover, as the governor told a conference of state foresters in December 1920, "the state stood ready to share in the [financial] burden if demanded."[17]

16. "Aerial Forest Fire Patrol in Oregon and California," *Journal of Forestry*, vol. 19 (November 1921).

17. Pennsylvania State Department of Forestry, *Proceedings of the State Foresters' Conference*, Bull. 23 (Harrisburg: 1922).

But any considerable extension of the air patrol to more western states and to other regions was precluded by cuts in the appropriations of the peacetime Army. In a memorandum sent to the commander of the Air Service, in January 1921, the air officer of the 9th Corps Area, Presidio, San Francisco, noted that a request had been made for air patrol in Montana, but he doubted that it would be undertaken because army enlistments about to be discontinued by Congress limited the Air Service to personnel inadequate for its operations.[18] Meanwhile additional requests for the patrols were mounting. According to a War Department memorandum of February 19, 1921, such requests had been received from Pennsylvania, Minnesota, Idaho, and Montana, as well as other requests for the continuation of patrols in California, Oregon, and Washington.

The Season of 1921

The agreement for the season's operations was signed on behalf of the Air Service by Major Arnold (presumably his official rank at that time) and for the Forest Service by Paul G. Reddington and George H. Cecil. Patrols would be flown in California, Oregon, and Washington. The Forest Service agreed to provide two qualified observers (reserve officers when possible) for each patrol in Oregon and Washington. In California, thirty-eight planes operated from four fields; in Oregon sixteen planes operated from two fields; and in Washington four planes operated out of one field. All fifty-eight were De Haviland 4 B's. Radio apparatus was again used; one plane at each station was equipped with "magnavox" for direct communication with lookouts or fire fighters. Of the army personnel on duty, 19 were officers and 243 were enlisted men and flying cadets.

During 2,779 flying hours, 260,291 miles were flown on 746 patrols. Twelve million acres were protected. Of the 1,035 fires reported, 373 were reported first by the planes. There were twelve forced landings and twenty-five crashes.

Interest in the patrol program was high. Citizens and communities in Oregon and Washington spent $75,000 on the preparation of landing fields so that the patrols could operate. Landing fields were established as the direct result of the forest patrols in all three states: thirty-three in California, ten in Oregon, and seven in Washington.

In 1921, at the urging of the California Forest Protective Association and individual lumbermen and foresters, the California legislature asked that the air patrol be continued and expanded. But Congress refused to appropriate the necessary funds, and military aerial fire detection ceased.

During the three years the project was in operation, 3,837 fires were detected. Nearly 1 million miles were flown. That even peacetime flying was not without its hazards during that developing period of aviation is shown by the record of several hundred forced landings and the accidental death of two Forest Service employees and an army pilot in a takeoff crackup.[19]

18. War Department Records, National Archives.
19. For an interesting account of how the air age came to California, see C. Raymond Clar, *California Government and Forestry*, California Department of Natural Resources (Sacramento: 1959).

Closing the Communications Gap

For a decade following the first aerial fire patrol, the Forest Service had not devised a satisfactory method of radio communication between airplanes and ground forces, nor between fire dispatchers' headquarters and the field. Canadian forestry agencies and some state forestry departments had also experimented with the development of radio equipment, but efficient apparatus still had to be designed for communication in remote mountain areas inaccessible except by pack animals and men afoot.

In studying this problem, fire control officers found no existing sending and receiving sets able to meet the need for communication under field conditions. The ideal set had to be rugged, yet light enough to be transported by truck over rough roads or by pack animals over steep, rocky trails. Moreover, since the sets would be used under emergency conditions during fires, they would have to be simple in operation so that personnel lacking both technical knowledge of codes and complicated equipment could transmit and receive messages.

In 1927, the Forest Service undertook to design its own portable equipment. D. L. Beatty, a forest inspector in the Northern Region, Missoula, Montana, was assigned to supervise the radio project. Three years later, a specially built combination transmitter-receiver was given field trials after having been tested by the U.S. Bureau of Standards and the Naval Research Laboratory. The complete set weighed just under eighty pounds, including the batteries that provided power for the receiver sufficient for a whole field season and approximately twenty-five hours of transmitting.

During a fire season in the state of Washington, the practicability of radio communication between a radiophone center and portables in operation at distances of twenty-five miles was proved. The central station used voice to transmit to the portables; the latter used continental code to communicate with each other and with the central station at prearranged times.

In 1931, the Forest Service was experimenting also with radio communication between airplanes and fire patrol and ground crews, a form of communication that was being researched by engineers in other branches of government, by the air transportation industry, and by commercial manufacturers. Meanwhile, the Forest Service, with its 37,000 miles of telephone lines, and the state forestry departments continued to rely on the telephone.

By 1937, the Forest Service had developed at its Radio Laboratory in Portland, Oregon, shortwave radio equipment of several kinds under the direction of A. Gael Simpson, radio engineer. In size, weight, and power the equipment ranged from units weighing only nine pounds and having limited range for use in extremely rugged country to radiophones of 15 to 125 pounds (depending on the type of batteries used), to ultra-high frequency radiophone transmitter-receivers of various capabilities. In addition, a special radiophone was designed to meet Forest Service needs for airplanes.[20] These special communications aids made possible further development of aerial fire control techniques.

20. A. Gael Simpson, "Forest Service Radiophone Equipment," *Fire Control Notes*, U.S. Forest Service, April 1937.

Aircraft Use Expands

Experimental use of aircraft in forestry in Canada began in June 1919. Ellwood Wilson, forester for Laurentide Paper Company, reported that two U.S. Curtiss seaplanes had been turned over to the Department of Naval Affairs of the Dominion Government.[21] These were borrowed for experimental flying in Quebec in late June. Most forest fires during that season had already occurred, but the plane was credited with discovering one late fire and two others of little consequence.

Two years later, Wilson reported on his experience in using a Curtiss flying boat for aerial mapping and timber estimating during 1921.[22] While on this duty, the plane detected and reported several forest fires in a remote area of Quebec.

One of the early recorded uses of the airplane in forestry for purposes other than fire detection and suppression was pioneered in Canada by Stuart Moir, forester for Laurentide Pulp and Paper Company at Grand Mere, Quebec. With 12,000 square miles of Crown land under lease, the company had the duty of preparing plans for cutting and obtaining approval from the Provincial Department of Lands and Forests.

On the advice of Ellwood Wilson, Moir induced the company to borrow two World War I aircraft (H-S seaplanes) from the Dominion Air Board. During 1921, 1922, and 1923, Moir developed techniques for aerial cruising of timber from photographs. He believed it to be the first time that pulpwood stands were estimated by air survey.[23]

In 1927, timberland owners in Maine authorized the Forest Commission to make a contract with a commercial flying company for the services of an airplane and pilot. Maine was the first eastern state to use aircraft (in this case, a seaplane) for forest patrol. Early in the fall of 1927, the plane crashed with its pilot and a passenger. In 1933, the State Forest Service bought its own seaplane and employed a full-time pilot. Since then the state and several private forest companies in New England have used aircraft regularly in their forestry operations.[24]

The New York State Conservation Department purchased its first airplane in 1931 and used it in systematic patrol for fire detection. The next year, two-way radio was installed. Aerial patrol supplemented the state's tower detection system. The planes were replaced periodically, and during the following eighteen years they logged 15,000 flying hours.

In 1931, the Forest Service contracted with a private flying company for the first aerial fire patrol in the Lake States national forests. Two planes based in East Tawas and Munising, Michigan, were subject to call for patrol duty, principally when visibility was poor from the fire towers and when

21. "The Use of Seaplanes in Forest Mapping," *Journal of Forestry*, vol. 18 (January 1920).
22. "Forest Mapping and Estimating from Aerial Photographs," *Journal of Forestry*, vol. 20 (February 1922).
23. From an unpublished interview with Stuart Moir by Elwood R. Maunder, November 12, 1958 (Forest History Society, Santa Cruz, California).
24. Austin H. Wilkins, "Use of the Airplane in Fire Protection," *Journal of Forestry*, vol. 39 (September 1941).

extensive danger conditions required better observation than was possible from the ground. Four national forests in the Upper Peninsula of Michigan were given this patrol service.

The period in which professional foresters experimented with aircraft and adapted them to their purpose was a pivotal time in the history of forestry. To be sure, the airplane is only one of many scientific and mechanical devices foresters have employed, but the manner and time of its employment helped publicize the conservation movement and the need to protect the nation's natural resources. By means of the airplane, forestry brought itself to public attention.

A valuable lesson foresters learned was that the airplane as an instrument for aerial detection and reporting of fires had limitations too. Except in remote areas difficult of access, an airplane would usually be supplementary to an efficient ground system of observation towers and lookouts serviced by telephone or radio. But regular aerial patrol flights over certain kinds of terrain—for example, the Boundary Waters Canoe Area in Minnesota—would continue, and here the float plane would replace both the fire tower and the motor truck.

During the 1920s and 1930s, experiments with aircraft continued, and new uses were found that further contributed to the development of forestry. Some of these uses will be dealt with in the next chapter.

CHAPTER 13

Smokejumpers:
The Elite Corps

Aerial forest patrol in the Northern Rocky Mountain Region (Idaho, Montana, and eastern Washington) of the Forest Service began in the summer of 1925. Organized by Howard R. Flint, regional forest inspector, the patrol was based at Spokane. Experiments were started also with the "free dropping" of specially packaged supplies from aircraft to ground forces. Techniques were worked out whereby food and equipment could be dropped without the use of parachutes.

Glenn E. Mitchell, a Forest Service officer, reported that the first air-drop delivery probably was made in 1926 when mail and food were dropped to a fire camp in the Chelan National Forest in Washington.[1] The first drop made by an autogiro, he noted, was in 1932 on the Siskiyou Forest. A bad fire on Red Mountain was only twelve miles from the end of a road, but the topography and ground cover were so rough and dense that a pack train required two days of hard travel to make the round trip. So, free dropping of supplies was tried. The regional office reported that the autogiro was excellent for observation but deficient in cruising range and expensive to operate.

In August 1929, food for fire fighters was dropped free fall into a high meadow near Deer Lick Springs on the Trinity (now Shasta-Trinity) National Forest in California and to the Mt. Constance fire in the Olympic National Forest in Washington. On May 31, 1936, equipment and food were supplied to a 100-man fire camp serving the Storm Creek fire in the Lolo National Forest in Montana. The drops were made from a trimotor Ford plane, the type of plane that would be used with efficiency and safety in fire duty for years to come. Within a few years, free-fall dropping had become a practical and routine method of supplying fire fighters in back country. The procedure had one disadvantage, however, in that the supplies required specially designed containers and skilled workmen to prepare the bundles to be dropped.

---

1. U.S. Forest Service, *Fire Control Notes*, January 1942.

In the beginning of its experiments with air-drop delivery of supplies to fire camps remote from landing fields, the Forest Service tried "tight packaging," a laborious process that often resulted in loss and breakage. "Loose packaging," tried out during the summer of 1936 in the Idaho National Forest, was found to be superior. During fourteen tests, mess outfits, fire tools, and bedding were dropped successfully. Because loose packages had more air resistance, they made slower and softer landings.

To reduce the amount of noneffective cargo, the fire control officers also experimented with parachutes. In 1933, Flint made possibly the first experiments with fabricated parachutes to drop supplies and equipment. Homemade linen chutes with four to eight shroud lines were tried. Then, in 1935, the service acquired some condemned army regulation chutes that gave better performance and dependability, especially in the size and weight of the load.

In October 1936, at Pearson Field, Vancouver, Washington, field tests were conducted of crude parachutes made of burlap sacks cut open and tied at the four corners with 17-foot shrouds. Similar experiments were made in 1937 in the Coronado National Forest in Arizona and near Winthrop, Washington. Operational drops of supplies were made during that year on the Siskiyou and Wallowa National Forests in Oregon. By 1940, the Forest Service was dropping hot meals in specially designed containers to fire fighters. No longer an experimental technique, delivery of supplies by air to fire crews now became routine.

An advance of great moment in the continuing search for improvements in the parachute was the invention of the static line, a device that automatically opened the parachute. This was conceived jointly by Howard Flint and Robert Johnson, president of the Johnson Flying Service, during early experiments with cargo dropping in the autumn of 1934. Later (about 1940), the line was adapted to personnel parachutes by Frank Derry while he was employed by the Forest Service, and smokejumpers of the service first used chutes equipped with static lines in 1941.

Meanwhile, however, the tests were to take a different form, one that would revolutionize fire control work in the West. Doubtless as a result of the experience of military fliers dropping bombs during World War I, various interested parties suggested that experimental bombs containing fire-suppressing agents be dropped on forest conflagrations. In Scientific American (August 2, 1919), it was proposed that airplanes be used to fight fires from the skies with bombs containing fire-smothering gas. On the magazine cover there was a colored drawing of a two-passenger biplane dropping the bombs on a woodland blaze. Fanciful though it may have seemed at the time, the proposal was neither impractical nor impossible, and techniques of fire bombing would in time be worked out.

Concurrently with the experiments in dropping supplies and equipment from airplanes, some forest officers were investigating the possibility of dropping water and fire-retarding chemicals from aircraft. Flint conceived the idea of developing water and chemical bombs, and in 1934 conducted the first experiments in aerial delivery of water. During the following spring, the water-dropping tests continued; in addition, experiments were tried with Foamite chemicals. Flint, who had a strong bent toward the imaginative and innovative, was unable to continue his research; he died in October 1935.

In December 1935, an aerial fire control experimental project was set up in the Washington, D.C., office. All Forest Service flying in the western regions was based on cooperative arrangements with the army or with private contractors. In 1938, the Forest Service purchased its own plane, a Stinson SR-10 fitted out for experimental work in fire control. The plane was assigned to the California Region and used in fire-bombing tests, a continuation of the experiments initiated by Flint. Despite the success of the experiments in parachuting and free dropping supplies, it became apparent that suppressing fires by water or chemicals from the air was impractical with the airplanes and equipment then available.

Beginning early in 1939, the aerial experimental work was transferred to the Pacific Northwest Region. David P. Godwin, assistant chief of the Division of Fire Control, was put in charge. When the service decided to abandon the bombing tests, Godwin recommended that the balance of the experimental funds be used to carry on a study of parachute jumping.

Fire Fighters with Parachutes

When a procedure becomes routine, however novel it may have been when first tried, it ceases to excite wonder, and inquiring minds seek new ways to utilize it. Thus, parachuting fire fighters themselves was a possibility that occurred to several Forest Service officers simultaneously.

According to Godwin, T. V. Pearson, an officer of the Intermountain Region of the Forest Service in Ogden, Utah, originated the technique of smokejumping in 1934. Pearson conducted limited experiments but could find no support for his idea. "Then due to lack of vision or timidity in setting forth on a course which seemed so loaded with human hazard," Godwin wrote, "a period of inaction ensued, which was not broken even when the Russians started their much publicized mass jumping of troops."[2]

It appears that Pearson's experiments leading to parachuting men to fires were conducted with the assistance of a professional jumper, one "Buddy" Bruce. Their first tests were made with a dummy dropped at low altitudes. In the spring of 1935, Pearson continued the experiments, and Bruce made two successful low-altitude live jumps. The project was then discontinued, mainly because of the high risk involved.

Godwin is believed to have got his conception of parachuting fire fighters from accounts of German and Russian military personnel who had engaged in mass jumps. He had some of this foreign literature translated into English.

During October and November 1939, the Forest Service undertook an experimental project to determine the conditions under which fire fighters could be trained to land safely in mountainous terrain. Parallel with this object, field tests of parachutes and protective clothing were made to find

2. "The Parachute Method of Fire Suppression," *Journal of Forestry*, vol. 39 (February 1941), p. 169.

suitable and safe equipment. Essentially, the purpose of the experiment was to reduce the travel time of fire fighters so that fires could be put out while still small in size.

The Intercity Airport near Winthrop, Washington, in the Chelan (now the Okonagan) National Forest, was the base of operations. Experiments began October 5 and terminated November 15. Assisting in this historic project, in addition to Godwin, were C. Otto Lindh, chief of fire control for Region 6; T. Albert Davies, a technician in the Forest Service regional office at Portland, Oregon; Harold C. King, engineer-pilot; Walter Anderson, fire assistant on the Chelan; Beach Gill, president of the Eagle Parachute Company of Lancaster, Pennsylvania; two riggers and professional parachutists; and several local "smoke chasers," as the fire fighters were called.[3]

After these successful experiments had been concluded, Godwin wrote an account of them for *Aero Digest*:

The first men [to jump] were professional parachute jumpers but soon they were followed by two local men of "smoke chaser" experience who had never seen a parachute before. All jumps were successful. In the two months during which the experimental work was in progress 58 live jumps were made. In no instance was anyone injured in landing, although they dropped into mountain meadows and onto slopes and ridges, landed in fir trees as high as 135 ft., in thick stands of pine and in tall dead snags. These landings varied in altitude from 1700 ft. to 7000 ft. . . . Its practical application in fire fighting is far from established, but hopes are high that this new device may develop into a useable means of reducing that all-too-bulky period of travel time.[4]

The first two men to parachute to forest terrain, as distinct from jumps to airport landing strips or to open meadows, were Francis B. Lufkin and Glenn H. Smith, the latter a professional jumper and rigger. Lufkin was a local forest guard without previous parachuting experience. Subsequently, he became a professional parachute fire fighter and later was put in charge of the Aerial Project (parachute training center) of the Forest Service near Winthrop, Washington.

The first operational smokejumper crew was organized at the Intercity Airport near Winthrop in May and June 1940. The personnel consisted of two professional jumpers, Glenn H. Smith and Virgil Derry, and two professional fire fighters, Lufkin and George Honey.[5]

A second crew of six men was organized at Missoula, Montana. On July 12, 1940, in the Nezperce National Forest near Martin Creek in Idaho, Rufus Robinson and Earl E. Cooley, members of this crew, were the first two jumpers to parachute to a going fire.

Lufkin and Smith were the first jumpers to a going fire in the Northwest Region[6]; they extinguished the fire on August 10, 1940. On August 11, a second fire was put out by Derry and Honey. Both fires were in areas where their control by conventional means would have been exceedingly costly.

---

3. "History of Smoke Jumping," *Fire Control Notes*, U.S. Forest Service, July 1950.
4. "The Parachute as an Aid to National Forest Protection," April 1940.
5. In May 1964, Lufkin received a presidential citation for his contributions to the development of smokejumping.
6. In a letter to the author, September 6, 1969, Glenn Smith wrote: "I spotted Lufkin on this fire and followed him out."

The New Technique Succeeds

Although the project was intended as wholly experimental in 1940, nine operational jumps were made to going fires. The average cost of extinguishing these fires was $247; if ground crews had been employed the estimated cost would have been $3,500. That this hazardous work had singular attractions for a certain type of young American is proved by the 100 unsolicited job applications received. Six of the applicants were chosen and began training. Their salary was $193 a month for two and a half months of duty. Training cost the Forest Service a total of $330 a man.[7]

During 1940, four staff officers from the U.S. Army visited the Forest Service smokejumper base at Missoula. One of the officers, Major William Cary Lee, later used techniques developed by the Forest Service when he organized the first paratroop training at Fort Benning, Georgia. Subsequently, he commanded the 101st Airborne Division and was the first chief of the Airborne Command.

All smokejumping during 1941 was operated out of the Northern Region (Region 1 with headquarters at Missoula), which provided jumpers on call for the Intermountain and Pacific Northwest Regions. Four squads totaling twenty-six men were organized. Thirty jumps were made to nine fires, with a benefit-cost ratio of 10 to 1; that is, savings of $33,875 were obtained at the expense of $3,510. It was during this fire season that the Ford Tri-Motor plane was found to be well adapted to smokejumping operations. Jumps were made on the Chelan Forest more than 100 miles from the operations base.

In 1942, the first full year of World War II, only five experienced jumpers were available for duty; thirty-three new recruits had to be trained. They parachuted to thirty-one fires at an estimated savings in suppression costs of $66,000. Their prompt handling of a concentration of lightning fires in remote areas in September more than paid for the entire cost of the project.[8]

Again, only five experienced jumpers were available in 1943, but numerous conscientious objectors drafted for civilian public service volunteered. In all, seventy inexperienced men were trained for duty, not only in the Northern Region, but also in the Intermountain and Pacific Northwest Regions. Jumps were made to forty fires at an indicated savings of $75,000.

Conscientious objectors provided most of the manpower during the 1944 season—60 percent of the 120 men who participated. Jumpers fought nearly 100 fires. At the end of the season, the fire control officers concluded that the program was no longer an experiment but a standard routine operation. In short, the Forest Service, after one year of experimental parachuting and five years of operational employment of parachutists, had successfully developed a technique of fire control that was unique in American forestry, and indeed in world forestry.

To be sure, improvements would continue in training, in clothing and gear design, in logistics, and in suppression tactics. But smokejumping was now an accepted and indispensable procedure, adopted not only by the Forest Ser-

7. Axel G. Lindh, "Parachuting Fire Fighters," *Journal of Forestry*, vol. 39 (February 1941).
8. The slotted chute, which reduces oscillation and provides greater maneuverability, was put into use in 1942. Frank Derry of the Forest Service invented the chute.

vice for fire suppression on western national forests but by the Department of the Interior for the protection of national parks, public domain lands especially in Alaska, and tribal forests under the jurisdiction of the Indian Service. Outside of government, emergency protection was being given to lands of private forest protection associations.

Of all the causes of forest conflagrations, the most difficult to attack is the lightning fire, which is frequently ignited during so-called dry storms, often on high peaks or mountain ridges remote from roads and trails. At such times, ground travel by fire fighters, whether by auto, truck, pack animals, or on foot, is usually slow and tiring. Small fires may become large ones. And when more than one blaze is touched off by the same storm—a common occurrence—the problems of logistics become magnified and complicated. The most critical months for lightning fires in the northern Rocky Mountains are June, July, August, and September.

Jack S. Barrows of the Division of Fire Research, Northern Rocky Mountain Forest and Range Experiment Station, compiled a record of lightning fires for the months of April through October for the period 1931–45 in the national forests of the Northern Region. During some years more than 1,200 lightning fires were reported.[9]

According to Barrows, only 4 percent of the lightning fires could be reached by road. Hence, the smokejumper program, designed primarily to control these back country fires, is effective to the extent that it prevents such fires from spreading over large areas. For the period under study, Barrows found that the average size of the smokejumped fires was 11 acres; the average size of lightning fires suppressed by surface-transported forces was 46 acres.

Individual lightning fires that spread beyond control during the two decades prior to Barrows's report reached sizes of more than 75,000 acres, and one burned 175,000 acres. With potential losses as great as these, one comprehends why fire control officers may be conservative in estimating the cost of extinguishing such holocausts by conventional ground crews as being many times the yearly savings in wages, supplies, and equipment required to finance a smokejumping operation.

At the end of the 1940–49 period of operation, the Forest Service summary of the program showed that 1,425 smokejumpers had descended on a total of 1,424 fires. By the end of the 1967 fire season, the number of jumps—for training, fire, and rescue—totaled 77,060.

Smokejumper Bases

As noted, the North Cascades Smokejumper Base near Winthrop, Washington, established by the Forest Service in 1939, was the first in the United States. It has been in operation ever since. A second facility in the Pacific Northwest Region, known as the Siskiyou Base, was set up in 1943 at Cave Junction, Oregon. A sub-base at La Grande, Oregon, was established in 1956. In 1964, a major base, designated the Redmond Air Center, began operating near Redmond, Oregon.

9. U.S. Forest Service, *Fire Control Notes*, July 1951.

In 1940, smokejumping crews were organized in the Northern Region, which had its headquarters at Missoula. The crews were based at various times at Seeley Lake, Moose Creek, Big Prairie, and Nine Mile. Hale Field on the southern outskirts of Missoula was a staging point. A sub-base, established in 1951 at Grangeville, Idaho, gave protection to the region's western national forests. In 1952, a $700,000 aerial fire depot was started near Missoula and completed in 1954.

In the Intermountain Region, with headquarters at Ogden, Utah, a smokejumper base was set up in 1943 at McCall, Idaho, in the Payette National Forest. In 1948, a base was established at Idaho City to serve the Boise National Forest.

A smokejumping unit was first organized in the Southwestern Region (headquarters, Albuquerque, New Mexico) in 1947 at Deming, New Mexico. The operation was moved to the Grant County airport at Silver City in 1953.[10] New facilities were constructed and put into use in 1961.

The National Park Service established a small base at Yellowstone, Montana, in 1951. Control of the crew was transferred to the Forest Service in 1965. Two years later a new Interagency Smokejumper Base was activated at West Yellowstone airport; it serves the National Park Service and adjacent areas—the Forest Service Northern Region, the Rocky Mountain Region, and the Intermountain Region. In addition to these facilities, the Bureau of Land Management, Department of the Interior, established a base at Fairbanks, Alaska, in 1959.

In order to improve efficiency in initial attacks on fires in northern California national forests, the Forest Service created a major smokejumper base at Redding in 1957. A sub-base was developed at Columbia in 1961 to serve forested areas farther south.

In the summer of 1947, the Canadian Province of Saskatchewan set up a smokejumper training headquarters at Prince Albert and a base at Lac LaRonge.

A new and radical departure from the conventional techniques of fire detection and control began as an experiment by the Northern Region of the Forest Service in 1945. Known as the "Continental Unit" project, it encompassed an expanse of 2 million acres of mountainous terrain in Montana, including the Bob Marshall Wilderness Area and other remote portions of the Flathead, Helena, Lewis and Clark, and Lolo National Forests. Protection against fire would be provided by aerial detection and smokejumper suppression. The use of ground forces—manned lookout towers and fire fighting crews transported over roads and trails—would be virtually discontinued.

The purpose of this experiment was to improve planning methods and to evaluate the possibilities of aerial detection and "smoke chasing" when used alone or in combination with ground detection from lookout stations. After three seasons of tests in the unit's extensive field laboratory, a system of combined air-ground detection and suppression was put into operation in several national forests in the West. Other agencies and states in the United States and Canada later introduced the system, modified to meet their needs.

10. For an interesting account of operations at this base during the 1955 fire season, see Randle M. Hurst, *The Smokejumpers* (The Caxton Printers, Ltd., 1966).

Other Uses of Aircraft Tried

In the summer of 1925, Howard Flint, the innovator of several imaginative uses of the airplane in forestry, experimented with aerial photography of woodland. These experiments were continued by the Forest Service and by other agencies and companies, and special aerial cameras and photographic equipment were designed by the military and by commercial firms. In February 1932, aerial photography was put on a production basis in the Northern Region of the Forest Service. Six years later, forest officers devised the technique of photographic fire scouting. During the summer of 1938, pictures were taken, developed, printed, and dropped to ground officers in a total of eighteen minutes.

Probably the first use of an airplane to survey insect infestation in forested areas occurred in 1930, when an airplane under contract to the Forest Service was used by the then Bureau of Entomology of the Department of Agriculture to examine infested timber stands in Yellowstone National Park. Rapid improvements, both in aircraft and techniques, made it possible through spraying and dusting to control destructive insect infestations that had caused untold damage under previous conditions. When a hurricane on September 21, 1938, blew down extensive tracts of timber in New England, two autogiros obtained from the bureau enabled the Forest Service, which had been charged with the timber salvage operation, to make a prompt survey of the acreage and forest growth involved. In 1947, the Forest Service supervised the first large-scale aerial insect control operation in northern Idaho and eastern Washington. Using contract airplanes, forest officers sprayed 400,000 gallons of DDT on some 400,000 acres of fir timber infested with the tussock moth.

Aircraft were put to another new use by forest officers in March 1931 when Orange Olsen, chief of wildlife management for the Intermountain Region of the Forest Service, first made population estimates from an airplane of the Nebo elk herd in central Utah. From this beginning, wildlife biologists developed the techniques widely used today to inventory and manage big game. In February 1932, a Forest Service contract plane dropped 3,000 pounds of hay to starving deer in the Coeur d'Alene National Forest in Idaho. Cooperating with the Idaho State Game Commission, the Forest Service in 1938 began experiments in the distribution of salt from the air. The next year, 88 tons of salt were distributed to inaccessible big-game ranges in the state. Olsen, who had initiated many of the experiments with airplanes in wildlife management, died in a plane crash in 1945 in Jackson Hole, Wyoming, while on a flight counting elk.

The first helicopter takeoff and landing was made by the U.S. Army in 1922. Improvements in the design and the performance of the helicopter were so hastened by World War II that by 1945 the Forest Service and the army were able to collaborate in tests of this aircraft in mountainous areas of California. It was used experimentally in various forestry operations, largely for short-haul delivery of personnel and supplies. Because of certain limitations inherent in the nature of the craft, the helicopter did not immediately become an acceptable machine for fire control. A Sikorsky model was used in 1946 for limited reconnaissance of a fire in the Angeles National Forest of California. A year later, the helicopter was considered as key working equipment in the national forests of the state. On one fire, eighty personnel, two at a time, were transported over rough terrain by helicopter, requiring only three and one-half minutes of flight time one way as against three and one-half hours that would have been required for ground travel. A Bell model 47B was field tested in 1957 and found suitable for carrying payloads up to elevations of 6,000 feet.

In the *Journal of Forestry* (July 1948), Jack C. Kern, a fire control officer in the Angeles National Forest in southern California, stated: "The helicopter was given its first acid test under critical California conditions during the Bryant fire, which started August 5, 1947, on the Angeles National Forest. Fifteen calendar days, and ninety-two operational flying hours later, it emerged a proven weapon for fire suppresion." He reported that two contract craft (Bell model 47-B) were used. They flew 300 fire fighters to critical areas, evacuated 15 casualties to first aid and medical care, and delivered supplies and equipment to the crews.

During the 1947 fire season, helicopters were used for the first time to retrieve smokejumpers from remote places and return them to airfields or other points of convenient access. They were used also for the first time in the Pacific Northwest Region for initial attack on a fire in the Snoqualmie National Forest of Washington.

In 1948, the Pacific Northwest Region contracted for use of a helicopter on the Chelan National Forest for fire detection, initial attack, and retrieval of smokejumpers in the North Cascades. Because roads, trails, and bridges had been washed out during the destructive floods of that year, the helicopter provided faster access to that area than any other form of transportation. The adjoining Northern Region had a contract with the Johnson Flying Service, which purchased a Bell model 47-D helicopter and used it during that fire season.

Helicopters were employed increasingly in 1949, especially to pick up smokejumpers and return them to places of access; in California, they were used for four different fires. Additional experience was gained in the operation of this type of aircraft for making initial attacks on fires in the Northern Region and in the Pacific Northwest Region.

Fixed wing aircraft made 5,636 flights during 1950 on fire control missions in national forests. The sixteen airplanes owned by the Forest Service made 41 percent of the flights; contract operators the rest. Helicopters, used principally in California, flew a total of 1,255 hours.

In 1956, a new technique was introduced in the constantly developing search for improved methods of fire control. A group of northern California pilots experienced in agricultural aviation undertook a different kind of fire fighting from the air. Their fleet of seven biplanes dropped 150,000 gallons of water and fire retardant on twenty-five fires in the state. By 1959, the fleet had grown to more than 100 planes, and about 4 million gallons of retardant chemicals were dropped on fires in the western states and Alaska that year.

Sodium calcium borate was the first retardant used. It was added to water in the proportion of four pounds to the gallon. Bentonite clay, material used as oil well drilling mud, was used effectively in 1959.

Improvement and expansion in the use of aircraft, both fixed-wing airplanes and helicopters, in fire control continued so that at the end of 1967 the Forest Service had set new records in all phases of air attack on fires. Aircraft were flown on fire missions for a total of nearly 75,000 hours. Smokejumpers made 4,400 jumps to 1,247 fires. Air tankers dropped almost 8 million gallons of fire retardant chemicals.

In short, from the first tentative experiments with aerial forest patrol in 1919, aircraft of all kinds became indispensable working tools of foresters, both in the United States and Canada. From detection and control of fire, their use was adapted to detection and control of insect and disease infestations, to mapping and inventorying timber volume, and finally to balloon logging. The adaptation of aircraft to forest management has immeasurably advanced the art and practice of forestry in America.

CHAPTER 14

Forestry on the Farm

Forestry extension, which has done so much to assist farm woodland owners, had its legislative beginning when Congress passed the Smith-Lever Act of May 8, 1914. This law provided for cooperative agricultural extension work between the state agricultural colleges and the Department of Agriculture. It defined the work as "the giving of instruction and practical demonstrations in agriculture and home economics to persons not attending or resident in said colleges in the several communities, and imparting to such persons information on said subjects through field demonstrations, publications, and otherwise. . . ."[1]

Under the terms of this act and its various amendments and of related federal and state laws, the Department of Agriculture, the land-grant colleges and universities, the states and territories, and the county governments share in both the financial administration and the subject-matter responsibilities of the program. The fundamental character of extension work has changed but little; it is still education carried on outside and beyond the classroom, principally in rural areas and communities.

At the beginning of the program in 1915, total expenditures for forestry extension work were about $4,000. A decade later, in 1924, they had risen to only $19,000. Four states were then participating in the program with full-time forestry specialists—Pennsylvania, New York, Maine, and Iowa. Part-time forestry specialists were doing extension work in several other states. Some states started a program but failed to continue it, at least on a full-time basis. For a decade after the passage of the Smith-Lever Act, the funds allotted annually for forestry were less than 1 percent of the total available for cooperative extension work.

Important as the Smith-Lever Act was in launching the agricultural extension movement, it had a less profound effect on the spread of forestry exten-

1. An account of the establishment of this movement is to be found in Alfred Charles True, *A History of Agricultural Extension Work in the United States: 1785-1923*, U.S. Department of Agriculture, Misc. Pub., no. 15 (1928).

sion. The law that induced the states to take up forestry as a cooperative extension activity was the Clarke-McNary Act of 1924. Prior to its passage, only six states had undertaken farm forestry extension work under authority of the Smith-Lever Act. Twenty additional states took up the work following passage of the Clarke-McNary Act.

Clarke-McNary specifically authorized educational assistance and advice to farm owners in establishing and improving woodlots, shelterbelts, and windbreaks. Federal-state cooperation in the production and distribution of forest planting stock for farmers was also provided. Within a decade most of the states and Puerto Rico were participating in this program.

By 1933, thirty-nine extension foresters were working in thirty-three states and two territories. According to the Natural Resources Board, the federal government apportioned about $70,000 annually to the support of forestry extension agents at state agricultural colleges. The states appropriated $90,000 as their share of this cooperative program. In addition, about $10,000 was contributed in behalf of private owners of woodland.[2]

Another legislative aid to farm forestry was the Cooperative Farm Forestry Act (also known as the Norris-Doxey Act) of 1937. It assigned to the Extension Service the administration of farm forestry education. The Soil Conservation Service was assigned the task of providing direct assistance to woodland owners in the management, harvesting, and marketing of their products; in 1945, the Forest Service took over this responsibility. The principal advantage of the law was that it enabled federal and state agencies to carry on a more intensive program in farm forestry throughout the nation than had been possible before, although funds authorized by it did not become available until 1940. By providing funds for additional extension foresters, it made possible the employment of a second, or assistant, extension forester in thirty-one states. By 1940, forty-three states and Puerto Rico were cooperating; fifty-eight extension foresters were employed.

A defect in the Norris-Doxey Act was its failure to define the role and authority of the land-grant colleges vis-à-vis the state forestry agencies. This issue was centered in the kinds of forestry services these agencies should provide to the private forest owners. It was resolved in 1948 by a joint policy declaration by the Association of Land Grant Colleges and the Association of State Foresters. All forestry educational activities that did not involve direct service to landowners on the ground would be carried on by the extension services. Service performed in the management, harvesting, and marketing of products would be the province of the state forestry agencies.

The Cooperative Forest Management Act of 1950 authorized financial assistance to the states to undertake management assistance to nonfarm owners of woodland as well as to farm owners. It also included aid to the processors of forest products.[3]

An extension forester is a specialist in both education and forestry who works with, and through, county extension agents in his state. He demon-

2. Natural Resources Board, *Supplementary Report of the Land Planning Committee*, pt. 8, "Forest Land Resources, Requirements, Problems, and Policy" (1935).
3. See chap. 7 for a further account of these activities.

strates to farm groups methods of planting, tree marking, timber harvesting, and other techniques of managing woodland. Generally, the state extension forester holds professorial rank in the agricultural college with which he is associated. The grade is customarily professor or associate professor.

Prior to the Smith-Lever Act the Forest Service provided to private woodland owners the kind of services later to be designated extension forestry. Wilbur R. Mattoon, a Yale forestry graduate who had been with the Forest Service since 1904, was chosen to develop the southern farm forestry program in 1912. He was the first forester in the service to become an extension forester. When the States Relations Service was set up in the Department of Agriculture, Mattoon became the forestry extension specialist, but he maintained his office in the Forest Service.

In a memorandum dated November 29, 1921, Mattoon noted that, according to the records of the Forest Service and the States Relations Service, "the situation is about as follows":

Pennsylvania and New York appear to be the only States regularly employing extension specialists. The specialist in North Carolina recently resigned and is now with the Timber Section of the Internal Revenue Bureau in Washington.

In a number of other States informal cooperation exists between the two organizations, as shown by concrete results in 1920 in California, Colorado, Minnesota, and Michigan. It appears that up to about a year ago Michigan devoted Smith-Lever funds to farm forestry and was obliged to discontinue the work. In addition, the records show that county agents carried on forestry work ... in Nebraska and Montana ... and in South Carolina, Mississippi, and Louisiana.[4]

During 1942, Joshua A. Cope, a Yale forestry graduate and extension forester for the New York State College of Agriculture at Cornell University, made a study of methods used by public and private agencies to interest farmers in the proper management of their woodlands. Noting little accomplishment in the promotion of extension forestry as a result of the Smith-Lever Act, he called 1924, when the Clarke-McNary Act was passed, the significant year in farm forestry education. According to Cope:

Prior to 1924 there had been very little activity on the part of either the federal government or the state colleges of agriculture in the field of farm forestry education. It was permissible, of course, for the college, under Smith-Lever funds, to take on extension specialists in forestry as well as in any other subject matter relating to farming, but with few exceptions this was not done. During the decade 1914-24, Pennsylvania and New York were the only states continuously carrying on their staffs an extension specialist in forestry.[5]

In order to identify the problems of getting more farmers to practice forestry, the Committee on Farm Forestry of the Society of American Foresters queried professional foresters by mail, receiving 167 replies from

---

4. Quoted in C. R. Anderson, "Some Phases of Forestry Extension Work," *Journal of Forestry*, vol. 20 (March 1922), pp. 264-71.

5. *Farm Forestry in the Eastern United States* (Washington: The Charles Lathrop Pack Forestry Foundation, 1943), p. 11. Cope was wrong; in addition to Pennsylvania and New York, Iowa and Maine also had forestry extension specialists during this period.

forty-two states. The results of the questionnaire, as reported by Cope,[6] showed that it was difficult to arouse the farmers' interest in forestry; half of them failed to see possible profits in farm woodland management. The respondents believed that the agricultural colleges should offer more courses in farm forestry and that county agricultural agents should be required to take them. Personal contact and service by foresters was deemed essential in getting farmers to practice forestry, a position with which Cope strongly concurred. It is pertinent to observe that personal service was the policy being followed by the Soil Conservation Service and the one that would be authorized by the Cooperative Forest Management Act of 1950. According to the annual report of the Extension Service for 1931, "Several counties in New York have appointed assistant county agents whose sole work is in forestry."

The first extension professor of forestry at Pennsylvania State College was Clarence R. Anderson, who became the commonwealth's first full-time extension specialist in forestry in 1919. Prior to that year, Anderson carried on forestry extension work on a part-time basis. Actually, he began the work in 1916 when he was an instructor in the Department of Forestry and spent one month each year as a temporary forestry specialist. In 1919, the Agricultural Extension Service at the college funded his work and appointed him extension forestry specialist. Calls on Anderson for advice in farm woodland management rapidly increased, and Frank T. Murphy was appointed his assistant in 1923.

Irwin T. Bode, a forestry graduate of Iowa State College, became extension forester for Iowa in September 1921.

Maine acquired an extension forester during the summer of 1923 when Myron E. Watson, a forestry graduate of the University of Maine, was appointed forestry specialist in the Extension Service of the College of Agriculture.

In those states having schools of forestry in land-grant universities, the schools usually participate in the work of the extension foresters and often provide office quarters for them. In the beginning years of the program, the extension foresters frequently came from the ranks of the teaching faculty. From a professional standpoint, the liaison between the extension specialists and the teachers has added strength to both sectors.

New York was the pioneer state in extension forestry on a continuing basis. John Bently, Jr., was the first appointee, on January 1, 1912, in the Department of Forestry at Cornell University. On October 1, 1913, Frank B. Moody, a forestry graduate of the University of Michigan, was named professor and was given responsibility for the direction of the department's extension functions. Moody resigned in 1915 to become forest commissioner in Wisconsin. The work was then carried on by Bently and Cedric H. Guise, who was named extension forester October 1, 1915.[7]

6. Ibid., app.

7. The author believes the first of the state forestry extension bulletins was written by Bently and published by Cornell in 1914. Entitled *Methods of Determining the Value of Timber on the Farm Woodlot*, it was revised and reprinted in 1922, 1923, and 1926.

As a replacement for Moody, George Harris Collingwood, a forestry alumnus of Michigan State College, was designated assistant extension professor of forestry July 1, 1916. He went on sabbatical leave in 1923 to help the States Relations Service of the Department of Agriculture plan a cooperative program between the Extension Service and the state foresters. With the passage of the Clarke-McNary Act in June 1924, Collingwood was invited to join the staff of subject-matter specialists in the States Relations Service. He resigned from Cornell June 30, 1924, to become the first extension forester in the Extension Service in Washington, D.C.

On October 1, 1924, Joshua Cope, who had been serving as assistant state forester of Maryland, entered on his long and productive twenty-six-year career as extension forester of New York State.[8]

George Harris Collingwood resigned from the Extension Service in 1928 to become forester for The American Forestry Association. For a year following his resignation, the position of extension forester in the Office of Cooperative Extension Work was vacant. It was filled on July 1, 1929, by William K. Williams, who had been state extension forester in Arkansas. During the ensuing decade the work load expanded so that Arthur M. Sowder, formerly a forester in the Forest Service, was taken on as Williams's associate in November 1939. Thereafter, Williams supervised the federal interest in extension forestry in the eastern part of the United States, and Sowder looked after the work in the West.

On the retirement of Sowder in 1964 and of Williams a year later, the position of extension forester was filled by Ivan R. Martin, formerly state extension forester in Alabama, beginning June 6, 1965.

By October 1968, there were 150 state extension foresters and assistant state extension foresters employed in forty-four states and Puerto Rico.

Farm Forestry and Soil Conservation

In August 1933, the Soil Erosion Service, later to be named the Soil Conservation Service, was set up in the Department of the Interior to administer a grant of $5 million made to the Federal Emergency Administration for erosion control. Intended to be a temporary agency, the service was one of several created to provide relief employment under the authority of the National Industrial Recovery Act. Hugh Hammond Bennett, soon to become one of America's most effective conservation advocates, was appointed director of the new service on September 19, 1933.

Bennett decided to concentrate work on certain watersheds, each not less than 25,000 acres in area, where erosion was ruining the land or theatening to do so and where soil erosion control practices could be demonstrated to landowners and the public. Coon Valley in southwestern Wisconsin was the first demonstration project undertaken; work began there in October 1933. Within five years, Coon Valley would be attracting soil scientists and conservationists from all over America and from abroad. Nearly 40,000 acres

---

8. See Ralph S. Hosmer, *Forestry at Cornell* (Cornell University, 1950).

had been put under management. More than 12,000 acres of woodland were being protected from fire and grazing; 810 acres had been planted to trees.[9]

In organizing this project and others to follow, the service had the advantage of local participation and control. A participating farmer or other landowner would work with the technical staff of the service in planning the erosion control practices and their application on his property. An integrated farm plan was prepared by the staff, which usually included specialists in agronomy, biology, engineering, forestry, land-use planning, range management, soil science, and other specialties as needed.

Woodland was a component of most of the demonstration projects, hence foresters were recruited for the technical staffs to plan the forestry phases of the work. An important requirement was that the forestry practices recommended had to be integrated with the farm business.

In March 1935, when the Soil Erosion Service was transferred from the Department of the Interior to the Department of Agriculture, thirty-nine demonstration projects were in operation. (By 1940, the number would rise to 174.) On March 27, 1935, through the Soil Conservation Act, Congress created the Soil Conservation Service in the Department of Agriculture and gave civil service status to its 10,000 employees.

The Committee on Forest Influences and Erosion Control of the Society of American Foresters endorsed the act in the following manner:

This measure is a landmark in conservation in the United States. Under this act the Congress recognizes that the wastage of soil and moisture resources on farm, grazing, and forest lands of the Nation, resulting from soil erosion, is a menace to the national welfare, and that it is hereby declared to be the policy of Congress to provide permanently for the control and prevention of soil erosion and thereby to preserve natural resources, control floods, prevent impairment of reservoirs and maintain the navigability of rivers and harbors, protect public health and public lands, and relieve unemployment. . . .[10]

Walter C. Lowdermilk, a forester and soil scientist, was chairman of this committee. Joining the Soil Erosion Service at Bennett's invitation, he served as a special advisor, with the title of associate chief, on the scientific aspects of soil and water conservation. Later, he was chief of the Research Division of the Soil Conservation Service (SCS), and on his retirement in 1947 was assistant chief for foreign cooperation.

Forestry, as one of the SCS technical specialties, was most active during the first decade of the service's existence. At one period, 250 professional foresters were employed in various capacities—nursery production of planting stock and the establishment of plantations and shelterbelts, farm woodland and watershed protection, forest management, and so forth.

9. In area, two of the most extensive soil-erosion control projects in the program—indeed, the largest ever undertaken anywhere in the world—were the 16-million-acre project in Arizona, New Mexico, and Utah, involving work on the Navajo, Hopi, and Zuni Indian reservations, and the 15-million-acre Rio Grande project in New Mexico. Hugh G. Calkins, a career officer in the Forest Service, was recruited by Bennett to administer them.

10. W. C. Lowdermilk, "Forest Influences and Soil Erosion," a committee report, *Journal of Forestry*, vol. 34 (April 1936), pp. 391–94.

In 1937, the SCS began providing technical assistance to the soil conservation districts. This development came about when the states passed laws authorizing the creation of soil conservation districts administered by local farmers. The SCS changed its function from that of administering demonstration projects to that of directing, training, and supervising personnel working in individual districts. (By 1969, there were more than 3,000 soil and water conservation districts in the United States.)

SCS administrative regions were abolished in 1954, and the seven regional foresters were assigned elsewhere. The term *forester* was temporarily replaced by *woodland conservationist; forestry* became known as *woodland conservation*. The staff of foresters was reduced to forty. Heading up the work in the office in Washington, D.C., was the woodland conservationist; a field woodland conservationist was appointed in each of the five SCS regions. Later, the title became optional: forester or woodland conservationist. (By 1969, there were four regions with a regional forester in charge of the forestry work in each.)

As the soil conservation districts came into existence, the services of foresters were less sought after, and the number of foresters declined. Courtland B. Manifold, former chief of the Forestry Division, told what happened.

The number of foresters dwindled. They became farm planners. The few that were left as strictly forestry technicians had to get forestry into the woods, if at all, through the farm planners, most of whom knew little about forestry. They could, however, grasp the four essential ingredients of "wood as a farm crop" and use their skill and opportunities to get wood accepted as a farm crop. This didn't require much knowledge of technical forestry; it involved mostly getting farmers started systematically working or "farming" their woods. The technical help in forestry practices would come from the SCS foresters (where there were any) or from the foresters employed by other agencies such as the State and the Extension Service.[11]

The Appalachian Section of the Society of American Foresters at a meeting in Durham, North Carolina, on January 28, 1956, adopted a resolution requesting the Soil Conservation Service to desist from permitting farm planners who were not professional foresters to perform technical forestry practices on farm woodland. Specifically, the society members objected to farm planners who lacked forestry education making thinnings and undertaking salvage, release, and crop-tree methods of cutting.

A similar resolution was adopted at a meeting of the Allegheny Section of the society in Harrisburg, Pennsylvania, on February 11, 1956. This group of foresters pointed out that "the practical application of any woodland management system and related silvicultural treatments vary from tract to tract to the extent that the services of a professional forester are needed."[12]

In both resolutions, the foresters acknowledged the valuable work done by the SCS in disseminating forestry information to farm woodland owners.

11. "Forestry in the Soil Conservation Service," 1958 (Committee on the History of Forestry, Society of American Foresters).
12. "Forestry and the Soil Conservation Service," *Journal of Forestry*, vol. 54 (April 1956), pp. 281–82.

They approved the accomplishments of SCS in reforestation and in inducing private owners to protect their woodland from fire and grazing.

In addition to the objections raised at the two society meetings, the South Carolina Forestry Committee and the North Carolina Forestry Council addressed comparable recommendations to the SCS. These state groups recommended that the forestry services of nonprofessional farm planners not include silvicultural treatment of farm woodland. This issue was more than a local or an isolated instance of public employees undertaking to apply technical practices without educational or professional qualifications.

In February 1956, the Council of the Society of American Foresters unanimously directed President DeWitt Nelson to express its strong opposition against nonprofessional workers in public agencies performing silvicultural functions and similar forestry work. Nelson wrote to Donald A. Williams, administrator of the Soil Conservation Service, on March 2, 1956, and transmitted the two society resolutions. He made it clear that the criticism directed at SCS resulted from instances when farm planners who were not foresters departed from official policy by recommending silvicultural practices to private woodland owners. Emphasizing that the criticism was not to be construed as questioning the competence of the professional foresters in the service, he added, "Our members gladly acknowledge the technical ability of the S.C.S. foresters and wish there were more of them."[13]

Replying to Nelson on March 28, 1956, Williams did not deny infractions in SCS policy. He was pleased to have the SAF Council express confidence in the technical ability of the SCS foresters. He then went on:

There is no disagreement between the Soil Conservation Service and the Society of American Foresters on the point that non-professional personnel should not develop recommendations as to silvicultural practices. Even though our farm planners are professional soil conservationists, we do not expect them to assume responsibility for such recommendations. We do expect them, after being trained by our own and other foresters, to use technical specifications developed by foresters to assist land owners and operators in their choice of practices and in learning how to use those practices in their woods.[14]

In objecting to publicly employed, nonprofessional personnel engaging in silviculture on private land, the Society of American Foresters was not attempting to appropriate to its members the exclusive right to practice forestry. The purpose was to protect the private owner from the economic consequences of ill-planned and ill-applied practices. This objective was in accordance with the society's policy of striving to guard the general public against unqualified practitioners professing a competence they lacked, whether employed in government service or engaging in private consulting work.

Throughout the SCS, professional foresters have contributed substantially to the success of the field work, which was, and is, the foundation of the program. During the thirty-five years of SCS operations, silvicultural and other forest management practices have been applied to 45 million acres of

13. "Exchange of Letters between S.A.F. and S.C.S.," *Journal of Forestry*, vol. 54 (June 1956), pp. 414–17.
14. Ibid.

farm woodland. Plantings alone add up to the impressive total of 18 million acres. Three million farms are now included in soil and water conservation districts. Conservation plans have been prepared for about 1.7 million of these farms on which the proportion of land in woods is approximately 33 percent (553 million acres).

E. V. Jotter, a career forester in the Department of Agriculture, was appointed chief forester for the Soil Erosion Service in 1934 and served during the transfer of the service from Interior to Agriculture.

John F. Preston, a forestry graduate of the University of Michigan and lately chief forester for the Hammermill Paper Company, was appointed chief of the Forestry Division, Soil Conservation Service, in 1936, continuing until his retirement in 1946. Courtland B. Manifold then became chief of the Forestry Division and on his retirement was followed by Theodore B. Plair, whose title was head woodland conservationist. Carrow T. Prout, Jr., was appointed head forester in 1965.

The Prairie States Forestry Project

Another of the New Deal's soil conservation undertakings—one that would be as successful as it was originally controversial—was the Prairie States Forestry Project. Also known as the shelterbelt project, it was started by the Forest Service under an executive order of July 11, 1934, by President Roosevelt and was financed by emergency relief funds.

President Roosevelt initiated this project in a brief memorandum to Robert Y. Stuart, chief of the Forest Service, on August 19, 1933. He wanted to know the cost of a series of 100-foot shelterbelts planted five miles apart in portions of Texas, Oklahoma, Kansas, and Nebraska.[15]

In his reply of August 15, transmitted through Secretary of Agriculture Henry A. Wallace, Stuart outlined a plan whereby the Forest Service would seek the cooperation of the state foresters in the area in accordance with an enclosed memorandum on forest planting possibilities in the prairie region. Raphael Zon, director of the Lake States Forest Experiment Station, St. Paul, Minnesota, is believed to have been the principal author of this memorandum. Credited also with having been the chief planner of the shelterbelt plantings, he was charged with the technical supervision of the project in July 1934.

The timeliness of the proposal was emphasized by the terrible drought during the summer of 1934. Of unprecedented severity, it caused such widespread economic distress that an enormous and imaginative program of relief for the drought-stricken farmers and ranchers was called for. Under the plan developed by the Forest Service, trees would be set out in strips aligned to break the force of the prevailing winds and to help control the vast dust storms that caused ruinous soil losses. The shelterbelts were to extend from Canada to Mexico.

Nurseries were established and trees were grown for the particular soil and climatic conditions where they were to be planted. In general, the plantings were successful.

15. Nixon (ed.), *Franklin D. Roosevelt and Conservation: 1911-1945*, vol. 1, p. 198.

When the project terminated as an emergency activity in June 1942, its administration was transferred from the Forest Service to the Soil Conservation Service for liquidation. During the seven years it had been under Forest Service supervision, 217 million trees had been set out in 18,600 miles of shelterbelts with the cooperation of 30,000 landowners and the governments of six plains states.

But windbreak planting did not cease. Under the Soil Conservation Service, it continued in the six states of the original shelterbelt zone and was extended to other states where windbreaks were needed for wind erosion control. As the areas of shelterbelt planting in time became soil conservation districts, the SCS foresters expanded the planting of trees and shrubs for the protection of crops and livestock.

CHAPTER **15**

The Growth of
Industrial Forestry

During the 1800s, the lumber industry moved from New England to the Middle Atlantic States and to the Lake States, finally branching out to the South and to the Pacific Northwest. As the timber resource in one region was cut out, the industry moved on. In the early 1900s, it had reached the last frontier of virgin timber, both in the South and the Northwest, and had nowhere else to go. This is an oft told episode of American history and need not be repeated here in detail. More pertinent is the reversal in operating procedures that transformed a migratory, exploitive, destructive industry into one that is generally a stable, permanent, timber-growing enterprise.

The company whose stockholders or management considered its existence as perpetual adopted operating methods that would assure stability and permanence. The essentials for corporate permanence were (1) land, (2) a stand of commercial timber of volume and quality adequate to sustain the mills and other manufacturing plants, and (3) the application of scientific management so that continuous crops of forest products could be harvested in perpetuity. These conditions obtained when old established companies already owned extensive woodlands that could be put under forest management, or when new companies (or old companies moving into new territory) purchased sufficient timber holdings.

As early as 1921, Royal S. Kellogg, secretary of the News Print Service Bureau, was predicting that the growing paper industry was the most likely one to undertake an industrial forestry program. Although previously identified with the lumber industry and its resources (he wrote the first appraisal of the U.S. timber supply in 1909 while with the Forest Service), Kellogg had little expectation that the lumber industry as a whole would initiate sustained-yield forestry. He expressed the belief that "the production of large-size timber is too long an undertaking with too great hazards and too low a rate of return to attract the investor or to appeal to the practical sense of lumber manufacturers." The production of pulpwood was another matter, because it required "much shorter time than the growing of sawtimber, and the amount

197

of capital invested in a pulp and paper mill is so great as to require a long period of return." Therefore, he concluded that "it is to the pulp and paper industry that the professional foresters of the country turn most hopefully for the practical application of their principles."[1]

Certain forces and events during the first half of the present century welded many separate and tentative industrial forestry beginnings into an identifiable national movement. This movement was to comprehend the largest acreage of privately owned woodland ever to be put under silvicultural management anywhere in the world. The decades between 1930 and 1960 were particularly significant because of industry's spreading adoption of scientific silviculture. Unaccountably, this period has been only sketchily chronicled in the past. Throughout the rest of this chapter, an attempt is made to round out the details of these three vital decades and to present the highlights of the industrial forestry movement as a whole.

The National Lumber Manufacturers Association

On December 9–10, 1902, the National Lumber Manufacturers Association (now the National Forest Products Association) was organized in St. Louis. At this meeting the directors passed a resolution, the first of the association's long involvements in forestry policy. In this resolution, it was urged that Congress establish a national forest reserve in the hardwood regions of the southern Appalachian Mountains. The stated purpose was to preserve the mountains and to demonstrate how to perpetuate the hardwood forests. When presented to the directors, the resolution was attributed to a Dr. Holmes, who was not present and who was not further identified in the printed report of the meeting.

In his autobiography, Gifford Pinchot threw light on the genesis of this resolution when he told of a discussion he had had at Biltmore Forest in 1892 or 1893 with Joseph A. Holmes, at that time state geologist of North Carolina. During the course of their talk, Holmes suggested that the government ought to purchase a large tract of timberland in the southern Appalachians and practice forestry on it. "It was a great plan, and neither he nor I ever let it drop," Pinchot wrote. "Nearly twenty years later the Weeks Law was passed, Holmes's dream came true, and today Eastern and Western National Forests which cover eighteen millions of acres owe their origin to his brilliant suggestion."[2]

During its formative years, the National Lumber Manufacturers Association (NLMA) maintained a close and friendly relationship with the Bureau of Forestry. At its second annual meeting in Washington, D.C., April 20–21, 1903, Forester Gifford Pinchot gave an address, and the directors appointed a Committee on Forestry that made a report pledging cooperation with the bureau and urging industry members to work with state governments for laws to encourage forestry.

1. "Notes upon the Paper Industry and the Pulpwood Supply," *Journal of Forestry*, vol. 19 (May 1921), p. 495.
2. *Breaking New Ground*, p. 56.

Two years later, Pinchot sought the cooperation of NLMA in two areas. First, having explained the current work program of the Bureau of Forestry, he asked the directors to endorse it. Second, he asked the directors to solicit funds to endow a chair of "applied forestry and practical lumbering" at the Yale University Forest School.

A committee to "secure the funds" was authorized, with Frederick E. Weyerhaeuser as chairman, and by the time of the 1907 meeting it had raised $66,000, which was turned over to Yale. (Ralph E. Bryant was the first professor to occupy the chair.) At the 1910 meeting, Mr. Weyerhaeuser reported that the whole endowment fund of $100,000 had been raised.

In policy statements, in the testimony of its representatives at congressional hearings, and other public announcements during the past quarter-century, NLMA has consistently opposed additional acquisition of private forest land by the federal government. Its position was not always thus. The following resolution was adopted by the directors on July 10, 1920, at Chicago:

Growing timber crops must be largely, though by no means wholly, a Governmental and state function. Hence, both should acquire, by purchase and by exchange of stumpage for land, much larger areas of permanent forest land than they now possess. Such acquirement should be largely cut-over land, to assure proper care thereof as well as economy in public expenditure.
If private owners refuse either to sell for such purpose, or to take reasonable steps themselves to keep in timber crops, any deforested land competently classified as suitable chiefly for forest growing and not suitable for agriculture, Government and states should be permitted to condemn and pay for it at prices comparable to those paid in voluntary transactions.[3]

That this policy was continued in force is shown by its reiteration two years later when the NLMA Forestry Committee submitted recommendations for legislation to a Senate Special Committee on Reforestation. Item 4 of the recommendations stipulated "provision for a reasonable program of selection and acquisition by exchange and by purchase, through bond issues if necessary, of such lands as should be added to the national forest system to assure their best protection and management in the public interest."[4]

During the early 1920s, E. T. Allen, executive officer of the Western Forestry and Conservation Association, served also as part-time forester for NLMA. His influence on the adoption of such policies by the association may be inferred from his background as a former Forest Service officer and his knowledge of the need for protection and management of the nation's extensive logged-off areas. Many forest conservationists of that period, both inside and outside government, believed that public ownership afforded the most certain guarantee that those millions of cutover and burned-over acres would ever be reclothed with commercial timber stands.

Chamber of Commerce Survey

In November 1927, the Natural Resources Production Department of the Chamber of Commerce of the United States, Washington, D.C., published a

3. National Lumber Manufacturers Association, *Lumber Bulletin*, August 1, 1920.
4. *National Lumber Bulletin*, December 7, 1923.

survey of private forestry, *Progress in Commercial Forestry*. The report was prepared by Charles W. Boyce, a member of the staff of the department and a professional forester.

Some 1,200 individuals and companies said to be interested in forestry were invited to report on their activities, and 470 replied. Of the responses received, 174 were sufficiently complete to enable analysis of the major forestry activities of the senders. The total area of the timber holdings was 21 million acres.

In the North Atlantic states the survey accounted for fifty owners active in forestry. Pulp and paper companies had the largest acreage under management. Mention was made of progress in reforestation by coal companies in Pennsylvania, an activity not specifically attributed to, but clearly reflecting, early offers by the Pennsylvania Department of Forests and Waters to prepare planting plans without charge and to supply seedlings from state nurseries at minimal cost. In the region, 6.5 million acres of industrial property were under management, together with a large aggregate of small tracts, some of which were under intensive management, as it was understood during that period.

In the South in 1927, little accomplishment could be found; fifty-one owners holding 6.6 million acres were practicing forestry, including fire protection. Of these, thirty-eight were lumber companies, eight were pulp and paper companies, and five were naval stores operations. A decade later, the greatest forestry development in the United States would occur in the South.

In the North Central Region, forestry had barely begun. In all this vast wooded realm, only thirty-four commercial owners had their lands under management, and the acreage was minimal—1.8 million acres. Much planting was being done, however, especially on small ownerships, which were mostly farms. In the West, according to the report, the forests were still largely virgin, but thirty-nine companies had 5.8 million acres under management.

In conclusion, the Chamber of Commerce noted: "A more complete and detailed survey is being made by the Society of American Foresters as a basis for [a] continuous record of forestry activities in the United States." True, the society was engaged in a study of private forestry, but its findings as to progress were less than impressive and hardly encouraging, as we shall see.

A national conference on commercial forestry was sponsored by the U.S. Chamber of Commerce in Chicago on November 16–17, 1927. It was the first nationwide colloquium on the business aspects of forest management ever held. In addition to industrial timbermen, its 250 registrants included government foresters, representatives of trade associations, the press, and the general public. The year 1927 was one of stagnant lumber markets and overproduction in the industry, and these conditions were frequently mentioned as obstacles to capital investment in forest practice.[5]

Four main recommendations were made for encouraging industry-wide application of forestry: equitable and stable taxation of forest properties; adequate forest protection by public agencies; increased technical and eco-

5. Chamber of Commerce of the United States, *Report of Conference on Commercial Forestry* (1928).

nomic research; and education of forest communities so as to gain public understanding of, and cooperation with, industry's forestry undertakings.

Reading the proceedings of this conference four decades later, one is struck by the extreme conservatism, even pessimism, of some industry spokesmen and by the optimism of others. Everett G. Griggs, president of the St. Paul & Tacoma Lumber Company, was a keynote speaker who talked much of uncertainties, obstacles, and doubts. Pointing out that during the business depression the industry found forests already grown of doubtful profit, he questioned how far lumbermen could afford to go to assure forests for the future. His narrow viewpoint of forestry and its possibilities was shared by many industrialists of the 1920s. "Forestry is nothing but intelligent perpetuated lumbering," he said. "Entirely too long it has been preached, defined and calculated by everybody but lumbermen; led by leaders with nothing to lead, no lands, no trees, no mills to serve the public, no forces to do the work in the woods, no taxes to pay, no business solvency to meet, no responsibility, no obligations."[6] Although Griggs then called on lumbermen to assume this leadership, it was quite evident that he resented public criticism of the industry for its slowness in undertaking sustained-yield management.

It is not an unfair commentary on this conference to note that the four principal resolutions all called for action by the public; not a single recommendation called for greater exertion and investment in forest management by the industry itself. In summarizing the conference, D. C. Everest, president of the American Paper and Pulp Association, made a point of the need for education of the public so that larger governmental appropriations for research would be forthcoming. "To all the problems presented either in forest management or in utilization of forest products," he said, "there is but one answer—research. It is the panacea of all the ills." Moreover, Everest appeared to be speaking for all the business representatives in emphasizing the point of view that it was the government's obligation to conduct experiments in management and utilization for industry. Reminding the audience "that the subject of forest management is one in which the national and state governments are vitally interested," he went on:

The perpetuation of the timber supply in the United States is the most important question confronting our people today. It involves the health, happiness and prosperity of every person in the country. It is classed as the fourth industry in the United States today, but we must remember that no industry can carry on business unless forest products are available.

One reason for suggesting that governmental agencies carry on the work of research in forest management is the fact that the program must cover a long period. The results obtained are not patentable and the benefits accrue to all the people, therefore it seems only sensible that there be one continuing agency to coordinate and carry on the work and that it be a governmental agency not dependent on voluntary organization and support.[7]

On the optimistic side, several knowledgeable speakers cited examples of progress and accomplishment in industrial forestry from their own experi-

6. Ibid., p. 17.
7. Ibid., p. 20.

ence. On balance, the results of the conference were favorable to improvement in commercial forestry, a consensus stated in summation by Wilson Compton, secretary-manager of the National Lumber Manufacturers Association: "It is evident that commercial forestry is well on its way and that a generation hence we will see that our national worries over the problem of our forests, like our personal worries over so many affairs, were preventive rather than desperate."[8]

Industrial Forestry Defined

In an editorial, the *Journal of Forestry* (January 1928) posed the question, "What Is Industrial Forestry?" Calling the term a new slogan to conjure with, the editorialist explained, "It is an attempt to give an expression to a type of forest practice consistent with the business interests and the profitableness of the undertaking of the timber operator." In its simplest terms, he said, industrial forestry means "*treating timber growing as a business enterprise.* There is more substance to this definition than may appear on the surface. The admission that *timber growing* may be considered a business enterprise is a new, revolutionary idea."

The writer stated his belief that the most inclusive definition of industrial forestry had been proposed by Thornton Munger, who was then director of the Pacific Northwest Forest and Range Experiment Station, Portland, Oregon.

According to Munger, industrial forestry is the employment by an individual or corporate owners in woods operations of methods of silviculture and forest protection that are intended to promote the continued growing of forest crops. It may or may not imply sustained production. It ordinarily would imply at least the equivalent of such silvicultural and protection measures as are recommended for each forest region in the "minimum requirement" studies of the U.S. Forest Service.

Raphael Zon, director of the Lake States Forest Experiment Station, St. Paul, was then editor-in-chief of the *Journal of Forestry*. Assuming that he wrote the editorial, one comprehends why his accepted definition of industrial forestry had a Forest Service slant.

From personal knowledge, based on conversations with Munger and Zon, the present author can testify that they were profoundly skeptical of industry's good faith in its attempts to practice forestry. Throughout their long and useful careers, they believed that, even if certain progressive companies followed sound management programs, some form of legal compulsion by the public would be needed to put the bulk of industrial holdings under acceptable silvicultural standards. This was an opinion shared by many thoughtful foresters in the Forest Service and elsewhere. It was the official policy of five chiefs of the service: Pinchot, Graves, Silcox, Clapp, and Watts.

Certain prominent conservationists had no confidence in the willingness or ability of the corporate establishment to invest profits in the perpetuation of the resource from which it derived its income. A proposed solution began to be articulated by a group convinced that what was needed was a combina-

8. Ibid., p. 139.

tion of social management and public ownership. Among those advocating this policy were George Ahern, Earle Clapp, Edward Munns, Gifford Pinchot, and Raphael Zon. An uncompromising pleader of their cause was Robert Marshall.

Marshall, a forester of inherited wealth, was a graduate of the College of Forestry at Syracuse who had taken a Ph.D. at The Johns Hopkins University. Before entering the Forest Service in 1936 (he became chief of the Division of Recreation and Lands), he was employed in the old Office of Indian Affairs, Department of the Interior. He died in 1939.

In 1933, he called for nationalization of 562 million acres of the country's commercial forests, then estimated to total 670 million acres. Proleptically, he would make an exception to the 127 million acres in farm woodland because the farmers' woods "cannot generally be nationalized without nationalizing the farms." An indication of the extremity of his thinking (and it must be remembered that he was not alone in such radical views) is to be found in his argument: "Until the time is ripe for public ownership of all land, it will be impossible for the government to take over a large proportion of the farm woodland. . . . Nevertheless, at least 80 million acres of the present 127 million acres could safely remain in private ownership." He went on:

The only way that private forestry could be a success would be for the government to pay practically all the expense of starting, developing, and protecting the forests, leaving to the owners only the harvesting of the profit. Such a scheme is obviously preposterous, and there is no social justification for the government to use the resources of all the people simply to make possible the continuance of private ownership. Far better it is for the government itself to take over private woodlands and to manage them in that competent way which it has, during nearly 30 years of practical experience, more than amply demonstrated.[9]

During the Great Depression, some economists and social planners thought and talked that way. However abhorrent such beliefs may have been to the conservative forester and timber operator, they reached into the upper hierarchy of government where they were heeded and experimented with during the heady New Deal era. Marshall, though a friendly and personable man, was not generally accepted as a leader of, or spokesman for, the forestry profession. But the circumstance that his views got the attention of such officials as Clapp, Munns, Pinchot, Zon, and later Silcox, shows that they were not to be brushed off. As described in chapter 10, Marshall was able to transmit his—and Zon's—opinions directly to President Franklin D. Roosevelt through the friendly office of Gifford Pinchot, then governor of Pennsylvania.

It should be noted that although the socialization or nationalization of the commercial forests was never a probability, it was a policy vigorously advocated in some circles and was officially recommended by the Forest Service in *A National Plan for American Forestry* (the Copeland report of 1933). In this report, it was asserted without equivocation that "practically

9. *The People's Forests* (New York: Smith and Haas, 1933), p. 106.

all of the major problems of American forestry center in, or have grown out of, private ownership."

This skepticism in governmental quarters of industry's willingness and ability to install proper management of its lands is discussed at length in Chapter 11. It is mentioned here to emphasize a point. For a half-century examples of public regulation of other industries, together with the threat of regulation of the forest industry, hastened the decision of industrial executives to set up forestry departments in their companies. But it is no detraction from industry's success in the application of scientific forestry to its lands to stress the influence on its policy decision of adverse public opinion and the threat of regulation.

The Reports of the Society of American Foresters

In the late 1920s, Shirley W. Allen, later to become president of the Society of American Foresters (SAF), was on the faculty of the University of Michigan School of Forestry and Conservation (now the School of Natural Resources). He was appointed chairman of an SAF Committee on Industrial Forestry whose sixteen other members represented regional sections of the society. The committee was to determine how many companies owning more than 1,000 acres each were making a conscious effort to grow timber crops.

When issued on December 16, 1930, "The Report of the Committee on Industrial Forestry" was mimeographed. Apparently, the society did not consider it sufficiently worthwhile to print the report, either separately or in the *Journal of Forestry*, the official organ of the SAF. Allen himself had a depreciatory attitude toward it, explaining that it was not an exhaustive study, merely the best information that could be secured by a scattered and voluntary effort.

Despite its fragmentary findings, the report revealed a great deal about the status of corporate policy in forestry. For example, the committee found 288 companies and individuals making a conscious effort to grow timber commercially. The area under industrial forestry management was the same as that reported by the Chamber of Commerce—slightly under 21 million acres. But only 178 companies were using careful cutting methods designed to promote natural regeneration on 10.5 million acres.

Another revealing portion of the SAF document gave the number of foresters industrially employed in each of the major forest regions. New England had the most; thirty to forty foresters were so employed. In addition, some companies used the services of ten consulting foresters on a part-time basis.

In the New York Section, twenty-two foresters were industrially employed. The Allegheny Section reported thirty-two. California had twenty-two. The Pacific Northwest respondent gave no definite number, simply reporting "many." Proving that forestry had not yet arrived in the South, as it would in another decade, the Southeastern States had "few" foresters employed, and the Gulf States, fourteen.

Nationwide, the number of professional foresters industrially employed was low. Since the report itself did not give a definite total number, the best one can do at this late date is to estimate professional forestry employment by industry on the basis of the palpably incomplete returns. It probably did not exceed 200. In addition, an indefinite number of consulting foresters, probably less than two dozen, were utilized by industry.

In summing up, the SAF committee found 9 percent of the nation's industrial forest holdings under forestry management. Another 1 percent was in good condition, and a conscious effort was being made to grow timber. Ending the report on a note of encouragement, the committee concluded that industrial forestry was making appreciable progress.

Factors Affecting Industrial Forestry

To understand how and why industrial forestry developed in the United States one must understand the role of fire, which up to a quarter-century ago was the greatest obstacle to forestry. In many parts of the country, organized fire control agencies—federal, state, and private—are reducing the risk. In a few localities, insurance against forest fire is available, but premiums are often prohibitively high.

Hence, timber growing as a business is still a risky enterprise, menaced by destructive forces originating at sources that may be distant from the lands of an owner and consequently beyond his control. Without the cooperation of the law enforcement and fire suppression forces of government, together with the cooperation of the general public, the growing forest is exposed to almost constant danger. Although the worst danger has been fire, insect and disease attacks may be equally destructive, or more so.

For industrial forestry to survive and flourish in the competitive business world, fire risks had to be reduced to levels that would enable investment capital to participate. However conservative the financial policy of a company may be, capital investments in forestry always have a speculative side because of the risks involved in growing timber and the long interval—25 to 100 years—between crops. Only with acceptable levels of fire risk could silviculture begin.

The forest industry, as W. B. Greeley observed, had to go through a stage of trial and error before forestry was possible on its lands. "It had to cut off some of the surplus stumpage, open up the old forests so that new ones could start; get pulp and paper mills for better use of raw materials; see more stable timber values ahead; get a grip on the fire problem. With greater security in these essentials," Greeley said, "the change from liquidation to timber cropping became possible."[10]

Critics of industry's long delay in practicing forestry on its original holdings often forget, if they ever understood, that industry operated almost wholly on old-growth timber, that is, mature and even over-mature timber. It is a truism that one cannot practice silviculture—once defined as the art of the second growth—in old-growth stands. As Frank Sweeney, associate editor of the American Enterprise Association series of monographs on national economic problems, explained:

The cost of growing such timber was obviously not reflected in the cost of stumpage. So long as stumpage was abundant the cost of growing trees was prohibitive. However, with the gradual depletion of the virgin timber, the

10. *A Decade of Progress in Douglas Fir Forestry* (Seattle: Joint Committee on Forest Conservation, 1943), foreword.

growing of trees has become profitable. Even small owners now have an incentive for growing trees and adopting sound forest practices, whereas formerly the only assured source of income from woodlands was through the liquidation of the standing timber.[11]

In 1967, Zebulon W. White, a long-time student of private forestry, a consultant to industry, and director of the Yale industrial forestry seminars, summed up the conditions under which industrial forestry began.

American forestry, especially private forestry, has developed as the net result of many intricate, interwoven policies and pressures through education, encouragement, and economic return. The practice of timber-growing as a business enterprise can be successful only within the framework of certain conditions, and most of these conditions were not present early in the 20th century. It took two more generations to develop them, and they are still being refined.

Forestry, as it is now practiced on private lands, could not have developed merely through the will and wisdom of those who owned the properties. There was no single factor which was paramount in bringing about successful forest management, or sustained yield, or industrial forestry. The whole environment had to be favorable or made favorable, and many lines of endeavor have coalesced to provide the climate in which industrial forestry thrives today.[12]

Some of the factors that contributed to the favorable climate mentioned by White were peculiar to a particular region of the country and will be discussed in later chapters. The following factors were national in their significance and influence:

1. The Weeks Law of 1911 laid the foundation for federal-state cooperation in forestry and materially increased the acreage of state and private lands under protection from fire—from 61 million acres to 178 million acres. This law was a major influence in the advancement of private forestry.

2. Although the Clarke–McNary Law of 1924 gave impetus to state forestry, its effects on private forestry were beneficial also. Through the Forest Service, the secretary of agriculture entered into agreements with the states to protect privately-owned and state-owned forests against fire. State and private owners contributed one-half the cost, or more. Stimulated by this law, the production by the states of forest planting stock for state and private lands was markedly increased. Federal and state foresters stepped up cooperative assistance in forest management on private lands.[13]

3. Authorized by the Emergency Conservation Act of 1933, the Civilian Conservation Corps promptly put 265,000 men to work in the nation's forests, parks, and public lands. During its eight years of existence, the CCC brought about a notable public awareness of resource conservation. The enrollees constructed lookout towers and fire lines, truck trails and telephone lines, and established thousands of tree plantations that converted land from idleness to productivity. Many private timberland owners were influenced by

11. American Enterprise Association, *The Changing Forest Situation* (New York: AEA, 1950), p. 21.
12. "Growth of Industrial Forestry," *National Colloquium on the History of the Forest Products Industries: Proceedings*, p. 95.
13. See chap. 10 for additional discussion of the Clarke–McNary Law.

the example of CCC accomplishments to undertake similar improvements on their own holdings.

4. In order to lift the nation's battered economy from the depression that struck in 1929, Congress passed the National Industrial Recovery Act in 1933. The National Recovery Administration, created by this law, undertook to supervise all industry through codes of fair competition. A code for the lumber and timber products industry, written jointly by industry and government, contained an article that provided for the conservation and sustained production of the forest resources. Under this Article X, rules of forest practice were adopted by the industry. These rules set up minimum standards of forest management on private woodland and encouraged timber harvesting under the system of sustained-yield management. Although self-regulation by industry was under trial for less than a year when the NRA was declared unconstitutional, the promised benefits of the code were not entirely lost. Several lumber trade associations continued to promote better management of the lands of member companies and hired foresters to help do it. Lasting results of this short-lived law were the gradual adoption by industry of logging methods that aided silvicultural practice and the improvement of seeding and planting on cutover lands.[14]

Professional Foresters Available

By the time the first industrial forestry positions were opening, after World War I, eighteen colleges and universities were offering curriculums in forestry. Up to this period, most forestry graduates had found employment in the federal government, principally in the Forest Service, or in state forestry departments. A few lumber companies and railroad companies had hired foresters, but public service provided the main, almost the sole, opportunity for a career.

During the two decades 1900–1920, the forestry schools had granted some 2,000 degrees. Although it is not known how many graduates were actually working in forestry, probably less than 1 percent were privately employed as foresters. It was not until the 1930s that the forest products industry began to recruit foresters—and then mainly for the expanding pulp and paper mills.

In 1933, the so-called Copeland Report[15] gave an estimate of only 146 technically educated foresters employed by 79 companies. A mail survey conducted by the Society of American Foresters in 1934 showed that of a total of 2,076 members, 220 (11 percent) were privately employed. A similar survey in 1937 revealed that out of a total of 3,954 members, 368 (9 percent) were in private forestry work. Private owners, then controlling 75 percent of the nation's forest area, employed less than 10 percent of the nation's professional foresters. By 1941, 650 foresters were privately employed, according to an SAF estimate.

14. See chap. 10 for additional discussion of the NRA and its influence on private forestry.

15. *A National Plan for American Forestry*, 2 vols., S. Doc. 12, 73 Cong., 1 sess. (1933).

Another SAF study showed that the number of industrially employed foresters increased from 4,400 in 1951 to 6,050 in 1961.[16] These estimates included employment in forest management and wood processing. But, in addition, 950 foresters were self-employed as consultants and as managers of their own timberland and wood-processing plants. There also were 200 foresters engaged in private work for associations and foundations, or as editors, writers, and public relations specialists. Altogether, 7,200 foresters were privately employed, or 37 percent of the total professional work force.

In the absence of a precise record of the number of professional foresters in the United States and of their fields of employment, the author believes that, as of 1969, private and industrial employment, including self-employment and employment by associations, totaled between 7,500 and 7,800.

Tax on Capital Gains

Private timber growing as a long-term investment was given encouragement by a 1944 amendment to the Internal Revenue Code. Section 117K (now 631) of the code permits the increased value of timber held for six months or more to be treated as capital gain for the tax year in which it is cut or sold, rather than as ordinary income.

The federal revenue code discriminates between income from ordinary business transactions and the capital gain from the sale of property held over a period of time. The code provides for taxing capital gains—the excess of market value over cost—at a lower rate than ordinary profit. Prior to 1943, when an owner sold standing timber outright or in a lump-sum sale, profit could be treated as a capital gain. On the other hand, when an owner harvested his timber himself or sold it little by little over a period of years, the profit not only was taxed at higher rates but was subject to excess profits tax rates as well if it accrued to a corporation.

During the early period of World War II, tax rates were increased so rapidly that their effect was to appear confiscatory to the owner who harvested his own timber. Thus, for financial reasons that could be contrary to the best interest of good forest management, he often felt obliged to sell his standing timber outright for a lump-sum instead of cutting it himself. In other words, the prevailing tax policy encouraged the owner to liquidate his timber rather than hold it for long-term operation under scientific forest management.

Corporate owners, who held the largest blocks of commercial woodland, claimed that the taxes were both discriminatory and confiscatory. In November 1942, the directors of the National Lumber Manufacturers Association resolved that "the present methods of taxation in the lumber industry are inequitable" and set about securing a change. Timber owners, representing the paper industry as well as lumber interests, set up a Forest Industries Committee on Timber Valuation and Taxation.[17]

16. F. H. Eyre, "How Many Foresters?" *Journal of Forestry*, vol. 60 (July 1962), pp. 499–500.
17. An account of this committee's work was made available to the author by Henry Baker, who served as secretary of NLMA.

Wilson Compton, secretary-manager of the NLMA, who feared the effect of wartime excess profits taxes on the production of needed forest products for the war, developed the economic arguments on which the industry decided to seek revision of the law. David T. Mason, a consulting forester with experience in timber valuation and taxation, was retained by the committee to investigate the matter. He prepared a statement on timber tax reform that was presented by the industry before the House Committee on Ways and Means in October 1943. Congress voted the amendment on February 24, 1944, over President Roosevelt's veto.

William K. Condrell, executive secretary of the Forest Industries Committee on Timber Valuation and Taxation, has long been a student of the operation of the capital gain rate of taxation on the industry. It is his opinion "that the tax change removed an impediment to investment by timber owners in the critical management and reforestation measures which in turn halted the decline in timber inventory."[18] This tax amendment, then, was one of the favorable factors that helped advance the practice of industrial forestry. It encouraged the holding and acquisition of young growth for permanent management. In harvesting his own timber or in selling it as it grew under a cutting contract, an owner could now practice conservative logging techniques with assurance of less injury to the residual stand than was possible when he sold his timber outright.

At a hearing of the House Ways and Means Committee on March 21, 1963, President Paul M. Dunn of the Society of American Foresters presented testimony endorsing the principle of capital gains taxation. His presentation was based on a report of a special SAF committee appointed to study the influence of this tax principle on the practice of forestry. On behalf of the SAF Council—whose eleven members had approved the statement—Dunn urged the Congress to continue this tax treatment.

Pointing out that until World War II economic factors were adverse to private investment in forestry, Dunn told the congressman that only limited progress had been made in developing the permanent productive use of the three-fourths of the nation's forest land in private ownership. He then summed up the stimulus given to private forestry by the Revenue Act of 1943.

This action removed a major tax barrier to investment in forestry by timber-processing companies and by investors who retain an economic interest in the forest being cut as required by sound forest management. It was of fundamental importance in releasing the flow of investment into private forestry which has occurred during the post-war period. The major improvement in the nation's timber supplies, the large scale investment in wood-processing facilities with related permanent employment in many rural areas, and the watershed and recreational benefits derived from forest management which have been achieved on private lands during the past twenty years are directly traceable to this classification of timber revenues.[19]

18. "How Has Taxation Affected the Growth of the Forest Products Industries?" *National Colloquium*, p. 154.
19. "SAF Council States Policy on Timber Capital Gains Tax," *Journal of Forestry*, vol. 61 (May 1963), p. 402.

In concluding his testimony, Dunn explained that private woodland includes both small woodlots and large corporate holdings. He then asserted a fact well known to every forester: that the development of private forestry has progressed rapidly on large ownerships and less rapidly on the small ones. "Removal of capital gains treatment," he said, "would penalize the ownerships which have made the greatest progress in forestry."[20]

The conditions under which income from the sale or cutting of timber may qualify for capital gains treatment are too detailed to explain here. The point to be made is that the Internal Revenue Act recognized that timber growing may require long-term investment and is subject to risks. In consequence, the maximum tax rate on capital gains may be substantially less than the tax on ordinary income. Hence, since investment in the acquisition of woodland for management over an extended period of time is encouraged by the capital gains provision of the Internal Revenue Code, commercial forestry obtained a powerful economic incentive.

Forestry Is Big Business

American forest industries own nearly 67 million acres (13 percent) of the nation's commercial timberlands. For the most part, this ownership is in individual properties larger than 50,000 acres. By far the greatest single class of industrial owner is the pulp and paper industry, which has holdings in excess of 35 million acres.

During the decade 1953–63, industrial woodland ownership increased 10 percent, about 6 million acres. Most of this expansion was by the pulp and paper industry, whose investments in land kept pace with its investments in new manufacturing plants. As will be noted in the following chapters, numerous corporate land transfers occurred when paper companies bought or merged with lumber companies.

Two salient trends characterized the 1960s. Land prices reached new peaks. Timber tracts of sizable extent became so scarce that companies desiring to acquire substantial reserves resorted to the expedient of buying up other land holding companies. In addition, certain corporations increased their wood supplies by acquiring cutting rights or by negotiating long-term leases of surface rights on lands not operated for wood production by the owners. Customarily, under the leasing system the lessee is responsible for adhering to standards of cutting practices in the interest of maintaining the stand. In several instances when private owners assigned cutting rights to corporations, either the owners were professional foresters or they retained professional consultants to assure compliance with the silvicultural and logging practices specified in the contracts.

Within the wood-using industry a policy has evolved whereby the old custom of cut-out-and-get-out is as obsolete as the use of oxen and the crosscut saw. International Paper Company, for example, would no more skin off its own, or leased, land than it would revert to making paper by hand. Such companies, unlike the lumber companies at the turn of the century, have

20. Ibid.

too much at stake in their woodlands. Their economic roots are so deep that the practice of sustained-yield forestry on land supplying their plants with wood is an economic necessity. William Greeley, who in his lifetime said many wise things about forestry, summed up this condition in an aphorism that might be called Greeley's law: "Economic interest in forestry increases in proportion to the plant investment per unit of raw material."[21]

Let it be granted, then, that the most compelling reason for industry's adoption of an enlightened forestry policy is economic, based on the simple principle of keeping alive the goose that lays golden eggs. But there is another forceful reason. This is the influence on corporate policy of professional foresters who have attained executive and decision-making positions in their companies.

The author knows of foresters who induced their companies to undertake silvicultural practice, not only because it was guaranteed to pay off in profits, but also because it constituted good land stewardship. Put another way, some companies adopted the practice of scientific silviculture with no more than a hope, certainly with no assurance, that it would be economically justified. Some timber stand improvement work of past years—experimental plantations, tree genetics tests and seed orchards, prescribed burning, and management practices to increase wildlife as well as timber—were undertaken by industrial foresters with little, if any, expectation that they were at the time economically feasible.

The challenge to the skills of the industrial forester is illustrated by the insatiable demands for wood of just one company, and this not the largest in the forest products industry. During 1967, the St. Regis Paper Company consumed in its manufacturing plants the equivalent of 1.6 billion board feet in the form of sawtimber, pulpwood, and chips. To transport such a huge volume of wood at one time would require a train of 160,000 railroad cars 1,500 miles long. Half this wood was harvested from lands that St. Regis owned in fee or controlled through long-term cutting rights. The other half was bought locally from other producers.

St. Regis timberlands, owned or controlled by the company, total nearly 3.8 million acres in the United States and 2.1 million acres in Canada. The company's policy is to add to timber reserves by acquiring more acreage and cutting rights. Through the company's long-term management practices, the annual growth is increasing. Moreover, since the volume harvested from its holdings is less than the total annual growth, its basic raw-material reserves keep increasing too.

According to the company's foresters, St. Regis owns, or has the right to cut, 35 billion board feet of standing timber. This wood, together with the wood available for purchase on the open market, assures the company of sufficient volume to supply its mill operations for many years at present levels of operation; in addition, there is enough in reserve for the production expansion required by market growth. It should be added that the company's timber holdings, both in land and growing stock, have risen in value so that

21. *Forests and Men*, p. 173.

their present financial worth exceeds their balance sheet value. At the end of 1967, company assets in timberlands and cutting rights had a net value (after deduction of $25 million for accumulated depletion) of $45 million.[22]

The present favorable state of industrial forestry is the result of the labors of literally hundreds of foresters, who, frequently working alone, obscurely, and against the inertia of entrenched corporate conservatism, were able to introduce scientific forestry as a feature of company policy. They helped get the practice of forestry accepted as a corporate policy, not because it was good public relations, but because it was good business.

22. Much of the information about St. Regis was obtained from the company's 1967 annual report.

CHAPTER 16

Industrial Forestry
in the Northeast

In colonial America, timber resources were first harvested commercially in the Northeast—New England and the six states to the south, including Maryland and West Virginia. Many of the early important developments in forestry occurred in this region, which for more than three centuries has supplied a large measure of the lumber and other wood products used in the United States. Since the Northeast is characterized by shifting patterns of land use, expanding population, and rapid urban growth, a decimation of the forest resource might have been expected. But this has not happened.

The state of Maine, where the nation's first documented sawmill was built in 1634, is an interesting example of how industrial forestry has fared in the Northeast. In one of the truly fascinating books about American forest lore, *Forest Life and Forest Trees*,[1] John S. Springer reported on a survey of lumber production in Maine that he compiled for the year 1849. The data apply mostly to white pine and show production of some 525 million board feet.

A century later, Gregory Baker, a professor of forestry at the University of Maine, gave a capsule description of the lumber industry in the state.

The migratory nature of the sawmill industry in the past is well known. As the better and more accessible areas of old-growth timber were cut, the mills moved on to new forests. About 1850 New York became the leader in lumber production and the movement in search of new stands of old-growth white pine started. This movement was to continue to Pennsylvania and on to the Lake States.

The common impression is that once the leadership in production passed to another area, the industry declined to the vanishing point. Actually, many of these older areas continued to produce a substantial quantity of lumber which was obscured by the greater production in the newly opened forest areas. This is true of the State of Maine.[2]

1. Harper and Brothers, 1851.
2. Technical note, January 1952 (School of Forestry, University of Maine, mimeo.).

Baker then shows that 100 years after Springer's estimate of 1849, long after Maine had ceased to be a major lumber-producing state, the total cut in 1949 was 537.5 million board feet, of which 51 percent was still white pine. Further, he shows that the total cut of lumber and pulpwood in 1949 was equivalent to about 1.2 billion board feet.

No state better illustrates the regenerative capacity of native forest types and their inherent ability to grow repeated crops of commercial products than does Maine. After supplying lumber, pulpwood, and other products for more than 300 years, Maine is still a well-wooded state. Of its total land area (19.8 million acres), 87 percent (17.4 million acres) is clothed with trees,[3] a greater proportion of woodland than that found in any other state. The forest is still Maine's most valuable natural resource. Its forest-based industry yields more than one-third of the value of all the state's manufactured products and provides more employment than any other industry.

By 1966, more than 13,000 workers were employed in Maine's lumber and lumber products industry. (Of these, 4,647 were loggers engaged in cutting timber.) The gross wages of the 13,000 workers totaled more than $55 million. The industry's products were valued at more than $161 million.[4]

In the Northeast as a whole, the area of commercial forest land has actually increased. During the period 1953–63, for example, the commercial forest acreage in New England rose 1.4 percent, to 31.5 million acres; and in the Middle Atlantic States, 3.9 percent, to 43.9 million acres.[5]

It is perhaps no exaggeration to assert that the region's forest resources are more important today than at any period in its history—for recreation, water, and wildlife, as well as for commercial products.

The remainder of this chapter is devoted to a discussion of the salient factors that influenced the development of forestry as a business enterprise in this region, to examples of successful practice by companies that were pioneers in the field, and to a brief summary of the status of forestry in the Northeast today.

Renaissance in New England

A prospective investor in the forest industry during the 1920s, heeding the predictions of the U.S. Forest Service, would have avoided New England as a likely region to lay out capital with the expectation of permanency and profit. The commercial timberlands of New England were cut out and nearly exhausted, according to a Department of Agriculture report.

About half of the entire present stand of saw and pulp timber in New England is in commercial tracts; the remainder is in farm woodlots. It is particularly from the larger commercial tracts that the cut of most of the higher-grade material comes at present. Few of even the larger timber owners have more than a 20 years' supply. Most of the pulp mills will be cut out in 20 years. Not over four or five companies own stumpage enough to last for a

3. U.S. Forest Service, *Timber Trends in the United States*, Forest Resources Report no. 17 (1965).
4. Data supplied by the Maine Department of Labor and Industry, Division of Research and Statistics.
5. U.S. Forest Service, *Timber Trends*.

longer period. Unless Canadian wood is imported on an increasingly larger scale or effective forestry measures are introduced immediately, the pulp industry of New England will be largely a thing of the past within 30 years.[6]

Even well-informed Julian E. Rothery, forest engineer for the International Paper Company, accepted the current beliefs about the exhaustibility of the pulpwood forests of the Northeast. In 1929, he commented on the prevailing viewpoint.

Collectively, the paper industry controls a very substantial part of the remaining spruce forests. While a few owners have reasonably satisfactory supplies, the industry as a whole has not sufficient pulpwood to carry it over a long enough span to bring in a second crop; in fact, a study of spruce production recently completed by the Special Committee of the New York Section of the Society of American Foresters indicates that present and accruing supplies for all New England will last only about 35 years, a situation that forest management cannot avert.[7]

The predicted three-decade deadline for timber depletion in New England was never met. According to the Forest Service, the net annual growth on New England's commercial forest lands in 1962 was 1 billion cubic feet, hardly evidence of a declining resource.[8] Despite the presence in New England of literally hundreds of wood-consuming industrial plants, from large pulp and paper companies to small portable sawmills, the annual harvest from the forests was less than half the growth. In 1962, forest industries grew 291.5 million cubic feet of lumber on their properties while cutting 124 million cubic feet. After warning in 1928 that most of the pulp mills in New England would be cut out in twenty or thirty years, the Forest Service then found that the region had produced 2.5 million cords in 1962. How did this favorable result come about?

Forestry in New England got off to an early start. The region's state forestry departments were among the first in the nation to organize for intensive fire prevention and control. Cooperating with the large timberland owners, the state forest services detected disease and insect attacks early and applied control measures.

In a report to the American Pulpwood Association, Dwight B. Demeritt, former vice president of the Dead River Company of Bangor, Maine, once expressed the opinion that the loss of millions of cords of spruce and balsam fir by an outbreak of budworm between 1910 and 1920 probably had been more serious than all the fires of the previous fifty years.

Industrial tree-planting programs have been going on for a half-century. And in order to better both the quality and the quantity of second growth, some companies have invested in timber stand improvement, including the culling out of trees of poor form and quality and release cutting in natural stands and plantations. All these management programs on the industry's 8.1

6. U.S. Forest Service, *Timber Depletion, Lumber Prices, Lumber Exports, and Concentration of Timber Ownership* (1920), p. 16.
7. "New England's Pulpwood Supplies and Other Forest Possibilities," *Journal of Forestry*, vol. 27 (April 1929), p. 366.
8. U.S. Forest Service, *Timber Trends.*

million acres have reversed the trend toward depletion predicted by the Forest Service in 1928.

The Tree-Planting Crusade

Prior to World War I, great activity in reforestation occurred throughout the eastern part of the United States. The developing state forestry departments were establishing forest tree nurseries to grow planting stock for privately owned lands, as well as for public lands. Seedlings were made available to farmers in most states at nominal cost or at the cost of production, and in some states seedlings were given free to those who would guarantee to plant them.

In Pennsylvania, the state's first forest nursery was started in 1901 at Mont Alto shortly after George H. Wirt, forestry graduate of the old Biltmore Forest School, was appointed state forester. Within a few years this nursery was producing 1 million trees annually. Three additional nurseries were subsequently established by the Department of Forestry.

Corporations owning idle or open land began reforestation projects too—lumber companies, mining companies, paper companies, railroad companies, water companies, and many others. These companies obtained their planting stock from local state or private nurseries, but some also imported seedlings from Europe.

In 1899, a year after the establishment of the New York State College of Forestry at Cornell University, Filibert Roth, a member of the faculty, started a coniferous forest tree nursery containing 1.5 million plants at Axton, New York. During that year, he and the students set out 67,000 pine and spruce seedlings. A second nursery was started at Axton, and the two together were capable of producing 1 million plants annually. Trees from these nurseries provided the planting stock for the early plantations in the Adirondacks and Catskills. The nurseries were abandoned in 1908, when loss of state financial support for the College of Forestry caused its closing.

The Delaware and Hudson Company, one of the first railroads in the nation to become interested in forestry, started a nursery at Wolf Pond, New York in 1904. H. R. Bristol, a Yale forestry graduate, was employed by the company and had his headquarters at Plattsburg, New York. In 1914, he reported that he had set out more than 1 million trees and had over 5 million in the nursery.

Plantings on the municipal watershed of the city of Rochester at Hemlock Lake were started in 1902. These were the forerunners of extensive watershed plantings that would be made throughout the state during the next six decades.

New York State itself, which in time became the largest producer of planting stock for public and private reforestation, started plantations in the Adirondacks about 1902. These plantings were undertaken by the Forest, Fish and Game Commission (later the State Conservation Commission).

Largely through the drive of Commissioner J. S. Whipple, the legislature in 1908 granted the commission authority to distribute nursery stock at cost of production to private planters. Two years later, private owners in the state set out 2.7 million trees. Thereafter, the private tree-planting project in New York grew to such proportions that it became one of the nation's largest. By

1960, three state-operated nurseries were producing 45 million seedlings and transplants annually; nearly half of this production was from the world-renowned Saratoga Nursery at Saratoga Springs.

The International Paper Company and its subsidiaries early joined this tree-planting movement. During the four-year period 1909–12, the companies set out 1.5 million trees in Maine, New Hampshire, New York, and Vermont. The plantings in Vermont illustrate the experience of a corporation undertaking this new venture in reforestation.

In 1909, the Champlain Realty Company, an operating subsidiary of International Paper, began planting Norway spruce seedlings imported from Germany. The company continued to import German seedlings for several years. Also in 1909, the company started its own forest tree nursery at Randolph, Vermont, under the supervision of an experienced German nurseryman. This nursery was operated until 1926. Annual production was from 1.5 million to 2 million seedlings. In addition to supplying all the company's needs for planting open lands in New Hampshire, New York, and Vermont, the nursery produced trees for sale both in the United States and Canada. When Canada restricted the importation of trees, the nursery was discontinued.[9]

In Maine, a small forest nursery was started at Orono by the university when a curriculum in forestry was first offered in the new Department of Forestry. As the nursery was intended primarily for instruction, much of the work was done by students. In 1913, this nursery was put under state administration, and the legislature began modest appropriations (as little as $1,000 annually) for its operation. Seedlings were supplied to landowners at the cost of production. Generally, throughout the Northeast, this was the pattern of nursery development by the states. Seedling production was small and appropriations were minimal.

Here and there, commercial nurseries were started in an attempt to profit from the booming interest in reforestation. Only a few of these endured; most operated for a decade or less, then were abandoned. Unable to compete with publicly supported nurseries that supplied planting stock to landowners at cost, or slightly above, the commercial nurseries sometimes turned to growing ornamental stock. One of the successful private ventures was the Western Maine Forest Nursery at Fryeburg, started in 1918 by T. Clifford Eastman. Spread over 80 acres in Maine and adjoining New Hampshire, this business has been going for five decades, growing upwards of 4 million trees annually.

Illustrative of the industrial participation in growing trees for commercial planting was the Brown Company nursery at Oquossoc, Maine. In production from 1919 to 1933, it was about 30 acres in size and had a capacity of upwards of 17 million trees. Although most of its production was sold to private planters, Brown Company made good use of the planting stock in reforesting 1,200 acres of its own land.

During the 1920s, numerous private forest nurseries, many of them operated by industry, were growing planting stock to reforest land that had been burned, logged, or taken out of production of farm crops. Often these

9. G. A. Pesez, "Norway Spruce Plantings in Vermont," 1963 (Department of Woodlands, International Paper Company, Glens Falls, N.Y.).

nurseries were established by industrial foresters who desired to grow species of certain sizes or ages. With experience, the industrial operators found they could buy planting stock from state nurseries as cheaply as they themselves could grow it, or cheaper. With the depression years of the 1930s, much industrial forestry work was temporarily put aside; nursery operation was one activity that ceased.

Numerous additional examples of the beginnings of interest in tree planting throughout the East could be cited. The point to be made is that American forestry, which began in the eastern states, stemmed from public interest in two aspects of forest conservation: protection from fire and tree planting. Protection had great popular appeal because it involved the stopping of needless waste and destruction; reforestation, because it involved the restoration and rehabilitation of the resource. These were concepts that even school children could understand and support. Moreover, doing something practical about them appealed to the pragmatic side of citizens concerned about conservation.

Some foresters, with reason, have questioned the necessity and value of much of the early tree-planting work. Certainly, the results were often unsuccessful and wasteful in time and money. But all the same, reforestation had a significant part in the advancement of forestry.

During the 1920s, the author, while a forester with the Pennsylvania Department of Forests and Waters, drew up dozens of long-term planting plans for private landowners in the anthracite region, particularly for industrial landowners, such as mining companies, railroad companies, and water companies. The water companies were early converts to forest protection. But the mining and railroad companies had been traditionally indifferent to protecting their holdings from fire. They put fire suppression crews to work usually only when buildings, bridges, or similar structures were threatened. Once they had embarked on planting programs, however, they began to take a proprietary interest in the plantations.

After the industrial landowners had expended modest amounts in planting trees they were easily persuaded to protect them from fire, and from this simply beginning they were induced to make further investments in forest management. Thus, even though tree planting in numerous instances may have been unnecessary in order to bring about forest regeneration, its influence on the application of private forestry was in the long run beneficial and constructive.

Austin Cary: Early Industrial Forester

Prior to World War I, various companies and landowners in the Northeast employed foresters, either on salary or as consultants, to advise them on the wood volume and management of their holdings. Austin Cary was one of the earliest of these forestry consultants. His was true pioneering forestry experience, for he was cruising timber in northern New Hampshire as early as 1887 and in the Androscoggin basin of Maine a year later.

In a paper presented at a meeting of the Boston Society of Civil Engineers, May 10, 1899, he referred to himself as "forester to the Berlin Mills Company." He mentioned that in the autumn of 1896 he was employed by

Hollingsworth & Whitney Company of Waterville, Maine, "to make what I suppose is the first genuine topographical survey ever made of a New England timber township." His explanation of the relationship of forestry and business is as sound today as it was then:

Forestry should seek to ally itself with business, to promote the success of careful and foresighted concerns. The forester, if he would work directly on the problem of management, must work in private employ and in accordance with its fundamental conditions. First among these is the necessity of making profit. Should the forestry practiced lead to loss, the business goes down and the forester's position and opportunity go with it.[10]

Cary then told of "a movement among the paper mills, yet in its infancy, but apparently increasing, to back themselves with land enough to render them independent. With that movement has gone the purpose to treat these lands carefully and with foresight." As an example, he pointed to the International Paper Company—which controlled 80 percent of the U.S. output of newsprint—and to its employment of a professional forester "and the intention expressed of living, so far as forest supplies were concerned, within the limits of actual growth."[11]

In another paper, undated but probably written prior to 1904, Cary asserted, "I believe I am the first man calling himself a forester to be employed regularly by an American business firm." He was then with the Berlin Mills Company (later named the Brown Company). At that period, little if any of his work was concerned with silviculture; actually, his duties were those of a timber cruiser and logging engineer. He explained:

My work outside the logging season has been the survey and exploration of the lands as a basis for their operation. Topographical maps and models result from this, also sheets descriptive of the timber. As far as may be, the logging jobs are located on the territories that most need cutting, and we are careful while there to take all the defective but still usable timber. The tracts are kept under watch too, and no big blow down can occur, nor bug work get much of a start without our being aware of it.[12]

Although he had a university education (Bowdoin, Johns Hopkins, and Princeton), Cary did not have a degree in forestry. With scientific precision, he studied the technology of logging in the woods, and his approach to forest management was pragmatic. He was not lacking in imagination or ability to theorize, but his attitude was always that of a practical woodsman dealing with practical businessmen. He believed that forestry would be accepted by industrial owners when they better understood it, when the old-growth stands were harvested, and when economic conditions justified it. (This was the belief subsequently held by William B. Greeley, perhaps the most influential exponent of industrial forestry during the 1920s and 1930s.) Cary's written thoughts on these matters are interesting even six decades later.

10. "Forest Management in Maine," *Journal of the Association of Engineering Societies*, vol. 23 (August 1899), pp. 62–63.
11. Ibid.
12. "The Management of Pulpwood Forests" (Woodlands Division, Brown Co., Berlin, N.H.).

The main impression left on the writer by his experience to date is that the country is ripe for forestry. . . . What country ever set about repairing its mistakes with such energy as now characterizes public forest work in the United States: And say what we will about the altruism of the leaders of the movement, it never could be possible but for the support of large bodies of substantial businessmen.[13]

Like other early American foresters—Fernow, Pinchot, Graves, and Roth—Cary had acquired some of his forestry knowledge in Europe, not, however, by formal education, but by travel and observation. He saw forestry practice in the United States as an indigenous development, not one to be copied from European examples.

The first men, to be sure, had to learn their principles in Europe, and men may yet gain inspiration and suggestion abroad, but forms of management are not to be learned there. The German *Oberforster* swinging around his district in a stylish uniform, with a feather in his cap and a dachshund at his heels, is no model for the American forester.[14]

Information about Cary's career as a forestry advisor to industry will be found in chapter 17.

Industrial Forestry Failures

Industrial forestry enterprises sometimes floundered and sometimes failed when parent companies became the victims of adverse economic trends or poor management policies. The histories that follow illustrate the uncertain state of corporate forestry during its formative years.

Fearing a possible shortage of crosstie timber, the Pennsylvania Railroad Company began reforestation work in 1902, planting mostly black locust and red oak. A tree nursery was established at Morrissville, Pennsylvania. In 1906 the company asked the Forest Service to examine locust trees planted during the period 1902–1905 that were damaged by insects. In its report, the Forest Service recommended that the company employ a forester. E. A. Sterling and John Foley, both Forest Service officers, were hired in 1907. Sterling stayed only a short time before going into consulting practice. Foley was not a professional forester but had had experience in practical field forestry as well as in wood use. He served as company forester during most of his career, retiring in 1946.

Conservation, the official magazine of The American Forestry Association, reported in its issue of June 1909 that the Pennsylvania Railroad had planted a total of more than 3.4 million trees. According to the magazine, this constituted the "largest forestry plan yet undertaken by any private corporation."

In 1923, Foley described the work of a railroad forester.[15] By that year, the company had ten foresters on its staff who managed company woodlands, especially lands surrounding reservoirs in mountain territory where water was

13. "Forest Management as Applied to Northern New England," circa 1900 (Woodlands Division, Brown Co., Berlin, N.H.).
14. Ibid.
15. "The Work of Foresters of the Pennsylvania Railroad System," *Journal of Forestry*, vol. 22 (February 1924).

obtained for locomotives and shops. They operated a nursery of fifty acres, but, since there was little field planting on a large scale, the nursery produced mostly ornamental trees and shrubs for landscaping station grounds. Fire prevention and control was a major responsibility of the forestry staff, in cooperation with forestry officials of the eleven states traversed by the system. In addition, the foresters were involved in forest utilization and lumbering, forest engineering, forest management, and wood technology.

During the depression years of the 1930s, both the size of the Pennsylvania Railroad forestry staff and the scope of its operations were reduced. During World War II the staff was scarcely involved in forestry work at all. For the most part, the foresters' duties involved timber inspection, wood preservation, investigations of woods fires, and kindred activities, which, although technical in nature, were not professional forestry. The company continues to employ a few professional foresters, but their major activities involve duties other than the practice of silviculture and the field management of timberland.

In 1913, the New England Box Company, incorporated about the turn of the century, found that prices for the lumber it needed had risen and that, according to prevailing opinion, local timber supplies would be exhausted in another decade. The company hired a forester.

Guy C. Hawkins, a graduate of the Biltmore Forest School, went to work for the company in 1914. Ten years later, he reported that the company had ten factories and 30,000 acres of forest in Massachusetts, New Hampshire, and Vermont. His duties were planting, thinning, weeding, and experimental work to increase growth. In addition, he had a cooperative program with neighboring owners of pine forests, providing management service for their lands.[16]

In the end, the company's forestry policy was sounder than its business policy. New England Box was one of the companies whose forestry program ceased with the decline of business. In 1968 the company was in liquidation.

About 1919, Arthur C. Silvius, a graduate of the Biltmore Forest School, was engaged as the first forester for the Philadelphia and Reading Coal and Iron Company. The company owned some 180,000 acres, mostly in the anthracite region of Pennsylvania. Silvius organized the company's forest protection and wood harvesting operations. In 1923, he described how the company was trying to make forestry pay its own way. The holdings were administered in four districts, each in charge of a forester or a forest ranger. The forestry staff had planted 110,000 trees in 1922 and expected to plant 191,000 in 1923. In 1922, there were 141 fires on the company's woodlands; some 6,000 acres burned, with damage in excess of $10,000.[17]

Maintaining a fire-fighting organization of its own, the company built more than 100 miles of fire lines and trails. From its own small forest tree nursery, the company in time planted several million seedlings on its property. Later, the plantations were thinned for Christmas trees, and many

16. "How One Wood-Using Industry Has Made Use of a Forester," *Journal of Forestry*, vol. 22 (February 1924).
17. "Making Forestry Pay Its Own Way," *Journal of Forestry*, November 1923.

thousands of the trees were sold. At its peak, Silvius's forestry division had sixty employees, not including contract workers.

Although the company's forestry operations returned profits, its coal business did not. When the corporation went bankrupt, all forestry activities stopped. Most of the timberlands were lost by tax default or sold to the Commonwealth of Pennsylvania. Thus, in a span of less than two decades, a potentially permanent and profitable forestry enterprise was abolished, not because of its inherent economic weakness, but because of unprofitable management by the parent company. This was the frequent fate of industrial forestry as practiced by mining companies, railroad companies, public utility companies, and forest-based corporations struggling to survive under the business hazards of the 1930s.

Industrial Forestry Takes Root

Although a number of early industrial forestry programs were unsuccessful, many survived the depression years and surmounted the hazards of corporate reorganizations. Since some of these programs have now endured for more than a half-century, their longevity attests to their soundness. Numerous instances of successful industrial forestry could be described; those that follow are among the oldest.

Finch, Pruyn & Company. This company, formed in Glens Falls, New York, in 1865 as a sawmill and lumbering business, built a mill for the manufacture of newsprint in 1904. With timber holdings of some 100,000 acres in the Hudson River highlands, the company controlled its basic sources of wood and power. In 1910, it was one of the first to implement a planned program of forest management.

Howard L. Churchill, a forestry graduate of the University of Maine, joined the company in 1911 and organized a forestry department. He had been recommended for the appointment by Austin Cary. By 1923, the company had some 200,000 acres in Maine, New York, Vermont, and Canada, and in 1928 decided to go on a sustained-yield basis.

A decade later, George N. Ostrander, vice president of the company and foremost exponent of forestry in New York State, reported in the *Journal of Forestry* (February 1938) on the progress of the company's sustained-yield management. The forestry staff then consisted of two graduate foresters and five assistants. Ostrander was one of the few corporate officers of that era to make public an estimate of the cost, in terms of the raw material harvested, of the forestry work; he said it averaged 25 cents per cord cut. Another observation he made—informative then and equally interesting now—was that at least 50 percent of the forestry work was nonprofessional. He regarded the ability of the foresters to render nonforestry service as indispensable.

Great Northern Paper Company. After graduating from the Yale forestry school and spending seven years with the Forest Service in the West, Ernest F. Jones in 1919 became forester of the Division of Forest Engineering of the Great Northern Paper Company at Bangor, Maine. Later, he was made superintendent. He was responsible for supervising timber sales; cruising; land utilization; forest investigations of growth, yield, and regeneration; and the taking of woods inventory records. Jones's staff included from eight to ten foresters and up to forty scalers and timber cruisers. He handled the company's forestry operations until his retirement in 1952. John T. Maines, a professional forester and graduate of the University of Maine, went to work for the company in 1941 as a scaler and wood buyer; later, he became vice president in charge of woodlands and a board director.

By 1967, the company owned 2.25 million acres in Maine; moreover, it can draw on the production of an additional 5 million acres. It also owned or leased 178,000 acres in Alabama, Florida, and Georgia. Great Northern has had some of its forest lands under management for a half-century. Much of the area was under extensive management up to the period of World War II, but thereafter the company's forestry practices became more intensive as consumption of all species increased.

International Paper Company. In December 1908, Chester W. Lyman and C. H. Griffing, officials of the International Paper Company, conferred with Forester Pinchot of the Forest Service in Washington, regarding the adoption by the company of practical forestry methods. Griffing was then in charge of the company's woodlands—some 1 million acres in Maine, New Hampshire, Vermont, and New York.

Even before the conference with Pinchot, according to Lyman, International had practiced the kind of management that would preserve its woodlands as a perpetual source of pulpwood. But he and Griffing wanted Pinchot's suggestions for extending the application of forestry methods on the company's land. As a result of the conference, International proposed to limit cutting to the amount of annual growth and only to trees specified by trained foresters. Trees would be planted on burned-over land and on wastelands in order to increase the annual crop that could be cut.

At a directors' meeting held December 29, 1908, it was resolved that the company would "manage its timberlands and those of its subsidiary companies under the methods of practical forestry, so as to insure a permanent growth of spruce timber thereon." The Department of Woodlands was directed "to see that this policy is carried out, and that the most conservative and economical methods practicable are used." The directors further ordered that these operations were to be conducted in a manner that would minimize the danger of fire.[18]

International's decision to improve the quality of its land management undoubtedly was based on more than Pinchot's recommendation. The company already had information by competent authority that its logging methods were wasteful and destructive. In 1906, for example, H. H. Chapman, then assistant professor of forestry at Yale, investigated 20,000 acres of the company's lands in the Waterville Valley of Maine. His report was critical.

Logging in the past has been conducted without regard to the future condition of the forest, the only desire being, apparently, to log where it was easiest and to cut everything merchantable. There would have been an opportunity in the spruce and hardwood stands to leave all trees under 10 to 12

18. "Minute Book of the Board of Directors" (International Paper Co., New York City).

inches. In this case the rapid increase in diameter of these small trees would have more than paid the interest on the investment of leaving them, while the chances for spruce reproduction in this type of forest would have been vastly increased. This opportunity has now disappeared except on one side or two small areas. Upon the remaining slopes there is no choice but to cut the stand clean, according to the system now practiced, but even here reproduction can be greatly assisted without expense or serious modification of the system of cutting.[19]

Julian Rothery was another forester whose professional services were used by International to improve its forestry practices. In 1912, after four years as a forester with the Forest Service, Rothery went into consulting practice. For the next fifteen years, his services were utilized by industry, largely by the International Paper Company during the 1920s. At various times, he had sizable crews of from 100 to 150 foresters and timber cruisers inventorying timber for the company in Canada, New England, and the South and classifying the company's lands for tax purposes.

In 1927, Rothery became International's salaried forester, later chief forester. After the company bought its first two mills in Louisiana, he began a land purchase program to acquire sufficient southern growing stock to sustain the mills. Much of his work as company forester, however, was in timber cruising, inventorying, and classification in Canada and New England. In 1935, he returned to the Forest Service.

Although International was then, as it is now, one of the outstandingly progressive corporations in the nation in its protection of its forests, it did not start the application of technical management (as distinct from protection only) until much later. According to John H. Hinman, former president and board chairman, the reason the company was not active in silviculture until about 1940 was because it owned large tracts abundantly stocked with timber and was not concerned with its wood supply.[20]

An example of International's land management is the handling of its Phillips Brook conservation project, a 24,000-acre tree farm in northern New Hampshire. When the company was formed in 1898 by merger of twenty paper mills in Maine, Massachusetts, New Hampshire, New York, and Vermont, most of this property came into its ownership. It was a tract in a valley that had already been operated for lumber and other forest products for a half-century.

During the seven decades of International's ownership, only three fires, and those small in area, have burned on the property. Hinman and Rothery undertook some experimental tree planting there in the 1920s, but no silviculture as such was applied until a quarter-century later.

In 1945, a detailed inventory of the timber stand was made. Planned cuttings under the selection system of management were started the following year. The decision was made to have an annual harvesting budget of 5,000 cords of spruce and balsam fir pulpwood. Hardwood cuttings to the extent of about 1.5 million board feet were begun both for pulpwood and sawlogs.

Now, the application of intensive forestry on the tract is based on a grid of 5,000 quarter-acre permanent growth study plots, which provide a contin-

19. Chapman Papers, Sterling Memorial Library, Yale University.
20. Interview with John Hinman, December 5, 1967.

uous inventory of growing stock. The plot data are coded on cards for automatic recording and processing. Timber harvesting, under the supervision of professional foresters, is now automated and controlled by computers.

Armstrong Forest Company. In 1910, the Armstrong Forest Company of Johnsonburg, Pennsylvania, a subsidiary of the New York and Pennsylvania Company, was organized to manage timberland and procure wood for paper mills in New York and Pennsylvania. The parent corporation had started to acquire woodland in the northern tier counties of Pennsylvania during the 1890s as a source of wood and natural gas reserves for its paper mill operations. As early as 1905, the company employed a consulting forester to recommend forest management practices on its holdings. Four years later, experimental plantings of Norway spruce obtained from Germany were made on company land.

Edmund O. Ehrhart, a Penn State forestry graduate, was employed as Armstrong's first full-time forester in 1915. Under his direction, an extensive spruce-planting program was started and continued for nearly two decades. Silvicultural studies were begun in 1923 in the naturally regenerated northern hardwood type, and in 1930 the 2,500-acre Wolf Run Experimental Forest was dedicated to research in northern hardwood silviculture and to the testing of new harvesting techniques.

A change in ownership occurred in 1945 when the Curtis Publishing Company acquired the company, together with extensive timber holdings in Ontario. Ehrhart was elected president of Armstrong Forest Company in 1953, and on his retirement five years later the Pennsylvania property contained 140,000 acres and the Ontario property, 120,000 acres.

A sound forestry program continued under Arthur L. Bennett, who had joined the company in 1940 as Ehrhart's assistant, and who became its president in 1966. In that year, Armstrong and its Canadian subsidiary were purchased for $24 million by Texas Gulf Sulphur Company, following discovery of rich ore bodies in the Canadian woodlands. In January 1968, the subsidiary company became the Armstrong Forest Division of Texas Gulf Sulphur Company.

In addition to producing paper pulp for the various Curtis publications, Armstrong turns out high-grade cherry veneer logs; hard and soft maple logs for furniture; red and white oak for furniture, flooring, and veneer; ash for baseball bats; and hard maple for bowling pins. Recreation also yields financial returns; the company leases areas for hunting and cabin sites. For a half-century, this forest under progressive technical management has done well by its owners and its community.

Glatfelter Pulp Wood Company. Among the pioneer companies practicing improved forest management in the Northeast is the Glatfelter Pulp Wood Company, a subsidiary of the P. H. Glatfelter Company of Spring Grove, Pennsylvania. Although small in size, as such firms are rated in an industry of corporate giants, the Glatfelter Pulp Wood Company has followed a scientifically based forestry policy that is well regarded throughout the industry.

Its first woodlands were acquired in Maryland in 1908. Walter Schwab, the company's first professional forester, was employed in 1917. As the company acquired additional lands in Delaware, Pennsylvania, and Virginia, its foresters carried forward an intensive reforestation program, together with a high degree of advanced harvesting techniques.

Since the paper mill obtains much of its wood from small private tracts, the company has undertaken to help the owners reforest their idle land. Seedlings were purchased, beginning in 1951, from state nurseries in Pennsylvania and Virginia and freely given to landholders who would plant them. Nearly 10 million trees have been distributed to cooperating owners, and more than 10 million have been planted on the company's holdings.

In addition, eight professional foresters employed by the company provide free technical assistance to private owners in the four-state area serving its operations. These foresters advise on management plans and timber marking prior to cutting and help develop more efficient techniques for harvesting and handling pulpwood. D. E. Hess, vice president and general manager, and Harold W. Geiger, company forester, are responsible for this imaginative venture in corporate forestry extension.

St. Regis Paper Company. Founded in 1899, this company had headquarters in Watertown, New York, when it began experimenting with forest management about 1919. Although it owned 100,000 acres in northern New York State, the company had cut much of the merchantable timber, and its officials saw the approaching exhaustion of its Adirondack forest holdings. C. C. Burns, general manager, became interested in reforesting lands in the area. In 1920, a forest tree nursery of 37 acres was started near St. Regis Falls to provide planting stock to reforest the company's burned and open lands. Until it ceased operation in 1928, more than 7 million trees were raised in the nursery, mostly Norway spruce and white and red pines. The trees were interplanted on holdings near St. Regis Falls and Degrass; 1.7 million seedlings were sold to other planters. Burns made a sincere effort to establish plantations and to initiate pilot forestry projects, but with only partial success.

In June 1922, the company hired its first forester—Harold V. Hart, a graduate of the College of Forestry at Syracuse. He was assigned to company operations in Quebec. In 1939, he was transferred to the office in Deferiet, New York, and given responsibility for the supervision of lands in New Hampshire, New York, and Vermont, and subsequently of lands acquired in Maine and Minnesota.

In addition to its timberlands in New York, St. Regis acquired extensive forest holdings in northern New Hampshire and Vermont. In 1934, these holdings totaled nearly 335,000 acres. Arthur B. Recknagel, professor of forest management at Cornell University, was called into a conference in October of that year by President Roy K. Ferguson to consider the possible disposal of these lands to the federal government. No decision was made then, and in the summer of 1937 Recknagel undertook a reconnaissance survey of 125,000 acres of St. Regis lands in northern New Hampshire. In his report, he stated that the object of the survey was "to quicken interest of the U.S. Forest Service in possible acquisition of this area as a National Forest," and noted that such acquisition should be encouraged.[21]

---

21. Unpublished report in the files of the St. Regis Paper Co., New York City.

Fortunately, St. Regis held on to these lands. In the summer of 1940, Recknagel, representing the company, had a conference with officers of the Forest Service to consider a practical forest management program that could be recommended to the firm. One of the government foresters was Harold C. Hebb, who was designated to set up a 725-acre cutting area as part of a cooperative plan between the company and the Forest Service. Its purpose was to demonstrate practical forest management to company officials and to guide them in developing a management plan and a cutting policy.

In 1943, Hebb, who had left the Forest Service to go with the National Lumber Manufacturers Association, and Recknagel wrote a report entitled "Common Sense Forestry in Northern New Hampshire."[22] It dealt with the management possibilities on 100,000 acres of company land in the town of Pittsburg, Coos County. This land, which St. Regis had bought in 1927 from the Connecticut Valley Lumber Company, had been cutover for sawlogs but was in productive condition, and even contained 13,000 acres of old growth.

Notwithstanding optimistic opinions given the company by Recknagel, Hebb, and others, a forestry policy was not adopted. In a letter of August 4, 1947, Victor S. Jensen, a forest economist in the Forest Service, informed the company that it had "a wonderful opportunity to practice a more enlightened land policy on its extensive holdings in northern New Hampshire and Vermont."[23] Jensen reported that St. Regis was not realizing the maximum returns on its good lands that were possible under more intensive management. He recommended shorter rotations and shorter cutting cycles, at least for balsam fir.

These favorable recommendations together with rising land values and increasing profits in the paper industry brought about the policy adopted by St. Regis to practice long-range timber management and intensive forestry. In 1967 its forest holdings, owned and controlled, in the northeastern states totaled nearly 1.2 million acres.

By 1968, St. Regis Paper Company owned or controlled nearly 6 million acres in fifteen states and provinces—in the Northeast, the South, the Lake States, the Pacific Northwest, and Canada. Much of the success of its forestry program can be credited to two of the ablest professionals in North America: Paul M. Dunn, vice president in charge of forest operations (retired in 1968); and, in Canada, Desmond I. Crossley, manager of woodlands for the St. Regis subsidiary, North Western Pulp and Power, Ltd. Robert R. Hyde was appointed director of forestry in the company's New York City headquarters in 1968.

Industrial Forests and Tree Farms

Numerous additional corporations in the northeastern states have progressive forestry policies in force. Since their forestry programs began later than those previously described, detailed accounts of their management procedures would largely duplicate those already touched on. But mention of several more is appropriate, in recognition of their early forestry practices successfully continued.

22. *Journal of Forestry*, vol. 42 (December 1944), p. 925.
23. Correspondence files, St. Regis Paper Co., New York City.

In 1924, the Brown Company in Berlin, New Hampshire, hired Henry I. Baldwin, a forestry graduate of Yale. The company had extensive holdings in Maine, New Hampshire, Vermont, and Canada. Baldwin began experiments in girdling and poisoning hardwoods in Maine at a time when only softwoods could be utilized in the mill. He also investigated spruce reproduction and the rate of decay of slash. Later, tests were made by injecting dyes into living trees, logs, and lumber in an unsuccessful attempt to utilize hardwoods profitably. Baldwin set out about 100 sample plots to determine the effects of girdling hardwoods and of weeding, thinning, and methods of cutting. While supervising extensive reforestation operations, he instituted many tests of planting methods.

His work was thus a combination of practical field forestry and research, for which an excellent opportunity was provided on the 10,000-acre Jericho Experimental Forest under his management. Another development was a large seed extraction plant and a seed-testing laboratory which served the company nurseries and produced tree seed for sale to dealers and nurserymen. During the nine years that Baldwin worked for Brown Company, he was occupied with a variety of other forestry projects—cruising and mapping; handling logging contracts; marking selective cuttings; the sale of stumpage, cordwood, and other products; and the delivery of pulpwood to the mill. Probably few foresters of this period, whether publicly or privately employed, could match his experience in such a diversity of tasks.

One of the properties in Maine with a widely acclaimed record of conservative forest management is that of the Penobscot Development Company of Old Town. The company's 500,000 acres were as carefully husbanded by Louis J. Freedman as any in the Northeast. Freedman, a forestry graduate of Harvard, retired as woodlands manager in 1956 after long service and was succeeded by forester Edwin L. Giddings, who later became vice president. In 1967 Penobscot became a wholly owned subsidiary of Diamond International Corporation.

A giant among the industrial land operators is Scott Paper Company of Philadelphia, a business started in 1879 and incorporated in Pennsylvania in 1922. In 1968, Scott owned, held under purchase or cutting rights, or leased 360,000 acres in Washington and British Columbia, 425,000 acres in Alabama and Mississippi, 835,000 acres in Maine and New Hampshire, and 1.2 million acres in eastern Canada. In addition, Scott owns 50 percent of Brunswick Pulp and Paper Company, which holds 410,000 acres in Georgia and Florida.

Finally, there are hundreds of industrial tree farms under multiple-use management throughout the Northeast. They not only produce timber and wood fiber but also provide improved wildlife habitat, watershed protection, and outdoor recreation for the public. Today, industrial foresters do not think of the products of woodlands as limited to lumber, plywood, paper, and paper products; they make provision for other products and services—fish and game, open space for recreation, and water. Tree farms are now owned and managed by lumber, mining, paper, plywood, railroad, and water supply companies. To be sure, the intensity of applied silviculture varies from one property to another, but all subscribe to certain minimum standards which include protection of the stand from fire, insects, disease, and improper cutting.[24]

Three tracts in New Hampshire demonstrate the extent and intensity of scientific forestry that is being applied on industrial tree farms throughout the Northeast. One of the earliest in the state's tree farm system is the 33,000-acre property owned by the Draper Corporation, Beebe River. This tract is intensively managed, primarily for bobbin and shuttle stock.

Another intensively managed tree farm is a 38,000-acre tract owned by the Franconia Paper Corporation. Franconia uses integrated logging to maximize returns from its woodlands; in addition it carries on educational activities to promote improved forestry by other timber owners.

A smaller tree farm of 5,800 acres is owned in New Hampshire by the New England Power Company of Boston. It is managed by the New England Forestry Foundation, a nonprofit foundation organized in 1944 in Boston to increase wood production in New England by improved management of private forest lands. The foundation provides complete forestry services at cost to this company and to other owners of properties not large enough to justify employment of full-time foresters.

Forestry in the Northeast Today

Forestry is being practiced on industrial lands in New England and the Middle Atlantic States at a progressive rate. Encouraged by reasonably steady consumer demand for wood products and by generally favorable prices, the industry has continued to invest in timberland and to expand its holdings. As more woodland goes into corporate ownership and as the intensity of management increases in stands already owned, more foresters are recruited for industrial employment.

Since World War II, the rate of progress has been remarkable. With increased federal-state-private cooperative protection against forest fire, insects, and disease, industry has found that the natural hazards of sustained-yield management are decreasing. Likewise, the amendment of 1943 to the Internal Revenue Code that provided for more favorable capital gain treatment of income from timber operations continues to encourage investment in forest practices.[25]

As we have seen, corporate management recognizes that growing trees under scientific silviculture is financially profitable, or can be made so. Companies that have sizable investments in timber acreage seldom have a choice between practicing forestry to some degree or not practicing it at all. In a business as competitive as the forest products industry, with high land values, taxes, and protection costs, few owners can afford not to grow the maximum volume of wood their lands are capable of producing.

Over the years, as the demand for forest products kept rising and the expense of obtaining raw material kept increasing, some companies sought to

24. See chap. 20 for a detailed account of the tree farm movement in the United States.
25. See chap. 15 for an explanation of the effect on forestry of capital gains treatment of income.

solve the hard-core problem of wood supply by concentrating on more efficient labor-saving, cost-cutting techniques of logging and manufacture. Foresters viewed the problem from still another angle, as one of better silviculture, that is, increasing the volume and quality of the growing stock by more productive—not necessarily more expensive—land utilization. The future belongs to those corporations that understand what the foresters, through their technical education and woods experience, are capable of doing for them.

CHAPTER 17

Industrial Forestry in the South

One of the most productive forest areas in all the world lies in the vast 1,500-mile crescent of coastal plains, mountains, and river valleys that characterize the twelve states collectively known as the South. The southern pineries extend in dense ranks from Virginia south and west to the prairies of Texas; even after three centuries of agricultural development, urbanization, and woodland exploitation, the commercial forest area exceeds 201 million acres. During the past century, the South produced more timber products than any other section of the nation.[1] How the region managed to produce so much while simultaneously increasing timber growth represents a triumph of industrial forestry.

Early Forest Industries and Aftermath

The naval stores industry, dating back to 1600, was one of the earliest industries in the South. Its name was derived from the pitch, tar, and turpentine obtained from pine trees—products essential to the building and maintenance of wooden boats and ships. Although the industry once spread from New England to the Carolinas, by the turn of the present century it was largely confined to the coastal forests of longleaf and slash pines in Georgia and Florida. It was an exploitative industry, ruinously destructive of the resource on which it depended.

In a turpentine operation, workers cut one or more faces on the trunk of a pine tree. Often the tree was as small as six inches in diameter. The wounds, about an inch deep, let crude gum (oleoresin) flow down into metal gutters into cups fastened to the tree. Small trees might die; larger ones might be broken off by wind. Some were killed by insect attack.

To safeguard a turpentine woods from wildfire that might destroy the gutters and cups, fires were set periodically to burn off the grass and leaves on

---

1. U.S. Forest Service, *Timber Trends in the United States*, Forest Resource Report no. 17 (February 1965).

the ground. Because this deliberate burning also destroyed the small seedlings on the forest floor, the turpentine forest could not reproduce itself.

From this destructive practice of light burning evolved the method of prescribed burning, which in time became an accepted silvicultural technique. Prescribed burning is the controlled use of fire in woodland under conditions that make it possible to restrict burning to a predetermined area and intensity. The ground cover is burned off to accomplish a silvicultural purpose—perhaps to prepare a seedbed to aid reproduction, or to reduce a fire hazard.

Although the naval stores industry still contributes to the forest products economy of the South, its role is a minor one, and since World War II the industry has been declining. Considerable research has been carried on by the Forest Service to increase the gum yield of naval stores operations while reducing the damage to trees by the chipping process. Improvements in woods practices have eliminated many wasteful features of turpentine operations. It is no longer the destructive industry it was a half-century ago.

Sawmilling was another early industry in the South. From Virginia into Georgia, the primitive lumber industry was confined to the coast. Transportation of lumber was mostly by water because of the bulk and weight of the product. The industry developed slowly until the mid-1860s. Then, following the Civil War, as the Mississippi Valley began to expand industrially and the utilitarian southern pines found markets, an era of timber exploitation set in. Lumbermen moved into the South in two waves, beginning in the 1880s. One group migrated from the New England and the Middle Atlantic States; the other, from the cutover pineries of the Lake States. New companies were formed or old companies simply moved South. They bought great tracts of timberland on which they built hundreds of mills, together with towns for the workers and railroads to haul the logs to the mills and the lumber to market.

In 1909, lumber production in the South reached a peak; the harvest totaled almost 20 billion board feet, or 45 percent of all the lumber cut in the nation. Considerable virgin hardwood and cypress timber remained, but the old-growth stands of southern pine were being liquidated fast. Since lumber was the principal product of the timber resource, both in volume and in value, the future of the South's wood-based economy was uncertain and portentous.

During World War I, expanded needs for lumber speeded up the logging of the southern pineries. This was the flourishing period of southern lumbering, and it brought unaccustomed prosperity to established towns and new backwoods communities alike. A broader tax base resulted in new roads, new schools, new court houses, and other appurtenances of civic affluence.

This hungry industry swallowed the forests insatiably. The pineries, once thought to be inexhaustible, began to vanish. By the late 1920s, lumber production declined. All over the South, tax officials watched apprehensively, and often incomprehensively, the passing of the timber and the closing down of the mills. Their reaction was to raise taxes, in order to collect the maximum amount before the industry cut out and moved out. Many operators with timber mortgages and other debts to pay off simply ran their mills day and night, some even without profit, in order to liquidate their forest holdings quickly. Thus, the new prosperity and the fat tax rolls faded as rapidly as they had materialized.

From birth to decay, the average sawmill town lasted about two decades, rarely three. Most companies, after cutting off their timber, liquidated their operations and either quit or moved on, usually to the relatively untapped forests of the West. Meanwhile, the end of the South's "inexhaustible" timber was in sight. As the tide of logging swept onward, it left in its wake hundreds of thousands of acres, cutover and burned over, that nobody wanted at any price. The little sawmill towns disintegrated among the charred stumps.

Frank Heyward is a candid and perceptive student of southern forest history. No romantic glow obscures his description of the pre-forestry condition of southern woodlands.

At the turn of the twentieth century, millions of acres of bleak cut-over land, apparently useful for no gainful purpose, cursed and shamed every state in the South. Instead of attracting more people, the sawmills left "ghost towns," equalled in their bleakness and spirit of desolation only by the surrounding expanse of sun-baked land. People simply moved out, fading away with the lonely wails of the mill whistles which echoed for the last time over the endless land of stumps.[2]

First Steps toward Forestry

It would be a gross distortion of history to suggest that all naval stores operators, all lumbermen, all large forest owners were indifferent to what was happening to the forests of the South. Many were quite aware of a social and economic need to restore this resource. Since wildfire was the principal natural hazard to timber ownership, owners naturally sought ways to reduce or eliminate the danger. Early in the 1900s, several companies in scattered locations throughout the region attempted to organize forest protection forces for the detection and suppression of wildfire. But individually they could do little, especially in the absence of any public agency for forest protection.

Consequently, woodland owners in several southern states began lobbying for laws to suppress woods fires and for state forestry departments to enforce the laws. With the passage of the Weeks Law in 1911, the states were encouraged to enter into the cooperative forest fire protection arrangements with the Forest Service by authority given the secretary of agriculture.

The Southern Pine Association, founded in 1915, was for years the sole organization in the region representing industry's interest in forest conservation. Under the leadership of Joseph Hyde Pratt, the association initiated the first Southern Forestry Conference, held in 1916 to promote state legislation for forestry. Pratt, a director of the Geological Survey of North Carolina, was active in organizing the South for protection against fire. Only five of the twelve southern states then had forestry departments or commissions established by law.

In 1917, the Southern Pine Association was cosponsor of a Cut-Over Land Conference held in New Orleans. The other sponsor was the Southern

2. *History of Industrial Forestry in the South* (University of Washington College of Forestry, 1958), p. 14.

Settlement and Development Organization, formed six years earlier by several railroad companies serving the South. The purpose of the conference was to seek solutions to the economic and social problems resulting from the huge extent of nonproductive land from which the timber had been harvested without provision for new crops. It was attended by more than 300 persons representing railroads, agriculture, manufacturers of agricultural machinery, and real estate agencies. Only four foresters were present.

To extricate the region from the fix it was in, the conferees recommended that purchasers be sought who would put all suitable stump land into agriculture, especially into pasturage for livestock. Timber growing was proposed also, but not as a major solution. Although the land in question had produced some of the most utilitarian pine lumber ever harvested anywhere, the vision of the conferees did not extend to another tree crop, much less to repeated crops in perpetuity.

Their lack of vision is understandable when it is remembered that the old-growth trees cut from the land were 150 to 250 years of age. Even the shrewdest businessmen in 1917 could hardly have been expected to invest capital in reforesting and protecting land whose next crop—so they thought— would not be ready for harvest for 100 years or longer. The South's vast timber-growing potential was as yet unrealized by the forest industry. Professional foresters were yet to demonstrate it.

When, in 1919, the Southern Pine Association made an estimate of the acreage of cutover land in the South, the total was 92 million acres. This association had a Forestry Committee as early as 1920, although only a few of the member companies were attempting to practice forestry on their holdings. At best, their efforts were largely confined to fire exclusion. A. L. Clark, president of the association, expressed the opinion that broad-scale reforestation would need to be undertaken to restore the lands to productivity, but that it would have to be done by the state or federal government. During the formative years of forestry in the South, the Southern Pine Association was a constructive force in promoting fire control, in strengthening state forestry departments, and in working for progressive forestry laws.

The phenomenal growth of forestry in the South was not wholly an indigenous development, however. Certain outside influences guided and moved it along. In 1927, for example, the American Forestry Association launched an ambitious and imaginative project designed to change the in-grained compulsion of rural people to burn the woods every year. It was customary in the South to set fires to provide new grass for cattle, to drive game for hunters, to destroy insects, to keep the woods open and free of poisonous snakes for the protection of naval stores workers, to clear the forest floor of inflammable debris in order to prevent the loss of trees producing naval stores, and often for no reason at all except that burning the woods was a regional habit.

By means of a three-year educational program, the association sought to reduce forest fires and fire losses in the South, specifically in Florida, Georgia, Mississippi, and South Carolina. Named the Southern Forestry Educational Project, it was manned by teams of "Dixie Crusaders" traveling in a fleet of eight motor trucks to carry the forest fire prevention message everywhere, even to the most remote backwoods hamlets. Motion pictures and lectures (more than 7,000) were attended by 3 million people, children as well as adults, many of whom saw movies for the first time. Two million bulletins, pamphlets, and posters were distributed. During this operation, which in the parlance of today would be called a crash program, The American Forestry Association had the cooperation of the Forest Service, state forestry agencies, and the state forestry associations.

Another notable cooperative undertaking under the leadership of the association was the Southern Forest Fire Prevention Conference held in New Orleans in April 1956. Federal and state forestry agencies, state forestry associations, industrial and trade associations, and local conservation groups combined forces to arouse the public and stir up action throughout the region for better fire prevention and control. Among the direct beneficial results were improved law enforcement in several states and increased appropriations for fire suppression.

In 1928, Florida appointed its first state forester, Harry Lee Baker, a former Forest Service officer. To interest citizens in growing trees and protecting them, he had small plantations set out along roadsides with firebreaks around them. Earl Porter was district forester for the Florida Forest Service at Gainesville during the early 1930s. Two brothers, naval stores operators near Ocala, wrote Porter's office for instructions about planting trees on an extensive tract of pine they had under production for turpentine. A ranger was sent to advise the owners. He showed them thousands of seedlings on an area that had not burned that year and explained that with proper fire control they did not have to plant trees for a new crop. "They were astounded that it was so easy to grow trees by just not burning the woods," Porter said. "The planted roadside trees are what attracted them to inquire into how to have more trees."[3]

This casual example of on-the-ground education, to be repeated during the next three decades throughout the naval stores belt, first by federal and state foresters, then by industrial foresters, led in time to widespread fire prevention and control. Many owners, indifferent to the protection of their natural stands, took a more proprietary attitude toward their planted trees, protecting them not only from fire, but also from destructive grazing by cattle and hogs that ranged freely through the piny woods.

Patterns of State Forestry

In several of the southern communities, the organized strength of citizens advocating forestry laws was channelled through state forestry associations.[4] Credit is due the early associations for their effective support during the formative period when the need to get started was so crucial. They alerted legislators to the importance of fire control, of state tree nurseries for the production of planting stock to reforest idle land, and of general education of the public about the economic value of commercially productive forests.

Since the Georgia Forestry Association, founded in 1907, was the first in the South, the manner of its birth illustrates the tentative growth of southern forestry. George Foster Peabody gave the University of Georgia $2,000 in

3. Letter from Earl Porter, Mobile, Ala., to the author, November 18, 1966.
4. For a detailed account of state forestry associations, see chap. 7.

1906 to start a course in forestry, which began in the fall of that year. Alfred A. Ackerman, former state forester of Massachusetts, was the professor. In 1907, Ackerman called a meeting of citizens at the university to plan a forestry program for the state; one result was the Georgia Forestry Association. Upon Ackerman's resignation a few years later, the association went into a decline, but was revived in 1921 and has been active ever since.

Despite a small membership and limited finances, the association was largely responsible for the state's early forestry laws. It fostered the creation of an advisory State Board of Forestry in 1921, although the General Assembly did not get around to passing the act creating a permanent Board of Forestry until 1925, when the first state forester was appointed.

Louisiana was the first southern state to set up a state agency for forestry. A law of 1904 created a Department of Forestry, and a commissioner of forestry was given the supervision of fire protection. An act of 1910 superseded the 1904 law; it imposed the protection duties on a forester and designated as forester the register of the State Land Office, a political incumbent. Amended in 1912 and again in 1916, this law gave forestry statutory recognition; moreover, it provided for personnel and organized effort to detect and control fire. But at best, the effort was a feeble one, largely because of the political nature of the personnel and lax enforcement. In October 1917, Reginald D. Forbes, a Yale graduate, became the state forester of Louisiana, the first professionally educated forester to hold the position.

Alabama adopted a general forest administration law in 1907; it established a commission of forestry and provided for county forest wardens. Virginia, in 1914, created a geological commission, and the members were required to appoint a technically trained forester. In 1915, North Carolina authorized the state geological board to designate its forester as the state forester and forest fire warden. Texas also established the position of state forester in 1915; he was appointed by the board of directors of the State Agricultural and Mechanical College and was charged with the administration of laws for the protection, management, and administration of the forests.

During the first decade and a half of the present century, developments in these five states represented the total public effort in the South to establish a system of forest fire protection. The activity in these states was tentative and partially ineffective, but it helped arouse citizens and legislatures to the unnecessary, enormous loss of a rich and renewable resource caused by fire.

Henry Hardtner of Urania

Henry Hardtner, president of the Urania Lumber Company of Louisiana, was a pioneer leader in southern industrial forestry. During the early 1900s, the company began investing in logged-off land to grow another crop of pine. This venture was almost unheard of in the industry; lumber companies were selling their cutover land as fast as they could, if they could. Hardtner asked Gifford Pinchot, then with the Forest Service, for the services of a forester to advise the company on the management of its second-growth holdings. W. W. Ashe, a forest officer experienced in southern silviculture, inspected the company's woods in response to the invitation. He was the first of a number of professional foresters who, over the years, were consultants to the company.

Hardtner's plan of management was simple but effective: protect young timber during logging and cutover land from fire, and natural regeneration would follow. In 1932, he summed up the results of some two decades of forest husbandry at Urania: "I have been operating my sawmill on the same site since 1896 and there is now more timber tributary to it than ever. The mill is on a perpetual basis. . . . Its present size is just right to cut the same amount each year forever—the amount the land is capable of producing, or about 20 million board feet per year."[5]

Commenting on the fact that the company's 100,000 acres of pine and hardwoods had been under continuous production for nearly four decades, Stanley F. Horn, historian and editor, pointed out in 1943: "Here pine saw timber is being harvested from land which was planted to cotton within the memory of men who are now cutting the trees."[6]

The Urania Lumber Company was the true innovator in practical forestry in the South. It was one of the first to build a lookout tower for detecting fires and to organize crews for extinguishing fires. Another early forestry innovation was the fencing of company lands against the omnipresent razor-back hog, a scourge that ranked with fire in its ability to destroy seedling longleaf pines.

It is an interesting commentary on the persistence of regional customs that the Louisiana legislature did not get around to passing an effective law controlling the free ranging of the half-wild razorback hog until 1954. The law actually was an accomplishment of the Louisiana Forestry Association, which promoted it.

Great Southern-Gaylord-Crown

Throughout the South one or more progressive forest products companies in each state undertook to protect their properties from wildfire years before the states set up organizations for fire detection and suppression. But not all companies continued their efforts. Some gave up when recurring incendiary fires were more than they could cope with and when the good results of several years of protection were knocked out by one conflagration.

Fortunately, the early forestry programs of several companies were successful and persisted. A notable example is the program of the Great Southern Lumber Company of Bogalusa, Louisiana, which was incorporated in 1902. A. Conger Goodyear became president of Great Southern and of the Bogalusa Paper Company in 1920. Later, he reported on the problems he faced.

Our management had frequently discussed various possibilities of saving Bogalusa from the common fate of sawmill towns—decay and desolation after the timber was gone—but until 1920 nothing had been done about it. By then it had become evident that the building of a paper mill and other wood-using industries would not alone make permanence possible. Quite clearly we were going to run out of our raw material—timber—the very reason for our existence.[7]

5. "Forestry at Urania, Louisiana," *Journal of Forestry*, vol. 30 (March 1932), pp. 310–11.
6. *This Fascinating Lumber Business*, p. 59.
7. *Bogalusa Daily News*, March 29, 1949.

In 1920, a group of company directors visited Urania for an inspection of Henry Hardtner's forestry work. They were so impressed by what they saw that they decided to put their cutover lands under forestry management. Austin Cary was brought in for consultation. "More than any other man Austin Cary was responsible for the spread of the gospel of reforestation in the yellow pine lands,"[8] according to Goodyear.

Lacking a forestry staff and a supply of seedlings, the company nevertheless immediately fenced 800 acres of denuded land, plowed furrows eight feet apart, and planted pine seed in them. The next year, seedlings were obtained from the woods and hand planted on 380 acres. In 1922, a company nursery was started at Bogalusa; 1.2 million seedlings were grown and set out in 1,200 acres. Paul M. Garrison was employed as forester in 1925 (he became head of the Forestry Department in 1934). By the end of 1929, some 23,000 acres had been reforested.

According to Philip C. Wakely, former silviculturist at the Southern Forest Experiment Station in New Orleans, the Experiment Station made Bogalusa its planting research center in 1923 because the company offered cooperation and the new enterprise afforded an opportunity to learn. Twenty-five years later, Wakely could report that the results had been gratifying.

The company's extensive plantations have served as a vast observation ground and pilot plant to supplement the station's small plots. Out of the combination came much of the technical information that guided the planting of many millions of pine trees by the Civilian Conservation Corps throughout the South, and has guided the operation of State Forest Nurseries in a dozen states, much of the routine planting of the Soil Conservation Service, and the forest planting on thousands of farms from Maryland to Texas.[9]

Great Southern's reforestation operations were soon on a scale never before attempted in the South, and indeed probably not anywhere else in the United States by a private company. Wakely noted that by 1926 the company had 12,700 acres of thriving plantations. "At that time," he said, "there wasn't another 100 acres of successful southern pine plantation in any one place south of the Biltmore Estate in North Carolina."[10]

When, in 1937, Gaylord Container Corporation acquired the forest properties, then totaling 260,000 acres, it continued planting 1,000-2,000 acres yearly, and increased the timber holdings to 344,000 acres. By 1949, the company had a staff of ten graduate foresters, a fleet of mechanical tree planters, a system of two-way shortwave radio communication for fire control, and an airplane for forestry use that was equipped for aerial photography.

In 1955, ownership passed to Crown Zellerbach Corporation, whose record of forest management on its western holdings augured well for the continued management of its newly acquired southern lands. Garrison managed Crown Zellerbach's southern timber operations from 1955 until his

8. Ibid.
9. Ibid.
10. Ibid.

retirement in 1961. His career was different from that of most other American foresters in that he practiced silviculture in artificial plantations that were among the most extensive in the country.

By 1967, Crown Zellerbach and its predecessor companies had planted 236 million trees in the South, and additional acreage was being regenerated by direct seeding. Owned outright or under long-term lease are 700,000 acres in Louisiana and Mississippi, all receiving scientific forest management. Over the past half-century, Great Southern, Gaylord, and Crown Zellerbach created one of the largest industrially owned, man-made forests on the continent. A living demonstration of the productive capacity of southern woodlands under scientific silviculture, these pineta are a convincing example of the economic soundness of growing trees for profit.

Chesapeake Corporation

Incorporated in 1918 for the manufacture of pulp and paper, the Chesapeake Corporation of West Point, Virginia, acquired an engineer, Elis Olsson, who later became president. Although the mill was located in an area of extensive second-growth pines, Olsson became concerned about the plant's future supply of pulpwood long before the problem became critical.

In 1922, the company's timber holdings amounted to only 4,500 acres. But in that year, it began a policy of leaving seed trees to provide natural regeneration following cutting. Three years later, the stockholders approved "a policy of acquiring timber lands as fast as the finances of the Corporation would permit."[11]

By 1929, the company owned nearly 24,000 acres and began planting abandoned farmland with pine seedlings. During 1930, a year of serious drought, the forests of Virginia suffered extensive fire damage. Chesapeake Corporation cooperated with the State Forest Service in financing and erecting four steel fire towers in the mill's wood procurement area.

Winslow L. Gooch, a forestry graduate of the universities of Maine and Michigan and a former district forester in the Virginia Forest Service, was appointed company forester in 1932. During the next twelve years, he cruised and mapped the company's timber stands, developed a management plan for woods operations, laid out experimental plots, established a nursery for seedling production, and set up demonstration plots along roadsides where forestry techniques could be seen by other landowners and the general public. Landowners in the counties from which the company obtained wood were given free technical advice in the handling of their stands.

When Gooch resigned in 1944 to become a forestry consultant to the federal government, he was succeeded as chief forester by his assistant, James H. Johnson, a Yale forestry graduate. During Johnson's tenure, the company acquired additional timberland, stepped up its reforestation work, and undertook a program of tree improvement to raise genetically superior trees. In a seed orchard, the foresters are growing pine seed to produce superior forests that will yield increased volumes of wood and cellulose per acre.

11. Alonzo Thomas Dill, *Chesapeake, Pioneer Papermaker: A History of the Company and Its Community* (University of Virginia Press, 1968), p. 152. Much of the account of the company's forestry operations has been drawn from this book.

In addition to producing income from trees, part of the corporation's woods are rented to sportsmen's clubs for hunting. Wildlife management areas have been set up in numerous tracts. By 1969, the Chesapeake Corporation owned 278,000 acres of well-managed forests in Virginia, Maryland, and Delaware.

Riches from Ruin in Arkansas

Commercial lumber production began in Arkansas during the closing years of the 1860s, when the state's woodlands were estimated to total 25 million acres of so-called yellow pines and hardwoods.

In 1907, Samuel J. Record, later to become dean of the Yale School of Forestry, gave a discouraging report on the future of the forests of Arkansas. He noted that the state had approximately 100 billion feet of standing timber, one-fifth of it pine. In 1906, the total cut was nearly 2 billion feet, the largest in the state's history.

At this rate 50 years will be required to cut off all the timber, assuming that the factor of growth will be offset by deterioration and waste. In all probability the rate of cutting will increase so materially that the available timber supply will be largely exhausted within 20 years. Most of the pine mills will cut out within 10 years, while the cypress industry is rapidly nearing an end.[12]

After 1909, when 2 billion board feet were harvested from virgin stands, a gradual decline set in. Two decades later, as Record predicted, most of the old-growth timber had been cut, and Arkansas appeared to be through as a major timber-producing state.

Most sawmill owners had operated on a wholly exploitative basis. Since virgin timber was both plentiful and cheap, they logged off all trees over a foot in diameter at the stump. The remaining smaller trees had a slim chance to regenerate a new stand; most were broken during the logging operation. Those not broken might be made into crossties to build and maintain the logging railroads that were the sole means of log transport in that era. Finally, the residual trees not broken or utilized were destroyed by the fires that almost invariably followed when the fallers moved on.

Lumber companies throughout the state hired real estate or agricultural agents to sell the land as fast as the timber was removed. But much of the soil was unsuited for farming, hence tens of thousands of acres remained unsold at any price.

With the advent of the depression years of the 1930s, the future of the state's forest resource appeared doubtful—with a few exceptions to be noted later. If the cutover land could not be cultivated for crops or converted to pasture for cattle, it was deemed worthless. Few citizens believed that another crop of trees could be grown with profit.

But not all people were blind to the possibilities of renewing the resource. Officials of the Crossett Lumber Company, for example, were shown by H. H. Chapman and other early foresters that the seedlings and saplings that

12. "The Forests of Arkansas," *Forestry Quarterly*, vol. 5 (September 1907), p. 301.

escaped death by logging and fire responded to their release from competition by putting on rapid growth. Three decades after the virgin trees had been cut, the stands had grown to small sawlog size. With fire control, less destructive logging, and reforestation where necessary, the forest industries need not wither away. They might even look to a prosperous future.

William L. Hall, an early Forest Service officer, became a consulting forester in the early 1920s. During most of his career he operated in Arkansas, where he managed a sizable tract of his own timber. He was intimately acquainted with the beginnings of forestry in the South and with the attempts of industry to handle the fire problem in the absence of state assistance or responsibility. In 1927, he reported:

In many instances the southern timber land owners themselves have shouldered heavy responsibilities, both in fire protection and in education of people as to the fire menace. In Arkansas, with no state forestry or fire organization, without a cent of state or federal aid, substantial headway in fire control is being made. There it is the leading timber land owners and lumber and paper companies who have undertaken measures of fire protection. And they are getting results. Fire is being controlled over a large part of the 10-million-acre pine belt of Arkansas. The companies doing this own less than 20 per cent of the pine lands of the state. They are actually protecting a very large acreage that they do not own.[13]

Then, in 1933, several encouraging things happened. The Arkansas Forestry Commission was created by law, and state-organized fire protection was started. More companies organized their own fire crews to cooperate with the state forces. They even began experimenting with selection cutting to hasten natural regeneration and thus obtain fully stocked stands. Some large owners stopped selling their cutover lands, deciding to hold them for timber growing. A few who had been selling their lands began buying them back.

Industrial forestry had begun in Arkansas. In a 1949 report, Russell R. Reynolds, silviculturist in charge of the Crossett Experimental Forest of the Southern Forest Experiment Station, stated that most of the large owners were on a sustained-yield basis by 1940. Some accomplished the change without a reduction in production. Others found that output had to be reduced until growth caught up to the cut, or exceeded it. "In some other cases, in which the mills had practically cut out before it was decided to try for sustained yield," Reynolds said, "it was not only necessary to reduce the mill cut for a number of years but also to purchase from other sources most of the logs necessary to keep the mill running."[14]

Charles A. Gillett was the first state forester of Arkansas, appointed May 23, 1933. During the next three years, nearly one-third of all the state's privately owned timberland was put under organized protection from fire. Over a period of thirty-five years, the State Forestry Commission built up its permanent personnel to more than 450. Nearly 17 million acres of private

13. "Commercial Forestry and the South," *Report of the Conference on Commercial Forestry*, Chicago, November 1927 (Chamber of Commerce of the United States, 1928), p. 162.
14. "Industrial Silviculture in Arkansas," September 26, 1949 (Southern Forest Experiment Station, Crossett, Ark.).

woodland were given full protection. One hundred and two modern steel lookout towers were put into operation and tied into a communication system of 4,300 miles of telephone lines supplementing a two-way shortwave radio installation of 79 fixed stations, 414 mobile units, and 26 portable sets.[15] In less than four decades, fire ceased to be the principal obstacle to the practice of silviculture on the private holdings in Arkansas.

The Forest Service reported that the woodland area of Arkansas in 1959 was 20.8 million acres, some 1.4 million acres greater than in 1951.[16] The downward trend in growth had been reversed. Softwood volume (mainly pine growing stock) had increased nearly one-third to 5.4 billion cubic feet.

The greatest advances in forestry had been made on industrial holdings and on publicly owned woodlands; together these totaled 7 million acres. On the private nonindustrial holdings—160,000 of them, comprising 14 million acres—progress was slower.

Four years later (1963), the Forest Service estimated the forest area in Arkansas to be 21.5 million acres.[17] Industrial holdings totaled 4 million acres. The net volume of softwood growing stock had risen to 5.9 billion cubic feet.

During the transition period of the past three decades, companies that adopted intensive forestry practice as a permanent operation have stayed with it. In 1969, Arkansas had 1,740 tree farms with an area of 4.1 million acres.

In 1968, 149 professional foresters and 24 forest technicians were employed by industry in Arkansas. Nine consulting foresters were in practice.

Crossett Lumber Company

The productive capacity of timberland under improved management also has been convincingly demonstrated by the experience of the Crossett Lumber Company. The company, which in 1899 had built a sawmill at Crossett, Arkansas, early sought technical advice, and a report on a portion of its holdings was prepared by the 1912 class of the Yale Forest School. The report contained a summary and recommendations by Professor H. H. Chapman.

An estimate of the mature timber indicated that at the then rate of cutting—over 200 million board feet annually—harvesting could continue eighteen or twenty years. According to the report: "The land cannot be kept permanently in forest by the present company and it is planned ultimately to dispose of it as farm lands."[18] The stands were in an unsatisfactory condition; severe fires had burned through the slash, destroying immature pole timber, and worthless oaks and scrub sweet gum were coming up.

Nevertheless, Chapman asserted, "It would be possible under proper management to maintain a perpetual supply of timber on the holdings of this

---

15. Fred H. Lang, "Two Decades of State Forestry in Arkansas," *The Arkansas Historical Quarterly*, vol. 24 (Autumn 1965).
16. Herbert S. Sternitzke, *Arkansas Forests*, U.S. Forest Service, Southern Experiment Station (1960).
17. U.S. Forest Service, *Timber Trends*.
18. A copy of the typewritten report of the Yale Forest School is in the possession of Walter H. Meyer, Hamden, Conn. Professor emeritus of the school, Meyer formerly was consultant in forest management to the Crossett Lumber Co.

company, but the present output could not be maintained." He added, "The forest itself is admirably adapted to continuous production."[19] Finally, he recommended that a forester familiar with southern pine should be employed, at least temporarily.

Another report on the company's cutover lands, then totaling 197,396 acres, was made by Chapman on July 1, 1912. He found that 63,000 acres, or 32 percent, chiefly in Louisiana, had been ruined by unrestricted fires and would produce no second cut. Stands of poles that would have provided a cut of 73 million board feet in fifteen years had been destroyed by fire. Stands of seedling pines capable of producing a cut of 743 million board feet in 30 years also had been destroyed by fire. Most of this damage had occurred in the five-year period following logging. Chapman made the following recommendations:

Fires should be absolutely kept out of recently cut-over areas after slash is burned, for a period of at least five years, by employing rangers and providing an organization to fight and put them out.
The company should employ a forester and an assistant to determine the growth on cut-over land, to supervise brush disposal and burning, to study utilization in the woods, to be responsible for fire protection and to determine methods of cutting and diameter limits.[20]

In January 1923, W. K. Williams, having been employed as company forester, made a survey of the cutover lands. He recommended the acquisition of additional cutover lands so that the total would be 200,000 acres and suggested limiting the yearly cut to one-half the capacity of the mill.

Following another inspection of the holdings, Chapman informed the directors in June 1923 that the work done in organizing fire control forces was more important than all the other forestry measures combined. But in a follow-up report to the directors in May 1926, he was not optimistic about the results.

In my opinion, the effort to prevent fire has not succeeded and unless the company intends to handle this question along more modern lines than have been pursued to date, it will never succeed.
While the company has been expending nearly two million dollars in increasing the size of their holdings by purchasing lands stocked with second growth, they are at the same time burning up probably three times as great a value in restocking on lands they already own, in the form of seedlings and young saplings which would make the subsequent cut when these new purchases are cut over.[21]

In about 1926, the company's forest operations were put on a sustained-yield basis. Following an inspection of a portion of the Crossett forest in May 1930, Chapman noted that "the organization for fire protection has reached a high state of efficiency."[22]

A. E. Wackerman, forester for Crossett from 1927 to 1932, asserted that "fire protection can be made effective at a moderate cost of not more than

19. Ibid.
20. A copy of the Chapman typescript is in the possession of Walter H. Meyer (see fn. 18).
21. See fn. 20.
22. See fn. 20.

four cents an acre a year" and cited reductions in acreage burned on 350,000 acres as follows: 1928, 25,000 acres; 1929, 18,000 acres; 1930, 12,000 acres; and 1931, 4,800 acres.[23]

During the fall of 1933, the forestry staff started the first marking of timber for cutting under the selection system of management. Surveys and inventories of the stand were made by professional foresters, and in 1940 Chapman presented still another report in which he recommended that the company study alternatives to railroad logging in order to build up the pine stands in certain blocks instead of liquidating them. The annual cut was then 35 million board feet, less than half the estimated annual growth. In a subsequent inspection in May 1942, Chapman noted that brush growth was occupying cutover land in the absence of fire.

Forestry paid off. A half-century after Chapman had predicted the company would lose its woodlands unless it changed its policy, Crossett was still producing forest products from the same holdings, now increased to 565,000 acres. For these assets, together with the company's manufacturing plants, Georgia-Pacific Corporation paid $127 million in 1962.[24]

Forestry by Foresters

Austin Cary first visited the South in 1917. As a roving extension specialist for the Forest Service, his missionary work on behalf of improved forest management profoundly influenced the spread of forestry knowledge and its application.

As a consultant in silviculture and logging engineering, Cary influenced the woods management policies of a number of leading companies. He did not tell lumbermen what they should do or how to run their business. By example and demonstration, he showed them how certain methods would help perpetuate and build up the stand, all within the economic realities of the times. His ideas were accepted, and among the companies that acknowledged indebtedness to his teachings were the Alger-Sullivan Lumber Company, the Allison Lumber Company, the Brooks-Scanlon Corporation, the Crossett Lumber Company, the Great Southern Lumber Company, the Vredenburg Lumber Company, and the W. T. Smith Lumber Company.

Frank Heyward summed up Cary's role in two sentences: "Austin Cary dedicated the last 19 years of his life to awakening southern wood-using industries to the possibilities of timber growing. He was successful to a remarkable degree, and his accomplishments in the fields of fire protection and forest management comprise the greatest contribution by any single person to southern forestry."[25]

The work of men like Cary and Chapman had great influence on company officials who began to realize that they should have their own full-time foresters to manage their lands under scientific forestry principles. Walter J. Damtoft, a Yale forestry graduate, was the first industrial forester employed

23. "Forestry at Crossett, Arkansas," *Journal of Forestry*, vol. 30 (October 1932), pp. 747–48.

24. *Standard Corporation Descriptions* (Standard & Poor's Corporation, 1968).

25. *History of Industrial Forestry in the South*, p. 28.

in the South; he went with the Champion Paper and Fibre Company in 1920 and spent his entire career with this company.

Another early industrial forester was Inman F. Eldredge, a native of South Carolina and a 1905 graduate of the Biltmore Forest School. After employment by the Forest Service in the West and in Washington, D.C., he left the government in 1926 to take charge of some 170,000 acres of longleaf and slash pine in southeastern Georgia that had been acquired by the Superior Pine Products Company. Although this forest had been ruinously cut over, burned, and misused, the site was naturally productive. Under a working plan that included planting, thinning, and prescribed burning, the second growth responded to management and protection from fire.

Eldredge stayed with the company six years, leaving it to head up the Forest Survey of the South, a project begun by the Forest Service in 1932. The survey was undertaken because little was actually known about forest conditions in the South. Data were utterly lacking as to the total woodland acreage; the volume of the principal tree species; and the amount of net growth after deducting for the estimated drain by cutting, fire, insects, and disease. As the former manager of a large private holding, Eldredge understood that factual data were important if the timber resource was to become the base for economic expansion.

Survey headquarters were in the Southern Forest Experiment Station at New Orleans. It took four years to complete the field work alone. Included in the data collected was information of particular value to the pulp and paper industry—the volume in cords of wood by species, by sizes, and by location. According to Eldredge, the presence of this growing stock and its availability for utilization induced the paper industry to move into the South during the 1930s.

The Southern Forest Experiment Station had been established in July 1921. Reginald D. Forbes was the first director. He was succeeded by Elwood L. Demmon, who served during the period of the Forest Survey of the South. The research findings of this station, together with those of the Southeastern Forest Experiment station at Asheville, North Carolina, contributed much to the advancement of southern forestry.

Eldredge was succeeded at the Superior Pine Products Company by his assistant, William M. Oettmeier, who later became president and general manager. Oettmeier, a graduate of the Pennsylvania State Forest School at Mont Alto, built up the growing stock under modern silvicultural practice and developed the Suwanee Forest, later enlarged to more than 200,000 acres, into one of the valuable timber properties of America. Foresters and others acquainted with this tract, which is now leased and managed by the St. Regis Paper Company, consider it to be a striking example of profitable industrial forestry based on scientific management, sound economics, and progressive administration. Oettmeier, incidentally, was possibly the first industrial forester to use radio for forest administration. Although primarily set up for reporting fires, his radio system handled all aspects of communication, replacing the telephone.

The Suwanee Forest is representative of private forestry as practiced by the forest products industry throughout the South. Within a half-century, this industry adopted a policy of responsibility to the land and to the public. The destructive logging and carelessness with fire so typical of the industry prior to World War I would not be tolerated in the 1960s, either by society or by the industry itself.

In 1942, Joseph E. McCaffrey, woodlands manager of International Paper Company's Southern Kraft Division, reported on information he had obtained from forest industries throughout the South. His survey showed that, in 1925, 82 properties totaling 4.7 million acres had started forestry practices to make their lands more productive. In 1925, the southern pulp and paper industry owned less than 500,000 of those acres; in 1940 it owned 4.5 million acres, almost all under intensive management. Other corporations in 1940—lumber companies, naval stores operators, power companies, oil companies, steel companies, and others—owned 12 to 15 million acres "so handled that the growing stock is being materially increased each year." McCaffrey pointed out: "The latest figures available show that prior to 1925 less than one-half dozen technically trained men were employed by industry in strictly forestry work. The picture in 1940 is greatly different; the industry now employs a total of 220 trained foresters."[26]

In 1946, Earl Porter, then chief forester of the Southern Kraft Division, estimated that 484 technically trained foresters were working on 167 million acres of privately owned woodland in the South. Mississippi, he noted, had three technical foresters privately employed in 1936 and twenty-seven in 1946. Louisiana in 1936 had four foresters in private employ and thirty-eight in 1946.

Porter, who had started his woods work in the Adirondacks and whose long career included experience in the Northwest and New York State, commented on opportunities in the South: "There is no better place in the world for a private forester to practice."[27]

Paper Production Boom

Industrial forestry had an eloquent and indefatigable missionary in Charles Holmes Herty of Georgia, by profession a chemist and by conviction a promoter of the economic possibilities of southern pines. His first notable contribution was to the naval stores industry when he devised and introduced a more efficient and less destructive method of extracting resin from the trunks of pine trees. Beginning in 1931, he operated a privately supported pulp and paper laboratory at Savannah for research in the utilization of southern pine species for newsprint. His demonstration of how newsprint could be manufactured from the southern pines dramatized the economic possibilities of forestry for profit.

In the words of Jonathan Daniels, editor of the *Raleigh News and Observer*: "Few men have contributed more to the possibilities of the pines than Dr. Herty. . . . In 1931, at the close of a distinguished career as a chemist, he not only made important discoveries in the use of pine in the production of

---

26. "Progress in Industrial Forestry," *Journal of Forestry*, vol. 40 (February 1942), p. 90.
27. "Private Forestry and the Private Forester in the South," *Journal of Forestry*, vol. 44 (November 1946), p. 909.

newsprint, but made himself an evangel of the planting and protection of the pines."[28] Because Herty was a persuasive speaker and publicist, as well as a scientist, his personal campaign for improved protection of the southern forests against fire influenced legislators and industrialists, teachers and farmers, newspapermen and citizens of all classes. He died two years before the South's first newsprint mill was built by the Southland Paper Company at Lufkin, Texas, in 1940.

However, most of the southern pulp and paper mills were engaged almost wholly in the manufacture of kraft paper—the product responsible for the spectacular growth of the paper industry in the South. Originated in Germany in 1884, the sulphate process of making unbleached, or kraft,[29] paper was adopted commercially in the United States in 1909. In that same year, the Roanoke Rapids Paper Company began manufacturing kraft paper from pine. Another kraft paper mill started operating in Texas in 1911.

In Bogalusa, the Great Southern Lumber Company introduced the kraft process into Louisiana in 1918. Then, in 1920, a new kraft mill was built at Bastrop, in northeastern Louisiana. This mill is notable because it was bought by International Paper Company in the mid-1920s, thus providing the opening for International's advent into the southern paper industry, with benefit both to forestry and to the people and the economy of the whole South. When International Paper Company moved into the South in 1925, it bought three kraft mills and built three.

Credit for the development and woods application of International's broad-gauge southern forestry policy is shared by many company officers, from presidents on down. But the chief proponents were Joseph McCaffrey, who joined the company in 1928 and retired in 1963 as vice president in charge of the Southern Kraft Division's woods operations; and Earl Porter, who rose through the ranks to become manager of woodlands for the division.

During the 1930s, the few foresters employed by International were mostly engaged in fire control and timber cruising. No real forest management was being practiced. In 1937, with McCaffrey in charge, the company set up a separate woodlands organization at Camden, Arkansas, and started an intensive management program, although on a fairly small scale. It gradually expanded, and a year later a central woodlands organization for the whole division was created at the headquarters in Mobile.

In 1948, the Southern Kraft Division employed 100 foresters for its 2 million acres. In that year, the company observed its fiftieth anniversary, and in a commemorative book published for the occasion it was noted that during the depression years of the 1930s International's southern mills "provided vital earnings for the company, and later helped provide capital for full-scale financial reconstruction." An important part of company policy was stated in the following way:

Underlying all paper making is forestry. I-P men are first woodsmen, and increasingly today teachers and exponents of scientific tree farming. . . . The

28. *The Forest Is the Future* (New York: International Paper Co., 1957), p. 11.
29. *Kraft* is the German word for strong.

goal of International companies is about 5,000,000 cords a year. The modern paper maker is a conservationist by instinct and by necessity.[30]

International Paper Company provides an outstanding example of large-scale industrial forestry that has benefited both the corporation and other owners as well. In 1967, the company employed 330 foresters in the nine states of its Southern Kraft Division. Most of these foresters supervise management and harvesting operations on company lands. In addition, the company maintains the Southlands Experiment Forest near Bainbridge, Georgia, a center for applied research in forest, wildlife, and related resource management. Not all the foresters work exclusively on company lands; some are specially assigned to give technical advice to other landowners who sell pulpwood to the company's mills.

Throughout the South in 1968, 100 pulp and paper mills used the equivalent of 37 million cords of wood. Whereas four decades earlier the industry employed less than a dozen full-time foresters, in 1968 these companies employed 1,647 foresters.[31] Although the South produces half the wood pulp and a third of the paper manufactured in the United States, the timber resource has not declined. On the contrary, under widespread silviculture and with almost complete organized fire protection in the states, the volume of wood grown exceeds the annual drain from all causes—cutting, fire, insects, and disease. And industry's intensive forestry programs are still expanding.

Success Preceded by Stress

Up to the early 1930s, about fifteen paper mills had been built in the South. Their combined wood requirement was barely equal to that of one of the large mills operating today. Several of the older mills were built to utilize the waste wood from sawmills. But the mill operators soon learned that the sawmill waste was insufficient to fill the need for raw material to supply pulp mills of a size to be run economically. Banks and other financial institutions were reluctant to lend money to build mills unless the mills had adequate timberland reserves to support the operations. Thus, mill owners began to back up their operations by obtaining timberland.

The Southern Paper Company at Moss Point, Mississippi, built to utilize the waste from the Dantzler Lumber Company sawmills, acquired timberlands from Dantzler to help sustain the paper mill. International Paper Company's extensive holdings in Alabama, Arkansas, the Carolinas, Florida, Louisiana, and Mississippi were used to obtain bank loans for financing mill contruction. For years West Virginia Pulp and Paper Company had a woodland purchase program in the Carolinas before building a mill there. Crossett Lumber Company in Arkansas built a pulp and paper mill to utilize its timber more completely. These and other early paper company woodlands were put under the supervision of foresters whose first job was to organize fire prevention and control facilities.[32]

---

30. *International Paper Company after Fifty Years* (New York: IPC, 1948).

31. Southern Forest Institute, *A Statistical Report on the Pulp and Paper Industry in the South* (Atlanta: SFI, 1969).

32. The author is indebted to Earl Porter for information pertinent to this discussion.

When the Forest Service's survey of the South resulted in an inventory of more timber than anyone imagined or thought possible, the ever-alert financial interests were attracted, and expanding investments in paper manufacturing inevitably followed. In time, what with the establishment of new mills and the expansion of existing plants, a bullish market for sizable blocks of timber, heretofore of little value, developed wherever mills were planned or even rumored.

Consequently, increasing land values justified, and indeed required, more intensive management of the corporate forest than it had ever had before. Thus, the practice of silviculture, which previously could not be economically justified in second-growth stands with little or no sales value and without markets for products, now became an integral aspect of industrial policy.

In short, paper mills required a guaranteed supply of raw material for permanent operation; competition for raw material increased its value; foresters were needed to grow the raw material in sufficient volume and at an acceptable cost. These conditions brought industrial forestry to the South. But before this advent, a period of adjustment had to be hurdled.

As prices of forest land mounted, and the companies competed with each other to buy acreage, the stumpage returns to private owners who held on to their land increased excitingly. Thinnings, previously unsalable, were now profitable. An investment in a young pine stand located within hauling distance of a paper mill assured quick and handsome profits. Even worked-out trees in naval stores operations, in the past absolutely worthless, found a market. Although the outlook appeared rosy, actually it was bleak. Frank Heyward wrote:

For the most part, little or no thought was given to forest practices when cutting pulpwood. The main idea was to satisfy the gargantuan appetite of the big mills which ran 24 hours a day seven days a week. As a result many privately owned timber tracts were stripped as thoroughly of their second growth pines as had been the original virgin forests by steam skidders. There was an immediate outcry from the public, the press, and public foresters. Was the South again to see its forests reduced to waste stumpland?[33]

By the late 1930s, this industry, whose coming to the South had been welcomed with enthusiasm, was under attack from several quarters for its baleful consequences. It started another round of disorderly and wasteful liquidation of the forest resource. Although the chief of the Forest Service did not have only the South in mind, he asserted that public control of the management and harvesting of private timber would be necessary to stabilize the forest industries and the forest communities. He advocated that the supervision of forest practice on private lands be done by public agencies, because it could not safely be left to industry.

Inman Eldredge summed up the confused and ominous sequelae of events resulting from the impact of the paper industry on the region.

This sudden and spectacular development was a source of much gratification to the fortunate millsite communities, upon which the rich payrolls fell like manna from heaven in the years of the depression, as well as to thousands of cash-hungry farmers and jobless men; but it sent a tremor of alarm through

33. *History of Industrial Forestry in the South*, pp. 38–39.

the South as a whole. The lumber, pole, tie, and naval stores industries saw in the well-financed newcomers from the North new and powerful competitors for the raw materials they must use in common. The conservationists, too, and many segments of the general public feared that the region's providentially and none too plentiful resource of second-growth pine timber was gravely threatened. This general apprehension was reflected in the press and in the state legislatures throughout the South, and for awhile it was the topic of conversation of the man on the street and the suggested subject of hostile legislation in several of the states.[34]

On March 25, 1935, from Lake City, Florida, Austin Cary wrote President Roosevelt a seven-page single-spaced typewritten letter. Although mainly devoted to the history of the forest industry of New England and New York, it was descriptive also of developments in industrial forestry in the South. Identifying himself as "the oldest forester in the country," Cary explained that he wrote in his private capacity as a citizen, but signed the letter "A. Cary, Logging Engineer, U.S. Forest Service." Because of his extensive knowledge of southern forest conditions, his comments on industrial forestry progress are significant.

In 1920 the Capper report so-called of the Forest Service summarized the state of affairs in this particular region, of the production of naval stores, in a way that clearly indicated the exhaustion of available timber at just about the present date. . . . What, however, has been the outcome? In the time that has elapsed the naval stores industry has produced some of the largest crops in its history; the government is today urging and helping it to control production; its well-informed members are apprehensive of a surplus of timber arising in from one to two decades hence, expecting in fact the appearance of several times the amount it can possibly use unless it expands its markets. . . . The unreliability of figures of this kind is, however, strongly illustrated.
The Copeland report of 1933 is much more elaborate and impressive. It was, however, produced by much the same men, with the same bias and one-sided training. Inevitably much of its material is estimate or guesswork.[35]

Cary then went on to explain "the real motive behind this letter."

The policy I suggest is that public ownership be kept out of sections in which private initiative promises to meet public need and in which there is no other clear reason for its introduction.[36]

This unusual letter was referred by the White House to the Forest Service. It is doubtful if Cary ever received an acknowledgement. Chief Silcox is

34. "Forestry in the Southern Region," *Problems and Progress of Forestry in the United States* (Washington: Society of American Foresters, 1947), p. 69.
35. Cary sent a copy of this letter to H. H. Chapman, Yale School of Forestry. It is now among the Chapman Papers, Sterling Memorial Library, Yale University. The Capper Report, *Timber Depletion, Lumber Prices, Lumber Exports, and Concentration of Timber Ownership*, was prepared by the Forest Service and submitted by the secretary of agriculture to the Senate on June 1, 1920 in response to a Senate request initiated by Senator Arthur Capper of Kansas. The secretary recommended legislation for (1) federal-state cooperation in fire control and in promoting the growth of timber on cutover lands, and (2) increased acquisition of land to enlarge the national forest system. The Copeland Report, *A National Plan for American Forestry*, was prepared by the Forest Service and transmitted to the Senate by the secretary in 1933 in response to a resolution by Senator Royal S. Copeland.
36. Ibid.

known to have been annoyed because Cary wrote directly to the White House, but did nothing about it, probably in view of Cary's venerable years and approaching retirement. Cary died a year later, in 1936.

During the depression years, the Forest Service greatly extended its land acquisition program in the South. (In 1967, national forests in the twelve southern states totaled 10.5 million acres.) Many owners, faced year after year by tax bills and low profits, if any, from their cutover properties, considered themselves lucky that the federal government wanted to buy their land. As Heyward pointed out, when forest products companies elected to sell out "no pressure was brought to bear on these companies to influence their decisions towards selling their land. This is a fact that should be remembered when private groups criticize the government for national forest ownership in the South."[37] Cary's ingenuous if sincere attempt to influence national policy had no effect.

Union Bag and Paper Corporation (now Union Camp Corporation) started building a mill at Savannah in 1935; two years later it was one of the world's largest pulp mills. Conscious of its public reputation, the corporation outlined its forestry program at a meeting of the Georgia Forestry Association in Athens in May 1937. It would adopt a constructive forest policy to perpetuate its pulpwood supply and would inaugurate a program that would insure permanent forestry operations on both company lands and other privately owned lands.

Over the past three decades, Union Camp has so faithfully adhered to this policy that the quality of its forestry accomplishments is the equal of any company in the industry. But in 1937, not many companies were willing or able to follow its example.

Technical Aid for Forest Owners

Southern Pulpwood Conservation Association. Faced with justified public criticism, threatened with government regulation of its woods operations, and challenged by the forestry profession to apply minimum standards of silviculture, the paper industry responded by forming a highly effective association. The Southern Pulpwood Conservation Association (SPCA), organized in 1939 with headquarters in Atlanta, had a simple but broad charter: through education it would strive to improve the utilization and conservation of the South's forest resources. SPCA would accomplish its mission by getting its members to recognize and voluntarily apply sound forestry principles and by initiating an educational program directed to forest owners and the public.

The industry agreed to undertake self-regulation of cutting practices on its lands, and SPCA recruited a staff of field foresters, who, working with company foresters, held demonstrations for landowners and pulpwood procurement operators. They demonstrated harvesting methods that would maintain the growing stock in permanently productive condition.

SPCA and company foresters taught timber owners how to mark trees for cutting. They explained the function of seed trees left standing after logging and the techniques of partial cutting, selection cutting, and the various kinds

37. *History of Industrial Forestry in the South*, p. 32.

of thinnings. Over the years management assistance was given to tens of thousands of landowners who collectively owned millions of acres. In addition, so-called pilot forests, maintained by companies throughout the region, were visited annually by hundreds who came to see demonstrations of approved forest practices.

Frank Heyward, then state forester of Georgia, was selected as SPCA's first general manager. He served during the period 1939–45 and was succeeded by Henry J. Malsberger, who guided the organization to maturity and status. By 1967, it was supported and financed by twenty-six pulp mill members. Its success has attracted well-merited acclaim.

In mid-1967, Malsberger noted that the twelve southern states were producing 61 percent of the nation's supply of pulpwood raw material. He attributed the South's preeminence in paper production to two factors: continual improvements in forest management practices and new developments and increased efficiency in the utilization of southern pines.

In 1968, the Southern Pulpwood Conservation Association changed its name to the Southern Forest Institute. On Malsberger's retirement, he was succeeded by another forester, George E. Kelly.

Forest Farmers Association. In 1941, at Valdosta, Georgia, with William Oettmeier as president, an association of southern private timberland owners was organized for the purpose of promoting the maximum yield of forest products on their holdings. Named the Forest Farmers Association, it grew into an institution with thousands of members representative of both large and small ownerships, but with the small owners in the majority. The association early began serving as a forum for communication between the individual landowner, the forest industry, and the forestry profession. Through the *Forest Farmer*, the association's monthly magazine, and its yearly *Manual*, members are informed about the business and technical aspects of timber growing for profit.

The association's special contribution to the advancement of private forestry stems from its educational work among small woodland owners. Guided by the association, many forest farmers have learned to establish successful wood-growing operations based on sound financing, modern harvesting methods, timely knowledge of market trends and prices, and practical forest management techniques.

Despite the years of educational efforts by the Forest Service, Soil Conservation Service, state forestry services, and state agricultural extension services, the South's woodlands in farms and other small ownerships were generally poorly managed. Inman Eldredge noted in 1947: "There has been a great deal of planting on vacant or eroded acres, thinning in sapling stands, and improvement cutting in rural sections in all the states. In time this will add both to the farmers' cash income and the wood supplies needed to support industry." He added:

All this is encouraging, but the increase in timber production on farms probably may not materialize soon enough to contribute more than modest support to the program for rapid industrialization of the lower South. The many millions of feet of lumber and millions of cords of pulpwood that will be needed in the next 20 years must come in the main from well-placed, well-chosen lands upon which technically directed, soundly financed forest management is practiced as a stable business policy.[38]

Eldredge's predictions came true only in part. The educational functions performed by the Forest Farmers Association and by the staff foresters of the Southern Pulpwood Conservation Association, coupled with the extension services given small owners by foresters employed by the paper companies, made tree farming an expanding and profitable enterprise.

Industrial Forestry after World War II

During 1945 and 1946, under the general direction of Raymond E. Marsh, assistant chief, the Forest Service made a reappraisal of the nation's forest situation. Of 302 million acres of privately owned woodland then being operated, it was estimated that the character of the cutting was of high order on only 1 percent of the acreage; it was good on 7 percent, fair on 28 percent, and poor on 64 percent. The following comment is revealing:

Differences in cutting practices between the three great geographical sections—North, South, and West—are important. Insofar as the large owners are concerned, the best performance is in the South. Lumber companies of the South lead those of other sections by a wide margin. Pulp-company performance, generally better than that of the lumber companies, is also best in the South.[39]

Regarding the character of the cutting by pulp companies in the South, the report revealed that an estimated 77 percent was either of high order or good; 12 percent was fair; and 11 percent was poor and destructive. Lumber companies were doing a less satisfactory job. Forty-three percent had good cutting practices; 23 percent, fair; and 34 percent, poor and destructive.

In 1958, Walter H. Meyer, professor of forest management on the faculty of the Yale School of Forestry, traveled through the South interviewing the forestry personnel of twenty-one industrial organizations about their forestry operations. These companies controlled 9.5 million acres and employed more than 500 technically trained men. Meyer summed up his observations thus:

The visitor cannot fail to be impressed by the great strides that have been made by industrial foresters of the Southeast, especially within the past ten years. Equally impressive is the energy, time, and money being spent to correct past mistakes in forest land management. There is a strong sense of urgency to get the forest into full production; there is commonly a lack of patience with nature's slowness and unreliability and a substitution therefor of forceful, artificial methods of getting new full stands started. There is above all, the spirit that forestry has come of age and that the forest lands will be handled for the long future for their best use, namely the production of wood in its most useful forms.[40]

The region-wide application of scientific management on the forests owned by industry is the oustanding success story of southern forestry. By 1969,

38. *The 4 Forests and the Future of the South* (Washington: Charles Lathrop Pack Forestry Foundation, 1947), p. 39.
39. "The Management Status of Forest Lands in the United States" (U.S. Forest Service, 1947, mimeo.).
40. "Impressions of Industrial Forestry in Southeastern United States," *Journal of Forestry*, vol. 58 (March 1960), pp. 179–87.

more than 2,000 professional foresters were industrially employed in the twelve southern states.

The South's 201 million acres of commercial forest comprise 39 percent of the nation's total. Practically all of the southern commercial forests have been logged over, not once but several times. Even so, because of improved harvesting methods, more effective fire protection, and extensive reforestation, timber growth exceeds in volume the amount cut.

Of all the industrially owned woodland in the nation, nearly 60 percent (37.5 million acres) is in the South. Pulp and paper companies with nearly 29 million acres are mainly concentrated there and are now the nation's largest class of industrial owners. It is on the industrial holdings that the best quality of silviculture is to be found. In general, the degree of management on these lands is equal to that on the national and state forests, and indeed in many instances is even more extensive.

In pine especially, the prevailing excess of growth over cut results in greater timber volumes throughout the South. "If continued," according to the Forest Service, "this will in time permit production of better quality and lower cost products, and thus add to the competitive strength of the forest industries in that section."[41]

Assuming continued advancement in protection from fire, insects, and disease; in reforestation; and in improved harvesting techniques that will reduce damage to the growing stock, the South's commercial forests will support even greater industrial expansion. Southern foresters have several advantages that justify the application of intensive silviculture: a number of valuable tree species with favorable growth rates, short cutting rotations, terrain generally accessible for mechanical logging, and active markets for products. All in all, if the experience of the past four decades may be taken as an indication, the future of industrial forestry in the South is bright indeed.

41. U.S. Forest Service, *Timber Trends.*

CHAPTER 18

Industrial Forestry in
the North Central Region

In its administration of research, the Forest Service groups seven states under the designation "the North Central Region." These states are Michigan, Minnesota, and Wisconsin (the Lake States), and Illinois, Indiana, Iowa, and Missouri. Of the region's 77 million acres of commercial forest land, nearly 70 percent is in the Lake States. Forest industry holdings total only 3.5 million acres; more than 95 percent of this acreage is in the Lake States and more than 70 percent is owned by pulp and paper companies.[1]

In view of the dependence of the regional economic structure on the wood-connected industry, the manner in which industrial forestry programs developed in the North Central Region provides an outlook for trends in the future. Although the progress in industrial forestry discussed in this chapter is not intended to apply only to the Lake States, because these states contain the bulk of the region's industrial timberland, the focus is on corporate forestry in Michigan, Minnesota, and Wisconsin.

The Effect of Economic Pressures

In 1954, at a meeting of the Society of American Foresters, M. B. Dickerman, director of the Lake States Forest Experiment Station, described changing forest conditions in the Lake States.

Perhaps the most striking change in the situation is on private land. Whereas in the thirties the private owner's primary aim was to salvage what he could from the land and then under economic pressure to dispose of it to a public agency, today many private companies are in the process of acquiring forest land and building up sustained yield properties. This change has come about through a combination of improved economic conditions, better fire protection and resulting greater timber growth, and a growing realization

1. U.S. Forest Service, *Timber Trends in the United States*, Resource Report no. 17 (1965), p. 141, table 2.

upon the part of the industries and the general public that to maintain permanent and profitable industries requires attention to forest management.[2]

In March 1961, George B. Amidon, then director of woodlands for the Minnesota and Ontario Paper Company, gave the fifth and final lecture of a series on industrial forestry at the University of Washington College of Forestry. In this account, he described how industrial forestry in the Lake States had its beginnings in 1926 or 1927 and by 1940 had become firmly established in the programs of most of the leading companies in the region.

As noted earlier, private forestry almost everywhere needed first of all the benefit of public leadership in protection against fire. With the passage of the Clarke-McNary Act in 1924, W. B. Greeley, then chief of the Forest Service, and other prominent foresters both inside and outside government believed— or at least hoped—that timber growing as a commercial enterprise would soon be generally adopted. During the post-World War I years, industrial leaders and other large private landowners were investigating the possibilities of applying improved management practices to their lands. But distressed economic conditions in the forest industry, notably the lumber market, were formidable. Almost a full decade before other major segments of American business began to suffer the consequences of depressed markets and financial desiccation, two key industries were in poor straits—agriculture and lumber.

In the Lake States, widespread tax delinquency on logged-off lands was an economic and political phenomenon of the 1920s and early 1930s. Some 6 million acres passed from private ownership to counties and municipalities. The cause of this dislocation in ownership was the application of the general property, or ad valorem, tax. Since the tax, as applied in many counties, ignored the income-producing capacity of the land, it not only discouraged private forestry, but also discouraged private forest ownership, and millions of acres were simply abandoned.

The breakdown of forest taxation is nowhere better illustrated than in Oneida County, Wisconsin, where tax delinquency during the decade 1921–30 rose in gross area to 261,600 acres, or 34 percent of the total land area of the county. It was a period of financial crisis for local government; some towns had as much as 40 percent or more of their land tax delinquent.[3]

Specific statistics revealing the scope of conditions were published in 1934 by the Natural Resources Board.

The northern cut-over sections of Michigan, Minnesota, and Wisconsin probably present the most striking picture of permanent tax delinquency and reversion at the present time. In Michigan, in addition to the 2 million acres to which the State has acquired title through tax delinquency, there are approximately 3 million acres of State tax lands, that is, lands which have been offered for sale for taxes but which have been bid in by the State in the absence of private purchasers. [In Wisconsin] two and one-half million acres in 17 northern counties were sold in the 1927 tax sale, and in that year the same counties were eligible to take deed to 492,642 acres unredeemed after

---

2. "The Forests of the Lake and Central States Region," *Proceedings: Society of American Foresters' Meeting,* October 24–27, 1954 (SAF, 1955), p. 3.

3. Erling D. Solberg, *New Laws for New Forests* (University of Wisconsin Press, 1961).

previous sales. . . . In the northeastern Minnesota counties 6,830,840 acres of land were delinquent on January 1, 1931, on levies of 1929 or before.[4]

Weyerhaeuser's Dilemma

The economic and political problems of a corporation attempting to grow new forests in the Lake States are illustrated by the experience of the Weyerhaeuser group of industries in Minnesota during 1929 and the 1930s. Under a state law of 1927, known as the Auxiliary Forest Tax Law, private owners were authorized to make application to have their cutover lands classified as auxiliary forests for reforestation purposes. The application required the approval of the State Forestry Commission and the Board of Commissioners in the county in which the lands were located. If the application was approved, the land was subject to a flat tax of 8 cents (reduced in 1929 to 5 cents) per acre plus 3 cents added for fire protection. This land tax would then be in force for a period of fifty years and would be renewable by agreement for another fifty-year period. Meanwhile, all timber cut from the auxiliary forest would be taxed at 10 percent of its value at the time of harvest.

In 1929, the Northern and Cloquet Lumber Companies, Weyerhaeuser subsidiaries, made application to put into auxiliary forest 172,000 acres of cutover land in St. Louis County. The county commissioners denied the application on the ground that, if granted, it would result in local communities having insufficient funds for necessary governmental business over long periods of years. Moreover, local opposition to the growing of forests arose in the belief that the woodland might be needed in the future for agricultural development.

According to a Weyerhaeuser official, taxes up to 16 cents per acre had been paid on the land until 1928. Fire protection cost an additional 11 cents per acre. The value placed on this cutover land by Weyerhaeuser was not disclosed, but it may be estimated from a company report showing that Weyerhaeuser had received offers of $1.25 per acre for some of its holdings.

Following the rejection of its application, the company declared that its land would be abandoned and no more taxes would be paid; expenditures for fire protection would also have to cease. When this decision was announced, it was explained that the lands in question had no merchantable timber. According to the official statement, the lands "are coming back to trees in various stages of growth from the seedling trees to trees that in 20 years from now should be ready for pulpwood. The species coming back are aspen, balsam, birch, spruce, white and Norway pine and in volumes are about in the order named. . . . Ninety percent of the lands covered by the application are reported as coming back into forest without artificial replanting." Furthermore, he declared that there was no sale whatever of these lands for agricultural purposes, presumably because they were not suited to farming.[5]

---

4. *Supplementary Report of the Land Planning Committee*, pt. 8, "Certain Aspects of Land Problems and Land Policies" (1935), pp. 44–45.
5. "Weyerhaeuser Reforestation Blocked," *Journal of Forestry*, November 1930, p. 1003.

Ten years earlier, on October 12, 1918, Cloquet, a city of 9,000 population whose economy was based on forest products industries, was almost totally destroyed by one of the most destructive woods fires in Minnesota's history. During the following decade, wood-using companies invested $93 million—in timberlands, logs and pulpwood, supplies and equipment, logging operations, and experimental work—to restore the industrial plants. Denied its tax relief in 1929 through the Auxiliary Forest Tax Law, Weyerhaeuser announced that the planned expansion of one of its Cloquet wood-working plants, involving an investment of $1.25 million, was now abandoned. An equivalent project would be developed on the West Coast where the company had large interests. "No further important extensions of the Cloquet wood industries can be made," it was pointed out, "without reasonable assurance of an adequate permanent supply of raw materials."[6] Actually, in later years the company would invest many millions in plant and equipment in Cloquet when economic conditions improved. And even in 1930, when The American Forestry Association held its annual meeting in Minnesota, Cloquet was hailed as "the greatest wood conversion city in the world."

In extenuation of the company's decision in 1929, one must realize that the Great Depression had set in. Moreover, Weyerhaeuser's principal subsidiary in Cloquet—Northwest Paper Company, into which the other companies had been consolidated—was operating at a loss, whereas the company's pulp plants on the Pacific Coast were earning profits. Northwest Paper Company incurred deficits during the 1930s but began to make profits in the following decade and was paying dividends and making handsome earnings by 1948, two decades after the decision not to invest in plant expansion in Cloquet.[7]

But since this account is concerned mainly with the forest resource and not with the manufacture and sale of wood products, it must be put into the record that much of Northwest's land that had been proposed for auxiliary forest status was permitted to revert to the state for unpaid taxes. Some of this area is now in St. Louis County's Cloquet Valley Memorial Forest.[8] But that was not all the land let go. In 1937, the Weyerhaeuser companies in Cloquet chose to give up 63,656 acres of their land rather than pay the confiscatory taxes. More land was forfeited later, because of the prohibitive state levies.

Twenty years after the passage of the Auxiliary Forest Tax Law, less than 228,000 acres were classified as auxiliary forests. Thus, auxiliary forests have not been significant in providing tax relief or in advancing the application of scientific forestry. In the case of the Weyerhaeuser organization, this law and the attitude on it taken by a county board of commissioners delayed for nearly two decades the practice of scientific forestry on a substantial acreage of industrial holdings in Minnesota. In 1964, Northwest Paper Company was merged with Potlatch Forests, Inc., whose holdings in Minnesota in 1968 totaled 236,000 acres, all under scientific management.

6. Ibid.
7. Ralph W. Hidy, Ernest Hill, and Allan Nevins, *Timber and Men*.
8. Samuel T. Dana, John H. Allison, and R. N. Cunningham, *Minnesota Lands* (Washington: American Forestry Association, 1960).

Still, interest in commercial forestry in the Lake States was kept simmering by public discontent with industry's failure to improve the protection and management of its lands. This interest was also kept alive by promotional activities, such as the 1927 Conference on Commercial Forestry in Chicago, sponsored by the Chamber of Commerce of the United States.[9] Despite the hazards of fire and the handicap of economic stress and strain, several leading Lake States companies undertook the practice of sustained-yield forestry about this time. In the following pages will be found brief accounts of the beginnings of forestry by these companies and of its development over the years.

Industrial Forestry in Action

Goodman Lumber Company. During the late 1800s, the virgin forests of northern Wisconsin and the Upper Peninsula of Michigan—white pine intermingled with hemlock and northern hardwoods—were a powerful attractor to lumbermen. After loggers cut the timber, settlers cleared the land for agricultural crops. Pure stands of pine often yielded 30,000 board feet of the highest quality wood to the acre, and individual trees might scale from 2,000 to 3,000 feet. Down the creeks and tributaries of the Menominee River floated pine, basswood, and hemlock logs to Marinette and Menominee where they were held and sorted for a dozen sawmills. Cargoes of lumber were shipped on Lake Michigan schooners to distributing yards at Chicago, then loaded on railroad cars for consignment to the prairie states.

Within three decades the pine was mostly cut out, and new mills were built to manufacture lumber from the remaining hardwood and hemlock stands. One of these mills was that of the Goodman Lumber Company, built in 1908 at Goodman, Wisconsin.

Clearcutting of the old-growth timber was accelerated, even though the operators realized it was a destructive system. State and federal agencies advocated selective logging as a method of preserving the second growth. But often local property taxes on the timber forced the owners to liquidate it as rapidly as they could skin the land. To illustrate: the annual tax on virgin timber in one county increased from an average 12 cents per acre in 1894 to $1.80 per acre in 1922.

But high taxes were not the sole obstacle to conservative logging and the practice of forestry. Fire was a major one. The Pestigo holocaust of 1871 should have awakened state and local government to the need for protection from fire, but during the next half-century little protection by public agencies was provided. The sawmill at Goodman was built to salvage several million board feet of white pine killed and damaged by a fire in 1907. As late as 1931, during a season of drought and searing winds, the company lost by fire nearly 15,000 acres of promising second growth.

In 1927, the citizens of Wisconsin approved an amendment to the state constitution. It permitted a special method of taxing forest land. The legislature implemented it by enacting the Forest Crop Law which made an important distinction between land as capital and the timber as income. Under this

9. See chap. 15 for an account of this conference and its aftermath.

law, there is an annual tax of 10 cents per acre on lands legally entered. Timber cut from the land is subject to a severance tax of 10 percent of the stumpage value when the income is obtained.

With the enactment of the Forest Crop Law, the practice of forest management was encouraged on lands previously subject to tax-prompted exploitation. In 1931, the State Department of Conservation set up a reorganized system of fire prevention, detection, and suppression for the 12 million acres of woodland in central and northern Wisconsin.

Meanwhile, pulp and paper mills began to move into the region. Their considerable financial investment in plants and equipment required a permanent supply of raw material. With the application of sustained-yield forestry at last economically feasible, it became the policy of the industrial timber owners.

In the public sector, the U.S. Forest Service started an acquisition program in Wisconsin that resulted in the Nicolet National Forest, which has a present net area of 600,000 acres. Under a cooperative acquisition program by the counties and the state, large blocks of cutover land that had reverted to the counties for nonpayment of taxes were managed by the Conservation Department. By 1937, as a result of the depression and other economic factors, twenty-five counties owned and managed more than 1.6 million acres. By 1968, more than 90 percent of this vast forest region was under scientific forest management by governmental, industrial, and farm owners.

Returning to the Goodman Lumber Company, we note from the record that for two decades following the building of its sawmill in 1908 its timber was clearcut and the cutover land was sold to settlers when buyers could be found. Timber cutting was at the rate of 20 to 24 million board feet annually. The end of the operation was in sight when, in 1927, the company adopted the enlightened policy of managing its holdings of some 65,000 acres under the selection system. Selective logging, however, required that the annual cut be reduced to 12 million board feet, and later to 10 million. A veneer plant was built in 1928 to utilize the older timber removed in selective cutting. Logging by horses and railroad was replaced by tractors and truck hauling. By operating at a reduced cutting rate, the company assured itself of a permanent supply of logs. Moreover, since the kind of selective cutting practiced was also an improvement cutting, the company's future log supply promised to be of higher quality.[10]

A major influence in bringing about this change in policy was a study made for the company by W. S. Bromley and Calvin B. Stott of the Forest Service. In their report, released in 1937, they concluded that the company was close to meeting all the technical requirements of a sustained-yield policy. Although they admitted that plans of liquidation seemed to offer higher profits than conversion to sustained-yield operation, they favored the latter course.

10. This account of the Goodman Lumber Company is based on three articles: R. B. Goodman, "Forestry in Northeastern Wisconsin"; George A. Houghton, "Forest Industries at Goodman"; and John A. Carr, "Forest Management by the Goodman Lumber Company," all in the *Journal of Forestry*, vol. 37 (September 1939).

Plans of sustained yield, however, show present worth values that are very close to the most profitable plan of liquidation and offer 3.0 to 6.0 per cent annual return indefinitely on the investment. This is as much as can be earned on most large sums of capital over long periods, and is not accompanied by the enormous economic and social losses which follow liquidation.[11]

Bromley and Stott recommended that the company cut no more than 10.3 million board feet log scale of its own timber and purchase about 1.6 million annually for the next ten years.

In a privately printed brochure, *A Wisconsin Forest-Farm Working Circle*, dated July 1944, R. B. Goodman summarized the results of the company's sustained-yield operation. The first cycle of selective cutting, started in 1927, was completed in 1944. The annual logging budget had been reduced, and the company was buying logs outside the working circle in order to maintain normal operations. In a striking affirmation of the accomplishments of scientific forest management, Goodman claimed that after thirty-seven years of such practice the company had timber reserves substantially equal to its initial forest capital.

Goodman Lumber Company was acquired by Calumet & Hecla, Inc., in 1955 and is now the Goodman Lumber Division of this mining corporation. The division's 300,000 acres were continued under sustained-yield management supervised by a professional forester.

The Bruce G. Buell Tract. Bruce G. Buell, the first forester hired by industry in Michigan, went to work May 1, 1930, for Patten Timber Company, which then held title to some 24,000 acres near Amasa. At that time, the company was a wholly owned subsidiary of Northern Paper Mills of Green Bay, Wisconsin. Buell's assignment was to manage the woodland so as to help provide a permanent supply of pulpwood for Northern.

Since the property was located in a region without public roads, the company built a railroad to get the logs out of the woods. Buell's first difficulty was in determining a cutting cycle. The difficulty was compounded by the relative inflexibility of rail logging, as compared with modern truck logging. Moreover, he had little growth data on which to base estimates of allowable cut. The first selective logging began in the winter of 1930-31.

During the 1930s, about 70 percent of the mature hardwood and hemlock growth was removed. A second cut, largely a salvage operation, was started at the end of twenty-four years; it was about completed in 1968, and the third cycle was ready to start. Log transportation by rail was superseded by a truck operation in 1948.

The original unit of 24,000 acres has been increased to 120,000 acres. Ownership, however, passed in 1953 to Marathon Corporation when it merged with Northern Paper Mills. The assets of Marathon Corporation were in turn acquired in 1957 by American Can Company. Meanwhile, the Patten forest had been named the Bruce G. Buell Tract, in recognition of the pioneer

11. "Timber Management and Financial Plans for the Goodman Working Circle," U.S. Forest Service, Division of State and Private Forestry, Milwaukee (1937, mimeo.).

work of its first forester. It is one of the well-managed industrial forests of the Lake States.

Consolidated Papers. Corporations have often been successful in their forestry operations because their decision-making executives were men of imagination and discernment who sensed, even if they could not foretell, the future influence of technical forest management on their business. A company whose directors had foresight and a willingness to experiment was Consolidated Water Power & Paper Company of Wisconsin Rapids, Wisconsin. (Having adopted this name in 1902, the company changed it to Consolidated Papers, Inc., in 1962.)

It took considerable imagination, together with faith in the future, for a board of directors to embark on a forestry venture in 1930 in Wisconsin. For one thing, a plentiful supply of pulpwood was already at hand. For another, the state's sad history of poor fire protection was less than encouraging. Moreover, since the whole country was in the grip of a business depression, few companies were willing to invest in a forester's modest salary and the equally modest outlay needed to start a forestry program.

Emmett R. Hurst, a young professional forester, reported for duty on November 1, 1930. Little woodland was owned by the company—about 5,000 acres in Wisconsin and twice as much in Minnesota. None of it was under technical management.

Hurst's first assignment was to start a forest tree nursery to grow white and Norway spruce, at that time the preferred species for pulping. But over the years spruce was superseded in consumption by aspen, birch, and associated hardwoods. Other species of increasing value for pulp were balsam fir, hemlock, and the pines. During the next quarter-century, the company's reforestation work resulted in the planting of some 7 million trees. And in 1957, pulpwood was being thinned from spruce and jack pine plantations set out on abandoned farmland.

Much cheap land was available for purchase in northern Wisconsin during the 1930s. The company began an acquisition program, but, even with land values as low as they were, business was slow and money was tight. Nevertheless, during the first twenty-five years of forestry operations, the company accumulated 220,000 acres in the three Lake States.

Although these lands were maintained primarily to produce pulpwood for the company's five mills, they yielded other products as well. Sawlogs, fence posts, poles, tie cuts, and Christmas trees were grown and sold at a profit. But pulpwood continued to be the main goal of the forestry work. Hence, in order to learn how best to manage stands for maximum pulpwood yield, Consolidated established an experimental forest. Since data on the silvical characteristics of the region's mixed forests had already been gathered by the Lake States Forest Experiment Station and university research stations, the experimental forest was established for the application of these findings, rather than as a basic research center.

The Gagen Forest Management Unit, as it was called, was set aside in 1948, an area of 2,032 acres in eastern Oneida County, Wisconsin. It is a tract typical of the 90,000 acres of Consolidated timberlands within twenty-five miles of the unit. Conceived as a demonstration small enough to be managed economically and efficiently, it is also large enough to serve as a model for the conditions common to the operation of an extensive industrial property.

Through this pilot unit the company sought to determine the kind of management that is feasible to practice under various growth conditions, species distribution, and logging methods. Economics governs the degree of management too; utilization practices are tested so that the company may, for example, avoid incurring costs of $100 to grow a unit area of pulpwood and then only harvest $80 worth of it.

Consolidated's timber holdings in 1968 totaled 635,000 acres in Wisconsin, Minnesota, Michigan, and Ontario. The company employed fifteen professional foresters in the United States and one in Canada. On Emmett Hurst's retirement as manager of timberlands in 1968, he was succeeded by John W. Macon, former research forester.

Kimberly-Clark. Anyone with the sniffles who has ever wiped his nose with a piece of Kleenex has used one of the many forest products manufactured by the Kimberly-Clark Corporation. A major producer of paper and cellulose products, the parent company began making paper shortly after the Civil War. Its daily output was then two tons of newsprint fabricated from rags. In 1878, the company started making paper from groundwood pulp. Wood has been its raw material ever since.

But it was not until 1903 that the company began the operation of its own woodlands. In that year, 17,000 acres were bought in Wisconsin. Through mergers, the organization of new companies, and the purchase of other companies over the past six decades, Kimberly-Clark and its subsidiaries now own or have cutting rights on millions of acres in Wisconsin, Michigan, Minnesota, California, Alabama, and Ontario.

In hiring its first professional forester, the company selected an able Canadian—Robert W. Lyons who had previously been with the Laurentide Company in Quebec. As woodlands manager of Kimberly-Clark's Ontario operations, Lyons put foresters in charge of the company-operated pulpwood producing camps and set up a separate accounting system to control the costs of pulpwood production. The foresters proved that they were more efficient producers of wood than the contract loggers previously employed. When wood produced by the foresters was delivered at the mill at less cost than under the former system, foresters and forestry were recognized as essential functions in the establishment.

Convinced of the soundness of the forest management in Ontario, the corporation, put Lyons in charge of a similar operation in the Lake States. In 1936, he became vice president and general manager of two subsidiary companies in Michigan and Minnesota (William Bonifas Lumber Company and North Star Timber Company). Foresters were hired to make an inventory of the timberlands and to purchase sizable additional acreages. Experimental and research projects were begun; permanent sample plots were set out, growth studies were started, and management plans were written.

Lyons moved his headquarters from northern Michigan to Neenah, Wisconsin, the company's home office, in 1940. Two years later, when he was appointed general manager of the Woodlands Department to oversee all company forestry operations in the United States and Canada, forestry became an element of top management. In 1941, he was appointed a vice president and also became a company director in 1947.

As part of the research in forestry, an early and continuing study was undertaken of the silvical characteristics of the species utilized. Another was of damage by insects and disease, both of living forests and wood in storage. A forest pest control laboratory was created in 1952; a forest entomologist and a forest pathologist were employed. During Lyons's incumbency, the corporation had on its payroll 126 foresters who were graduates of nine schools of forestry. Now deceased, Lyons retired from active administration in 1958.[12]

Nekoosa-Edwards Paper Company. Incorporated in 1908, the Nekoosa-Edwards Paper Company operates pulp and paper mills at Port Edwards and Stevens Point, Wisconsin, and since 1968 at Ashdown, Arkansas. The combined capacity of the mills is nearly 290,000 tons of wood pulp annually. To help sustain this enormous consumption, the company in 1968 owned 237,000 acres of managed woodlands and 65 acres of forest tree nurseries.

F. G. Kilp was the company's first forester, starting in October 1925. About 3,500 acres of land were owned, largely for riparian rights. Kilp's first assignment was to establish a nursery for seedling production and to acquire lands for reforestation in order to assure future pulpwood supplies. Kilp set out to create an industrial forest within economical hauling distance by truck and rail to the mills. Thus, the company could control pulpwood transportation costs, at least to a large degree. During his twenty-eight years as chief forester, Kilp purchased more than 230,000 acres of forest for the company.

Two nurseries were operated in Wisconsin: one of 60 acres in Wood County, the other of 5 acres in Oneida County, the latter for the production of red pine only. Originally, the acquisition program was directed toward pine lands, though spruce and balsam fir were the preferred species, with hemlock next, followed by aspen and the dense hardwoods.

As the use of spruce declined, the hardwoods, aspen especially, increased in consumption, illustrating the changing utilization of species brought about by developments in pulp and paper technology. "In the early history of the Nekoosa mill," according to Kilp, "jack pine was used to fire the boilers to make pulp from spruce. It is difficult to believe such a procedure ever existed; yet it is true."[13]

According to Kilp, the pulp and paper industry forester is in an enviable position as a forest manager. "He can remove a very considerable amount of cull wood from his company's forest and receive revenue for it from the pulp mill. Sanitary cuts of the kind he can plan and execute are difficult for the sawmill and government forester to have approved because of the economic feature involved."[14] Although the Nekoosa-Edwards Paper Company's lands

---

12. Information about Kimberly-Clark's forestry operations was obtained from an article by William J. Brown, "Forestry and the Growth of the Kimberly-Clark Corporation," *Journal of Forestry*, vol. 51 (November 1953); from personal communication with Robert W. Lyons; and from other sources.
13. Letter to the author from F. G. Kilp, April 3, 1968.
14. Ibid.

are managed primarily for pulpwood, the foresters also grow good-quality saw logs and veneer wood. In short, the best economic value of the species is not overlooked. Robert A. Petry succeeded Kilp as woodlands manager on the latter's retirement in 1963.

Minnesota and Ontario Paper Company. The Minnesota and Ontario Paper Company (merged in 1965 with Boise Cascade Corporation) was founded in 1910. It was started on the basis of a timber cruiser's estimate that 18 million cords of spruce were available by water drive to International Falls, Minnesota, the mill site. In 1910, the pulp and paper industry was just beginning to become established in the Lake States; all the paper mills in Minnesota consumed slightly more than 40,000 cords that year.[15] With an abundant raw material supply available, the pioneer paper companies of the 1920s were not worried about wood procurement and, hence, saw no need to practice silviculture to grow more for the future.

But by the 1930s, Mando, as the company was then familiarly known, began to engage in cooperative forestry projects with the U.S. Forest Service Division of State and Private Forestry, which had headquarters in Milwaukee. F. E. Boeckh, a forestry graduate of Iowa State College, was employed in 1936 and began a modest forestry program with the help of the Forest Service and the Minnesota Division of Forestry. A forest management plan was developed, tree planting was carried on, and partial cutting operations were started.

George Amidon, a forestry graduate of the University of Minnesota, joined the company as director of woodlands in 1944. He expanded the forestry work so that the program would lead to sustained-yield management. By 1950, the company employed eleven foresters, and by 1960, thirteen. The company's holdings then totaled 286,000 acres, and the forestry personnel averaged out at one forester for 22,000 acres.

During the first decade of Amidon's service, an experimental forest was established, the planting program was stepped up, and forest management advisory assistance was provided to other private timber owners in the area. As a new and useful technique to guide the company's silvicultural policy, a continuous forest inventory system was begun in 1953.

From the first plot measurements the foresters estimated the gross growth was 0.44 cord per acre per year, whereas the net growth was 0.23 cord only.[16] The reason for this disparity was the condition of the stands, many of which contained diseased and overmature trees. Good forestry practice required the prompt removal of those old-growth trees to make room for younger and more vigorous growing stock. In 1968, the growth information obtained from the forest inventory plots showed that the increment was 0.38 cord per acre per year, compared with only 0.23 cord fifteen years earlier. In 1960, the allowable annual cut was 60,000 cords, then about 20 percent of

15. James D. Studley, *United States Pulp and Paper Industry*, U.S. Department of Commerce, Bureau of Foreign and Domestic Commerce, Trade Promotion Series no. 182 (1938).
16. Gross growth is the increment uncorrected for losses by cull or deterioration; net growth is the increment after such losses have been deducted.

the wood consumed in the International Falls Mills. The allowable annual cut in 1967 was calculated to be 77,000 cords on the company's Minnesota lands, which totaled 325,000 acres.

Throughout the Lake States generally, the pulp and paper industry is practicing sustained-yield forestry. The former Mando woodlands provide excellent examples of an intensity of silviculture that was literally unknown three decades ago.

Continuous Forest Inventory

Continuous forest inventory (CFI) is a system based on the periodic measurement of permanent forest plots and the calculation of growth by the use of computers. Using CFI, the forester obtains data on both gross and net growth. This scientific approach to the inventory of timber stands was devised in 1934 by foresters in the Division of State and Private Forestry, North Central Region of the Forest Service, with headquarters at Milwaukee, Wisconsin. Calvin Stott, a staff forester in the division, is credited with having been the principal author of CFI. His definition tells both what it is and what it does.

It is a proportional sampling system based upon circular plots [one-fifth or one-seventh acre in size] within which all living trees 5 inches and larger [in diameter] are measured, described, recorded on punch cards or tape, machine compiled and analyzed finally in whatever segregations of the data are needed. . . . In substance, the method results in periodic, comparable trial balances of forest growing conditions.[17]

CFI field work began late in 1934 on holdings of the Fisher Body Company in the Porcupine Mountains of northern Michigan. Additional timber cruises were made on other industrial tracts in northern Lake States woodlands. Foresters realized that intensive inventory was a requisite for the practice of intensive management. One of the first industrial management plans based on a complete inventory of forest holdings was the one prepared in 1937 for the Goodman Lumber Company by Bromley and Stott. A similar inventory was completed during the same year for the woodlands of the Ford Motor Company in Michigan.

During the three decades since these first operational applications of CFI, the system has been adopted by managers of industrial and publicly owned forests elsewhere in New England, the southern states, and Canada. In the North Central Region where it was first conceived, approximately 6 million acres of active inventory control are in effect, involving up to 20,000 permanent plots. Nationally, there are more than 50,000 permanent plots on 20 million acres of industrial and public woodlands.

Interest in inventory control methods of forest management has been encouraged by successful early applications now in their fourth remeasurement period in the Lake States. Publication of a periodical newsletter, *Forest Control by Continuous Inventory*, has helped to sustain this interest. This

---

17. "A Short History of Continuous Forest Inventory East of the Mississippi," *Journal of Forestry*, vol. 66 (November 1968), p. 834.

series, started in 1954 by the Forest Service, has been prepared principally by Stott and his associates.[18]

The growing interest in CFI as a scientific technique in forestry was indicated by the attendance at a conference on this subject held at the Ford Forestry Center of Michigan Technological University in May 1965. More than 100 participants from twenty-two states and three Canadian provinces were present. In addition to providing an opportunity to review progress in CFI and to examine problems of data processing, the conference served as an occasion to honor Stott, the protagonist of the movement, who retired from the Forest Service in 1965.[19]

Trees for Tomorrow

Trees for Tomorrow, Inc., is an industry-supported, nonprofit undertaking that demonstrates the extent to which wood-converting corporations, inspired by enlightened self-interest, can extend the practice of forestry to other private lands. In 1944, nine Wisconsin paper companies formed Trees for Tomorrow, whose purpose was—and is—to help develop the timber growth of the northern portion of the state where the forest resource is basic to the economy.

Briefly stated, the organization's program encompasses three principal activities: (1) the machine planting of trees for landowners whose seedlings are purchased from state and private nurseries; (2) the preparation of management plans for landowners by professional foresters and the supervision of timber harvesting and sales; and (3) the operation of a resource education center at Eagle River. Fees are charged landowners for the technical services rendered by a staff of four professional foresters.

At the education center, known as the Trees for Tomorrow Camp, short courses, conservation workshops, and field practice in resource management are provided for teachers, university and high school students, and community groups, who are drawn from all over the North Central States. Attendance at the education center, beginning with forty adult students in 1945, totaled 75,000 through 1968. A special training program for young woods workers was started in 1966 with instruction provided in logging methods, operation of woods machinery and equipment, tree felling, timber estimating, and land surveying.

Supported financially by seventeen paper and hydroelectric companies, Trees for Tomorrow offers its services in thirty-four counties of north central Wisconsin and upper Michigan. During its twenty-five years of operation, the organization has distributed 9 million trees, machine planted 14 million trees for landowners who bought their own planting stock, prepared management plans for 370,000 acres of privately owned woodlands, and supervised the harvest of 400,000 cords of wood.

18. The newsletter is issued by the U.S. Department of Agriculture, Forest Service, 6816 Market Street, Upper Darby, Penna. 19082.

19. Ford Forestry Center, *Proceedings: A Conference on Continuous Forest Inventory* (Michigan Technological University, 1966).

Trees for Tomorrow was one of the nation's most successful industry efforts for the improvement of private forestry by the small woodland owner. It has proved to be a practical and successful solution of the problem of getting the small woodland proprietor to practice simple forms of silviculture and thus keep his lands reasonably productive.[20]

Corporate Forestry Progresses

Karl A. Swenning was the first of a growing corps of industrial foresters in the North Central States. On his graduation in 1920 from the New York State College of Forestry, he was appointed forester and manager of the Woods Department of Mead Pulp and Paper Company (now the Mead Corporation) at Chillicothe, Ohio. In 1909, this company had begun the planting and short rotation management of hardwood species—cottonwood, poplar, silver maple, and willow—suitable for the manufacture of soda pulp. By 1923, the company had under management 500 acres of plantations. Meanwhile, Swenning began the acquisition of additional woodland. In 1935, he was appointed general woods manager for the company. (Later, he became director of timberlands for Scott Paper Company.) By 1968, Mead Corporation owned or controlled 470,000 acres of well-managed woodland in Michigan and Ohio.

Subsequently, as noted earlier, other companies in the region put their extensive holdings under management. Among those not previously mentioned that have undertaken silvicultural practices with professional foresters in charge are the Blandin Paper Company, the Celotex Corporation, Cleveland-Cliffs Iron Company, Mosinee Paper Mills Company, Owens-Illinois Glass Company, Packaging Corporation of America (a subsidiary of Tennco Corporation), St. Regis Paper Company, and U.S. Plywood-Champion Papers.

At a meeting of the Society of American Foresters in September 1946, E. B. Hurst estimated that about 100 foresters were employed by the wood-using industry in the Lake States.[21] Industry-owned timber under management totaled about 1.5 million acres.

In 1960, the American Pulpwood Association released the results of a survey of forestry progress by the region's forest products companies. Included were data from nine companies (two lumber companies and seven paper companies); these firms owned 2.2 million acres. According to George B. Amidon, then president of the association, the number of technical foresters employed in forestry and woods work by these companies was 19 in 1940, 66 in 1950, and 108 in 1960. Employment of foresters had increased by 470 percent in twenty years.

Incomplete as these data are known to be, they denoted consistent expansion in the employment of foresters by industry, which in turn denoted an increase in the practice of sustained-yield forestry on industry-owned lands. In 1969, the number of foresters industrially employed in the North Central Region, both on a full-time basis and as consultants, was believed to be nearly 500.

20. See Ernest Swift, "Trees for Tomorrow: A Study in Grass Roots Conservation," *American Forests*, April 1968, pp. 20–26, 46, and May 1968, pp. 32–35.
21. "Industrial Forestry and the Forester in the Lake States," *Journal of Forestry*, vol. 44 (November 1946), pp. 920–22.

CHAPTER 19

Industrial Forestry
in the West

For statistical purposes, the Forest Service records the distribution of commercial forest land in the West in two zones. The four Pacific Coast states (Alaska, Washington, Oregon, and California) contain 70 million acres of commercial forest. In the eight Rocky Mountain states (Idaho, Montana, Wyoming, Nevada, Utah, Colorado, Arizona, and New Mexico), 66 million acres are classified as commercial forest. The West's aggregate of commercial forest—136 million acres—represents 27 percent of the nation's total.[1]

The earliest and most extensive applications of forestry practice on corporate timberlands in the West occurred in Washington, Oregon, California, Idaho, and Montana. Since these five states now contain the largest acreages of industrially owned timberland under intensive management in the West, the discussion in this chapter will be, for the most part, about developments in industrial forestry in these states.

Within these five states, there are certain well-defined forest regions so extensive in area, so important economically, and so valuable as resource bases for the continuous production of wood supplies, that the author finds it convenient to explain the growth of industrial forestry in terms of these geographic regions. The Douglas-fir region of the Pacific Northwest is notable for its high yield. Under intensive management, this region has the potential for the most abundant productivity and the greatest volume growth of any region in the nation with a comparable forest type. The sizable ponderosa pine region extends from eastern Washington and eastern Oregon into California and thence throughout the Rocky Mountains. Northern California's timber region is characterized by magnificent stands of softwoods, including the useful and valuable sugar pine and western white pine and the well-known redwood, in addition to ponderosa pine and Douglas-fir. The Northern Rocky Mountain region is richly endowed with forests, particularly in northern

---

1. U.S. Forest Service, *Timber Trends in the United States*, Resource Report no. 17 (1965), pp. 76–78.

Idaho and western Montana, where the dominant species are the western pines, true firs, and spruces, together with larch and Douglas-fir.

Throughout the West, as in other timber regions of the United States, forestry began with fire control. Indeed, there could be no forestry without fire control. For example, as the old-growth forests of western Washington and Oregon were logged off, the danger of fire in the cutover stands and oncoming second-growth became a deterrent to even the simplest silvicultural practices.

Destructive fires had raged through the virgin Douglas-fir forests long before the region's lumber industry started. Although logging operations caused some fires, many more were started by settlers clearing land, by railroads, and by the carelessness of the general public. But cutover areas, logging's aftermath, with their residues of inflammable slash, enormously increased the hazard.

Forest fires were a fact of life in the Northwest, to be controlled when possible, which was rarely the case; in bad seasons they were to be survived, if those in the path of the fire were lucky. The year 1902 was a year of terror for many settlers and woods workers. More than 100 fires on the western Cascades and southern Olympics burned three-quarters of a million acres. During that awful September blowup, the loss of timber alone, not to mention other property, was incalculable.[2]

Despite the appalling losses to a great resource and to the economy of the state, Washington did not get around to enacting legislation for a board of forest commissioners and a state forest fire warden until 1905. Oregon's state board of forestry was not set up until 1907.

During this formative period, state laws and state aid in fire control helped scarcely at all. Settlers who deliberately set fires to clear land for crops were rarely subject to punishment for this misdemeanor in the local courts. It was the era of agricultural development; the setting of wildfire that spread to the timber property of others, if done in the name of land improvement for farming, was dealt with lightly.[3]

Industrial woodland owners began to form private associations for mutual protection against fire. The associations set up patrols for fire detection during seasons of high fire risk and equipped and trained crews for fire suppression. In the early 1900s, forest protection associations were organized in California, Idaho, Oregon, and Washington.

The Western Forestry and Conservation Association

Among the groups formed during the first decade of the century to advance forestry, and particularly forest protection, on private lands was a regional body that ever since has effectively promoted the conservation of the forest and related resources through cooperative effort. This is the Western Forestry and Conservation Association (WFCA), with headquarters in Port-

2. See Stewart H. Holbrook, *Burning an Empire*, for a vivid description of this holocaust.
3. Elwood R. Maunder, "Forest Protection Comes under the Microscope," interview with Charles S. Cowan, retired manager of the Washington Forest Fire Association, *Forest History*, vol. 2, nos. 3 and 4 (Winter 1959).

land, Oregon. It was organized January 4, 1909, in the office of A. L. Flewelling of the Milwaukee Land Company in Spokane. George S. Long, western manager of the Weyerhaeuser Timber Company, Tacoma, and president of the Washington Forest Fire Association, was a leader in establishing the association. The Forest Service was represented by William B. Greeley and E. T. Allen, then district forester of the Pacific Northwest District (now Region).

A declared association objective was to obtain the membership of all the forest fire protective associations in the territory comprising California, Oregon, Washington, British Columbia, Idaho, and Montana.[4] This region contains one of the world's most valuable commercial timber stands; the dominant species are Douglas-fir, ponderosa pine, western white pine, sugar pine, western red cedar, western hemlock, white fir, and Engelmann spruce.

At the association's first regular meeting on April 1, 1909, Flewelling was elected president, and the trustees, having voted to employ a permanent secretary-forester, selected Allen. Although not a professionally educated forester, Allen had entered the old Bureau of Forestry in 1898, becoming the first forest ranger in the Pacific Northwest and rising to the position of district forester.

Greeley credited George Long with having been the prime mover in creating the association. He described Long as being "endowed with rare foresight and a practical gift of getting things done," and said that Long "grasped the full proportions of the protection job which confronted the forest regions of the West and its many ramifications in state laws and cooperation between public and private agencies."[5]

It is probable, however, that the conception of a strong central forestry association for the whole Pacific Northwest originated with Allen. He presented a proposed outline for the organization and work of a regional conservation association to Long in 1909. One thing is certain: the association promptly took effective action in regional forestry matters. Its records show, for example: "In 1910 President Taft ordered out Federal troops to fight forest fires at the request of the Western Forestry and Conservation Association. Also *World's Work*, a widely read magazine, called WFCA 'The greatest good influence in America on private forest management.' "[6]

In providing a central forestry forum in the Northwest, WFCA enlisted the cooperation not only of the forest products industry but of federal and state forestry agencies and of educational institutions as well. It sponsored the training of forest protection workers, held review investigations of fires that were incompetently fought, promoted improvements in meteorological forecasting of fire weather, and fostered the improvement and testing of fire-fighting tools and equipment. Two helpful publications prepared under the association's aegis were the *Western Fire Fighter's Manual* and the handbook *Practical Forestry in the Pacific Northwest*.

4. Minutes of the association's first meetings and other original documents pertaining to its early history are in the Manuscript Division, Oregon Historical Society Library, Portland.

5. *Forests and Men*, p. 21.

6. WFCA document (Manuscript Division, Oregon Historical Society Library, Portland).

Among the association's most effective incursions into forestry policy was its influential participation on the National Forestry Program Committee, organized in 1920 to combat legislation to put timber cutting on private land under federal supervision. The committee's counterproposal—a bill providing for federal assistance to those states that passed laws requiring private owners to maintain their woodlands in productive condition—failed to pass.[7] But a successor bill did pass—the enormously efficacious Clarke-McNary Act. According to Greeley: "The success of the Western Forestry and Conservation Association and its constituent patrol associations in organized co-operation inspired the Clarke-McNary Act of 1924, which carried the same ideas into federal policy."[8]

As an educational force in forestry, the association soon became influential in numerous ways. Besides publishing books and bulletins, it conducted research on the insurance and taxation of timberlands and helped work up forest codes for the states. As a coordinating force, it became a clearinghouse for information on all aspects of western forestry among federal, state, provincial, educational, and industrial bodies. Through its annual meetings and proceedings, the latest data on forest tree diseases and insects, on fire statistics, on protection equipment development, and on related topics were made available to all interested parties.

The Western Forestry and Conservation Association has long filled a place in the practice of industrial forestry in the Northwest. Although its member companies are concerned with growing, protecting, and harvesting forests as a business, the association has served to point up the opportunities and responsibilities of private ownership in the public interest. Its influence has been considerable, but nowhere more significant than in helping guide a great industry from a policy of exploitation of a great resource to scientific management of it.

The Pre-Forestry Situation

During World War I, demands for forest products brought about an increase in lumber production. In 1919, the national total was 34.5 billion board feet. West Coast (Washington, Oregon, California, and Nevada) production was 8.8 billion board feet. Generally, throughout the 1920s, West Coast lumber mills yielded annual increases; from 7.2 billion board feet in 1921, production rose to 14.1 billion feet in 1929.[9]

West Coast industry has been criticized by some conservationists for its delay in applying scientific forestry to its considerable holdings during the 1920s, a boom period of rising production and prices. When one considers the economic conditions under which most of the industry was struggling during those years, it is not difficult to understand why the time of forestry had not yet arrived. David T. Mason, who was on the scene as a consulting forester, has described these conditions:

7. See chap. 10 for a detailed discussion of these bills.
8. *Forests and Men*, p. 21.
9. Dwight Hair, *Historical Forestry Statistics of the United States*, U.S. Forest Service, Statistical Bulletin 228 (October 1958), table 15.

Back as far as I can remember, and no doubt earlier, the lumber industry—the main consumer of saw timber—was plagued by its chronic tendency to produce more lumber than consumers needed. For many years there was continuously available for annual cutting far more than enough standing timber to satisfy market demand. As an outstanding example of the western situation, let us look at the Douglas fir region of western Oregon in the mid-1920's. At that time there was still standing most of the great store of timber provided by nature. The readily accessible timber was mostly in private ownership; the less accessible was mostly in the national forests or in the Oregon & California Railway land grant revested into government ownership [in 1916]....

The private timber owners were carrying a heavy load of investment, of debt, and of taxes, and they were in fear of destruction of their timber by fire. These pressures were so great that the private owners constantly pressed their timber on the glutted market.[10]

Several companies made tentative starts in industrial forestry in the three coastal states during the 1920s. Their financial investment in silviculture was minuscule in comparison with the investments that would be made decades later; but, considering the uncertain returns that could be expected then from scientific forest management, the capital risked was impressive. It was an era of notable expansion of manufacturing plants and equipment. Companies went heavily in debt to increase mill capacity. New and bigger markets, as well as higher prices for lumber, apparently justified their borrowing. As millions in capital became available for new mills and logging machinery, a little of it was channeled to forestry.

Because of extensive reserves of old-growth timber and readily available supplies of stumpage, economic conditions for silviculture in the West were unfavorable almost until World War II. Not until old growth began to be scarce and more expensive did industrial management begin to think of growing trees.[11] Cutover areas, once tax liabilities and fearful fire hazards, in time became financial assets. Companies that let such lands revert to the state for nonpayment of taxes often bought them back at inflated prices. Well-stocked cutover lands having commercially valuable species protected from fire and insects could be managed at a profit. When this economic fact of corporate life was understood and accepted, the era of industrial forestry opened up.

Most of the major companies operate forest properties for a permanent raw-material supply, and now have forestry departments staffed by professionally educated foresters. In almost every company at least one forester holds a position of general responsibility as an officer or a director, or is in some similar policy-making post.

10. "Six Decades of Change in the Forest Products Industries: Personal Recollections," in Forest History Society, *National Colloquium on the History of the Forest Products Industries: Proceedings*, p. 89.

11. *American Lumberman* (August 16, 1919) reported that the sawmills of Grays Harbor County, Washington, had a lumber output of 1 billion board feet in 1918. Assessment records showed that 414,295 acres of timberland remained to be logged in the county. In an editorial comment on this news item, it was predicted in *American Forestry* (October 1919): "This means only 16 years' cut remaining in one of the biggest timber producing districts of the Pacific Northwest."

In the West, the forest products industry is still a dominant industry, notably so in Oregon and Washington, less so in California, Idaho, and Montana. As long as the industry maintains this essential role in the regional economy, foresters will be needed to grow the wood and fiber for it.

Tentative Beginnings

In 1920, the Everett Pulp and Paper Company (later owned by Simpson-Lee Paper Company) started reforesting all its logged-over lands, planting cottonwood to supply its mill at Lowell, Washington. Its planting program, never on a large scale, continued sporadically until World War II.

Apparently, the next company in the Douglas-fir region to undertake a tree-planting program was the firm of Merrill & Ring. Its reforestation operations, started in 1924 near Port Angeles, Washington, were largely experimental and not generally successful.

In July 1926, the Long-Bell Lumber Company, Longview, Washington, employed three technical foresters: John B. Woods, a Biltmore graduate; Arthur D. Read, a Yale graduate; and Omar Undseth, who had studied forestry at the Agricultural College of Norway. Woods was chief forester. He distributed his time between the Ryderwood holdings and the Weed Lumber Company in California, a large tract of ponderosa pine near Klamath Falls. He also worked on large Long-Bell properties in the Southeast.

Read worked on the Ryderwood holdings where the company owned 80,000 acres. According to information he gave the Committee on Private Forestry for the Society of American Foresters' North Pacific Section, the company had fifteen years to operate at its then rate of cutting—3,500 acres annually—but planned nevertheless to go on a sustained-yield program and purchase the additional virgin timber and logs needed to operate its mills. Read's duties included planting trees, sowing seeds, making utilization studies, acting as fire warden, and inspecting cutover lands that the company might wish to buy.

Long-Bell made the first large-scale plantings by a lumber company in the Douglas-fir belt. In 1926, it started a 12-acre tree nursery and seed extraction plant near Ryderwood, Washington, with Undseth in charge. Two years later, trees from the nursery were set out. During this period, the company was planting 850,000 trees per year on cutover lands that failed to show satisfactory natural regeneration two to three years after logging. In all, the company raised more than 8 million seedlings and transplants, mostly Douglas-fir, Port Orford cedar, and redwood. A total of 13,330 acres of company-owned lands were planted during a period of four years. The reforestation work stopped in 1931 with the onset of the financial depression. Of the 13,330 acres planted, fire destroyed all but 5,400 acres in one conflagration in 1938.[12]

Christopher M. Granger of the Forest Service told the Society of American Foresters Committee on Private Forestry in 1927 that he was unable to report any real forestry developments on the Olympic Peninsula, including Grays Harbor and Mason Counties, Washington. He credited the timber

12. Axel J. F. Brandstrom, *Development of Industrial Forestry in the Pacific Northwest* (College of Forestry, University of Washington 1957).

owners with accomplishment in protection from fire and noted that they were showing interest in their cutover lands, but that was the extent of their participation in forestry.

David Mason gave a similar report on western Oregon, noting that the lack of interest in forestry was general in that part of the state. Aside from the tree-planting operations of the Crown Willamette Paper Company and the Booth-Kelly Lumber Company, he knew of no other operators performing any forestry work of consequence.

C. S. Chapman, forester for the Weyerhaeuser Timber Company, listed forty-four companies in the Douglas-fir region that controlled 2.5 million acres. Of these, twenty companies were showing interest in forest management. Some hired consultants as needed or depended on the Western Forestry and Conservation Association for technical advice. Very few had their own foresters.

When the final report of the Committee on Private Forestry for the Pacific Northwest was completed, it listed only ten companies that had forestry programs. These companies had total holdings of slightly more than 1 million acres. As elsewhere in America, industrial forestry beginnings in the Pacific Northwest were few, small, and tentative. Another decade or more would pass before corporate forestry would become established on a permanent basis.

In the redwood region of California, a few progressive companies, led by the Union Lumber Company of Fort Bragg, began extensive reforestation work in the 1920s. Several company-operated nurseries were established to raise seedlings for the plantations. In all, 12 million seedlings were grown. Some 26,400 acres were planted at a cost of nearly a quarter-million dollars.[13] But this program also was stopped by the economic depression of the 1930s. Another reason for dropping industrial reforestation projects, according to the Society of American Foresters Committee on Private Forestry, was the low survival rate of the planted stock, and after $350,000 had been spent, the planting program ended.[14]

With the employment of Swift Berry in 1924 as forester and timber cruiser, the Michigan-California Lumber Company of Camino, California, started a policy of forest management that has endured to this day. A former timber management officer and logging engineer for the California Region of the Forest Service, Berry developed the company's method of cutting under the selection system, which was well adapted to sugar and ponderosa pines. He was one of the first foresters to become general manager of a large company; he had charge of all forestry, land management of the firm's 90,000 acres, logging, sawmilling, and lumber distribution.

In 1942, Myron E. Krueger, professor of forestry at the University of California, made a survey of privately owned cutover forest land in that state. He found that cutting practices had improved during the previous ten to twenty years in both the redwood region and the pine region, notably in the

13. Emanuel Fritz, *The Development of Industrial Forestry in California* (College of Forestry, University of Washington, 1960).

14. A. E. Wackerman, "Report of Committee on Private Forestry," *Journal of Forestry*, vol. 38 (February 1940).

latter. Logging methods were still unsatisfactory, however. But he encouragingly reported: "Capable leadership on the part of a few progressive operators, and the increasing employment of foresters in positions of responsibility, promised continued improvement in the situation."[15]

The Weyerhaeuser Story

The Weyerhaeuser Company[16] of Tacoma, Washington, is a widely known name in the forest industry because of the variety of its products and the quality of its advertising. Featuring forest and wildlife resources, tree farms, and forestry research, the advertisements have attracted much public attention; even people who may never have seen an industrial forest are aware that scientific forest management exists, although they may only dimly comprehend what it is.

This corporation was one of the first industrial landowners in the West to organize personnel and equipment for fire control. Through George Long, its western manager, Weyerhaeuser was a leader in the cooperative attack on the fire menace made by lumber companies and the federal government. However, Long did not believe that the practice of forestry in second growth was economically feasible. Weyerhaeuser then controlled more than 3 million acres in Idaho, Oregon, and Washington. In 1910, when asked whether the company was making an effort to reforest cutover land and if it intended to pay taxes on this land, Long replied:

We believe that the only way in which the forests are likely to be replaced is for the state either to buy the lands from the lumber companies and replant the cut-over areas or remit the taxes. It is a simple mathematical demonstration that it will not pay the lumber corporations to keep up tax payments and wait for a new crop of trees on cut-over lands. When the taxes are added and the value of the land is computed, it is only a two per-cent investment and business men are not looking for that kind.[17]

Weyerhaeuser's entry into technical forest management, as distinct from forest protection activities like fire prevention and control, occurred in 1924. In that year, the company created a subsidiary corporation, the Weyerhaeuser Logged-Off Land Company, with capital of $1 million to manage the parent company's cutover timber holdings totaling some 200,000 acres. C. S. Chapman, a Yale forestry graduate, resigned in July 1924 from the Western Forestry and Conservation Association to become manager of this company. Surveys were started to classify the lands as to site quality, degree of stocking of commercial species, and timber-growing potential.

Within the following decade, Weyerhaeuser adopted the policy of managing its timber under the principle of sustained yield. Major credit for the change is due David T. Mason, a professional forester and senior member

15. "Condition of Privately Owned Cutover Lands in California," *Journal of Forestry*, vol. 41 (September 1943), p. 665.

16. Incorporated in Washington as Weyerhaeuser Timber Company. The present name was adopted in 1959.

17. "The Weyerhaeuser Idea as to Reforestation," *American Forestry*, March 1910, p. 194.

of the consulting firm Mason & Stevens, which he had formed in Portland, Oregon, in 1921.[18] Having convinced officers of the company of the feasibility of sustained-yield management, Mason saw the policy started on Weyerhaeuser operations in Idaho. In getting the plan implemented, he was seconded by C. Lee Billings, a forest engineer newly appointed as assistant manager of the Clearwater Timber Company. Edwin C. Rettig, chief forester for Clearwater, developed a plan of selective logging for the second-growth stands that assured continuation of the merchantable growing stock.

Another large Weyerhaeuser tract was put under this type of management in the 1930s. This was the St. Helens sustained-yield unit, created to provide a permanent supply of raw material for the company's extensive manufacturing complex at Longview, Washington. According to Axel Brandstrom, "the transfer of these huge timber areas plus many smaller ones that followed, from the category of timber open to unrestricted cutting to timber regulated by sustained yield, was psychologically an important step in straightening out the current timber-supply situation in this region."[19] But this development had another significant influence: industrial administrators began to comprehend the meaning and opportunities under sustained-yield operation, and often took the initiative in setting up sustained-yield units as a corporate policy.

During the critical 1930s, many companies were abandoning their harvested woodlands and letting the counties take them for nonpayment of taxes. Weyerhaeuser officials, after becoming delinquent in tax payments on some cutover lands in Idaho, Oregon, and Washington, developed faith in the economic value of second growth; they kept their land taxes paid up and even purchased additional acreage.

Because cutover timberland appeared to have promising production possibilities, Weyerhaeuser liquidated its Logged-Off Land Company in 1936. The parent corporation absorbed the assets of the company, assigning them to a new Reforestation and Land Department. C. S. Chapman, chief forester of the department, set up extensive reforestation projects on areas so badly burned that planting was the only way to get trees back on the land promptly. Logging operations were planned so as to insure natural seeding.

During the decade prior to World War II, several western wood-using corporations began hiring foresters for duties other than forest management. Apparently, two reasons prompted their employment. Foresters were eagerly hunting jobs; they were willing to start as laborers or perform forestry-related duties with the hope of later working into forestry positions. At the same time, certain companies that already employed foresters and found them satisfactory recruited new graduates for training in other departments of their organizations.

Weyerhaeuser, for example, early began employing forestry graduates for other duties. In 1940, the company's Longview branch alone employed more than fifty foresters scattered throughout various departments—falling and bucking, yarding and loading, accounting, engineering, research, sales, and

18. Carl M. Stevens joined the firm in 1923.
19. Brandstrom, *Development of Industrial Forestry in the Pacific Northwest*, p. 17.

pulp production. Some held executive positions; some were in forestry.[20]

With the establishment of the 120,000-acre Clemons Tree Farm in Washington in 1941,[21] the first tree farm in America, the company accelerated its forestry activities under the direction of Clyde S. Martin,[22] chief forester; Edwin F. Heacox, who subsequently succeeded him and became vice president; and Thomas J. Orr, branch forester at Klamath Falls, Oregon. In 1944, the Forestry Research Center was set up at Centralia, Washington, with Donald G. McKeever in charge. Thus, committed to a policy of timber growing under scientific silviculture, Weyerhaeuser was one of the first companies to start a research unit in forest management staffed with full-time professional foresters.

In 1967, Weyerhaeuser owned 3.7 million acres of woodland, largely in the West and the South. That year, the company officially announced that its forestry program, which up to that time had been mostly experimental, would be put on a wholly commercial basis.

Crown Zellerbach Corporation

Faith in the potentials of scientific forestry to yield profits was early demonstrated by Crown Zellerbach Corporation. In 1892, the company started reforesting cottonwood lands in the Willamette River Valley of Oregon to supply wood to a paper mill at Oregon City. Under a policy of insuring a permanent wood supply for all its operating mills, the corporation has been purchasing land stocked with young growth over a period of seventy years. Often, this was cutover land with young growth left after lumber companies had harvested the old growth—land that no one else wanted.

In 1926, Crown Zellerbach began operating a forest tree nursery to provide seedlings for planting partially stocked land that it was acquiring. Although fire destroyed some of the planted trees, Crown Zellerbach reforested 4,689 acres between 1926 and 1933. In the 1940s, its corps of foresters started to make inventories of the extensive young-growth stands. Commercial thinnings of these stands began in 1947. Two decades later, the area of these annual thinnings and partial cuttings was 33,000 acres.

By 1967, Crown Zellerbach Corporation owned 810,000 acres in Oregon and Washington, much of it young growth. A new paper mill built on the lower Columbia River in 1967 cost more than $90 million. Its production is 1,200 tons daily. Logging has been going on in this area for more than a century, but the land is so productive under silvicultural practice that the wood supply for this big mill is obtained from young growth.

---

20. Robert P. Conklin, "Trends toward Improved Cutting Practices on Private Lands in the Douglas-Fir Region," *Journal of Forestry*, vol. 39 (November 1941), pp. 954–56.

21. See chap. 20 for more information about this pioneer forestry development.

22. Martin may have been the first professionally educated forester to be employed by industry in the Pacific Northwest. After graduating from Yale in 1907, he went with the Weyerhaeuser Timber Company as a logging engineer, not as a forester, because little forestry work was involved in his duties. Five years later, he became logging engineer for the Saginaw Timber Company; he returned to Weyerhaeuser in 1914 and in 1920 went to India as a logging engineer.

Potlatch Forests, Inc.

Elers Koch, former assistant regional forester of the Northern Region of the Forest Service, once declared that the Clearwater Timber Company of Lewiston, Idaho, owned "probably the largest body of white pine in the world." As previously mentioned, this company, since merged with Potlatch Forests, Inc., in 1927 hired the firm of Mason & Stevens, well-known consulting foresters in Portland, Oregon, to make an analysis of its timberlands and to recommend cutting practices for the company to follow.

C. L. Billings, general manager of Clearwater and later of Potlatch, discussed the progress and difficulties of corporate forestry at a meeting of the Society of American Foresters in San Francisco in 1927. Among the difficulties he listed were taxation, protection costs, and fire losses; the high cost of logging improvements; overbuilt sawmill capacity; and the meagerness of research data. Progress, he reported, was being made in protection and brush disposal, in preliminary experiments with conservative cutting and in forest management. He noted that the state law of 1925 creating the Idaho Board of Forestry and the office of state forester was calculated to aid the advancement of industrial forestry.[23]

As Ralph Hidy et al. noted in *Timber and Men*:

Clearwater's emphatically successful experience with selective logging led the associated companies to expand their forest management projects. This was an important factor lying behind the 1931 merger of Clearwater, Potlatch, and Edward Rutledge companies into Potlatch Forests, Inc. In the combined operations, Phil Weyerhaeuser and C. L. Billings could develop the forestry methods started by Clearwater Timber—with the result that Potlatch Forests soon offered one of the best examples of forestry in the West. The Mason & Stevens plan was used to guide the new undertaking.[24]

In 1942, Billings said the company's shelterwood system of cutting "has been the keystone of our marking practice." He emphasized the role of the forester in the company's operations.

Our timber is marked for cutting by foresters. Many men in our organization are foresters. The general manager of our company, meaning me, is a forester. . . . One of our assistant general managers is a forester. Our slash disposal is handled by a forester. Our research work in the various fields of forestry is handled by a forester. Altogether, the company employs 20 to 30 university-trained foresters plus a score of undergraduate foresters.[25]

St. Paul & Tacoma Lumber Company

In 1888, a group of Minnesota and Wisconsin lumbermen organized the St. Paul & Tacoma Lumber Company and built a sawmill in Tacoma,

---

23. "Industrial Forestry in the White Pine Region of Northern Idaho: Its Progress and Difficulties," *Journal of Forestry*, vol. 26 (February 1928).

24. P. 493.

25. "Forest Management by Potlatch Forests, Inc.—Prospects and Policies," *Journal of Forestry*, vol. 40 (May 1942), p. 364. The foresters in management, slash disposal, and research to whom Billings referred were E. C. Rettig, John T. Baggs, and E. R. Rapraeger.

Washington, at the mouth of the Puyallup River. After nearly four decades of logging its old-growth stands, the company sought the advice of a consulting forester for ways to protect the young growth on its cutover lands from fire and to perpetuate the timber resource by harvesting the trees as a crop.

Norman G. Jacobson, a forestry graduate of the University of Minnesota, had entered the U.S. Forest Service in the Pacific Northwest and had become supervisor of the Deschutes National Forest in Oregon. Having set up practice as a private consulting forester, he was retained in 1924 by several lumber companies in the region. One of these was St. Paul & Tacoma. In 1934, the company employed Jacobson full-time as a forester. Later, he became chief forester, a position he held for two decades.

According to *Growing New Forests*, a brochure published by the company in 1927, the condition of all company lands had been analyzed with a view to assuring reforestation or regeneration of the timber stands as they were logged. Future yields had been calculated. Announcing that its policy would be the growing of new forests on its lands, the company admitted active concern with forest conservation, because its future existence depended on it.

As one of the large private landowners in the Douglas-fir region, the company had timber of all ages—uncut stands of old growth, recently logged-off areas, and second-growth tracts up to forty years of age. These holdings provided an opportunity to install a system of conservative cutting in the old growth and to begin the practice of sustained-yield forestry in the second growth. Unfortunately, the economics of the lumber industry was out of joint with the times. Throughout the industry during the 1920s, loggers and mill operators were cutting ruthlessly in an attempt to compete in a widely fluctuating market. During the 1930s, most companies were more concerned about survival than about forestry innovations that would result in added expense; financial benefits, if any, would not to be realized until far in the future.

Despite these and other obstacles, the company supported Jacobson in his forestry program. This program encompassed three main activities: the organization of a comprehensive fire protection plan for all lands; tree planting on cutover areas that were not reproducing naturally or were burned so severely that artificial regeneration was necessary to ensure a new stand; and the adoption of cutting methods that would provide for natural regeneration from existing seed sources and would facilitate artificial seeding or planting.

With the support of President E. G. Griggs and General Manager Corydon Wagner, Jacobson helped to make St. Paul & Tacoma an industrial leader in intensive forestry in the Douglas-fir region. Two phases of the work added to the growth inventory and increased the productive capacity of the holdings. The first of these was a planting program that reached large-scale proportions during the early 1940s; more than 13,000 acres were hand planted. Then in the late 1940s, thinnings made in second-growth stands were put on a commercial basis. Such thinnings, in 1968, were on an annual schedule of 10 million board feet. This phase of the forest management program is being expanded as additional areas of second growth reach economic maturity.

Jacobson's faith in the financial possibilities of second growth under sound forest management led him to persuade the company to purchase cutover tracts as they came on the market. When the company's holdings were certified as a tree farm in 1943, they totaled 81,000 acres. Under Jacobson's vigorous land acquisition program, the acreage had risen to more than 137,000 acres when St. Paul & Tacoma was merged with St. Regis Paper Company in 1957. Under St. Regis, the policy of intensive forest management continues.

J. Neils Lumber Company

While chief of the Forest Service, Lyle Watts was critical of industry's slowness in applying forestry practices on its lands. When he singled out a company for commendation, it was certain that the corporation was a top performer. In the *Journal of Forestry* (November 1943) he declared: "Out in Oregon and Montana the J. Neils Lumber Company has a sustained-yield program fully equalling in intensity national forest operations in the ponderosa pine type."[26]

What manner of operator was this, to win praise from a federal forestry officer who throughout his career found much to criticize and little to commend in private forestry? The J. Neils Lumber Company, incorporated in 1895, with sawmills at Cass Lake, Minnesota, and Libby, Montana, bought out the Western Pine Lumber Company of Klickitat, Washington, in 1922. Within a few years, the company dominated the timbered area tributary to Klickitat, and acquired additional holdings tributary to Libby. Ponderosa pine and Douglas fir were the principal and most valuable species logged.

Like most business firms during the Great Depression, the J. Neils Company had acute financial problems, but it overcame them. Then, as consumption of lumber and other forest products picked up again, company officers saw the need for long-term planning in order to establish the Klickitat operation on a permanent basis. On the advice of Ernest L. Kolbe, then with the Pacific Northwest Forest and Range Experiment Station, the company undertook a study, with Forest Service supervision, to determine whether selective logging would be feasible.

In 1936, at the invitation of the company, Walter H. Meyer, professor of forest management at the University of Washington College of Forestry, had his students make check cruises of selected stands and prepare a comprehensive plan for the permanent management of the Klickitat woodlands. This survey was followed by a log-grade output study made by the Pacific Northwest Forest and Range Experiment Station at the Klickitat mill, and by additional studies in subsequent years by the forestry students. As a result of favorable findings in 1939, the company adopted a program of intensive economic selection logging. It proved so successful that, within a year or two, the selection system was modified to incorporate more silviculture and thus became truly silvicultural in pattern. A similar program was started on the Libby operations in 1942.[27] A. T. Hildman, a forestry graduate of the Univer-

26. "Comprehensive Forest Policy Indispensable," p. 786. Watts meant to say Washington instead of Oregon; the company had no holdings in Oregon.

27. Much of the information in this section is from "Biography of Julius F. B. Neils and History of J. Neils Lumber Company," by Paul Neils, former president and now a director of St. Regis Paper Company, Portland, Ore.; and from the personal papers of Walter H. Meyer, Hamden, Conn.

sity of Washington, was hired as company forester, serving until 1941 when he was succeeded by Elmer W. Lofgren, another graduate of the university.

This sustained-yield program has been continued under the forestry policy of St. Regis Paper Company, which acquired the J. Neils Lumber Company through a merger in 1957.

Western Industrial Associations

As industrial trade associations came into existence in the West, they promptly interested themselves in forestry matters, usually those related to taxation and land law. But in time, the associations supported improved forestry practices and did missionary work to induce the industry to adopt them.

One of the most active of these trade groups was the West Coast Lumbermen's Association, organized in 1911. During William B. Greeley's term as secretary-manager (1928–45), the association was an effective educational force in improving cutting practices and management on its members' holdings. A forestry department headed by a professional forester—Russell Mills—was established in 1934.

Improvements in logging practices resulted also from educational work by the Pacific Northwest Loggers Association and two professional foresters: secretary-manager E. T. Clark (1938–56), and his assistant Kenneth M. Murdock (1956–63).

In 1931, the Western Pine Association was formed by the merger of two older established pine groups, with David T. Mason as secretary-manager. A forestry department was established in 1934, with Clyde Martin in charge as forest engineer. In 1935, the association made a valuable contribution when it drew up forest practice rules for its subscribers, who then operated in twelve states.

From its inception in July 1909, the Pacific Logging Congress was involved in the mechanics of timber cutting and transportation in the interest of both greater economy and efficiency. In time, the congress became concerned with techniques beneficial to forestry. These techniques, such as selective cutting in pine, were instituted when logging became motorized. The old logging railroad, with its high-lead and skyline cable methods, was displaced by motor trucks and permanent road systems made possible by the development of the bulldozer and the introduction of tractors and mobile log loaders. The former destructive practice of clearcutting with no restriction on the area logged gave way to the practice of intermediate cuttings. Many of the improvements advocated by the congress were brought about by the personal drive of foresters and logging engineers who served as president and directors of the congress. George L. Drake, logging engineer and later vice president of the Simpson Logging Company, was a professional forester who, as president, helped get the Pacific Logging Congress behind techniques to advance forestry.

As we have seen, industrial forestry on the West Coast was started during the 1920s in a desultory, modest, and tentative way. But an event occurred in 1933 that was to establish it on a firm and lasting foundation. The National Industrial Recovery Act was passed that year, and one purpose of the lumber code provided by the act was the conservation of forest resources.[28] Acceptable rules of forest practice were to be set up by April 15, 1934.

Acting for the Douglas-fir region, the West Coast Lumbermen's Association and the Pacific Northwest Loggers Association created a Joint Committee on Forest Conservation. In its handbook on forest practice, the committee described techniques for protection from fire and for the maintenance of seed trees for natural regeneration—two key needs for a permanent timber supply. Three foresters, hired by the committee, worked with operators in the field to show them how to reduce fire hazards and, by snag falling and proper slash disposal, to leave standing blocks of mature timber as seed sources.

Although the Supreme Court declared the National Industrial Recovery Act unconstitutional in 1935, the industry continued the Joint Committee with a staff of three foresters assigned to advance the application of forestry on private lands in the Douglas-fir region. The Joint Committee was separated from its two parent associations in 1949. It operated as an independent forestry organization until 1952, when its name was changed to Industrial Forestry Association (IFA). In 1956, it was incorporated as a nonprofit corporation to work exclusively in forestry. With headquarters in Portland, Oregon, it has a staff of eight foresters who provide technical assistance to its subscribers and to other private forest owners.

The association operated two forest tree nurseries; one started in 1941 at Nisqually, Washington, the other in 1961 at Canby, Oregon. By 1969, these nurseries had produced more than 200 million seedlings for planting on industrial tree farms in the Douglas-fir region. IFA helped launch the tree farm movement in June 1941, and approved the first properties for tree farm certification on January 20, 1942.[29] Since then, it has added 7.25 million acres to the tree farm system, an area making up 55 percent of all the private forest land in the Douglas-fir region. It should be added that IFA was also a pioneer in forest tree genetics in the region, having started a program in 1954.

The Douglas-fir industry employed about 100 foresters in 1934. By 1964, the number had increased to 1,500. Modern harvesting methods, improved silvicultural practices, and more efficient utilization of the raw material are now standard operating procedures. Through direct seeding and planting, the industry reforests more than 100,000 acres each year.[30]

The Sustained Yield Act

In 1938, the Pacific Northwest Regional Planning Commission issued a report entitled *Forest Resources of the Pacific Northwest*.[31] Largely based on economic considerations, the report included recommendations for action by the federal and state governments and by landowners and the forest industries. As was traditional in documents dealing with the forest problems of this region, the proposed remedies emphasized increased protection against fire,

---

28. See chap. 15 for a discussion of this act and its influence on private industry.

29. See chap. 20 for an account of the tree farm movement.

30. From reports by W. D. Hagenstein, IFA executive vice president, to IFA subscribers in 1959 and 1964.

31. National Resources Commission, Washington, D.C., 1938.

insects, and disease. Reflecting the contemporary local viewpoint, another recommendation called for federal legislation to make the Civilian Conservation Corps a permanent organization and for the assignment of more CCC camps to the region. (Within five years this proposal would be forgotten as completely unnecessary, and the CCC would be, in the parlance of the day, "phased out.") One recommendation, advanced with strong argument by the commission's Forest Advisory Committee, was for the promotion of sustained-yield management of private woodland by the creation of sustained-yield units on federal and state-owned forests.

David T. Mason, chairman of the Forest Advisory Committee, was an indefatigable advocate of the sustained-yield principle. He helped obtain the passage of the Sustained Yield Forest Management Act of March 29, 1944, which was hailed by influential spokesmen in government and industry as a new instrument of policy and practice to stabilize forest industries and employment in the communities dependent on the industries. Under the act, stabilization would be accomplished by assuring a continuous supply of raw material for the manufacturing plants. The act was also designed to benefit streamflow, to control erosion, and to improve wildlife habitat.

Christopher M. Granger, assistant chief of the Forest Service, was not much given to enthusiasm on behalf of untried forestry legislation and policies. But of this law he expected great results:

> The act is in effect a sustained yield magna charta for the purpose of supporting and stabilizing forest-dependent communities. It has been skillfully drawn to meet a complex situation. It is a great trust on the part of Congress in the integrity and wisdom of the public and private foresters who will have the responsibility of developing units and agreements and thereafter administering them. [32]

Senator Charles McNary of Oregon introduced the bill. Its advocates intended it as a device to halt the creation of ghost towns, those forest-based communities that died or declined when wood processing ceased with the exhaustion of the local timber supply. For example, a lumber manufacturer who owned timber, but in insufficient volume to sustain his plant permanently, might enter into an agreement whereby he would be assured of an adequate log supply, partly from his own land and partly from the nearby national forest. He would be permitted to buy the government timber noncompetitively, but in no case at prices lower than those appraised by the Forest Service. As a quid pro quo, the operator would then agree to adopt cutting practices and silvicultural systems calculated to maintain and improve the stand. In short, what the operator could not do alone, he would be enabled to do with government assistance. The community would be supported economically and socially, and the forest resources would be perpetuated.

Following enactment of the law, the Forest Service drew up rules for its application. After a public hearing, in 1946 the service set up Cooperative Sustained Yield Unit Number 1 jointly with the Simpson Logging Company

32. "The Cooperative Sustained Yield Act," *Journal of Forestry*, August 1944, p. 558.

on the Olympic Peninsula in Washington. George L. Drake, then assistant to the president of the company, was instrumental in bringing about the agreement designed to stabilize the employment and economic base of the towns of Shelton and McCleary.

A forestry graduate of Pennsylvania State College, Drake had been employed by the Forest Service as a logging engineer in Alaska and the Pacific Northwest before he joined the Simpson Logging Company in 1930. During the depression, Simpson retained the company's cutover lands and continued to protect them from fire when other companies were letting their lands revert to the counties for unpaid taxes. The company logged as much as 200 million board feet annually during the 1920s and in the early 1930s was logging more than 100 million feet. According to Drake, the company could operate from fifteen to twenty years on its own old growth and had started buying national forest timber in 1930.[33]

The unit is comprised of 111,000 acres in the Olympic National Forest and 158,000 acres of company land. Under the terms of the contract, the agreement will be in effect 100 years from 1946. The volume and methods of cutting on both parts of the unit are determined by the Forest Service. The company maintains the growing stock on its land by planting when necessary and by silvicultural practices approved by the government foresters. In return, the company has first opportunity to purchase such stumpage as the Forest Service determines may be cut from the national forest within the unit at the government's appraised prices.

This sustained-yield unit was the only one ever established cooperatively between the federal government and a private forest owner.[34] Additional agreements have been proposed or considered but failed to gain approval. Opposition was voiced by small operators who feared unfair competition or monopoly as a result of the alleged advantages that might accrue to large operators. In some cases, after investigation, anticipated advantages were believed to be outweighed by disadvantages.

The J. Neils Lumber Company, for example, made studies over a period of years leading to a possible cooperative sustained-yield unit for its operation at Libby, Montana. In 1945, Harold F. Kaufman and Lois C. Kaufman, rural sociologists then with the University of Missouri, conducted a special investigation of the proposed sustained-yield unit. The study was sponsored jointly by the Montana Study of the University of Montana and the Forest Service. In their report, the Kaufmans noted that the proposed agreement was endorsed by citizens, unions, and civic organizations in Libby but was opposed by the same groups in the town of Troy. According to the opposition, the company would acquire a monopoly of timber resources, and labor would be at a disadvantage in dealing with one principal operator. The Troy Rod and Gun Club objected on the basis that logging roads might be closed to deer hunters. Thus, the conflict between Libby (whose population in 1940 was

33. Interview with George Drake by E. R. Maunder, January 19, 1968 (Forest History Society, New Haven, Conn., typescript).
34. See David T. Mason and Karl T. Henze, "The Shelton Cooperative Sustained Yield Unit," *Journal of Forestry*, vol. 57 (March 1959), pp. 163–68.

1,800) and Troy (population 800) was abetted by those who feared Libby would be favored at the expense of the other communities. The J. Neils Company offered to build a mill at Troy, and did so.

Meanwhile, the company and the Forest Service attempted to draft an agreement that would be mutually satisfactory. The seventh draft, as revised August 12, 1947, was reedited November 7, 1947. The proposed contract was for a duration of sixty years. But the company was dissatisfied with the terms and was doubtful about the numerous regulations contained in the agreement, because the regulations could become onerous with changes in Forest Service personnel. And so the proposal was dropped.

Pope & Talbot, Inc., a company that had begun sawmilling at Port Gamble, near Seattle, as early as 1853, was another applicant for a sustained-yield unit. Having built a modern mill at Oakridge, Oregon, in 1948, the company had an annual payroll of $1.5 million and employed 450 men in logging and milling.

In July 1946, the company had paid $2.5 million for 30,000 acres of virgin timber (1.124 billion board feet) along the Middle Fork of the Willamette River. By 1951, Pope & Talbot had spent $2.9 million for plant and equipment, $1.7 million for roads, and $874,000 for housing for employees. Other expenses had brought the total to $10.9 million for the Oakridge project.

In 1951, the company made application to the Forest Service for a sustained-yield unit in the Willamette National Forest where company land and Forest Service land were intermingled. In furtherance of its plans the company published a twenty-page illustrated booklet that described the purpose of the unit, with an explanation of the resources available in the area for a pulp or by-products plant. The unit, it was claimed, would insure permanence of operations and open the way for further industrial development. Despite the economic, technical, and publicity preparations, the agreement was never consummated.

Another corporation that made formal application to the Forest Service for a cooperative agreement was the Soper-Wheeler Company in California. At the public hearing, strong opposition to the agreement was voiced by other companies that feared their opportunities to buy public timber in the area might be reduced. No contract was forthcoming.

Such, in brief, is the history of a sincere, though unsuccessful, attempt by industry to work out an arrangement with government under democratic safeguards to make permanent forest management an economic reality. To be sure, industrial forestry has become an economic reality in the West, as elsewhere, but the Cooperative Sustained Yield Act of 1944 has had little influence on it.

CHAPTER 20

Tree Farming in America

More than a century ago, Alexis de Toqueville wrote: "I have often admired the extreme skill with which the inhabitants of the United States succeed in proposing a common object to the exertions of a great many men, and inducing them voluntarily to pursue it."[1] So it has been with the voluntary tree farm movement, an indigenous American phenomenon whose origin is rooted deep in the traditions of free enterprise. Tree farming developed wholly without government support, and indeed in the face of official skepticism, even opposition.

The account begins in the 1880s when loggers started felling the virgin stands of Douglas-fir, Sitka spruce, western hemlock, and western red cedar in Grays Harbor County, Washington. It took them fifty years to harvest the original forest. In the wake of their axes and saws, nature restocked the soil with seedlings that developed into second-growth stands.

By 1939, the Clemons tract, for example, had been logged over. Owned by the Weyerhaeuser Company, this property of 120,000 acres showed such favorable regenerative prospects that the company decided to utilize it for intensive research in tree reproduction and growth. In a sense, it was to be a pilot project whose results would guide the future management of all the company's extensive holdings.

As always, both fires set deliberately and those caused by the carelessness of hunters, fishermen, and other recreation seekers would threaten the success of the experiment. A considerable investment was made in lookout towers and telephone lines for fire detection, in roads and trails for access by fire trucks, and in water supplies for fire control. But public understanding of the significance of the Clemons tract was even more essential for effective fire prevention. Company officials faced the dilemma of how to inform neighbors and the public in general that this cutover land was a forest being managed

---

1. *Democracy in America*, vol. 2 (Knopf, 1960), p. 106.

under scientific silviculture, not a wasteland growing up to worthless brush. They needed a name for the project that would attract popular support.

"Reforestation area" or "forest management area" would have been accurate enough, but they lacked popular appeal. Then, a couple of foresters, a public relations man and a county newspaper editor, hit on the term *tree farm*. They hoped the public would instinctively think of a tree farm as land where trees are grown as a crop and would deem such land worthy of the respect customarily given to land growing conventional agricultural crops. Their hopes materialized.

The Clemons Tree Farm, the first in the United States, was established in the state of Washington in June 1941. During the following year, Alabama, Arkansas, California, and Oregon joined the movement.

Early Days of the Tree Farm Movement

During its first two years, the tree farm movement was sponsored largely by local industry groups. In the Douglas-fir region of western Oregon and Washington, the movement was led by the predecessor organization of the present Industrial Forestry Association.[2] In the western pine region of Oregon, Washington, California, and other states, the Western Pine Association undertook to guide the program. In Alabama, joint sponsors were the State Chamber of Commerce and the State Division of Forestry; and in Arkansas, the State Forestry Commission started the program.

Soon, national aid and direction were being given by American Forest Products Industries, Inc. A subsidiary of the National Lumber Manufacturers Association, AFPI had been created in 1932. Its original purpose was to promote trade in lumber products and research and development in wood manufacture and utilization.[3] Assuming a new role, AFPI pushed the tree farm program in cooperation with other interested organizations. For example, in the South the Southern Pine Association was an effective cooperator, as were the state forestry associations that sponsored and administered local tree farm systems.

When the National Lumber Manufacturers Association was reorganized in 1945, AFPI became a separate entity.[4] William Greeley was elected chairman of the board of trustees. Chapin Collins, a former newspaper editor in Montesano, Washington, became managing editor, and Charles A. Gillett became chief forester. Henceforth, AFPI's main concerns would be forestry and public information.

In New York City on March 1, 1946, AFPI launched an information campaign to promote forestry, fire prevention, and similar activities. A major objective of the campaign was to encourage the growing of more trees in the United States. This goal was to be achieved by securing the cooperation of both small woodland owners and industrial timber owners to improve forest protection and to grow perpetual tree crops. They would be asked to cooper-

2. W. D. Hagenstein, "Tree Farms, How They Started," *Western Conservation Journal*, vol. 14 (July–August 1957), pp. 7–9, 56, 58.

3. W. B. Sayers, "To Tell the Truth," *Journal of Forestry*, vol. 64 (October 1966), pp. 652–63.

4. In 1968, AFPI changed its name to American Forest Institute.

ate by dedicating their lands as certified tree farms that would be operated according to recognized standards of management.

William Greeley defined a tree farm as "an area of privately owned, tax-paying forest land, protected and managed for repeated crops of forest products,"[5] and he helped write the policy under which the tree farm system has thrived. He, himself, had a tree farm on Gamble Bay in Washington, and he believed tree growing could be a profitable business.

The American Tree Farm Program has an objective as simple as it is direct—to grow trees as a crop on private lands dedicated to this purpose. From one tree farm of 120,000 acres the first year, the number had grown to 3,500 comprising 25 million acres ten years later.

In 1969, 74 million acres were certified as tree farms by the American Forest Institute. The number of tree farmers exceeded 33,000. Forty-eight states (all except Alaska and Hawaii) were participating.

Mississippi leads with more than 3,900 tree farms; Alabama follows with some 2,800; Georgia has more than 2,400; Louisiana more than 1,800; and Arkansas and Texas more than 1,700 each. These figures reflect the burgeoning interest throughout the South in growing trees for profit. On thousands of acres of southern farm land, pines are now more profitable than cotton.

In tree farm area, Georgia and Alabama lead with 7.7 million acres in each state. Florida has 6.9 million, Oregon has 5.4 million, Louisiana and Washington each have 5 million, and Arkansas has 4.1 million.

Although tree farms are sponsored nationally by the American Forest Institute, the states administer the program locally. In each state, a committee representing the forest industry and other forest interests directs the program and sets standards for certification to meet local requirements for growing, protecting, and harvesting the trees.

A landowner may become a certified tree farmer in one of two ways. He may apply to the state committee for an inspection of his property and get a certificate if his land meets the qualifications. Or, if his property is one known to a local forestry inspector to be well managed in accordance with tree farm standards, the owner may be invited to apply for an inspection leading to certification.

Every tract is inspected by a forester prior to certification and is reinspected periodically as to compliance with the standards. Hundreds of the farmers have had their certificates cancelled for improper cutting or for failing to protect the stand from fire, insects, disease, or injurious grazing by cattle.

The Program Criticized and Defended

Unlike Greeley, who believed that the tree farm system would bring about improved management of millions of acres of private woodlands, Lyle F. Watts, chief of the Forest Service during the early years when the program was getting under way, doubted the honesty of its declared intentions. In his

5. "Growing Trees to Meet the Nation's Needs—Silver Anniversary of Tree Farms, 1941–1966" (American Forest Products Industries, Washington, D.C., 1966, mimeo.).

official report of 1941, he made known his opinion that the real object of the movement was to ward off public regulation. It will be recalled that government policing of private forest management was deemed essential by Pinchot, Graves, Silcox, Clapp, Watts, and others in order to maintain the nation's private, particularly industrial, lands in productive condition.

In its annual report for 1940, the Committee on Private Forestry, Society of American Foresters, warned: "Undue cynicism or distrust of the intentions or achievements of private owners is not conducive to cordial and pleasant relations between forest owners and foresters."[6] In an editorial about the tree farm movement in the SAF's *Journal of Forestry* (August 1942), the editor declared: "That one of its purposes is frankly to forestall federal regulation is certainly not to its discredit." His candor reflected the attitude of many members.

Watts, who was often critical of industry for failing to take positive action to promote forestry, was likely to be skeptical when it did. Within two years after AFPI started its public education campaign to publicize industry's participation in improved forest practices, he called its efforts misleading and exaggerated.

It is unfortunate that a well-financed publicity campaign sponsored by the forest industries during the recent past should tend to cultivate public complacency when the situation with respect to our forest resources is so unsatisfactory. As head of the agency concerned with the public interest in maintaining the productivity of our forests, I cannot let the misleading publicity of the forest industries pass unchallenged.

This campaign creates the impression that little not already being done on private land is needed to assure the nation ample timber supplies for the future. It implies an inevitable increase of annual growth when as foresters we know that the usable growth depends upon merchantable growing stock and that it cannot increase if destruction of the productive growing stock is indefinitely continued. It exaggerates the extent and adequacy of industry progress in good forest practice.[7]

In an article addressed directly to SAF members, C. Edward Behre, assistant to Watts, claimed that the SAF had a responsibility to the public to expose misrepresentation in forest industry publicity that discounted forest depletion and implied that the growth outlook was satisfactory. Behre was known as a red-hot regulationist, and he was even more caustic than his chief in questioning the good faith of industry's educational work.

The American Forest Products Industries are now engaged in a well-financed campaign aimed at cultivating public complacency with the nation's forest situation. The theme of this campaign is that we have plenty of timber, and that the "tree farm" movement among the forest industries gives assurance that the nation will be amply supplied with timber in perpetuity.

Some of the conceptions being propagated with all the pressures known to a modern industrial promotional organization are so questionable as to constitute a challenge to the forestry profession. If the Society of American

6. "Report of the Committee on Private Forestry, Society of American Foresters," *Journal of Forestry*, vol. 39 (February 1941), p. 116.

7. "Comprehensive Forest Policy Indispensable," *Journal of Forestry*, vol. 4 (November 1943), p. 787.

Foresters is worthy of public confidence it should not be content to let the misleading information being circulated by industry pass unchallenged.[8]

Paul F. Sharp of the Department of History at Iowa State University undertook a study of the tree farm movement during the late 1940s under the sponsorship of the Forest Products History Society (now the Forest History Society). In a paper summarizing his findings, presented at a meeting of the Agricultural History Society on April 23, 1948, he commented on the criticism directed at the movement. Some of the criticism, he found, resulted from "overenthusiasm by partisans of the movement" and from publicity presented "in a loose and misleading fashion." But not all the carping was justified.

These critics overlooked the fact that the tree farm movement was accomplishing a feat of indoctrination unparalleled in conservation history. Ninety percent of America's forest fires are annually caused by a careless public. Previous efforts to arouse the public to this tragic waste had failed badly, though conservation organizations and the Forest Service itself had sponsored elaborate publicity drives. Tree farm committees, working with the "Keep Green" movement, performed a signally successful task of indoctrination in a field marked by previous failures.[9]

W. F. Ramsdell, professor of forest management at the University of Michigan, made an inspection of tree farms in various parts of the nation during 1950. His report contained this opinion:

... Millions of Tree Farm acres are already getting more intensive forest management than is available to most of the publicly-owned lands and recognition of these accomplishments is gradually reaching the public. Advertising backed up by the goods is part and parcel of America. It is my conviction, based upon my look at 103 properties in 17 states, that America's Tree Farm acreage has and is keeping the goods on its shelves to back up its advertising. It needs still more well-stocked shelves and that of course is the goal.[10]

In contrast to the suspicious attitude of Watts in 1941, Edward P. Cliff, appointed chief of the Forest Service in 1962, recognized that the American tree farm system sponsored by the forest industries has made a contribution in meeting the great need to stimulate the interest of private forest landowners in doing a better management job on their own lands.

Samuel T. Dana's appraisal of the development of private forestry, as exemplified by the tree farm system, is pertinent: "Enlightened self-interest, rather than public compulsion or private altruism, is basically responsible for the upsurge of interest on the part of private owners who have previously regarded it as impracticable. A more favorable economic climate resulting from higher stumpage prices and improved technology in the use of woods are primarily responsible for the change."[11]

8. "Forest Industry Spreads Dangerous Assumptions on Annual Growth," *Journal of Forestry*, vol. 42 (January 1944), p. 17.

9. "The Tree Farm Movement: Its Origin and Development," *Agricultural History*, vol. 23 (January 1949), p. 44.

10. "Growing Trees to Meet the Nation's Needs."

11. *Forest and Range Policy*, p. 312.

From the author's own knowledge of the movement, gained from personal association with it over the past quarter-century, the overwhelming majority of tree farmers are making an honest attempt to practice good forest management. Nevertheless, criticism continues, although not always from informed sources. David R. Brower, former executive director of the Sierra Club, a critic of what he calls saw-log forestry, described a tree farm as a forest where 1,000 trees were cut down and one sign was put up. Despite those who mistrust the movement, it marches on with an average of more than 2.5 million net acres added each year.

Greeley realized that, as he put it, "There is bound to be a certain amount of 'window dressing' or bunkum in a movement of this kind which seeks popular support."[12] In rural districts, tree farm dedications attract gatherings of people who come to hear prominent orators and high school bands and to see pretty tree farm queens. As "American Tree Farm" signs become more noticeable along country roadsides, they also become status symbols. A farm woodlot owner, for example, presented with his tree farm certificate by the state forester in a ceremony honored by the presence of his governor or congressman, is more likely than not to take seriously the dedication of his land to the growing of tree crops.

Tree Farms as Timber Reserves

Two classes of forest land are recognized in statistics of the nation's timber resources—commercial and noncommercial. Noncommercial lands have little or no possibility for timber production. They either are not suited by reason of climate or terrain to the growing of merchantable trees or are reserved for such purposes as national parks and wilderness areas. Three-fourths of the country's forest land is classified as commercial and one-fourth as noncommercial.

According to the Forest Service, commercial forest land in the United States, including Coastal Alaska, totals 508.8 million acres. This is the timber estate to which America must look for its future supplies of forest products.

Of this priceless domain, 366.9 million acres are in private ownership. The remaining 141.9 million acres are in public ownership, principally in national and state forests, certain lands held by the Department of the Interior, and other woodlands under the jurisdiction of federal, state, and county agencies.

Earlier it was pointed out that the tree farm system totals 74 million acres. Some conception of the vastness of 74 million acres may be had from the fact that this acreage is equivalent to the area of all the New England states, together with Delaware, Maryland, New Jersey, and West Virginia. It is significant that 20 percent of all the privately owned commercial forest land is in tree farms. Because the farms have the capacity to produce permanent timber crops, and moreover are dedicated to such production, they are of incalculable economic importance to the welfare and security of the nation.

On the Clemons tract in Washington—the first certified tree farm in America—the Douglas-fir seedlings that sprang up following logging in the 1930s are now upwards of 100 feet tall. Of sawtimber quality, these trees will

12. *Forests and Men*, p. 163.

be ready for harvest in another decade. Cutting will continue through the year 2000 and beyond.

Wood production, however, is not the only benefit of this and other tree farms. Silviculture is a technique that can be used to increase water yield from watersheds. Extensive road systems, developed to facilitate forestry work and to make all sections of the forest quickly accessible to fire-fighting forces, also open the properties for recreational use. Felling operations form openings in the forest canopy. Increased sunlight in the clearings stimulates the growth of plants on which deer browse; hence deer populations in the West and elsewhere are now larger than ever. In general, wildlife species benefit from thinnings and selection cuttings, which improve their habitat.

The diversity of tree farm ownership indicates the spreading interest in increasing land productivity by growing trees. To be sure, a sizable acreage is held by corporate owners—lumber, mining, paper, plywood, and railroad companies. Such participation, it should be noted, is evidence of industry's transition from the old cut-out-and-get-out attitude to a policy of permanent sustained-yield management.

Significantly, most of the tree farms are small and belong to farmers, or to Christmas tree growers, or to professional men whose farms give them a stake in the land and offer possible hedges against inflation. Some tree farms are properties that have been in the same family for generations. For example, the Robert H. Lawton farm woods, dedicated in 1948 as the first tree farm in Massachusetts, have been in the same family for 200 years. Consisting mainly of white pine and hemlock, the tree farm covers 740 acres in Worcester County in the Connecticut River Valley.

If a property meets the standards for certification, it may be a three-acre shelterbelt for producing fence posts in North Dakota; a 20-acre sugar bush in Vermont; a 200-acre farm woodlot in Tennessee; a 1,000-acre Christmas tree operation in Minnesota; or a half-million-acre industrial holding in the Northeast, the Lake States, or the West. It may be a young coniferous plantation under protection for some indefinite future use. Or it may be the operating forest of a paper company that employs a careful logging plan under the selection system of management in order to permit either natural reseeding or artificial reforestation.

By any criterion, a sober evaluation of the tree farm program shows that it is accomplishing its major objective—to encourage woodland owners to practice improved management by publicly recognizing their work. Its success is attested by the steady increase in the number of certified tree farms. Although the program is privately financed and administered, it deserves public recognition because it is in the public interest. Consider just one example.

Nowhere in the United States is forest land being diminished by the encroachment of urbanization as rapidly as in the New England and Middle Atlantic States. In consequence, as population pressure mounts, the demand for the products and services of the forest rises, not only for lumber, plywood, paper and paper products, but also for fish and game, open space for recreation, and water—above all, water. Tree farms in the eastern states are helping to supply a portion of these consumer needs and will supply more as their number and acreage expand. If this movement had nothing else to its credit, it would still be a notable contribution to the conservation of U.S. forest resources.

But most tree farms throughout the country are under multiple-use management; that is, they provide improved wildlife habitat, watershed protection, and outdoor recreation, as well as timber. They have been a major force in restoring the nation's forests to a condition of productivity; more timber and wood fiber are now being grown than are being harvested and lost to fire, insects, and disease. In truth, the green and white tree farm sign is the symbol of another historic advance during this century in the conservation of a priceless natural resource.

Tree Farming's Worldwide Possibilities

Although American in conception, the tree farm movement has international potentialities. A tree farm program could be put into operation in almost any nation that has developed a forest policy, or is developing one. It could be sponsored by industry, as in the United States. But it also could be sponsored by government, by a trade association, or by a forestry society—working either singly or cooperatively.[13]

Tree farming has possibilities for improving the practice of forestry and for increasing the economic benefits from forest land wherever private owners can be induced to manage their timber stands in accordance with silvicultural standards. But it is not a quick cure for the evils of long periods of forest misuse, nor can it produce instant profits from woodland lacking merchantable growing stock. Over a reasonable length of time, however, tree farming, properly applied, can build up the economic wealth of individual timber owners as well as of nations.

13. Henry Clepper, "Tree Farming in America," *Unasylva*, vol. 21 (February 1967), pp. 3-8.

CHAPTER **21**

Forest Renewal
in the Tennessee Valley

The Tennessee River and its tributaries form a drainage area of 41,000 square miles in seven states. Potentially a region of wealth and opportunity, with abundant natural resources and a river system capable of extensive development, the Tennessee Valley nonetheless was a depressed area by 1930. More than 100 years of wasteful agricultural practice, forest exploitation, destructive logging, and fire had ruined millions of acres of once-productive land. Moreover, the basin—a region of high rainfall—had a shameful record of floods and soil erosion.

The woodland domain, estimated in 1934 to be 14 million acres, was widely dispersed throughout the valley states of Alabama, Georgia, Kentucky, Mississippi, North Carolina, Tennessee, and Virginia. About one-third of the acreage was in small woodlots scattered in the lower elevation of the valley; the bulk of it was in the higher mountains of the Appalachian range. In a contemporary description of the forests, it was noted that they were culled, burned, neglected, and reduced to low productivity.

A new federal agency, the Tennessee Valley Authority (TVA), was created by Congress in May 1933. Charged with the development of the river system for navigation, electric power, and flood control, TVA was given the added responsibility of rehabilitating the land. Among the techniques that would be used were improved agricultural and forestry practices for the control of soil erosion and floods. TVA was also given the duty of promoting industries for the utilization of the area's resources.

Abused and neglected as they were, the valley's forests covered more than half the land area. They constituted a resource that, although practically dormant, had promising possibilities for improving the income of the people and thus the economic growth of the region. As stipulated in the preamble, the purpose of the TVA Act was "to provide for reforestation and the proper use of marginal lands in the Tennessee Valley."

Edward C. M. Richards, a consulting forester with land holdings in Pennsylvania, was appointed chief forester of TVA when its Forestry Division was set up in 1933.[1] Within a few months after becoming chief forester, Richards wrote a paper on the scope of the rehabilitation project and the opportunities it offered foresters. "This is the first time in modern history that any democratic government in the world has undertaken to set aside the entire watershed of a great river and all its tributaries, totaling nearly twenty-six million acres of land, for the purpose of a unified experiment in regional planning on a gigantic scale," he wrote. "In friendly, uncoerced cooperation with private individuals," the government would be engaging in "a systematic attack upon the problem of bringing the whole economic life of a region into coordination and of permanently setting up a plan for its constructive management."[2]

A Forestry Staff Organized

By the spring of 1934, the new Forestry Division had a professional staff of nineteen foresters and seven soil erosion control specialists. It was organized into four sections: planting, lands, forest operations, and forest investigations. The Forest Investigations Section undertook a major study to find out precisely what the valley's economic conditions were.

The outlook was not promising. More than 700 wood-using plants were operating in the region. Nearly 500 of these were sawmills, and much of their output was shipped elsewhere for fabrication. Only seventy-five manufacturing plants gave employment to skilled workers in the valley. The condition of the timber resource was serious; annual growth was estimated to be not more than 25 percent of the annual cut.

A tenet of TVA policy was to make permanent jobs through resource development for the valley's population of 2 million. The forest resource was expected to contribute its share of work opportunities in this "pocket of poverty." Yet, the misuse of this resource had resulted in cutover, fire-scarred hills that had been stripped of their erosion-checking forests; in thousands of acres gutted with gullies; and in from 2 to 3 million acres in need of reforestation before they could produce any wood at all.

The TVA forestry staff initiated a program of applied research in order to obtain data essential for the planned rehabilitation and utilization of the region's forest resources. Consisting mainly of resource and industry surveys, the research also included investigations of ways to obtain better protection from fire, to improve watershed and woodland management practices by private owners, and to increase the economic returns from timber. Because much of the acreage supported second-growth stands of hardwood species, generally of poor quality, research in hardwood silviculture and cutting techniques was undertaken. In time, these studies would include the breeding and growing of superior hardwood species as a necessary aspect of the division's forest tree improvement policy.

---

1. Later, for a brief period the Forestry Division was known as the Division of Forestry and Erosion Control. Subsequently, the name was changed several times—to the Department of Forestry Relations, the Division of Forestry Relations, the Division of Forestry Development, and finally to the Forestry, Fish, and Wildlife Development Program.

2. "The Tennessee Valley—A Challenge to Foresters," *Journal of Forestry*, vol. 32 (March 1934), p. 329.

Getting a forestry program under way and overcoming the obstacles facing the division called for imaginative planning by a staff of competent and experienced foresters. It also called for a big labor force to do the necessary field work.

The problem was as sizable as any ever tackled by a group of foresters. For example, as many as 10,000 fires might burn over 10 percent of the woodland in a single year. Lookout towers for fire detection, telephone lines for reporting fires, and organized fire suppression crews were essential, though in most valley counties they were nonexistent or inadequate. One million acres were so badly eroded that a massive reforestation effort was needed immediately. What little there was of a new forest industry—largely sawmilling—exploited and degraded the timber stand. Under existing conditions, there was no prospect of attracting permanent forest businesses based on local sustained-yield operations.

Fortunately, the forestry staff had the benefit of a labor force to start the essential work of forest and soil rehabilitation. Initially, twenty-five Civilian Conservation Corps camps were assigned to the valley; later, there were thirty-eight. At one period, 7,600 CCC workers were available for duty. They built forest nurseries and planted seedlings. They plugged gullies and put in erosion control installations on reservoir property. They erected fire lookout towers, eliminated fire hazards, and fought woods fires, vigorously tackling the forestry job that needed to be done. Until the CCC was terminated in 1942, the corps had helped produce 173 million nursery-grown trees planted on 137,000 acres of valley land.

Richards was a man of high integrity. He believed sincerely in the social doctrines of the New Deal and was dedicated to the TVA cause on behalf of the valley and its people, but in his capacity as administrator and forester he never won the confidence of TVA's three directors. He disagreed with the directors on policy as it affected the forest resources, and in January 1938 he resigned.

Willis M. Baker became chief forester and director of the Department of Forestry Relations in 1938. During his career, he had been assistant state forester of New Jersey, director of the Pennsylvania State Forest Research Institute, and director of the Central States Forest Experiment Station of the Forest Service. By the year of Baker's arrival, TVA had gained an international reputation as an agency developing waterpower and transportation on a gigantic scale. It was noted also for its development of agriculture through the use of fertilizers and modern farm practices.

But Baker found that higher TVA officialdom tended to vilipend some of the most vital tasks associated with forests and related resources. His department was primarily concerned with woodland, but not exclusively. The related resource activities for which the staff had responsibility were fish and wildlife, watershed protection, soil conservation, and other services of woods and waters. Late in life, long after his retirement, Baker told of the obstacles the foresters and biologists faced when he first joined TVA.

. . . At that time, few of the top TVA officials appeared to understand conservation problems and objectives. Their attention was then focused on agriculture rather than on the timber industry; the influence of forests on water resources was generally disregarded and there was little recognition of the recreational assets inherent in the region's mountains, forests, lakes and streams. It took us a long time to convince the engineers who operated the dams and reservoirs that they should avoid, as far as possible, sudden, drastic fluctuations of water levels that destroyed aquatic life. A serious disturbance was created when we protested vigorously against the killing of fish and wildlife by the oils and poisons sprayed along the reservoir margins by the Health and Safety Department to destroy the larvae of anopheles mosquitoes that spread malaria. . . .[3]

Emphasis on Cooperation

Henceforth, the forestry activities of TVA would be in the nature of regional extension services, gaining results largely through cooperative efforts with others. The "others" would range from individual farmers and small landowners to state forestry departments and federal agencies like the Forest Service; they would include such diverse cooperators as county agricultural agents and state agricultural colleges, furniture plants and great pulp and paper companies. In short, the Department of Forestry Relations would work with every interested individual, governmental body, and industrial corporation that could contribute to the development of the forest and related resources.

By 1939, the foresters had determined that, of the valley's woodland area of 13.5 million acres, at least 2 million acres needed reforesting. Two nurseries producing 24 million trees annually were in production at Clinton, Tennessee, and at Muscle Shoals, Alabama. Baker noted that the major problem was one of watershed protection on privately owned lands. Still, less than 20 percent of the forest received adequate protection from fire.

At the close of the spring planting season of 1941, the CCC camps had set out 118 million trees, and private landowners had planted 16 million—a total of 104,000 acres reforested. That year, TVA foresters began giving management assistance to woodland owners. At the same time, production services were made available to timber operators and industries. Demonstration areas of management practices were being established in farm woods.

In an address early in 1947, Director Gordon R. Clapp reported that more than 140,000 acres had been reforested with 156 million trees provided by TVA. The valley now had 15,000 farmer tree planters. The number of wood-using industries, including sawmills, had increased to 3,400. They gave employment to 100,000 workers and accounted for $100 million of the region's annual income. Clapp predicted that in the future the basin's forests under scientific management could account for $500 million in annual income.[4]

After fifteen years in charge of TVA's forestry program, Baker retired in 1953. His successor was his former assistant, Richard Kilbourne, who had had two decades of experience in all phases of TVA forestry work.

In 1954, the Division of Forestry Relations issued a brief report, *Private Forest Management in the Tennessee Valley*, in which it announced the results of a survey made in 1953 of the quality of forest management on the

3. "Reminiscing about the TVA," *American Forests*, May 1969, p. 58.

4. "Our Forests and the Future of the Tennessee Valley," *Journal of Forestry*, vol. 45 (May 1947), pp. 329–34.

14 million acres of valley woodland. It was noted in the report that the forest products industries owned more than 1 million acres and that their brand of management rated higher than that of any other class of ownership. But the large private ownerships practicing good management, together with the public ownerships, represented only 12 percent of the valley forests.

Small private holdings predominated; 99 percent of all ownerships were under 500 acres. Only 4 percent of the private owners practiced satisfactory management; 64 percent, owning more than half the area, did little or nothing to improve the resource.

Valley industries using wood as raw material turned out products valued at $350 million annually. According to the report, proper management and reforestation would make it possible to triple timber production, and the value of forest products could be boosted to over $1 billion a year.

Within six years after his appointment in 1954, Kilbourne could report that TVA foresters, working with state forestry and extension personnel, had established 300 forestry demonstration areas aggregating 560,000 acres. Reforestation continued to increase; since 1933, 45,000 landowners had planted 427 million seedlings on 400,000 acres of idle and eroded land. Most of the seedlings had been raised in TVA nurseries. State forestry agencies were providing organized protection on nearly all the region's woodland. Moreover, the annual fire loss had been reduced from as much as 10 percent of the entire forest acreage to less than 1 percent.[5]

After seven years as director of forestry, Kilbourne became director of TVA's Division of Tributary Area Development. Kenneth J. Seigworth, another TVA career forester, was designated director of the Division of Forestry Relations.

Reporting on the state of forestry in the valley in 1968, Seigworth announced that 60 percent of the region was then forested, with 80 percent of the acreage held by 235,000 private owners. Since 1933, the wooded area had been increased by 2.4 million acres. Fire losses averaged less than one-half of 1 percent annually. "Foresters can take much credit for the Tennessee Valley's progress in forest resource development," Seigworth wrote, "but they must also acknowledge the vital contributions made by others. Progress has been a team effort and it opens up a future with great promise."[6]

On Seigworth's retirement in 1969, he was succeeded as director of the Forestry, Fish, and Wildlife Development Program by Thomas H. Ripley, formerly of the Branch of Research of the Forest Service. Now, in the fourth decade of TVA's existence, the prevailing attitude of the valley's people toward woodland is one of appreciation for the social and economic benefits that flow from it and its associated fish and wildlife resources. No longer is the forest viewed as useful only for short-term exploitation. Moreover, forestry, whose possibilities in the early days of TVA were little understood and whose progress was at times hampered by obstacles within TVA itself, has become a functional integrant of the organization and the region.

5. See "Tennessee Valley Authority," in Henry Clepper and Arthur B. Meyer (eds.), *American Forestry: Six Decades of Growth*.

6. "Forestry Plus in the Tennessee Valley," *Journal of Forestry*, vol. 66 (April 1968), p. 328.

Appendix

American Forestry
in International Context

Two centuries ago, the youthful United States was a developing nation from whose "inexhaustible" woodlands products of the forests made up an important share of the nation's modest export commerce. A scant century later, thinking persons had begun to express alarm at the waste and destruction of the nation's timber resource, which was not inexhaustible after all. Among the articulate proponents of action to arrest the trend of devastation were several transplanted Europeans who advocated the novel concept of timber preservation. Carl Schurz, Bernhard E. Fernow, and Carl A. Schenck were supported by a group of native Americans who, after travel and study in Europe, were able to present a case to the people and the government. Prominent among these citizens were George P. Marsh, Franklin B. Hough, Gifford Pinchot, and Henry S. Graves.

Thus, the initial impetus behind the forest conservation movement was as much external as it was internal. Moreover, the effect of foreign stimulus on forestry in the United States was both beneficial and lasting.

When technical education in forestry began at Biltmore, Cornell, and Yale, there were no American textbooks. Consequently, the texts written by Fernow, Schenck, and Filibert Roth, for example, showed the influence of European techniques and practices. This same influence was evident also in the burgeoning professional literature; for example, in the *Forestry Quarterly*. The useful foreign influence did not cease with the creation of the forestry profession in the United States. It continues to this day. In education, research, and practice, American forestry has made certain advances because of the knowledge and techniques freely available from colleagues in foreign places.

It is understandable, then, that American foresters would want to return in kind the benefits their profession has received from overseas. Hence, forestry as an art and a science was barely established in the United States before American foresters began to participate in international spheres of action. The manner of this participation and its consequences are outlined briefly in this appendix.

Forestry in the Philippines

Following the Philippine insurrection during the Spanish-American War and the occupation of the islands, the U.S. Army assumed responsibility for the administration of the forests, which were almost wholly government owned. In April 1900, Captain George P. Ahern was put in charge. Ahern's long and deep interest in forestry, an interest encouraged by Gifford Pinchot, was unusual in a career army officer of that period. Indeed, few Americans other than a small group of scientists and other public-spirited citizens were concerned about it.

At once, Ahern was confronted with the colossal task of administering about 50 million acres of timberland whose species were only partially known to botanists and whose woods were mostly untested. But the resource had valuable timber trees that could be profitably harvested and marketed. Obviously, the first need was for a corps of technically qualified botanists, foresters, and forest products specialists.

During the early years of the 1900s, Ahern recruited several young American botanists and foresters—the latter, recent graduates of the few forestry schools then in existence—for duty with the newly organized Philippine Bureau of Forestry. Among these men were Ralph C. Bryant, Hugh M. Curran, F. W. Foxworthy, Wallace I. Hutchinson, Donald M. Matthews, Melvin L. Merritt, and H. N. Whitford.

As there were no native Filipino foresters, in 1910 the Bureau of Forestry established a Forest School at Laguna. Curran, who went to the islands in 1907, later became director of the school, where he served until captured by the Japanese invaders in 1941. Now the College of Forestry, the institution offers a four-year undergraduate curriculum in professional forestry and a two-year ranger course and carries on research in silviculture and forest products.

Captain Ahern's administration continued until 1914,[1] when he was succeeded by Arthur F. Fischer. As it progressed, the work of the bureau attracted the attention of government officials from other countries in the Asia-Pacific area and thus served as a guide for the organization of forestry in several nations of the region (China, for example). As Filipino foresters acquired technical training and obtained administrative experience, they supplanted the Americans. Within two decades all but a few of the several hundred technical personnel in the bureau were Filipino nationals. By 1946, the year of Philippine independence, the forests of the republic were entirely administered by its own foresters.

International Union of Forestry Research Organizations

The oldest international body in which American foresters have participated is the International Union of Forestry Research Organizations (IUFRO). European in origin, it antedated the beginning of forestry research in the United States. At an assemblage of the Congress for Agriculture and

---

1. See Lawrence Rakestraw, "George Patrick Ahern and the Philippine Bureau of Forestry, 1900–1914," *Pacific Northwest Quarterly*, vol. 58 (July 1967).

Forestry in 1890 in Vienna, a suggestion was made for the formation of an international organization of research scientists working in forestry. A committee was appointed (Austria, France, Germany, and Switzerland were represented), and, at a conference in Baden in September 1891, it proposed that interested governments form an international federation of state-supported forest experiment stations. Accordingly, the federation was created in 1892 at a meeting in Eberswalde, Germany. Thus, the International Union of Forest (later changed to Forestry) Research Organizations came into existence. It was composed of member experiment stations, and scientists were chosen as associate members. Its first congress was held in Austria in 1893.

Subsequent congresses were held in Germany in 1896, in Switzerland in 1900, in Austria in 1903, in Germany again in 1906, and in Belgium in 1910. Then, as a result of the dislocations in research caused by World War I, IUFRO, like some other small international organizations, became a casualty of the times. In 1926, however, research workers attending the First World Forestry Congress in Rome decided to reactivate the union.

IUFRO underwent reorganization in July 1929 at the congress in Sweden. The scope of the membership was broadened to include all kinds of forestry research organizations and institutions other than those maintained by the state.[2] Representatives were present from 141 member bodies from 35 nations. Edward N. Munns and Joseph Kittredge of the U.S. Forest Service were present as observers, but since the Forest Service was not a member they could not serve as officers.

Although no agency of the U.S. Government was a member, several American forestry schools took up membership. In IUFRO's annual report for 1931, forestry schools at Harvard, Michigan, Yale, and the University of California were listed as members, as was the Brown Company of Berlin, New Hampshire, represented by Henry I. Baldwin, research forester. In 1932, the congress was held in France, and that year three additional American universities were on record as members—Duke, Idaho, and Syracuse.

But it was not until 1933 that the U.S. Forest Service was listed. Then, the Branch of Research, together with the thirteen regional forest experiment stations and the Forest Products Laboratory, held membership. E. N. Munns was made a vice president, an office he held until 1948.

Following the congress in 1936 in Hungary, no further meetings were held until after World War II, although annual reports were issued during the war years in the three official languages: English, French, and German. In April 1954, the Interim Commission on Food and Agriculture adopted a resolution proposing that the Food and Agriculture Organization (FAO), then in the process of being created by the United Nations, take over the functions of IUFRO and serve as the world coordinator for all forestry research. Although this resolution was not implemented, IUFRO's influence and activity languished following the formation of FAO's Division of Forestry and Forest Products. A special Committee on Research met in Paris in May 1947 and proposed the reactivation of IUFRO. The nations represented on

2. Barrington Moore, "International Congress of Forest Experiment Stations," *Journal of Forestry*, vol. 27 (November 1929), pp. 875–78.

this committee were Finland, France, Italy, United Kingdom, United States (by Edward I. Kotok), and Switzerland. The conferees unanimously advocated the preservation of IUFRO's autonomy.

When IUFRO held its 1948 meeting in Switzerland, it underwent a second reorganization. American financial participation was withdrawn the following year when the U.S. Congress authorized contributions to FAO only. Clarence F. Korstian of Duke University succeeded Vice President Munns as a member of the Permanent Committee. At the congress held in Italy in 1953, 101 institutions, both public and private, in forty-three countries held regular membership.

A conflict between FAO and IUFRO over which organization should coordinate world forestry research was gradually resolved beginning in 1949; FAO agreed to serve as the secretariat for the IUFRO, and the latter agreed to designate an FAO staff officer as an observer to attend IUFRO committee meetings and congresses. In 1955, Irvine T. Haig, an American forester on the staff of the Division of Forestry and Forest Products, was named the observer (now known as the permanent representative) of FAO.

While serving as president of IUFRO, James MacDonald of the United Kingdom wrote a brief history of the organization. "The arrangement whereby the Secretariat resided with FAO at Rome, while the President was elsewhere, was not an easy one to operate," he commented, "and that it worked as well as it did was due largely to the skill of FAO's representative, I. T. Haig, who rendered great service to the Union, and indeed to forest research the world over during those difficult postwar years."[3]

By 1956, when IUFRO held its congress in Great Britain, the U.S. Forest Service was financially authorized to resume membership. In 1957, Verne L. Harper, chief of research, became a member of the Permanent Committee, and in 1962 he was elected vice president of IUFRO. During this period, IUFRO was becoming less Europe-oriented than it had been, and American research institutions were more influential in shaping its programs and more active in supporting its activities.

The secretariat arrangements with FAO did not last long, not only because of the difficulty of the operation mentioned above. Most of the reasons stemmed from IUFRO's cherished independence. In 1956, at the IUFRO Congress in Great Britain, it was decided to relieve FAO of its obligation to provide a secretariat for IUFRO and to seek other avenues of cooperation. Two years later, FAO gave IUFRO status as a consultant. Since then, the two organizations on occasion have jointly sponsored international symposia in specific research areas; through special grants, FAO has supported other research projects.

At the World Forestry Congress in Madrid in 1966, the president of IUFRO, Julius Speer of Germany, spoke of the new relationship between his organization and FAO: "Thus the responsibilities and operational spheres of both FAO and IUFRO are clear-cut and this is leading to a smooth working relationship that is at once stable and flexible to meet changing needs and

3. "The International Union of Forest Research Organizations," *Unasylva*, vol. 15 (January 1961), p. 30.

conditions." Speer concluded by quoting Verne Harper, vice president of IUFRO, who had said, "There is need for both organizations—indeed, in this technological society of ours, we cannot do without either, for they are essentially complementary."[4]

As the union's name implies, the purpose of IUFRO is to advance international cooperation in all branches of forestry and forest products research. Among its functions are the exchange of information about experimental programs and their results, the establishment of cooperative programs of research among different countries, the standardization of scientific nomenclature, and the improvement of international bibliography. About eighty working groups in twelve research sections carry on these activities. The sections have to do with bibliography and terminology, the history of forestry, watershed management, site factors, tree physiology and genetics, silviculture and reforestation, forest protection, forest growth and yield, forest economics, forest engineering, forest products and utilization, and recreation and wildlife management.

One of IUFRO's activities, initiated by the Section on Bibliography and Terminology, is the compilation of a multilingual glossary of forestry terms. Started originally by small grants from FAO, the five-year project was later financed jointly by the Forest Services of the Canadian and U.S. Governments and administered by the Society of American Foresters. Its director is F. C. Ford Robertson of Oxford, England, formerly editor of the Commonwealth Forestry Bureau's *Forestry Abstracts*.

By 1969, IUFRO had 225 institutional members in sixty-one countries. Together they comprise the major portion of the world's forestry science capability. The United States was represented by twenty-eight forestry schools, four federal organizations (including the eight regional stations of the Forest Service, the Forest Products Laboratory, and the Institute of Tropical Forestry), two industrial research units, one privately endowed research center, and one association with a research program.

IUFRO's fifteenth congress, the first outside Europe, was held at the University of Florida, March 14–20, 1971.

Forestry in FAO

While war raged throughout the world, representatives of the free nations met in May 1943 in Hot Springs, Virginia, to create an international organization within the structure of the United Nations to advance food and agricultural production. The U.N. Interim Commission on Food and Agriculture, composed of members from forty-six nations, was set up to plan the new organization.

Although forestry was not specifically represented on the Interim Commission, it had a spokesman. Anders Fjelstad of Norway, an agricultural delegate of his government in the United States, was a forest owner who practiced scientific silviculture. He contended that forestry should have a place in the proposed Food and Agriculture Organization. President Franklin

4. *Proceedings of the Sixth World Forestry Congress*, Madrid, Spain, June 1966, vol. 1, "Forestry Research" (1968), p. 935.

Roosevelt, an ardent tree planter and conservationist, authorized the American member (Paul H. Appleby, undersecretary of agriculture) to include forestry in the FAO charter.

The manner in which Roosevelt's approval was obtained makes an interesting addendum to the FAO chronicle. Appleby was favorable to Fjelstad's advocacy of forestry as one of FAO's functions. But Roosevelt had outlined the scope of the proposed organization prior to the Hot Springs conference and had not mentioned forestry. Uncertain then as to his authority to commit himself with respect to forestry, Appleby decided to refer the question to the president for decision. He wrote the following letter:

November 2, 1943

The President
The White House

Dear Mr. President:
    In the work of the Interim Commission planning a permanent International organization for food and agriculture, the question has been raised whether this organization should include functions in the field of forestry. I believe the general judgement of the members of the Commission is rather strongly in favor of including forestry, and to include forestry probably would add to the political appeal of the proposal. Would you have any other judgement?

Sincerely yours,
Paul H. Appleby
Under Secretary

On a carbon copy of this letter returned to Appleby, Roosevelt made a historic notation: "P. A. Yes. I think forestry should be included. F D R."[5]

At a conference of the Interim Commission held in Washington, D.C., in July 1943, an Economic Panel and a Scientific Panel advised the commission on the scope of the work that might be undertaken by the proposed Food and Agriculture Organization. Although no forestry expert served on either advisory panel, forestry and forest products were among the recommended activities.[6]

Accordingly, in December 1943 the Interim Commission agreed to include forestry in FAO's functions. A Technical Committee on Forestry and Primary Forest Products was designated in March 1944 to plan for the work of FAO in this field.

Chairman of this Technical Committee was Henry S. Graves, dean emeritus of the Yale School of Forestry. All thirteen members were appointed as experts in their fields, not as representatives of nations. Three additional American foresters were on the committee: Tom Gill of the Charles Lathrop Pack Forestry Foundation (acting as the expert on Latin America); Walter C. Lowdermilk of the Soil Conservation Service (acting as the expert on the Far East); and Lyle F. Watts, chief of the Forest Service.

    5. A copy of this letter and Roosevelt's approval is in the Paul H. Appleby Collection, Maxwell Graduate School of Citizenship and Public Affairs, Syracuse University.
    6. U.N. Interim Commission on Food and Agriculture, *First Report to the Governments of the United Nations by the Interim Commission on Food and Agriculture* (Washington: August 1, 1944).

The committee held meetings in Washington, D.C., in May, June, and September, and its report was unanimously adopted on November 4, 1944.[7] The committee's proposals for organizing the world's work in forestry and forest products were soundly conceived; when incorporated into the structure of FAO, they would serve as permanent guiding principles.

Gill described the report as "one of the world's important forestry documents. . . . It is the first integrated effort by foresters of many nations to define the place of forestry in the world's economy." He added: "The committee envisaged an organization equipped to undertake missions, advise the nations concerning their forest policies, and make universally available the results of investigations into silviculture, management, and wood utilization."[8]

During FAO's formative period, two forces were exerting an influence on American participation in world forestry. One was the impact of the national interest in the search for peaceful means to improve the living standards of people everywhere through international cooperation. The other was a surge of professional confidence experienced by U.S. foresters who believed in the ability of forestry to contribute to higher production of the world's goods and services.

World War II had been ended less than six months when representatives of thirty-seven nations assembled on October 16, 1945, in Quebec for the first session of the Conference of the Food and Agriculture Organization of the United Nations. At the close of the session on November 1, the FAO membership totaled forty-two countries. A constitution and a budget had been adopted. Sir John Boyd Orr of the United Kingdom had been named director-general.

Six committees worked during the two-week period to propose policies and recommendations for handling the major world problems in nutrition and food, agriculture, forestry and forest products, fisheries, marketing, and statistics. Henry Graves was chairman of the Committee on Forestry and Forest Products. The rapporteur was Marcel Leloup, director-general of the French Forest Service. Tom Gill was secretary. Two assistant secretaries well known in international forestry were Egon Glesinger of the Comité International du Bois, and William N. Sparhawk of the U.S. Forest Service.

Although thirty-seven nations had official delegates at the Quebec conference, only nine countries were represented on the Committee on Forestry and Forest Products. These representatives, assisted by nonofficial forester-delegates from Canada and the United States, drew up the policy and administrative structure for what then became FAO's Division of Forestry and Forest Products (now the Division of Forestry and Forest Industries).

Several American foresters contributed effectively to the committee's work: Lyle F. Watts; Edward I. Kotok, assistant chief of the Forest Service; and Walter C. Lowdermilk.

7. U.N. Interim Commission on Food and Agriculture, *Third Report to the Governments of the United Nations by the Interim Commission on Food and Agriculture, Transmitting the Report of the Technical Committee on Forestry and Forest Products* (Washington: April 25, 1945).

8. "Forestry Joins the United Nations," *Journal of Forestry*, vol. 44 (March 1946), pp. 159–63.

In its comprehensive report, the committee made fifty specific recommendations; nearly half were designated "for urgent action." They were grouped in nine general categories: forest policy, forest management, forestry in relation to rural welfare, forest products and living standards, forest research, forestry education, forest products research and utilization, and forest industries and marketing. Practically no major condition in world forestry that needed attention, especially in the developing countries, was overlooked.[9]

The program needed to implement the far-reaching recommendations might have been too ambitious and expensive for even a giant organization, adequately financed and staffed. To achieve the infrastructure envisioned by the committee, to obtain personnel qualified to function on a global basis, and to fund the work would take time; hence years would pass before some of the recommendations marked for urgent action would be carried through.

When subsequently created, the Division of Forestry and Forest Products was directed by Marcel Leloup. S. B. Show, career officer in the U.S. Forest Service, was appointed head of the Branch of Forestry, and Egon Glesinger, head of the Branch of Forest Products. Washington, D.C., was the division's headquarters until 1951, when FAO headquarters were permanently moved to Rome. For the first two years, FAO's total budget was slightly less than $4.2 million, of which the United States contributed 25 percent.

One of the first projects undertaken by the division was to determine the scope of the job it had to do. Data had to be gathered on the extent of forestry needs in developing nations, and in many of these nations statistics were inadequate or lacking altogether. Thus, priorities of technical assistance were hard to assign in the face of such widespread need. Moreover, sufficient personnel was unavailable even if funds had been. Governments without forestry policies had to have help in formulating them. Model laws had to be written in order to halt timber exploitation and to provide elementary protection against trespass, fire, and other destructive agents. Many nations requiring foresters with professional education and technicians with vocational training utterly lacked facilities to provide such instruction to their nationals. The obstacles might have appeared insurmountable if the opportunities had not been so great.

Although many of FAO's forestry activities have been criticized—and some have been wasteful and inefficient—FAO has adhered to its main function of serving nations in need of technical forestry assistance. Particularly effective have been its publications, its regional staffs, its special assistance programs, and its periodic resource commodity reports.

In 1947, FAO began publication of *Unasylva*, a quarterly journal devoted to world developments in forestry. The journal is under the editorial supervision of the Division of Forestry and Forest Products. During its relatively short existence, the magazine has become both a repository and a contemporary record of the science and art of forestry throughout the world. It has provided especially useful information on policy matters and on instrumentation and mechanization. As *Unasylva* makes clear, no nation stands pre-

9. Food and Agriculture Organization, *Report of the First Session of the Conference* (Washington: January 1946).

eminent in all phases of forestry, and every country may benefit from progress attained in others. *Unasylva* has performed a highly useful function out of all proportion to its modest circulation.

Every two years, a meeting of the Technical Committee on Forestry and Forest Products is held in Rome. Consisting of delegates from member nations, the committee reviews the division's activities for the past biennium and advises on a program of work for the biennium ahead. Through its recommendations to the FAO Conference, the committee helps set general policy in forestry and specifies major problems and areas most critically in need of attention.

During the past two decades, American foresters on the official delegations to the FAO Conference have been deeply involved in policy decisions in international forestry. They have helped guide the division's principal field projects for the advancement of forestry in the developing nations and for the establishment of soundly based forest industries in regions where such industrial growth is calculated to contribute to higher living standards.

Late in 1969, the Division of Forestry and Forest Industries was raised in status and renamed the Forestry Department. B. K. Steenberg, division director, became assistant director-general in charge of the new department.

Regional FAO offices have been set up in Africa, in the Asia-Pacific Region, in Europe, in Latin America, and in the Near East. The regional forestry officers perform staff functions for six regional forestry commissions. An example of such a working arrangement is the North American Forestry Commission, of which Canada, Mexico, and the United States are members. The regional forestry officer for the commission has headquarters in Mexico City.

FAO, which began in 1945 with 42 member nations in 1970, had 121 member nations, many of which did not exist when FAO was created. Because they are new states, often without experience in the administration of government and of resources, their survival has frequently depended on the political and scientific aid provided by the United Nations and on the financial support provided by international banks and similar financing agencies. In forestry and forest products, FAO has provided essential advisory services in policy and technical matters, in professional education and technician training, and in surveys of resources as bases for industrial development.

In 1968, FAO employed 636 forestry and forest products specialists. Of these, 52 had their headquarters in Rome; 11 were posted to regional offices; 455 were assigned to sixty-eight special projects throughout the world; and 188 were technical assistance officers, whose projects were largely financed from funds outside FAO's regular budget and who worked mostly in the newly created developing nations. About sixty of the total personnel were American specialists. Only six of these were career officers with FAO; the others were on leave, ranging from a few months to several years, from permanent positions at home.[10]

Marcel Leloup served as director of the Forestry and Forest Products (now Forest Industries) Division during the period 1946–58. He was suc-

10. Robert K. Winters, "Forestry in FAO," *Journal of Forestry*, vol. 66 (November 1968), p. 872.

ceeded by his deputy, Egon Glesinger of Austria, who was director during the period 1959–63. Nils R. Osara of Finland became director in the latter years, serving until late in 1968, when he was succeeded by Borje K. Steenberg of Sweden.

World Forestry Congresses

From the beginning of forestry in the United States, American foresters went out to other nations as students and occasionally as workers. The first organized international activity in which they participated was the World Forestry Congress held in Rome in April 1926. The 1,500 delegates in attendance represented governments, educational institutions, industry, and forestry and forest products associations in 60 nations. Samuel T. Dana headed the thirty-member American delegation. Tom Gill, who attended this congress, has the distinction of being the only American forester who was present at all five subsequent congresses.

Although not notable for accomplishment, this first congress provided an opportunity for foresters throughout the world to become acquainted, to exchange information, and to hear technical papers. Resolutions were passed, one of which resulted in the establishment of a Silvicultural Section in the International Institute of Agriculture. This institute, formed in 1905 under the sponsorship of the Italian government, had its headquarters in Rome. It was, incidentally, a predecessor of FAO. The Silvicultural Section never became an effective instrument in advancing world forestry; its staff was chiefly concerned with gathering statistics and publishing papers in the institute's bulletins.

Convened in Budapest, Hungary, in September 1936, the Second World Forestry Congress attracted only about one-third as many delegates as the first; forty nations were represented. F. A. Silcox, chief of the Forest Service, headed the American delegation of fourteen.

An interesting, if short-lived, outcome of the second congress was the setting up of an International Forestry Center, an autonomous unit of the International Institute of Agriculture. The International Forestry Center, housed and largely financed by the German government, was in Berlin. During its brief existence, the Forestry Center published a quarterly journal and a monograph series.

Originally scheduled to be held in Finland in 1940, the Third Congress was postponed because of World War II. It finally convened in Helsinki on July 10, 1949. More than 500 persons from twenty-seven countries attended. The head of the American delegation was Christopher M. Granger of the Forest Service. In addition, twenty-two U.S. observers and associates were present.

Since some nations lacked forestry policies, the congress called on them to formulate such policies and charged FAO with the duty of cooperating in this program so essential to improving standards of land use throughout the world. FAO also was asked to call a special international conference on tropical forestry.

Dehra Dun, India, was the site of the Fourth Congress, held in December 1954. Approximately 350 delegates from forty-seven nations attended. For the first time, the United States was not represented by an official delegation. The U.S. Government had cancelled the authorization of its delegates because the host nation had officially invited Red China and East Germany. Seven American foresters having no affiliation with the federal government represented American forestry unofficially.

Two permanent committees were recommended for FAO action: a Committee on Bibliography under the chairmanship of Hardy L. Shirley of the College of Forestry at Syracuse University, and a Committee on Higher Forestry Education under the chairmanship of H. G. Champion of Oxford, England. This congress was the first to publish its proceedings.

The United States was the host nation for the Fifth Congress, which was held in August 1960 at the University of Washington in Seattle. The president of the congress was Richard E. McArdle, chief of the Forest Service. There were nearly 2,000 registrants from sixty-five countries and six international organizations. This congress featured hundreds of educational and industrial exhibits set up by forestry societies, educational institutions, book publishers, and equipment manufacturers. The 450 papers presented at the meetings, together with a record of the tours and other congress activities, were published in three volumes.

Spain was the host for the Sixth World Congress, which opened in Madrid on June 6, 1966, with ninety-three nations represented. Of the 2,787 registrants, 2,000 were congress members; the remainder, associates. There were 376 registrants from the United States (237 members and 139 associates). Edward P. Cliff, chief of the Forest Service, headed the official American delegation. It was the largest gathering dealing with forest resources and forest products ever held.

Although the interest of FAO and some congress members was focused on the growing world demand for wood as a raw material, the resolutions adopted reflected the need for increased education and increased research in finance, productivity, and protection. Of all the problems considered, that of ways to increase forest productivity was foremost—for example, forest development in the tropics. Governmental and private agencies were urged to create more national parks and natural areas representative of the world's ecosystems and to provide for more wildlife and recreational development.

Since their beginning, the World Forestry Congresses have served a necessary function in international affairs. They have been a friendly medium for the exchange of professional and technical information. They have promoted cooperation in the scientific management and utilization of the world's forest resources. In addition, they have provided a forum for personal discussion among foresters and forest industry leaders. Ever seeking more scientific knowledge to increase the earth's forest resource wealth for the benefit of mankind, foresters of all nations have something to teach and something to learn. The congresses have contributed much to the learning process.

Special U.S. Assistance Abroad

Following the close of World War II, military units of the United States Government assumed responsibility for forestry programs in several nations. In the zone of American occupation in Germany, the army recruited Joseph

S. Kircher, a former regional forester in the Forest Service, to supervise timber production in the German forests. Kircher and his assistants conducted harvesting operations so that adequate growth remained for future stands, despite the heavy cuts demanded by the military.

In Japan, the supreme commander of the allied powers set up a Natural Resources Section in which there was a Forestry Division responsible for increasing the production of timber, fuelwood, and other products for essential civilian needs. Colonel Arthur R. Spillers and Colonel Harold B. Donaldson, two American foresters then in military service, planned and carried out the work.

But the most momentous effort to help organize long-term forestry projects abroad was assigned to various civilian agencies of the government. An early one was the International Cooperation Administration (ICA), set up in the Department of State by Congress in 1952. Although it had certain military policies, in general its object was to help friendly nations develop their human and natural resources by providing them with financial grants and loans, machinery and equipment, and the advice of scientific and technical experts. Thus, in addition to logging equipment, trucks, and sawmills, the United States made foresters and forest engineers available to cooperating countries. By the late 1950s, about fifty such technical experts were employed by ICA abroad.

Despite the absence of a forestry policy and an administrator at the executive level in the agency, worthwhile forestry programs were started that helped economic growth in the developing nations. In addition to the traditional forestry practices, work was done in range, watershed, and wildlife management. Courses were set up to train local nationals in these fields. To help ICA recruit Americans for the foreign assignments, the Forest Service created a special personnel unit in its international forestry staff.

Since this program started, the Forest Service has helped hundreds of foreign nationals who have come to the United States to study forestry conditions and to visit the major forest regions. Not all of these callers have been on ICA-sponsored visits. Some have been participants in educational programs of the Department of State. Some have been under the aegis of FAO, of their own governments, or of privately financed interests.

Under the authority of the Foreign Assistance Act of 1961, President Kennedy established the Agency for International Development (AID) in the Department of State. AID was given responsibility for carrying out U.S. nonmilitary foreign assistance programs. One of its programs was set up for making loans to promote the productive use of economic resources in less-developed friendly nations. Among other things, the grants were used to aid technical education in resource management, to make surveys of investment opportunities, and to evaluate new or improved techniques for the utilization of natural resources.

With the creation in 1958 of the United Nations Special Fund, to which the United States was a major contributor, additional money was made available to FAO for fisheries, forestry, land and water use, and related agricultural programs. In 1965, for example, more than $62 million was budgeted to FAO for forestry and forest products projects alone. Meanwhile, AID began to shrink its forestry activities; at the same time FAO, financed by the U.N. Special Fund, by the Expanded Program of Technical Assistance, and by appropriations from trust funds of other sources, began to enlarge. Whereas FAO formerly had only limited money to use to assess needs in developing nations, it now was able to send out teams of technologists and specialists to prepare and initiate forestry working plans.

SAF Support of World Forestry

In order to cultivate friendly, as well as professional, relations with foresters in other countries, the Society of American Foresters set up a Committee on International Relations in 1924. Through this committee, SAF promoted informal exchanges of information with scientific and technical forestry societies in other nations. The committee stimulated attendance by American foresters at international conferences, particularly in meetings of the International Union of Forestry Research Organizations and the World Forestry Congresses.

The *Journal of Forestry* acquired its first associate editor for world forestry in 1946. He was J. W. B. Sisam, dean of the Faculty of Forestry at the University of Toronto. Although articles on silviculture and forestry policy in other nations had appeared in the *Journal* and its predecessor, *Forestry Quarterly*, since 1902, the appointment of Sisam emphasized and heightened the interest of American foresters in forestry abroad. A department on world forestry continues to be a feature of the *Journal*.

In 1953, FAO published a directory of forestry schools throughout the world. Many of the institutions then offering forestry instruction were listed. Since the listing was incomplete, and since new schools of forestry were coming into existence, FAO began gathering data for a new edition.

Because of the important role assigned to forestry education at the Fifth World Forestry Congress in 1960, an up-to-date reference book on schools of forestry was needed. As FAO, for internal reasons, could not publish the new directory in time for the congress, SAF undertook its publication. The revised edition of *World Directory of Schools of Forestry* was published by the society in 1960 with an introduction by Hardy L. Shirley, chairman of the FAO Panel on Education in Forestry.

In 1964, the Council of the Society of American Foresters authorized its Committee on International Relations to explore the feasibility of forming an international association of professional foresters. A proposal for such a body was presented to the representatives of forestry societies of thirty nations during the Sixth World Forestry Congress in Madrid in June 1966. Briefly, its purpose, as outlined by Verne Harper, chairman of the SAF committee, and Tom Gill, vice chairman, would be to advance the progress, competence, status, and effectiveness of professional foresters throughout the world.

Two subsequent organizing meetings were held by Harper and Gill in Helsinki, Finland, and in Munich, Germany, with representatives of forestry associations in other nations. The consensus was that the new body should consist of societies whose membership is composed primarily of professional foresters with university educations.

As finally adopted, the name of the organization is International Union of Societies of Foresters. In order to effect an administration for the new union, officers were named provisionally to serve during its developing period. Accordingly, Verne Harper was designated president; V. J. Palosua (Finland), vice president; and Tom Gill, executive director.[11]

In 1968, the Society of American Foresters adopted the following policy on world forestry:

The Society is aware of our nation's opportunity and responsibility to cooperate with other nations of the world in the advancement of forestry and conservation of natural resources. We encourage the development of professionalism in forestry among the nations of the world. The Society and its members should participate in the international exchange of personnel, knowledge, and ideas.[12]

On March 28, 1968, the Council of the Society of American Foresters, representing the forestry profession in the United States, voted to become a charter member of the International Union. In addition, the Council voted to sponsor the organizing congress for the union to be held in Washington, D.C., August 18–19, 1969. Finally, in a referendum held in December 1969, the members approved the society's affiliation with the union.

International Society of Tropical Foresters

The International Society of Tropical Foresters was created in 1950 by a small body of professional foresters who had need for an organization to represent their special interests. Its specific aims are to promote the practice, science, and standards of tropical forestry throughout the world; to act as a center of professional information and communication; and to make available to its members notices of important additions to the literature of tropical forestry and the dates and places of relevant meetings.

Although most of its members are professionally educated in forestry, membership is open to all those who are technically concerned with tropical forests and their products. The membership roster totals more than 450, including many of the world's most distinguished tropical foresters and representing every nation possessing tropical forests.

The American Forestry Association

A recommended program for more energetic American participation in world forestry improvement was adopted in 1963 by the Fifth American Forestry Congress, called by The American Forestry Association in Washington, D.C. Recognizing that forest resources can be utilized to raise human living standards, the conferees urged that the United States Government enlarge its support of the forestry and conservation work of the United Nations.

Having benefited from knowledge and practices brought from abroad, American foresters and resource managers are in the fortunate position of

11. Tom Gill, "World Union for Forestry," *Journal of Forestry*, vol. 66 (March 1968).
12. Society of American Foresters, *Forest Policies of the Society of American Foresters* (Washington: SAF, 1969), p. 7.

being able to reciprocate by assisting other countries, especially the emerging nations, with personnel and materials to develop their natural resources so that their peoples may enjoy higher living standards—an essential basis for lasting peace.[13]

Increased participation by the United States in the development of instruction in forestry in nations lacking adequate educational facilities was a major recommendation. Another recognized the need to help guide forestry policy in developing nations where governmental policies are inadequate or nonexistent. Still another was a call to aid in the conservation of soil and water, wildlife, and recreational resources, particularly in nations lacking requisite regulations or legislation. Free exchange of information among scientists and resource managers and increased cooperation among forestry and conservation associations throughout the world are considered necessary to advance sound resource management for special welfare.

13. American Forestry Association, *A Conservation Program for American Forestry* (Washington: AFA, 1963), p. 31.

Selected Bibliography

Because the historical literature of forestry is extensive and varied, it would be impossible to present a comprehensive bibliography here. This list is intended simply to identify the important books that were consulted during the preparation of this one. Not all the works catalogued below are cited in the text, but they constitute excellent sources of background information and suggestions for further reading. For example, Samuel Dana's selected bibliography in *Forest and Range Policy* is still valuable, although it was compiled fifteen years ago.

The periodical literature on the history of forestry is proportionately comprehensive. Two indispensable periodicals and reliable chronological guides are *American Forests* and the *Journal of Forestry* together with their predecessors. In addition, I relied heavily on the organs of the state forestry associations; for example, *Pennsylvania Forests* and its predecessor *Forest Leaves*, which began publication in 1886. *Agricultural History* and *Forest History* are also sources of balanced and accurate data.

Trade journals yield information on the development of forestry policy and practice. Among these, *The American Lumberman, Southern Lumberman, Lumber Trade Journal*, and *Northwestern Lumberman* are particularly useful for their accounts of the start of industrial forestry.

Original typescript reports on early forestry investigations and experiments by lumber and paper companies were generously made available to me by Brown Company, International Paper Company, St. Regis Paper Company, and others.

I have made use of many official reports and bulletins issued by federal and state governmental agencies. The early reports of the U.S. Forest Service and the state forestry commissions are illuminating and, on the whole, historically accurate. Many of these are referred to in the text.

Ahern, George P. *Deforested America: Statement of the Present Forest Situation in the United States*. S. Doc. 216. 70 Cong., 2 sess. Washington: 1929.
_____. *Forestry Bankruptcy in America*. Washington: Privately printed, 1933.
Allen, Shirley W. *Conserving Natural Resources: Principles and Practices in a Democracy*. New York: McGraw-Hill, 1966.

American Forest Products Industry. *Government Land Acquisition: A Summary of Land Acquisition by Federal, State and Local Governments up to 1964*. Washington: AFPI, 1965.

Bennett, Hugh Hammond. *Elements of Soil Conservation*. New York: McGraw-Hill, 1955.

Blauch, Lloyd E., ed. *Education for the Professions*. U.S. Department of Health, Education, and Welfare, Office of Education. Washington: 1955.

Brink, Wellington. *Big Hugh: The Father of Soil Conservation*. New York: Macmillan, 1951.

Brockman, C. Frank. *Recreational Use of Wild Lands*. New York: McGraw-Hill, 1959.

Brown, William Robinson. *Our Forest Heritage*. Concord, N.H.: New Hampshire Historical Society, 1958.

Burton, Ian, and Kates, Robert W. *Readings in Resource Management and Conservation*. Chicago: University of Chicago Press, 1965.

Butler, Ovid, ed. *American Conservation: In Picture and in Story*. Washington: American Forestry Association, 1941.

Callison, Charles, ed. *America's Natural Resources*. New York: Ronald Press, 1967.

Cameron, Jenks. *The National Park Service—Its History, Activities and Organization*. New York: Appleton-Century-Crofts, 1922.

_____. *The Development of Governmental Forest Control in the United States*. Baltimore: Johns Hopkins Press, 1928.

_____. *The Bureau of Biological Survey—Its History, Activities and Organization*. Baltimore: Johns Hopkins Press, 1929.

Carstensen, Vernon, ed. *The Public Lands: Studies in the History of the Public Domain*. Madison: University of Wisconsin Press, 1963.

Cheyney, E. G., and Schantz-Hansen, T. *This Is Our Land: The Story of Conservation in the United States*. St. Paul: Webb Book Publishing, 1950.

Clar, C. Raymond. *California Government and Forestry*. Sacramento: California Department of Natural Resources, 1959.

Clawson, Marion. *Uncle Sam's Acres*. New York: Dodd, Mead, 1951.

_____. *The Federal Lands Since 1956: Recent Trends in Use and Management*. Washington: Resources for the Future, 1967.

_____. *The Land System in the United States: An Introduction to the History and Practice of Land Use and Land Tenures*. Lincoln: University of Nebraska Press, 1968.

_____, and Held, Burnell R. *The Federal Lands: Their Use and Management*. Baltimore: Johns Hopkins Press, 1957.

_____, and Knetsch, J. L. *Economics of Outdoor Recreation*. Baltimore: Johns Hopkins Press, 1966.

Clepper, Henry, ed. *Careers in Conservation*. New York: Ronald Press, 1963.

_____, ed. *Origins of American Conservation*. New York: Ronald Press, 1966.

_____, ed. *Leaders of American Conservation*. New York: Ronald Press, 1971.

_____, and Meyer, Arthur B., eds. *The World of the Forest*. Boston: D. C. Heath, 1965.

_____, and _____. *American Forestry: Six Decades of Growth*. Washington: Society of American Foresters, 1960.

Connery, Robert H. *Governmental Problems in Wildlife Conservation*. New York: Columbia University Press, 1935.

Conover, Milton. *The General Land Office—Its History, Activities and Organization*. Baltimore: Johns Hopkins Press, 1923.

Cook, Harold O. *Fifty Years a Forester*. Boston: Massachusetts Forest and Park Association, 1961.

Coolidge, Philip T. *History of the Maine Woods*. Bangor: Furbush-Roberts, 1963.

Cowan, Charles S. *The Enemy Is Fire*. Seattle: Superior Publishing, 1961.

Coyle, David Cushman. *Conservation: An American Story of Conflict and Accomplishment*. Brunswick, N.J.: Rutgers University Press, 1957.

Dana, Samuel T. *Forest and Range Policy: Its Development in the United States*. New York: McGraw-Hill, 1956.

_____, ed. *History of Activities in the Field of Natural Resources, University of Michigan*. Ann Arbor: University of Michigan Press, 1953.

_____, and Johnson, Evert. *Forestry Education in America: Today and Tomorrow*. Washington: Society of American Foresters, 1963.

Dasmann, Raymond F. *A Different Kind of Country*. New York: Macmillan, 1968.

Defebaugh, James E. *History of the Lumber Industry in America*. 2 vols. Chicago: American Lumberman, 1906–07.

Egleston, Nathaniel H. *Report on Forestry*. Vol. 4. U.S. Department of Agriculture. Washington: 1884.

Fernow, Bernhard E. *Report upon Forestry Investigations, 1877–1898*. H. Doc. 181. 55 Cong., 3 sess. Washington: 1899.

_____. *Economics of Forestry*. New York: T. Y. Crowell, 1902.

_____. *A Brief History of Forestry in Europe, the United States, and Other Countries*. Toronto: University Press, 1911.

Forest History Society. *National Colloquium on the History of the Forest Products Industries: Proceedings*. New Haven: FHS, 1967.

Frank, Bernard. *Our National Forests*. Norman, Okla.: University of Oklahoma Press, 1955.

Freeman, Orville, and Frome, Michael. *The National Forests of America*. New York: Putnam. 1968.

Frome, Michael. *Whose Woods These Are: The Story of the National Forests*. Garden City, N.Y.: Doubleday, 1962.

Gates, Paul W. *History of Public Land Law Development*. Public Land Law Review Commission. Washington: Government Printing Office, 1968.

Gill, Tom, and Dowling, Ellen C., comps. *The Forestry Directory*. Washington: American Tree Association, 1949.

Graves, Henry S. *Problems and Progress of Forestry in the United States*. Report of the Joint Committee on Forestry of the National Research Council and the Society of American Foresters. Washington: Society of American Foresters, 1947.

_____, and Guise, Cedric H. *Forest Education*. New Haven: Yale University Press, 1932.

Greeley, William B. *Forests and Men*. Garden City, N.Y.: Doubleday, 1951.

_____. *Forest Policy*. New York: McGraw-Hill, 1953.

Gulick, Luther H. *American Forest Policy: A Study of Government Administration and Economic Control*. New York: Duell, Sloan and Pearce, 1951.

Gustafson, A. F. *Conservation in the United States*. Ithaca: Cornell University Press, 1949.

Guthrie, John D. *Saga of the CCC*. Washington: American Forestry Association, 1942.

Hair, Dwight. *The Economic Importance of Timber in the United States*. U.S. Department of Agriculture, Forest Service. Washington: 1963.

Havemeyer, Loomis, ed. *Conservation of Our Natural Resources*. New York: Macmillan, 1930.

Hayes, Samuel. *Conservation and the Gospel of Efficiency: The Progressive Conservation Movement, 1890-1920.* Cambridge, Mass.: Harvard University Press, 1959.

Held, Burnell R., and Clawson, Marion. *Soil Conservation in Perspective.* Baltimore: Johns Hopkins Press, 1965.

Hibbard, Benjamin H. *A History of the Public Land Policies.* Madison: University of Wisconsin Press, 1965.

Hidy, Ralph W.; Hill, Frank Ernest; and Nevins, Allan. *Timber and Men: The Weyerhaeuser Story.* New York: Macmillan, 1963.

Highsmith, Richard M. *Conservation in the United States.* Chicago: Rand McNally, 1962.

Holbrook, Stewart H. *Burning an Empire: The Story of American Forest Fires.* New York: Macmillan, 1943.

_____. *Holy Old Mackinaw: A Natural History of the American Lumberjack.* New York: Macmillan, 1956.

Horn, Stanley F. *This Fascinating Lumber Business.* Indianapolis: Bobbs-Merrill, 1943.

Hough, Franklin B. *Report upon Forestry.* 3 vols. U.S. Department of Agriculture. Washington: 1878-82.

Illick, Joseph S. *Outline of General Forestry.* New York: Barnes & Noble, 1939.

Ise, John. *The United States Forest Policy.* New Haven: Yale University Press, 1920.

_____. *Our National Park Policy: A Critical History.* Baltimore: Johns Hopkins Press, 1961.

Jarrett, Henry, ed. *The Nation Looks at its Resources: Report of the Mid-Century Conference on Resources for the Future.* Washington: Resources for the Future, 1954.

_____, ed. *Perspectives on Conservation.* Baltimore: Johns Hopkins Press, 1958.

Kaufert, Frank H., and Cummings, William H. *Forestry and Related Research in North America.* Washington: Society of American Foresters, 1955.

Kaufman, Herbert. *The Forest Ranger: A Study in Administrative Behavior.* Baltimore: Johns Hopkins Press, 1960.

Kauffman, Erle, ed. *The Conservation Yearbook, 1961-1962.* Baltimore: Monumental Printing, 1962.

Kinney, J. P *Forest Legislation in America Prior to March 4, 1789.* Agricultural Experiment Station Bulletin no. 370. Ithaca: Cornell University, 1916.

_____. *The Development of Forest Law in America.* New York: John Wiley, 1917.

_____. *A Continent Lost—A Civilization Won: Indian Land Tenure in America.* Baltimore: Johns Hopkins Press, 1937.

_____. *Indian Forest and Range: A History of the Administration and Conservation of the Redman's Heritage.* Washington: Forestry Enterprises, 1950.

Korstian, Clarence F. *Forestry on Private Lands in the United States.* Durham: Duke University Press, 1944.

Leopold, Aldo. *Game Management.* New York: Scribner's, 1933.

_____. *A Sand County Almanac.* New York: Oxford University Press, 1949.

Lillard, Richard G. *The Great Forest.* New York: Knopf, 1947.

Loehr, Rodney C. *Forests for the Future: The Story of Sustained Yield as Told in the Diaries and Papers of David T. Mason, 1907-1950.* St. Paul: Minnesota Historical Society, 1952.

McArdle, Richard E. *Timber Resources for America's Future: A Summary of the Timber Resources Review.* U.S. Department of Agriculture, Forest Service. Washington: 1955.
McGeary, Nelson M. *Gifford Pinchot: Forester-Politician.* Princeton: Princeton University Press, 1960.
McPhee, John. *The Pine Barrens of New Jersey.* New York: Farrar, Straus and Giroux, 1968.
Malone, J. J. *Pine Trees and Politics.* Seattle: University of Washington Press, 1964.
Marquis, Ralph W. *Economics of Private Forestry.* New York: McGraw-Hill, 1939.
Mason, Alpheus Thomas. *Bureaucracy Convicts Itself: The Ballinger-Pinchot Controversy, 1910, and Its Meaning for Today.* New York: Viking, 1941.
Morgan, George T. *William B. Greeley: A Practical Forester, 1879-1955.* St. Paul: Forest History Society, 1961.
Munns, Edward N. *A Selected Bibliography of North American Forestry.* U.S. Department of Agriculture. Misc. Pub. no. 364. Washington: 1940.
Nash, Roderick. *The American Environment: Readings in the History of Conservation.* Reading, Mass.: Addison-Wesley, 1968.
National Conservation Commission. *Report of the National Conservation Commission.* 3 vols. S. Doc. 676. 60 Cong., 2 sess. Washington: 1909.
Neiderheiser, C. M. *Forest History Sources of the United States and Canada.* St. Paul: Forest History Foundation, 1956.
Nixon, Edgar B., ed. *Franklin D. Roosevelt and Conservation, 1911-1945.* 2 vols. Hyde Park, N.Y.: Franklin D. Roosevelt Library, 1957.
Peffer, E. Louise. *The Closing of the Public Domain.* Stanford, Calif.: Stanford University Press, 1951.
Pinchot, Gifford. *The Fight for Conservation.* Garden City, N.Y.: Doubleday, Page, 1911.
_____. *The Training of a Forester.* Philadelphia: Lippincott, 1937.
_____. *Breaking New Ground.* New York: Harcourt, Brace, 1947.
Pinkett, Harold T. *Gifford Pinchot: Public and Private Forester.* Urbana, Ill.: University of Illinois Press, 1970.
Platt, Rutherford H. *The Great American Forest.* Englewood Cliffs, N.J.: Prentice-Hall, 1965.
Powell, Fred W. *The Bureau of Plant Industry—Its History, Activities and Organization.* Baltimore: Johns Hopkins Press, 1927.
Puter, S. A. D. *Looters of the Public Domain.* Portland, Ore.: Portland Printing House, 1908.
Richardson, Elmo R. *The Politics of Conservation: Crusades and Controversies, 1897-1913.* Berkeley: University of California Press, 1962.
Robbins, Roy M. *Our Landed Heritage: The Public Domain, 1776-1936.* Princeton: Princeton University Press, 1942; New York: Peter Smith, 1950.
Roberts, Paul H. *Hoof Prints on Forest Ranges: The Early Years of National Forest Range Administration.* San Antonio, Tex.: Naylor, 1963.
Rodgers, A. D., III. *Bernhard Eduard Fernow.* Princeton: Princeton University Press, 1949.
Rohrbaugh, Malcolm. *The Land Office Business: The Settlement and Administration of American Public Lands, 1789-1837.* New York: Oxford University Press, 1968.
Sakolski, A. M. *The Great American Land Bubble: The Amazing Story of Landgrabbing, Speculations, and Booms from Colonial Days to the Present Times.* New York: Johnson Reprint, 1966.

Salmond, John A. *The Civilian Conservation Corps, 1933-1942: A New Deal Case Study*. Durham: Duke University Press, 1967.

Saunderson, Mont H. *Western Land and Water Use*. Norman, Okla.: Oklahoma University Press, 1950.

Schenck, Carl Alwin. *The Biltmore Story: Recollections of the Beginning of Forestry in the United States*. Edited by Ovid Butler. St. Paul: American Forest History Foundation, Minnesota Historical Society, 1955.

Schiff, Ashley. *Fire and Water: Scientific Heresy in the Forest Service*. Cambridge: Harvard University Press, 1962.

Shankland, Robert. *Steve Mather of the National Parks*. New York: Knopf, 1951.

Smith, Darrell H. *The Forest Service—Its History, Activities and Organization*. Washington: Brookings Institution, 1930.

Smith, Guy-Harold. *Conservation of Natural Resources*. New York: John Wiley, 1965.

Society of American Foresters. *A National Program of Forest Research*, prepared by Earle H. Clapp as the report of the Special Committee on Forest Research of the Washington Section, SAF. Washington: American Tree Association, 1926.

———. *World Directory of Forestry Schools*. Washington: SAF, 1960.

Stoddart, Laurence A., and Smith, Arthur D. *Range Management*. New York: McGraw-Hill, 1955.

Swain, Donald C. *Federal Conservation Policy, 1921-1933*. Berkeley: University of California Press, 1963.

Swift, Ernest. *A Conservation Saga*. Washington: National Wildlife Federation, 1967.

Tilden, Freeman. *The National Parks—What They Mean to You and Me*. New York: Knopf, 1951.

Udall, Stuart L. *The National Parks of America*. New York: Putnam's, 1966.

———. *Agenda for Tomorrow*. New York: Harcourt, Brace and World, 1968.

U.S. Congress, Senate. Select Committee on Reforestation. *Reforestation*. S. Rept. 28. 68 Cong., 1 sess. Washington: 1924.

———. Joint Committee on Forestry. *Forest Lands of the United States*. S. Doc. 32. 77 Cong., 1 sess. Washington: 1941.

U.S. Department of Agriculture. *A National Plan for American Forestry*. 2 vols. S. Doc. 12. 73 Cong., 1 sess. Washington: 1933.

———. *The Western Range*. S. Doc. 199. 74 Cong., 2 sess. Washington, 1936.

———. *Trees: The Yearbook of Agriculture*, edited by Alfred Stefferud. Washington: 1949.

U.S. Department of the Interior. *Forest Conservation on Lands Administered by the Department of the Interior*. Washington: 1940.

———. *Forestry on Indian Lands*. Washington: 1940.

———. *Land Management in the Department of the Interior*. Washington: 1946.

———. *A Century of Conservation, 1849-1949*. Conservation Bulletin 39. Washington: 1950.

Van Hise, Charles R. *The Conservation of Natural Resources in the United States*. New York: Macmillan, 1910.

Van Name, Willard G. *Vanishing Forest Reserves: Problems of the National Forests and National Parks*. Boston: R. G. Badger, 1929.

Weber, G. A. *The Bureau of Entomology—Its History, Activities and Organization*. Washington: Brookings Institution, 1930.

Widner, Ralph R., ed. *Forests and Forestry in the American States: A Reference Anthology*. Washington: National Association of State Foresters, 1968.

Wilbur, Ray Lyman, and Du Puy, William Atherton. *Conservation in the Department of the Interior*. U.S. Department of the Interior. Washington: 1931.

Winters, Robert K., ed. *Fifty Years of Forestry in the U.S.A.* Washington: Society of American Foresters, 1950.

Yard, Robert Sterling. *Our Federal Lands*. New York: Scribner's, 1928.

Index